A Practitioner's Guide to
The Court of Protection

A Practitioner's Guide to The Court of Protection

Third Edition

Martin Terrell TEP
Thomson Snell & Passmore

Tottel Publishing Ltd, Maxwelton House, 41–43 Boltro Road, Haywards Heath, West Sussex, RH16 1BJ

© Tottel Publishing Ltd 2009

A CIP Catalogue record for this book is available from the British Library.

ISBN: 978 1 84592 244 3

Typeset by Phoenix Photosetting, Chatham, Kent
Printed and bound in Great Britain by M & A Thomson Litho Ltd, East Kilbride, Glasgow

Foreword

In his preface to this book Martin Terrell laments the fact that, since 1 October 2007, when the Mental Capacity Act 2005 came into force, life has become more complicated. Instead of simply updating the previous edition with a few minor amendments, such as the current practice direction on fixed costs or the latest statutory instrument revising the court fees, or disseminating snippets of gossip he has gleaned during one of frequent his visits to Archway Tower, Martin has had to rewrite the book in its entirety and, as he says, it is considerably longer than the last one.

I had a similar experience with *Cretney & Lush on Lasting and Enduring Powers of Attorney*. The fifth edition, which was published in 2001 and was confined to EPAs, ran to 296 pages. The sixth edition, published in March 2009, is 606 pages long. One of the contributory factors is the sheer length of the new forms. An EPA rarely extended to more than four pages, whereas the prescribed LPA forms are twenty-five pages long, and the draft versions of the revised forms that are likely to be introduced in July 2009 are no shorter. LPAs are not an isolated example. Every file I open seems to be stuffed with Court of Protection forms, particularly the pointlessly prolix acknowledgment of service/notification (COP5) and certificate of service/non-service (COP20). Instead of reducing the carbon footprint in favour of more environmentally friendly processes, those who were responsible for implementing the Act have gone to the other extreme.

The cost to the environment pales into insignificance, however, when one considers the cost to the client. In October 2007 I chaired a conference in Holborn, and there were rumours buzzing around the audience that a West End firm was charging £1,500 for preparing and registering a standard LPA. A few weeks later, I mentioned this to a well-known elder law practitioner, when we were travelling on a train together to speak at a STEP conference in Manchester. 'That's nothing', she said, 'I have just charged £7,900 for a personal welfare LPA'. Admittedly, in this case there were inter-jurisdictional aspects, and she had four lengthy interviews with the client. The combined costs of the parties in the recent two-day statutory will hearing before Mr Justice Lewison on 27 and 28 January 2009, reported as *Re P* [2009] EWHC 163 (Ch), came to just under half a million pounds, and a firm of solicitors that handles a lot of personal injury claims and has its own dedicated Court of Protection team has reported a 50% rise in its turnover from this work during the first twelve months since the Act came into operation, principally because the procedure has become more convoluted and protracted.

Foreword

I must thank Martin for providing me with the platform on which to launch upon this little tirade. I am sure that the third edition of *A Practitioner's Guide to the Court of Protection* will be an invaluable detector in locating most of the hidden obstacles in what has unfortunately become a procedural minefield.

Denzil Lush

Senior Judge of the Court of Protection

1 April 2009

Preface

It is not everyone who finds the work of the Court of Protection a fascinating subject but few of us can afford to ignore it or treat it as an obscure backwater of the law. The persons directly affected by the Court's jurisdiction are some of the most vulnerable persons in our society. They deserve the best support and protection that the law and the legal profession can provide. With increasing longevity, the number of elderly persons and the complexity of their affairs continue to increase, especially at a time of economic uncertainty. Since I began work on this edition, the interest paid on special account has halved to 3% and even that appears to be a generous rate of interest.

It is more than five years since the second edition of this work was published. I had hoped for a break after that, perhaps with no more than the occasional polish to reflect new fees or a couple of interesting cases. But life is more complicated and the Mental Capacity Act 2005, which came into effect on 1 October 2007 has lead to a largely rewritten and much more lengthy publication. The Mental Capacity Act 2005 has brought some benefits, especially the best interests' test and the ability of the Court of Protection to make welfare decisions. But whether the vast complexity of the legislation and the Court of Protection Rules has made for better justice for those who need it is another matter. As a writer, professional deputy and user of the Court of Protection, the feeling is that we all need to work a great deal harder to achieve the same results. As one colleague put it mildly, we may have a better system of justice, but the end results are much the same and the costs have risen enormously.

This does not even take account of the endless bureaucratic changes to the administrative framework that have been a regular backdrop to this area of work since I first visited Stewart House in 1993. In less than two years we have already seen a new Public Guardian, a new supervision regime, new branches of the Office of the Public Guardian, a transfer of the Court administration to the Court Service, proposals for new Lasting Power of Attorney forms and the introduction of the Deprivation of Liberty Safeguards. It seems that nothing can stand still for too long. The law also continues to develop, with cases such as *S v S*, *Re P* and *Re J* being heard in the higher courts and reported. In the meantime, any publication has to reflect the law as it is at a particular date, which with this work is 1 April 2009. Unfortunately this is also the date the administration of the Court is transferred to the Court Service. Forms, practice directions and other information relating to the Court of Protection are in the course of being transferred gradually to the HMCS website. However, 'signposts' will continue to be provided from the website of the Office of the

Public Guardian. There will be other changes over time and it will not be long before a further edition is required to reflect them.

The new jurisdiction also requires us to address a person known as 'P.' It is a convenient shorthand for a man or woman who may or may not lack capacity in respect of a particular decision made at a particular moment in time. I have tried to avoid using this term where possible, in deference to the person who sadly does lack capacity, despite the effect of using longer words where one letter may have sufficed.

This work does however make no apology for aiming to emulate its title. It is a Practitioner's Guide. It reflects one solicitor's journey through what is now a complex legal and procedural jurisdiction. It is therefore biased towards my own area of practice as a professional deputy and in dealing with a person's property and affairs. Possibly a further (and even longer) edition is needed to do justice to the developing welfare jurisdiction of the Court of Protection and the new Deprivation of Liberty Safeguards.

Bearing in mind that this began as a practical guide, I have drawn on my experiences and those of colleagues. As the experience of others may be equally or more illuminating or up to date I would be happy to receive any comments (of a constructive nature) which could be incorporated into another edition.

A sincere debt must be paid to those who have helped me with this work: Denzil Lush, now Senior Judge of the Court of Protection, for encouraging me to write on this subject and writing the foreword, helping with numerous queries, and ensuring that with tales of Louis the Poodle, a somewhat hideous statue in Italy, the toilets at Archway and the client who could not afford her return fare to Brighton the subject-matter could never be dry; Sarah Blair and Heather Saward at Tottel, Sarah for her persistence and good cheer at ever increasing deadlines and Heather for her speed and skill in making the text look so good; Richard Frimston of Russell-Cooke who is the only person who understands the Hague Convention and assisted me with chapter 16; David Rees at 5 Stone Buildings and Caroline Bielanska for their unhealthy knowledge of the intricacies of the Mental Capacity Act; Niall Baker of Irwin Mitchell for his cheerful cynicism; Eddie Fardell and my other partners at Thomson Snell & Passmore for allowing me the time to write and Christine Keevil, Amy Paxton and Charlotte Parsons for running my office in my absence (even if some of them thought I was on holiday!) and above all my ever patient (and thereby wonderful) wife and children for providing endless distractions to writing and for eventually tiring of my excuses and forcing me to finish the job.

Martin Terrell
Partner
Thomson Snell & Passmore
Tunbridge Wells
1 April 2009

Contents

Table of Statutes

[All references are to paragraph number]

Table of Statutory Instruments

[All references are to paragraph number]

Table of International Material

[References are to paragraph number]

Table of Cases

[All references are to paragraph number]

Chapter 1

Capacity and best interests

The Mental Capacity Act 2005

The need for reform

1.1 The Mental Capacity Act 2005 (MCA 2005) came into force on 1 October 2007. It is an impressive, ambitious and comprehensive piece of legislation that sets out not just to clarify important legal principles and provide a range of legal remedies but also to consolidate the law relating to capacity and delegated and substitute decision making. Although the wide scope of the Act has created its own difficulties, not least in the detailed implementation, the need for wide-ranging reform was apparent for many years. The piecemeal development of the law and the lack of a readily accessible forum for welfare decisions were highlighted by the Law Commission in its detailed report *Mental Incapacity* (Law Com No 231). This report introduced a draft Bill setting out a single statutory framework to cover the treatment and care as well as the management of the property and affairs of incapable persons, replacing Part VII of the Mental Health Act 1983 and the Enduring Powers of Attorney Act 1985.

In more recent years, further problems were identified with the Court of Protection and its administrative branch, the Public Guardianship Office. New legislation would improve the status of the Court, bringing it into line with the court service and separating its judicial and administrative roles in line with the Human Rights Act. It would also promote the rights of those who lacked capacity. In 1997 the Government set out a clear agenda for reform in *Who Decides?* (CM 3803) announcing its belief that:

> 'there is a clear need for reform of the law in order to improve and clarify the decision-making process for those who are unable to make decisions for themselves, or for those who cannot communicate their decisions. These are some of the most vulnerable people in our society. The law in this area has developed in piecemeal fashion, and does not always offer sufficient protection either for mentally incapacitated adults, or for those who look after them.'

The statutory framework of the Mental Capacity Act

1.2 Although this work is principally concerned with the Court of Protection, the powers of the Court are just one element in a much wider framework created by the MCA 2005. The Act is centred around the needs of the individual person and provides a range of remedies to protect that person. Every person's needs and interests at any given time are different and the aim of the Act is to provide different remedies to suit different situations. There is therefore as much flexibility as possible so that the rights, dignity and freedom of the individual are supported as fully as possible. Where intervention is required, then it should be there as a last resort or emergency safeguard, and where possible provided in accordance with the individual's own wishes. The Act therefore provides for decisions to be made in different forms and at different levels:

- By the individual exercising his autonomous rights to make his own decisions (s 1).
- By an individual refusing treatment in advance, so that the earlier decision is valid and applicable at a later date when he lacks capacity (ss 24–26).
- By another person performing basic acts of care and treatment or paying for essential goods and services, where there is no other form of authority in place (ss 5 to 8).
- By another person to whom authority has been delegated by the individual under a lasting power of attorney (ss 9–14 and Sch 1).
- By another person to whom authority has been delegated by the individual under an enduring power of attorney made prior to 1 October 2007 (Sch 4).
- By the Court of Protection exercising its own authority or authorising another person to make a decision (ss 15–23, 48 and 49).

The core principles of the Mental Capacity Act

1.3   Although the MCA 2005 is centred around the individual person and provides a range of options to address his needs, the Act's fundamental concepts or principles are capacity and best interests. These must be understood clearly before the detail of the Mental Capacity Act is considered. The legal remedies supplied by the Act are merely tools to assist in making decisions in accordance with these principles. Their importance is emphasised by the first section of the MCA 2005. The first section of the Act sets out the core principles that underpin the entire legal framework of the Act. The first of these is the principle that a 'person must be assumed to have capacity unless it is established that he lacks capacity'. The right to 'capacity' is a fundamental liberty and human right, long recognised in common law. A person is presumed capable in common law (*Simpson v Simpson* [1989] Fam Law 20) and any interference with that is an inroad into his 'personal freedom and autonomy'. This principle that the right of a person to manage his property and affairs for himself is a basic right was repeated in the Court of Appeal case of *Masterman-Lister v Jewell* [2003] 3 All ER 162, in which Kennedy LJ, declared forcefully that this was a right 'with which no lawyer and no court should rush to interfere' ([2003] 3 All ER 162 at 173).

The MCA 2005 asserts this presumption of capacity in favour of the individual concerned and only when it can be displaced, can decisions be taken. If the person has capacity, then the Act confers no rights on any other person or body to make decisions on behalf of the individual. The Act has no role or function whatsoever, except in the preparatory sense of enabling decisions to be taken or measures put in place by someone who has capacity for use at a future time when he lacks capacity.

Determining whether or not a person has capacity can be a difficult exercise requiring skill, patience and tact. However, no assessment of capacity can be made without addressing the question of what the capacity is required for. The MCA 2005 operates on the basis that each and every decision is a separate legal act. Each decision must therefore be evaluated on its terms and capacity measured accordingly.

The second underlying feature and core principle of the MCA 2005 is the concept of best interests. Any person or any body, including the Court of Protection, which makes a decision on behalf of a person who lacks capacity must make that decision in the person's best interests. Section 1(5) directs explicitly that 'an act done, or decision made, under this Act for or on behalf of a person who lacks capacity must be done, or made, in his best interests'.

The MCA 2005 therefore sets out a logical process for making decisions on behalf of another person. The person or body engaged in that process must address the following propositions:

1   what is the decision that is being made?

2   does the person lack capacity to make that decision? and

3   if the person lacks capacity to make that decision, what decision can be made?

These three propositions or processes need to be considered in more detail.

Capacity is specific to the decision being made

1.4   The MCA 2005 clarifies and asserts the common law principle that capacity is specific to the decision being made. Clearly different decisions require different levels of understanding. Thus s 2(1) of the Act defines a lack of capacity in relation to a matter (ie the decision being made) at the material time. This principle has regard to the rights of the individual whose autonomy should be respected as far as possible, and to an understanding of human nature which shows that different levels of capacity are required for different acts.

Sir Owen Dixon CJ expressed this principle succinctly in the Australian High Court of *Gibbons v Wright* (1954) 91 CLR 423:

> 'The law does not prescribe any fixed standard of sanity as requisite for the validity of all transactions. It requires, in relation to each particular matter or piece of business transacted, that each party shall have such soundness of mind as to be capable of understanding the general nature of what he is doing by his participation ... The mental capacity required by the law in respect of any instrument is relative to the particular transaction which is being effected by means of the instrument, and may be described as the capacity to understand the nature of the transaction when it is explained.'

The ease with which the common law adopted the principles set out in an Australian case was shown in the case of *Re Beaney dec'd* [1978] 2 All ER 595 which concerned capacity to make a gift. The judge, Martin Nourse QC described a spectrum or range of capacity according to the function for which it is required:

> 'The degree or extent of understanding required in respect of any instrument is relative to the particular transaction which it is to effect. . . .

3

Thus, at one extreme, if the subject matter and value of a gift are trivial in relation to the donor's other assets, a low degree of understanding will suffice. But, at the other, if its effect is to dispose of the donor's only asset of value and thus, for practical purposes, to pre-empt the devolution of his estate under his will or on his intestacy, then the degree of understanding required is as high as that required for a will, and the donor must understand the claims of all potential donees and the extent of the property to be disposed of' ([1978] 2 All ER 595 at 601).

Thus different levels of capacity are required for different legal acts such as:

- consenting to medical treatment (see for instance *F v West Berkshire Health Authority* [1989] 2 All ER 545)

- contracting a marriage (see for instance *Sheffield City Council v E and Another* [2005] All ER (D) 192 and *Re SK (vulnerable adult: capacity)* [2008] All ER (D) 395))

- entering into a contract (see for instance *Boughton v Knight* (1873) LR 3 PD 64)

- making a will (still covered by the classic case of *Banks v Goodfellow* (1870) LR 5 QB 549)

- granting an enduring power of attorney (see *Re F, re K* [1988] 1 All ER 358 and *Re W (enduring power of attorney)* [2001] 4 All ER 88 and which is dealt with in more detail at **14.10**)

- making a gift (see *Re Beaney dec'd* [1978] 2 All ER 595)

- conducting and compromising legal proceedings (see *Masterman-Lister v Jewell* [2003] 3 All ER 162 which is dealt with in more details at **10.1**) and

- managing property and affairs.

The difficulty for any person dealing with another who lacks capacity is identifying the decision that is being measured. Some decisions are specific to a time and place, such as consent to an operation. Others may be insignificant in themselves but will be bound up with other decisions which together make for a more substantial issue that needs to be assessed. And even where there are interconnected decisions, some can stand alone and be acted upon, while others will need the assistance of a deputy or the Court.

Managing property and affairs

1.5   Most legal acts for which the required state of mind has been addressed by the courts are single transactions. Even though they have long-term consequences, they are still solitary legal acts. However, the law is less clear as to how to address the status of a series of acts which individually may be valid, but which taken together may indicate a lack of capacity. The ability to manage 'property and affairs' is one of the most important issues that often needs to be addressed in practice. The Court of Protection and anyone else acting for or dealing with the person concerned needs to know which actions are valid. If the person has capacity to make an individual decision, then the Court of Protection has no authority to act.

Neither the MCA 2005 nor case law provide any assistance. Under Part VII of the Mental Health Act 1983 (which has been repealed and replaced by the MCA 2005) the crucial test of capacity which justified the intervention of the Court of Protection or the registration of an Enduring Power of Attorney (EPA) was the ability of the person concerned to manage and administer his property and affairs. This test is still preserved where EPAs (created before 1 October 2007) become registerable. Schedule 4 para 4 of the MCA 2005 requires the attorney to register the EPA if he has reason to believe that the donor is or is becoming mentally incapable. Paragraph 23 then defines 'mentally incapable' as meaning:

> '... in relation to any person, that he is incapable by reason of mental disorder (within the meaning of the Mental Health Act) of managing and administering his property and affairs and "mentally capable" and "mental capacity" are to be construed accordingly'.

The provisions relating to EPAs are not, however, carried through into other areas of the MCA 2005. When the draft legislation was reviewed by Parliament, the Joint Scrutiny Committee recommended that there should be a definition of general incapacity. The Government's response was that this was unnecessary:

> 'the Government is completely committed to the functional approach to assessing capacity. As the Committee realised, it is not immediately easy to see how this can be reconciled with a recognition of 'general incapacity'. We do however recognise that for some people, in order to provide adequate protection, it is necessary to consider their ability to make inter-related or sequential decisions; or to consider their ability to manage a whole portfolio of assets, rather than each individual asset. We do not consider this inconsistent with the functional approach and envisage giving guidance to explain this.' (CM 6121)

Although guidance is still awaited, the policy set out in the MCA 2005 is logical even if it creates problems in practice. If the functional approach to decision making is to be followed, then it is right that a person should not be prevented from making one decision simply because he cannot make another decision. Just because a person cannot manage his investment portfolio and buy and sell investments does not mean that he cannot manage a weekly budget, or spend small sums of money on a drink, a packet of cigarettes or a box of chocolates.

A person's ability to manage property and affairs must therefore be treated in the same way as any other function for which capacity can be required. The person concerned is entitled to the presumptions and benefits afforded by the MCA 2005 such as the benefit of advice and information, before it is concluded that he cannot manage his property and affairs. If the person can manage certain elements of his property and affairs then it should also be possible to isolate those elements and allow him to go on dealing with those matters. This common-sense or compromise approach was recognised in the Court of Appeal decision in *Masterman-Lister v Jewell* where Kennedy LJ commented:

> '... the judge must consider the totality of the property and affairs of the alleged patient, and no doubt if it is shown that he lacks the capacity to manage a significant part of his affairs the court will be prepared to act, exercising control in such a way that the patient continues to have control in relation to matters which he can handle.' ([2003] 3 All ER 162 at 171)

The separation of seemingly interconnected decisions was followed by the Court of Appeal in the case of *Bailey v Warren* ([2006] EWCA Civ 56; [2006] WTLR 753). The case concerned a claimant in a personal injury claim where liability was compromised before the claim for quantum was determined. By the time the damages came to be assessed, it was clear that the claimant's injuries were more extensive than was first thought to be the case. His capacity also deteriorated to the point that a litigation friend was appointed. On an application to set aside the original compromise, it was held that the claimant had capacity in respect of that decision even though he could not deal with the claim for damages.

The approach required by the MCA 2005 is similar. The Court will act in this type of situation and exercise its powers in respect of those matters it needs to deal with and in respect of which the person concerned clearly lacks capacity, while reserving or leaving to him those matters which he is able to deal with. An assessment will also depend on the complexity of the person's property and affairs which may change over a period of time, for instance following the sale of a property or the receipt of a damages award. It may also be affected by matters such as the ability of the person concerned to take advice or the degree to which the person concerned is vulnerable to undue influence or abuse.

The practical problems this causes for others is a regular theme of this work. Although the Court can stand back and look at the 'totality' of a person's property and affairs it is harder for those making regular day-to-day assessments of capacity. Often it takes time for the bigger picture to emerge. A person may for instance decide to buy a dozen tins of beans or lottery tickets. The next day he repeats the exercise. Is he being eccentric or making an unwise decision? After how many days is it clear that he does not understand what he has bought, how much he has spent or what the impact is on his future financial security?

The problems affecting deputies are dealt with in Chapter 4. However, notwithstanding these problems, they are treated as being outweighed by the benefits of the Act's approach.

Capacity to make the decision

1.6   Having addressed the question of what the decision is for which capacity is required, the MCA 2005 requires an assessment of whether the person concerned is capable of making that decision. An inability to make a particular decision rests on two criteria:

(a)   there is a medical condition; and

(b)   as a consequence of that condition a person is unable to make that decision.

The medical or diagnostic threshold set by the Act is a straightforward one. Section 2(1) states as follows:

> 'For the purposes of this Act, a person lacks capacity in relation to a matter if at the material time he is unable to make a decision for himself in relation to the matter because of an impairment of, or a disturbance in the functioning of, the mind or brain.'

Section 2(2) goes on to state that the impairment or disturbance may be permanent or temporary. This emphasises the scope of the Act, permitting decisions to be made in a wide range of situations. At one end of the spectrum, a person who is unconscious due to alcohol or drug abuse or who has a psychiatric illness that will abate can be treated within the statutory framework. A person who has had an accident and is taken by a stranger to hospital while unconscious is covered by the Act. At the other end of the spectrum, a person with advanced senile dementia who has no understanding can also be treated. In each case the treatment must be proportionate and appropriate, but the MCA 2005 is still able to cover all such situations and the range of decisions across a broad spectrum.

Understanding required to make the decision

1.7   For the purposes of the MCA 2005 a person lacks capacity to make a decision at the material time if because of the impairment or disturbance in the functioning of the mind or brain he is unable to make that decision. Under s 3(a) a person is unable to make that decision if he is unable:

(a)   to understand the information relevant to the decision,

(b)   to retain that information,

(c)   to use or weigh that information as part of the process of making the decision, or

(d)   to communicate his decision (whether by talking, using sign language or any other means).

Section 3(4) further defines information relevant to the decision including information about the reasonably foreseeable consequences of (a) deciding one way or another, or (b) failing to make the decision.

The first three criteria in s 3(1) reflect common law tests and reflect a simple logical process. If the statutory test is applied to a common example, such as making a will, the testator must be able to understand the information relevant to the decision. He must understand the size and nature of his estate and whom he is benefiting or not benefiting. He must be able to hold that information for long enough to use it to make a decision. He must decide whether he wants to make the decision and understand the consequences of making or not making the decision. This is entirely consistent with the approach taken by the courts, following the reasoning of Cockburn CJ in *Banks v Goodfellow*:

> 'It is essential … that a testator shall understand the nature of the act and its effects; shall understand the extent of the property of which he is disposing; shall be able to comprehend and appreciate the claims to which he ought to give effect; and, with a view to the latter object, that no disorder of the mind shall poison his affections, pervert his sense of right, and prevent the exercise of his natural faculties – that no insane delusion shall influence his will in disposing of his property and bring about a disposal of it which, if the mind had been sound, would not have been made.' (LR 5 QB 549 at 565)

Further considerations in determining capacity

Information need only be retained for a short time

1.8   In determining whether or not a person has capacity, it is always reassuring to know that the relevant information is understood and that the person concerned can recall this when his capacity is questioned. In many cases there will be a delay between taking instructions and carrying out the action or there may be several meetings to discuss a particularly complex transaction. The recollection of relevant details between those meetings is a helpful and reassuring indicator. Section 3(3) however makes it clear that:

> 'The fact that a person is able to retain the information relevant to a decision for a short period only does not prevent him from being regarded as able to make the decision.'

This provision needs to be treated carefully. A short-term memory does not prevent a person from being regarded as unable to make a decision, but it may do so. Section 3(1) makes it clear that information must be retained for long enough to make the decision. Or to quote Stephen Smith QC, sitting as a Deputy High Court judge in the case of *Scammell v Farmer,* 'the possession of an imperfect memory is not to be equated with an absence of testamentary capacity' ([2008] EWHC 1100 (Ch) at paragraph 94). A person who makes a will should be able to remember the information between giving instructions and confirming them when executing the will (or as in the case of *Clancy v Clancy* [2003] EWHC (Ch) that the later decision gave effect to the earlier instructions). In practice a particular case will depend on its own circumstances and will depend on factors such as the importance of the information relevant to the decision. The Code of Practice issued pursuant to the Act provides an example (at paragraph 4.20) of an elderly man with dementia and short term memory problems. He cannot remember the names of his great-grandchildren but recognises them when they visit. He does nevertheless have capacity to buy premium bonds for them.

The short-term retention of information may also reflect a person's fluctuating capacity. In such a case the ability to assimilate and remember information will vary from day to day or different times throughout the day. This may be caused by a mental illness where the person lacks capacity for periods of time and has complete capacity in between. A person in the early stages of dementia may also have moments of lucidity and insight, in which specific decisions can be made. Despite the complexity of the medical and evidential issues this gives rise to, a decision made in a window of lucidity against a background of mental incapacity can be a valid one.

A valid decision made against a background of mental incapacity will generally be a specific or 'one-off' decision. A person in a lucid moment may for instance decide whom he wants to benefit, who is to administer his affairs or whether he wants a particular treatment. Generally an ability to make single decisions can be distinguished from an ability to make interconnected decisions over a period of time that affect the overall competence to manage property and affairs. As mentioned at **1.5**, there may in practice be a conflict between the two functions in issue, which are not always going to be easy to resolve.

A person is entitled to assistance in making a decision

1.9   Section 1(3) makes it a requirement that a person cannot be assumed to lack capacity 'unless all practicable steps to help him to do so have been taken without success.' Section 3(2) expands on this principle as follows:

'A person is not to be regarded as unable to understand the information relevant to a decision if he is able to understand an explanation of it given to him in a way that is appropriate to his circumstances (using simple language, visual aids or any other means).'

This approach is entirely appropriate. An elderly testator should not be left alone with a detailed written account of a complex legal document with the conclusion that he lacks capacity to make the decision. He has a right to clear and simple explanations, even if it requires time and effort to provide them at the right level and in the right form. However, where advice is given, the person concerned must be capable of understanding and acting on the advice. This issue was considered by Boreham J in the case of *White v Fell* (12 November 1987, unreported) who held that whether a person is capable of managing his property and affairs depends on whether or not he is capable of taking appropriate advice, considering it, and acting upon it. To establish whether or not the person concerned (who was a 'patient' for the purposes of the Mental Health Act 1983) could meet these requirements, the following questions should be asked:

- Does the patient have insight and understanding of the fact that she has a problem in respect of which she needs advice?

- Is the patient capable of seeking an appropriate adviser and instructing him with sufficient clarity to enable him to understand the problem and advise him appropriately?

- Does the patient have sufficient mental capacity to understand and make decisions based upon, or otherwise give effect to, such advice as he might receive?

The questions posed by the judge in *White v Fell* were followed in the Court of Appeal case of *Masterman-Lister v Brutton* [2003] 3 All ER 162 at 171 and reflect the logical sequence set out in s 3(1) of the MCA 2005, requiring a person to understand the relevant information and act upon it.

It should always be borne in mind that many younger adults would struggle to understand the same complex legal document that is placed before the elderly testator and it is important not to place greater obstacles in the way of an elderly person which would not be applied to someone younger. Most people go about their daily lives relying on simple explanations whether from their lawyer, doctor, stockbroker or electrician. The case of *Saulle v Nouvet* [2007] All ER (D) 08 (Dec) applied the MCA 2005 principles to a claimant who had suffered a brain injury in a road traffic accident. In deciding whether or not the claimant was a protected party for the purposes of the Civil Procedure Rules, the judge had to consider whether the claimant would have capacity to control the money he would recover. The judge, Andrew Edis QC, held that the claimant's capacity was relevant to the issues before the court at that particular time. There was no requirement to anticipate every eventuality and provide for situations which might arise in different circumstances. If those circumstances changed and the claimant lacked capacity then the situation could be reviewed and brought before the Court of Protection. In the meantime the claimant should have the benefit of any doubt in his favour.

All the MCA 2005 requires is that those who are capable and those who might not be capable are treated in the same way. Section 3(3) therefore sets out a further requirement as follows:

'A lack of capacity cannot be established merely by reference to—

(a)   a person's age or appearance, or

(b)   a condition of his, or an aspect of his behaviour, which might lead others to make unjustified assumptions about his capacity.'

One difficulty with this approach is that many individuals who potentially benefit from the MCA 2005 depend on the quality and objectivity of the advice they receive. Thus a person who has good advisers is perhaps more likely to have capacity than another person who has no advice or receives inadequate advice, even though their mental abilities are similar.

A person can make an unwise decision

1.10   Section 1(4) sets out the right of an individual to make a bad decision. Thus 'a person is not to be treated as unable to make a decision merely because he makes an unwise decision'. Again, this merely creates a level playing field between those who are capable and those who might not be capable. Many people make unwise decisions whether in their choice of jobs, cars, investments or holiday destinations. The law does not prevent them from doing so and the MCA 2005 merely reflects the common law approach. This was neatly set out in the case of *Bird v Luckie* (1850) 8 Hare 301, which concerned the interpretation of a will and its possibly unfair consequences. Knight-Bruce V-C pointed out that:

'no man is bound to make a will in such a manner as to deserve approbation from the prudent, the wise or the good. A testator is permitted to be capricious and improvident, and is, moreover, at liberty to conceal the circumstances and the motives . . .'

The right to make an unwise decision is an important one, and while an unwise decision is not necessarily one that cannot be made, the wisdom of a decision should not be overlooked in assessing capacity. A person who wishes to give away all his estate is certainly making an unwise decision. Although his right to make the decision is acknowledged, this may create a presumption or at least a concern that the decision is not a sound one. It may well be a decision that he does not fully understand or which is subject to undue influence. The unwise decision may therefore be evidence of or a symptom of a wider lack of capacity.

Likewise, an irrational decision may indicate a lack of capacity, but is not conclusive proof. The question must be: is the absence of reason due to a delusion that prevents the actual decision being made? Or to paraphrase Cockburn CJ in the case of *Banks v Goodfellow* (see **1.7** above) which dealt with a disposal of property by will, does the insane delusion influence the will in disposing of his property and bring about a disposal of it which, if the mind had been sound, would not have been made?

In the case of *Re C (Adult: Refusal of Treatment)* [1994] 1 FLR 31; [1994] 1 All ER 819 a patient suffering from chronic paranoid schizophrenia refused to consider an amputation which his doctors considered to be essential. Although

C suffered from several delusions, he also understood the risk of dying if he refused treatment. There was therefore no link between the refusal of consent to treatment and the persecutory delusions.

The same principle was applied in the case of *Re MB (Medical Treatment)* which concerned a pregnant woman who refused a necessary caesarean section due to a needle phobia. She wanted the operation but could not give consent to the injection that was vital to the operation. The Court of Appeal approved the decision in *Re C* but held that each case had to be dealt with on its own merits. A person who was competent could ordinarily make a decision that was irrational as well as rational. But sometimes the presumption of capacity had to be rebutted. Butler-Sloss LJ commented that:

> 'Irrationality is here used to connote a decision which is so outrageous in its defiance of logic or of accepted moral standards that no sensible person who had applied his mind to the question to be decided could have arrived at it … Although it might be thought that irrationality sits uneasily with competence to decide, panic, indecisiveness and irrationality in themselves do not as such amount to incompetence, but they may be symptoms or evidence of incompetence. The graver the consequences of the decision, the commensurately greater the level of competence is required to take the decision.' ([1997] 2 FCR 541 at 553)

Communicating a decision

1.11 A person may lack capacity for the purposes of the MCA 2005 if he cannot communicate a decision. The Act does of course require that there must be an impairment or disturbance in the functioning of the mind or brain and that all steps possible must be taken to provide an explanation that the person concerned is able to understand. However, if these two criteria are met, a person who has suffered a stroke or a 'locked in syndrome' may be treated as lacking capacity for the purposes of the Act notwithstanding the fact that he understands what is being done.

Before an inability to communicate is deemed to render a person incapable, all possible steps must be taken to assist in communication. Expert assistance should be obtained from carers who may have more experience in interacting with the person concerned as well as from speech and language therapists. The case of *Re AK (medical treatment: consent)* [2001] 1 FLR 129 concerned an application for a declaration that the person concerned, AK, could communicate his consent to the withdrawal of life-sustaining treatment through simple eyelash movements.

The age of the person concerned

1.12 Under s 2(5) of the MCA 2005, no powers can be exercised in respect of a person who lacks capacity if the person is under the age of 16. The rights and interests of a child are covered by family law principles and a separate jurisdiction. However, s 18(3) does extend the Act's scope to the property and affairs of a child 'even though P [the child] has not reached 16, if the court considers it likely that P will still lack capacity to make decisions in respect of that matter when he reaches 18'.

Vulnerability and undue influence

1.13   One of the principal aims of any legislation for persons who lack capacity is to provide those who are inherently vulnerable with a degree of protection. There is of course a difficult balancing act between the rights and autonomy of the majority on the one hand and the need to protect the interests of the vulnerable minority on the other hand. To the extent that a perfect balance between two competing objectives is not possible, the MCA 2005 is weighted towards the former group. While there is some limited formal protection where the Court of Protection and Public Guardian are involved with deputies and attorneys, the framework for understanding and assessing capacity makes no reference to undue influence. There is a harsh logic to this. Capacity must first be assessed in its own right. Undue influence is then a separate issue that applies to every person, regardless of his formal capacity. A fully capable professional man or woman may be as much a victim of undue influence (or fraud) as an elderly person with deteriorating capacity.

One of the issues considered by the Court of Appeal in the case of *Masterman-Lister v Jewell* was the question of whether the claimant's brain injuries made him more vulnerable and therefore more likely to be within the jurisdiction of the Court of Protection (for the purposes of the Mental Health Act 1983). In his judgment, Chadwick LJ confirmed that the first instance judge was right to reject this approach and commented that:

> 'Wright J held that he should follow that approach in the present case. He rejected the submission, advanced on behalf of the claimant, that a finding of incapacity was required "if the effect of the injury to his brain renders [the claimant] vulnerable to exploitation or at the risk of the making of rash or irre-sponsible decisions" (see [2002] EWHC 417 (QB) at [24], [2002] All ER (D) (Mar) at [24]). I think that he was right to do so. The courts have ample powers to protect those who are vulnerable to exploitation from being exploited; it is unnecessary to deny them the opportunity to take their own decisions if they are not being exploited. It is not the task of the courts to prevent those who have the mental capacity to make rational decisions from making decisions which others may regard as rash or irresponsible' ([2003] 3 All ER 162 at 189).

Although the judge may have been naïve in assuming that the courts have ample powers to protect the vulnerable – assuming that the exploitation is identified, investigated and challenged – the MCA 2005 requires the same logical approach to be followed. Notwithstanding this principle, the circumstances may justify the application of the Act or the involvement of the Court of Protection. A person's vulnerability will be a factor that brings his circumstances to the attention of a concerned relative, solicitor or statutory body. There may be other ways of protecting the person concerned without involving the Court of Protection. The vulnerability may also be a symptom of a lack of capacity to manage or make other decisions. A person who receives a damages award and is in danger of dissipating it is more likely than not to lack capacity to manage the award, regardless of whether there is a risk of exploitation and abuse. On those grounds, the case might be dealt with by the Court of Protection. However, the mere fact of vulnerability does not by itself show that a person lacks capacity, as was emphasised by the High Court in the case of *Lindsay v Wood*. In his judgment, Stanley Burnton J emphasised that:

'vulnerability to exploitation does not of itself lead to the conclusion that there is lack of capacity. Many people who have full capacity are vulnerable to exploitation, or more so than most other people. Many people make rash and irresponsible decisions, but are of full capacity. The issue is, ... whether the person concerned has the mental capacity to make a rational decision.' ([2006] EWHC 2895 (QB) at para 18).

The difficulty of making an assessment in such cases was acknowledged in the notes issued to doctors completing Form CP3 which was used to certify that a person was incapable of managing their property and affairs for the purposes of Part Vll of the Mental Health Act 1983:

'In many cases of senile dementia, severe brain damage, acute or chronic psychiatric disorder and severe mental impairment the assessment of incapacity should present little difficulty. Cases of functional and personality disorders may give more problems and assessment may depend on the individual doctor's interpretation of mental disorder. The Court [tends] towards the view that these conditions render a person liable to their jurisdiction where there appears to be a real danger that they will lead to dissipation of considerable capital assets.'

These guidance notes are no longer applicable and do not appear in the notes to the current Court of Protection assessment of capacity form COP3. However, they would be applicable if modified slightly to show that such conditions 'are likely to but will not necessarily render' a person liable to the jurisdiction of the Court.

Assessing capacity

Capacity is a legal test

1.14   Section 2(4) of the MCA 2005 restates the principle that any question as to whether a person lacks capacity must be satisfied on the balance of probabilities and it is not necessary to be satisfied beyond reasonable doubt. This is consistent with the principle of capacity emphasised by s 1(2) and referred to in more detail at **1.3** above.

Where there is a presumption of capacity in favour of any person and where an action appears to have been carried out correctly, then the burden of proof lies with the person challenging the apparent validity of that action (see for instance *Re W* [2001] 4 All ER 88). The ultimate responsibility, however, rests with the court to make a judicial decision that a person lacks capacity. The question of whether a person has or does not have capacity is ultimately a legal one. Medical evidence is supplied to assist the court in making an assessment. This principle was expressed in the case of *Richmond v Richmond* (1914) LT 273 which concerned a dispute over medical evidence to determine whether or not Miss Richmond was still a patient. Neville J stated clearly that:

'With regard to the question of whether in any, or what degree, she is capable of managing her own affairs, and being bound by her own contracts and by her own acts, that, in my opinion is always a question for the court to decide ... although the court must have the evidence of experts in the medical profession who can indicate the meaning of symptoms and give some general ideas of the mental deterioration which takes place in cases of this kind.'

Who assesses capacity?

1.15 Although capacity is often thought of as a medical issue, the responsibility for assessing capacity falls on whoever it is who is dependent on or acting in connection with the decision in question. Most assessments of capacity will take place in informal day-to-day situations. A care worker or nurse will explain to a patient that he needs a new dressing or to receive his medication; a bank clerk will act on a customer's authority to release funds from an account; a solicitor will act on a client's instructions to prepare a document such as a will. In all these cases, the person acting on the authority of the decision-maker, is making an assessment of capacity. In most cases, this will be subconscious and capacity will simply be taken for granted. In other cases however, the decision requires a degree of formality to be implemented or the circumstances require a considered but basic assessment of capacity. A doctor who asks his patient to consent to an operation will need to certify that the patient understands the nature of the procedure and any associated risks. A solicitor who prepares a will for a client and acts as a witness is in effect confirming his belief that the client has capacity to make that document. If the solicitor prepares a Lasting Power of Attorney (LPA) for the client, he may be required to give the certificate of capacity, explicitly stating that his client has capacity to execute the instrument.

The MCA 2005 aims to give those dealing with decisions the tools to assess capacity. It also provides a framework for assessing capacity where the issues are more complicated. However, even where the situation is more complicated and expert advice is obtained, the responsibility for the assessment still rests with the person acting on the decision. A doctor who performs an operation or a solicitor who prepares a will may obtain advice from experts or colleagues as to whether the person concerned can make the decision; it remains for them, however, to decide whether they can then act on that decision. Even if the question of capacity is referred to the Court of Protection, the Court will merely confirm that the person concerned has capacity to make the decision.

When is medical evidence required?

1.16 It is not always obvious when expert advice should be required. Often this is only clear with hindsight. The MCA 2005 does provide a mechanism for assessing capacity and raises the awareness and relevance of this issue of capacity to people and situations where it might have been avoided in the past. Even if the statutory framework for assessing capacity is not sufficient by itself, it should at least help in identifying the questions that need to be asked when making an assessment and prompting a more accurate or detailed assessment.

It goes without saying that in difficult or potentially complex or contentious cases, where capacity is in issue, expert medical advice should be sought. Any solicitor dealing with an elderly or seriously ill client should consider the 'golden but tactless rule' suggested by Templeman J in *Kenward v Adams* (1975) Times, 29 November that medical advice should be obtained and carefully recorded. However, it is not always obvious who should actually make that assessment. Although most questions of capacity are initially referred to a person's general practitioner or clinician (especially if the person is in hospital), it is also important that the person who carries out the assessment has the right skills. A medical qualification is no guarantee of a good assessment. An orthopaedic surgeon or a busy general practitioner may not have the time or information to fully comprehend the need to investigate the decision in question, the correct test of capacity and the person's ability to meet that test.

Under the former Mental Health Act 1983 jurisdiction, the Court of Protection could only act if it had considered medical evidence. Evidence could only be accepted from a registered medical practitioner. The MCA 2005 jurisdiction is more flexible, as the Act makes no reference to the nature of the evidence the Court must rely on. This may appear to be an omission from the legislation, but the new Act aims to allow more detailed evidence from someone who is looking at the person's capacity in the context of the decision proposed and his or her best interests. A tick box form or one line letter from a doctor who has spent a few minutes with the person concerned is not enough. Practice Direction 9A therefore specifies that the Court must have evidence in a prescribed form, COP3. This requires a great detail of information about the decision before the Court and the ability of the person concerned to understand that decision. The form also accepts that a medical practitioner might not always be the best person to complete such a form. The form can be completed by a psychologist or psychiatrist. In certain circumstances, it might be appropriate for a speech therapist to complete the form. In complex cases it is also appropriate for more than one person to assess capacity and a multi-disciplinary approach may be needed. A speech therapist may for instance work with a psychologist to look at communication skills as evidence of understanding. A social worker, lawyer, advocate or relative might also be required to provide background information about the person's financial, social or emotional context which will inform the assessment of capacity being made.

Although formal medical evidence is often vital in determining a person's capacity, and is required by the Court of Protection, in other cases it is not the only evidence that a court will rely on. In the Court of Appeal decision in *Masterman-Lister v Jewell*, Chadwick LJ commented on the fact that two experienced solicitors felt comfortable taking instructions from the claimant (whose capacity was in issue). Their direct and contemporary evidence in that case carried as much weight, if not more, than the subsequent deliberations of medical experts ([2003] 3 All ER 162 at 190). The evidence of a solicitor or other independent observer will therefore be very important in determining the validity of a decision. Many Court of Protection decisions prefer the evidence of a solicitor who was present at the time of the decision and addressed the relevant tests of capacity to a medical expert looking back at events that took place some time previously.

Obtaining medical evidence

1.17   An assessment that a person lacks capacity may result in that person being deprived of fundamental rights and freedoms, and medical and legal practitioners need to ensure that what appears to be a simple formality is carried out tactfully and correctly. Doctors must also consider issues of patient confidentiality and the extent to which the patient can be informed of the purpose of the assessment. A patient who has capacity must be advised of the need for the assessment and can provide his informed consent. A doctor who considers that his patient lacks capacity should act in his best interests by providing medical evidence to the Court of Protection or to a solicitor on the understanding that the evidence is confidential. Form COP3 allows the practitioner completing the form to confirm that it contains sensitive information and that it is being returned directly to the Court.

Form COP3 also states explicitly that the contents of the form are confidential and will be confidential to the Court and those authorised by the Court to see it.

There may be cases where it is impossible for an applicant to the Court of Protection to provide the Court with medical evidence. Practice Direction 9A covers such a situation, so that an application can be made:

'If the applicant is unable to complete an assessment of capacity form (as may be the case, for example, where P does not reside with the applicant and the applicant is unable to take P to a doctor, or where P refuses to undergo the assessment), the applicant should file a witness statement with the application form explaining:

(a) why he has not been able to obtain an assessment of capacity;

(b) what attempts (if any) he has made to obtain an assessment of capacity; and

(c) why he knows or believes that P lacks capacity to make a decision or decisions in relation to any matter that is subject of the proposed application.'

The applicant should provide details of how medical evidence can be obtained and it may be that some doctors will only respond to an express authority from the Court. The Court may also arrange for a Court of Protection Special Visitor (appointed under s 61 of the MCA 2005) to visit the person concerned (see **2.45**).

The Court will generally require its principle evidence in form COP3. In an emergency other forms of evidence might be accepted. An assessment in the prescribed form may also be supplemented by other evidence. In most cases the applicant will prepare the form. The form is designed to ensure that the medical practitioner or expert as well as the Court understand what decision or decisions the person concerned is unable to make so that an appropriate order can be made. The form is therefore set out in two parts: the applicant completes the first part and passes the form to the expert to complete his part by reference to the first part. Where a person's ability to manage his property and affairs is concerned, the applicant will need to provide some information about the nature and extent of the estate so that capacity can be assessed correctly.

An applicant or his solicitor may also need to consider which is the right expert or experts to carry out an assessment. As has been mentioned at **1.15** above, a medical qualification is no guarantee of a good assessment. Often it is appropriate to approach the person's general practitioner who may have known his patient for some years and is able to view his current condition in the light of earlier knowledge. However, if the person concerned has not had much contact with his own doctor, the doctor acts for other members of the family and is concerned about a conflict of interest, the person is in hospital or the assessment is a particularly difficult one then it may well be more appropriate to obtain a formal assessment from a consultant psychiatrist.

Completion of Form COP3 is dealt with at **5.8** below.

Assessing the person concerned

1.18   Any person assessing capacity should be able to examine the person concerned privately and in a manner conducive to the assessment. The consequences of that assessment can be extremely serious, either permitting or preventing a decision that may have far-reaching implications. Assessment requires a fair degree of skill: to know when an assessment is required and in what detail it needs to be conducted and then to conduct it tactfully and objectively.

Some assessments will be entirely straightforward. A person with advanced dementia may have no memory or insight whatsoever and an assessment of capacity is a formality. However, the MCA 2005 is aimed at those cases where there is some degree of capacity, where a lack of capacity should not be taken for granted and the assessment of capacity should be carried out with the care and attention it requires. In such cases, an assessment of capacity can be – and often needs to be – a time-consuming and hence costly exercise.

A person carrying out an assessment needs to take account of the following considerations:

- *The function or decision in issue and any relevant legal tests.* As is clear from form COP3 it is not enough to tick a box and state that someone lacks capacity. The assessment needs to relate to a specific function or decision, even if it is an extremely general one such as an ability to manage property and affairs. A solicitor instructing a doctor carrying out an assessment of capacity therefore needs to ensure that the doctor has enough information about the circumstances and relevant legal tests to complete an assessment.

- *Whether there are any relevant background issues.* It can be difficult for a specialist to meet the client for the first time and then conduct a detailed assessment of capacity. It helps to have background information from medical notes or discussions with carers, relatives and other professionals. There may be difficult behavioural issues that may affect capacity that are not immediately obvious. A person's decision-making abilities may be affected by cultural, religious or ethnic considerations, or by family and personal circumstances. A seemingly irrational decision may be logical in context. Thus a person may want to leave his estate to a particular person or charity, cutting out other existing beneficiaries. The decision may be more appropriate when it is known what the proposed new beneficiary and former beneficiaries have done. Some people present better than their understanding merits while others have a better level of understanding than is apparent.

- *The need to take an independent view.* While family, carers and other professionals may help with background information and in facilitating an assessment, they may also have their own strong views and even with

17

the best intentions, aim to steer an assessment of capacity towards a particular outcome. There may also be cases where those engaged in the process have their own interests. It is therefore essential that at least some time is spent alone with the person concerned.

- *Supporting or enhancing capacity.* Under s 1(2) of the MCA 2005 a person is 'not to be treated as unable to make a decision unless all practicable steps to help him to do so have been taken without success' and under s 3(2) is not to be regarded as unable to make a decision 'if he is able to understand an explanation of it given to him in a way that is appropriate to his circumstances'. The person concerned is entitled to all necessary steps to enhance or support his ability to make a decision. It is not just a case of providing the person concerned with information or taking the time to explain matters in easily comprehensible terms. It may also involve seeing him in his own more comfortable surroundings, taking time to put him at ease or visiting at the time of day when he is at his most alert. Specialist support should also be obtained, for instance from a speech therapist where there are communication difficulties.

- *Section 2(2) of the MCA 2005.* The impairment or disturbance may be 'permanent or temporary'. The person concerned may have 'good days' and 'bad days' and may respond differently to an examination in different moods, in different surroundings and at different times of day.

The MCA 2005 may appear to make assessment of capacity a bureaucratic and burdensome exercise. It is inevitable that many professionals will hide behind the Act and claim that they are not qualified to make an assessment of capacity or that they cannot act on a decision until a detailed assessment has been completed. There are for instance doctors who will no longer complete a Court of Protection medical certificate, claiming it is too specialised and too time-consuming. It will be a great shame if the Act's objectives of empowering and supporting the vulnerable has the opposite effect. If the Act's objectives are to work in practice, it will be because those assessing capacity have the confidence and the ability to know when an assessment is necessary as well as the time, effort and expertise that needs to be involved.

Best interests

1.19   Having determined that a person lacks capacity to make a particular decision, the MCA 2005 requires a further assessment to be made. If the person concerned cannot make the decision in question, and another person or body has to make a decision on his behalf, what should that decision be? The Act does not supply an answer, as every decision is unique to the circumstances of the persons involved, both the person making the decision, as well as the person for whom it is made. Instead, the Act provides a logical process that will assist in making a decision which as far as possible reflects the decision which the person concerned would have made if capable of making it.

Best interests and substituted judgment

1.20   In attempting to determine what a person would decide in a particular situation requires an objective approach. The MCA 2005 provides no definition of 'best interests' as such. It merely states that a decision made on behalf of a person who lacks capacity must be made in that person's best interests and in determining what is in a person's best interest there are several factors that must be considered.

The 'best interests' criteria laid down by the MCA 2005 can give rise to some confusion. It is often assumed that a decision-maker must do whatever the person concerned would have done, trying to stand in his shoes and make the decision he would have made had he been able to make it for himself. This contrasts with the paternalistic approach of the Mental Health Act 1983 jurisdiction which required the decision maker to act in the person's best interests.

The true picture is more complicated. A receiver exercising his powers under the Mental Health Act 1983 did indeed have a duty to act for the 'maintenance or other benefit of the patient' (s 95(1). He had a simple duty to do whatever was necessary to maintain and provide for the patient. This also reflected the fact that the jurisdiction was primarily concerned with property and affairs where receivers had fiduciary responsibilities towards a person's estate. However, the Mental Health Act 1983 also allowed the Court, on behalf of the patient, to make provision for other persons or purposes 'for whom or which the patient might be expected to provide if he were not mentally disordered.' The Court would therefore aim to make a substituted judgment for the person who lacked capacity, an approach that was highlighted by Megarry V-C in the leading case of *Re D(J)* which dealt with the authority of the Court to authorise a statutory will. As Sir Robert Megarry explained:

'... subject to all due allowances, I think the court must seek to make the will which the actual patient, acting reasonably, would have made if notionally restored to full mental capacity, memory and foresight. If I may adopt Dr Johnson's words, used for another purpose, the court is to do for the patient what the patient would fairly do for himself, if he could.' ([1982] 2 All ER 37 at 43)

The MCA 2005 however requires the decision-maker to act in a person's best interests. The Law Commission in 'Mental Incapacity' rejected any incompatibility between the two concepts:

'We explained in our overview paper [Consultation Paper 119] that two criteria for making substitute decisions for another adult have been developed in the literature in this field: "best interests" on the one hand and "substituted judgment" on the other. In Consultation Paper No 128 we argued that the two were not in fact mutually exclusive and we provisionally favoured a "best interests" criterion which would contain a strong element of "substituted judgment."' (LawCom 231 at paragraph 3.25)

Although it may be hoped that there is no conflict between what a person might want and what his best interests are, the two are not always the same. A person may well have wished to do something unwise or illegal. He may have chosen to neglect his person or his property. This potential conflict was considered in some detail by Lewison J in the case of *Re P* [2009] EWHC 163 (Ch), who drew attention to the explanatory notes to the Mental Capacity Bill to remind us (at paragraph 37) that:

'Best interests is not a test of "substituted judgment" (what the person would have wanted), but rather it requires a determination to be made by applying an objective test as to what would be in the person's best interests.'

Doctrine of best interests

1.21   The concept of 'best interests' has been used by the courts in developing the jurisdiction to make declarations as to whether particular treatment or lack of treatment could be carried out. Thus a physician would be entitled to treat a patient who lacked capacity in his clinical best interests. He could do whatever was necessary to prevent a deterioration in the patient's condition, a position clearly set out by Lord Brandon in the House of Lords decision in *F v West Berkshire Health Authority*:

'In my opinion, the solution to the problem which the common law provides is that a doctor can lawfully operate on, or give other treatment to, adult patients who are incapable, for one reason or another, of consenting to his doing so, provided that the operation or other treatment concerned is in the best interests of such patients. The operation or other treatment will be in their best interests if, but only if, it is carried out in order either to save their lives or to ensure improvement or prevent deterioration in their physical or mental health.' ([1989] 2All ER 545 at 551)

The courts confirmed that any treatment was subject to consent where a person had capacity to give consent and had to be carried out in accordance with a responsible and competent body of professional opinion (*Bolam v Friern Hospital Management Committee* [1957] 2 All ER 118). The concept of best interests could be applied to the withdrawal of treatment as much as to the continuation of treatment (see for instance *Airedale NHS Trust v Bland* [1993] 1 All ER 821).

In deciding whether an act was in a person's best interests, the decision maker would be expected to perform a balancing exercise, weighing up the advantages and disadvantages of the decision. As Thorpe LJ explained in *Re A (Male Sterilisation)* [2000] 1 FLR 549:

'There can be no doubt in my mind that the evaluation of best interests is akin to a welfare appraisal ... pending the enactment of a checklist or other statutory direction it seems to me that the first instance judge with the responsibility to make an evaluation of the best interests of a claimant lacking capacity should draw up a balance sheet. The first entry should be of any factor or factors of actual benefit. In the present case the instance would be the acquisition of fool-proof contraception. Then on the other sheet the judge should write any counter-balancing dis-benefits to the applicant. An obvious instance in this case would be the apprehension, the risk and the discomfort inherent in the operation. Then the judge should enter on each sheet the potential gains and losses in each instance making some estimate of the extent of the possibility that the gain or loss might accrue. At the end of that exercise the judge should be better placed to strike a balance between the sum of the certain and possible gains against the sum of the certain and possible losses. Obviously, only if the account is in relatively significant credit will the judge conclude that the applicant is likely to advance the best interests of the claimant.'

The section 4 checklist

1.22   The MCA 2005 adopts the 'best interests' approach developed by the courts in developing a welfare jurisdiction. Thus the same principles can be applied to financial as well as welfare decisions. To assist with the application of these principles in practice s 4 of the MCA 2005 provides a simple checklist of factors which a person or body such as the Court of Protection must apply in determining whether a particular decision made on behalf of a person is in his or her best interests:

'(1)   In determining for the purposes of this Act what is in a person's best interests, the person making the determination must not make it merely on the basis of—

    (a)   the person's age or appearance, or

    (b)   a condition of his, or an aspect of his behaviour, which might lead others to make unjustified assumptions about what might be in his best interests.

(2)   The person making the determination must consider all the relevant circumstances and, in particular, take the following steps.

(3)   He must consider—

    (a)   whether it is likely that the person will at some time have capacity in relation to the matter in question, and

    (b)   if it appears likely that he will, when that is likely to be.

(4)   He must, so far as reasonably practicable, permit and encourage the person to participate, or to improve his ability to participate, as fully as possible in any act done for him and any decision affecting him.

(5)   Where the determination relates to life-sustaining treatment he must not, in considering whether the treatment is in the best interests of the person concerned, be motivated by a desire to bring about his death.

(6)   He must consider, so far as is reasonably ascertainable—

    (a)   the person's past and present wishes and feelings (and, in particular, any relevant written statement made by him when he had capacity),

    (b)   the beliefs and values that would be likely to influence his decision if he had capacity, and

    (c)   the other factors that he would be likely to consider if he were able to do so.

(7)   He must take into account, if it is practicable and appropriate to consult them, the views of—

    (a)   anyone named by the person as someone to be consulted on the matter in question or on matters of that kind,

    (b)   anyone engaged in caring for the person or interested in his welfare,

    (c)   any donee of a lasting power of attorney granted by the person, and

    (d)   any deputy appointed for the person by the court,

as to what would be in the person's best interests and, in particular, as to the matters mentioned in subsection (6).

(8)   The duties imposed by subsections (1) to (7) also apply in relation to the exercise of any powers which—

(a)   are exercisable under a lasting power of attorney, or

(b)   are exercisable by a person under this Act where he reasonably believes that another person lacks capacity.

(9)   In the case of an act done, or a decision made, by a person other than the court, there is sufficient compliance with this section if (having complied with the requirements of subsections (1) to (7)) he reasonably believes that what he does or decides is in the best interests of the person concerned.

(10)   "Life-sustaining treatment" means treatment which in the view of a person providing health care for the person concerned is necessary to sustain life.

(11)   "Relevant circumstances" are those—

(a)   of which the person making the determination is aware, and

(b)   which it would be reasonable to regard as relevant.'

Determining best interests

1.23   An assessment carried out in accordance with s 4 of the MCA 2005 does therefore provide a method of determining the best interests of a person who lacks capacity. It is the working out of the balance sheet described by Thorpe LJ in *Re A*. It should however, be emphasised that it is not an infallible method. One person's view of someone's best interests may be completely at variance with another's. It may also be impossible to know what the person concerned would wish to do in circumstances he had never envisaged and about which he had never expressed any view whatsoever. What s 4 does do is ensure that a logical process is followed. Thus the right questions must be asked, the relevant information must be taken into account and a considered decision must be made which is itself open to scrutiny. The person making the decision cannot simply rush ahead and make a decision which he wants to make regardless of the 'best interests considerations'. A decision-maker who has applied this method and as a result of that reasonably believes that the decision is in the best interests of the person concerned is then afforded the protection of sub-s 4(9).

How decisions can be made in individual situations is dealt with in more detail in the parts of this work that deal with those situations that need to be addressed by the Court of Protection or persons making decisions under the Act. However, some general observations can be considered at this stage:

•   The person making the determination is required to consider or take into account certain factors. He cannot ignore them or impose his own judgment without having considered the factors that he is required to consider.

•   A person's past and present wishes and feelings are factors that must be considered, so far as is reasonably ascertainable. The decision-maker is not bound to follow those wishes and feelings; but neither should he seek to depart from them. They are matters that carry 'great weight' (see the decision of Hazel Marshall QC in *Re S v S* (25 November 2008, unreported a full transcript is available at www.publicguardian.gov.uk/forms/other-orders-cop.htm). As the judge points out (at paragraph 55):

> 'What, after all, is the point of taking great trouble to ascertain or deduce P's views, and to encourage P to be involved in the decision-making process, unless the objective is to achieve the outcome which P wants or prefers, even if he does not have the capacity to achieve it for himself.'

- The decision must take into account 'other factors that [P] would be likely to consider if he were able to do so (sub-s 4(6)(c)). Thus the decision-maker may take account of present circumstances that were not present when an earlier decision or expression of wishes was recorded. The decision-maker may disregard a previous advance directive when making a welfare decision or the provisions of an earlier will when making a new statutory will.

- The decision a person would have made might be constrained by a lack of proper advice and information. 'Other factors' the person might consider would include independent professional advice (see for instance the fourth proposition advanced by Megarry V-C in *Re D(J)* [1982] 2 All ER 37. After all, a person cannot be said to have capacity to make a decision unless he has all the relevant information necessary to make the decision in question. But the decision-maker must also remember that the decision is his decision. It is therefore the actual and present responsibility of the decision-maker to obtain appropriate advice and assistance.

- The balancing of competing factors and the weight that needs to be given to a person's wishes and feelings was considered in great detail by Lewison J in *Re P* [2009] EWHC 163 (Ch); [2009] All ER 160 (Feb)). (This important case is considered in more detail in the context of specific decisions at **4.10** and **13.15**). The judge set out three propositions (at paragraph 41):

> 'First, section 1 (6) is not a statutory direction that one "must achieve" any desired objective by the least restrictive route. Section 1 (6) only requires that before a decision is made "regard must be had" to that question. It is an important question, to be sure, but it is not determinative. The only imperative is that the decision must be made in P's best interests. Second, although P's wishes must be given weight, if, as I think, Parliament has endorsed the "balance sheet" approach, they are only one part of the balance. I agree that those wishes are to be given great weight, but I would prefer not to speak in terms of presumptions. Third, any attempt to test a decision by reference to what P would hypothetically have done or wanted runs the risk of amounting to a "substituted judgment" rather than a decision of what would be in P's best interests. But despite this risk, the Act itself requires some hypothesising. The decision maker must consider the beliefs and values that would be likely to influence P's decision if he had capacity and also the other factors that P would be likely to consider if he were able to do so. This does not, I think, necessarily require those to be given effect.'

The judge then cited in support of his propositions the Code of Practice (at paragraph 5.38):

'In setting out the requirements for working out a person's 'best interests', section 4 of the Act puts the person who lacks capacity at the centre of the decision to be made. Even if they cannot make the decision, their wishes and feelings, beliefs and values should be taken fully into account – whether expressed in the past or now. But their wishes and feelings, beliefs and values will not necessarily be the deciding factor in working out their best interests. Any such assessment must consider past and current wishes and feelings, beliefs and values alongside all other factors, but the final decision must be based entirely on what is in the person's best interests.'

An overly strict adherence to a person's 'wishes and feelings' may lead to some harsh results. This is illustrated by the case of a personal injury claimant who wishes to buy an expensive car and go on exotic holidays. Or the case of the elderly person who has lived frugally in his own home but whose family would like him looked after in a well appointed nursing home. The decision-maker must remember that it is his responsibility to act in the best interests of the person.

- Likewise, a person's whose known wishes or feelings are delusional or irrational might be disregarded or placed in a wider context. As Megarry V-C commented in *Re D(J)*:

'I do not think that the court should give effect to antipathies or affections of the patient which are beyond reason.' ([1982] 2 All ER at 43)

- Section 4 of the MCA 2005 does not go as far as creating a presumption in favour of giving effect to a person's known wishes and feelings. However, they should not be disregarded unless there is some 'extraneous consequence, or some other unforeseen, unknown or unappreciated factor. (*S v S* 25 November 2008, unreported, at paragraph 58). The decision can be tested by asking the question whether the person for whom the decision is made would have changed his wishes had he known of such new factors. Another approach is for the decision-maker to ask the question: why should a person's wishes and feelings be disregarded?

- If a person's likely wishes and feelings are unwise, it should not be in his best interests to adhere to them. This contrasts with the right of a person who has capacity to make an unwise decision (s 1(4)). Where a person has capacity then his right to make good and bad decisions cannot be supplanted. But where there is no capacity, the situation is altered. Where a person lacks capacity and another person or body must make a decision on his behalf, the decision-maker cannot be expected to make an unwise decision, even if P might have made an unwise decision for himself when he had capacity. As Lewison J commented in *Re P*:

'I would add that although the fact that P makes an unwise decision does not on its own give rise to any inference of incapacity (section 1 (4)), once the decision making power shifts to a third party (whether carer, deputy or the court) I cannot see that it would be a proper exercise for a third-party decision-maker consciously to make an unwise decision merely because P would have done so. A consciously unwise decision will rarely if ever be in P's best interests.' ([2009] EWHC 163 (Ch)) at paragraph 42).

- The importance of *Re P* cannot be understated. A decision-maker cannot adhere simply to a person's known wishes and feelings. He can – or indeed, should – take a more responsible and robust approach. A deputy could easily be failing in his duties if he failed to maintain a property just because the person had neglected it or failed to sell land to someone whom the person had disliked. A doctor could also be negligent if he failed to treat a patient who had an aversion to a particular treatment at a time when he had capacity but which cannot be said to apply subsequently when he lacked capacity.

- Subsection 4(7) requires the decision-maker to consult with others. This can cause an obvious conflict or difficulty. The persons consulted should be involved to provide evidence of the person's best interests; they are not necessarily required to provide their own opinions as to what they think is best or what the person concerned would think was best. Care must also be taken when consulting relatives and carers who have a financial interest in the outcome. In one recent case the judge considered the statements of family members who were also beneficiaries under a proposed statutory will. He would be very cautious about 'potentially self-serving evidence' – even though the judgment accorded with the views of the family members. The evidence of a doctor and an attorney who had no financial interest in the outcome was regarded as more persuasive.

- Despite the need to approach consultation carefully, it was strongly recommended by Lord Goff in *F v West Berkshire Health Authority*:

  'It must surely be good practice to consult relatives and others who are concerned with the care of the patient. Sometimes, of course, consultation with a specialist or specialists will be required; and in others, especially where the decision involves more than a purely medical opinion, an inter-disciplinary team will in practice participate in the decision. It is very difficult, and would be unwise, for a court to do more than to stress that, for those who are involved in these important and sometimes difficult decisions, the overriding consideration is that they should act in the best interests of the person who suffers from the misfortune of being prevented by incapacity from deciding for himself what should be done to his own body in his own best interests.' ([1989] 2 All ER 545 at 567)

The statutory checklist provided by the MCA 2005 does assume that the decision-maker using it is acting conscientiously and dispassionately. The less than scrupulous decision-maker can also use the s 4 criteria to use the facts to achieve the results desired by him. Subsection 4(5) concerning life-sustaining treatment may also be hard to explain when it is also claimed that it is in the best interests of the person concerned to bring about his death. Such decisions have yet to be scrutinised judicially and it is hoped that with time a body of law will develop to protect the vulnerable and to assist and guide those making difficult decisions on their behalf.

Chapter 2

The new Court of Protection

Context of the new Court

The Mental Capacity Act 2005

2.1   On 1 October 2007 the Mental Capacity Act 2005 (MCA 2005) came into force. As we shall see, this is an impressive and ambitious piece of legislation which sets out to consolidate in a single piece of legislation the law relating to legal capacity. This covers both the legal nature of capacity and the legal framework within which decisions can be made on behalf of persons who lack capacity. The Act aims to address not just the question of how to make decisions, but also when decisions can be made, what decisions can be made and what those decisions should be.

The starting point of the Act is the principle, set out in s 1, that a person must be assumed to have capacity unless it is established that he lacks capacity. The Act aims to enable or empower the individual person to make as many decisions as he is able, with as little interference as possible. Only when a person cannot make a decision for himself does the Act allow a decision to be made on his behalf. That such a decision should be a judicial decision or pursuant to a judicial order is a last resort. Decisions can therefore be made in different forms and at different levels:

- by an individual exercising his autonomous rights to make his own decisions (s 1);

- by an individual refusing treatment in advance, so that the earlier decision is valid and applicable at a later date when he lacks capacity (ss 24–26);

- by another person performing basic acts of care and treatment or paying for essential goods and services, where there is no other form of authority in place (ss 5–8);

- by another person to whom authority has been delegated by the individual under a Lasting Power of Attorney (LPA) (ss 9–14 and Sch 1);

- by another person to whom authority has been delegated by the individual under an Enduring Power of Attorney (EPA) made prior to 1 October 2007 (Sch 4);

- by the Court of Protection exercising its own authority or authorising another person to make a decision (ss 15–23, 48 and 49).

The different levels at which decisions can be made are a hierarchy. At the apex is the autonomous individual making his own decisions. An individual may then appoint another person to make decisions on his behalf. Decisions may be made in connection with care and treatment at a local or informal level. Only if there is no other remedy should the Court be involved.

When the Court of Protection is involved, it can either make decisions on behalf of an individual who lacks capacity or delegate authority to another person (a deputy) to make decisions on behalf of an individual who lacks capacity. The Court also has an important role in overseeing LPAs and EPAs and intervening where there are problems or disputes involving their validity or operation. Although the Court of Protection should therefore be a court of last resort, it sits at the heart of the new legislation, as its ultimate guardian and providing a remedy where an individual lacks capacity and there is no other way of enabling a decision to be made for that person. The fact that it should only intervene where there is no other remedy does not in any way diminish the importance of the Court. It has extensive powers to make decisions concerning a person's property and affairs as well as a person's welfare. These are vitally important decisions and as the Court can authorise the continuation or withdrawal of life-sustaining treatment, the Court may well have a power of life or death over an individual. However, any decision made by the Court will have a direct bearing on the individual's interests: the choice of deputy or a decision as to where a person will live may have a major impact on that person's quality of life; every decision goes to the heart of the person's identity and the Court of Protection deserves the consideration and respect that goes with its responsibilities.

History of the Court of Protection

2.2   Although the MCA 2005 creates an entirely new Court of Protection, the title of this body suggests some continuity with the past. Although its powers derive from statute, the Court of Protection continues to exercise the inherent jurisdiction of the Crown to manage the property and affairs of persons who lack the capacity to do so. This jurisdiction has evolved piecemeal since the Middle Ages. The origins of a distinct body or court that resembles the present Court of Protection go back to 1842 and the appointment of the two Commissioners in Lunacy. Despite these appointments the power to make orders was retained by the Lord Chancellor and the Lords of Appeal in Chancery. The Commissioners in Lunacy were renamed Masters in Lunacy in 1846 and acquired the power to make orders in 1891. In 1922 the number of Masters was reduced to one and in 1947 the Lunacy Office, which was briefly known by the unfortunate title of the Management and Administration Department, became the Court of Protection. This title was confirmed by the Mental Health Acts of 1959 and 1983, which established the Court of Protection with the form and status of an office of the Supreme Court.

The limitations of this body were, however, numerous and recognised by the various reports that led to the introduction of the new legislation, principally the 1995 Law Commission Report *Mental Incapacity* (Law Com) No 231. Although decisions could be made by nominated judges of the High Court, such decisions were extremely rare. Most decisions were dealt with by the

Master and nominated officers of the Court. As only the Master held a judicial office, many decisions were made by civil servants. While administration as such was carried out by the Public Trust Office and from 2001 by the Public Guardianship Office, these were in effect the administrative arms of the Court of Protection. The Public Guardianship Office itself had no statutory basis or authority, despite often giving the appearance of making many day-to-day decisions. Its performance also suffered from a combination of factors: its uncertain and lowly status, regular reforms and improvements, lack of funding and trying to do too much with limited resources.

The principal limitation of the Court of Protection was, however, that it had no jurisdiction to make decisions concerning a person's welfare (*F v West Berkshire Health Authority* [1989] 2 All ER 545). This led to two obvious difficulties. First, it was not always possible to distinguish financial decisions from welfare ones as one usually has a bearing on the other; and second, where welfare decisions had to be made, these could only be made by the High Court or, on appeal, by the Court of Appeal or House of Lords. As there was no formal or statutory basis on which welfare decisions could be made, the High Court would in effect use its inherent powers to make declarations as to whether or not a proposed treatment or action was lawful within the existing common law (*Airedale NHS Trust v Bland* [1993] AC 789*).* Furthermore, as decisions could only be made in the High Court, the expense and complexity of proceedings ensured that applications were only made in exceptional circumstances and usually by health authorities who could afford the costs involved.

There were therefore two separate structures for welfare and financial matters. While in purely pragmatic terms these arrangements worked reasonably well, they were not an ideal solution. The limited role of the Court of Protection meant that it was treated as a legal anomaly or backwater outside of the main court structure. As such, the Court only had one venue in North London, apart from an arrangement for some hearings from 2001 onwards being held at Preston. More importantly, the lack of a readily accessible forum for important welfare decisions was not acceptable in a society where access to justice for the vulnerable and disabled was of fundamental importance. The Human Rights Act 1998 and the culture that underpins it could not countenance the blurring of the boundaries between the judicial role of the Court of Protection and the administrative role of the Public Guardianship Office (regardless of any practical benefits in this arrangement). The Court of Protection was an administrative body, with most of its decisions being made by clerical officers rather than judges.

The new Act would therefore set out to address these historical anomalies and practical defects. It would aim to create a new Court of Protection with clearly defined and widely drawn powers, with a separation of powers between the judges of the Court and the supervisory and administrative functions of a separate body known as the Public Guardian. The new Court would meanwhile work within existing court structures and have the prestige and authority that this would bring.

Terminology

2.3   The MCA 2005 introduces a new vocabulary for persons without capacity. Unlike the Mental Health Act jurisdiction, which defined a person who was unable to manage his property and affairs by reason of mental disorder, as a 'patient', the MCA 2005 attaches no such label to a person. The aim is to demonstrate that no one has a label attached that connotes a permanent status. The Act is concerned with individual acts rather than the person as a whole and it is therefore inappropriate to alter the status of the person who may well be capable of some acts at some moments in time and incapable of other acts at other moments in time. The person who lacks capacity who is the object of the Court's powers is a person who lacks capacity in relation to a particular matter or matters and for that matter or matters when he is the object of the Court's powers he is generally defined by the Act and the Court of Protection Rules simply, if somewhat bluntly, as 'P'.

In applications made to the Court, 'P' is usually described in Court forms as 'the person to whom this application relates'. In proceedings he is described as P or where a litigation friend is acting on his behalf, as 'P (by AB, his litigation friend)'. Other terms and definitions used by the Act are set out at **3.4**.

The new Court of Protection

Statutory basis

2.4   On coming into effect on 1 October 2007, the MCA 2005 created the new Court of Protection and abolished the old court. Section 45 succinctly provides as follows:

'(1) There is to be a superior court of record known as the Court of Protection...'

'(6) The office of the Supreme Court called the Court of Protection ceases to exist.'

Various parts of the Act contain provisions for further regulations to be made to effect the detailed or practical implementation of the Act. While the Act contains the Court's principal powers, the detailed way in which those powers are to be exercised is covered by the Court of Protection Rules 2007. Thus the provisions of the Act are in effect supplemented by the following Orders, Rules and Regulations:

- Lasting Power of Attorney, Enduring Power of Attorney and Public Guardian Regulations 2007 (SI 2007/1253);
- Court of Protection Fees Order 2007 (SI 2007/1745) as amended by the Court of Protection Fees (Amendment) Order 2009 (SI 2009/513);
- Court of Protection Rules 2007 (SI 2007/1899) as amended by the Court of Protection (Amendment) Rules 2009 (SI 2009/582) ('the Rules');
- Mental Capacity Act 2005 (Transfer of Proceedings) Order 2007 (SI 2007/1989);

- Mental Capacity Act 2005 (Transitional and Consequential Provisions) Order 2007 (SI 2007/1898);

- Public Guardian (Fees, etc) Regulations 2007 (SI 2007/2051) as amended by the Public Guardian (Fees, etc.) (Amendment) Regulations 2009 (SI 2009/514); and

- the Civil Procedure (Amendment) Rules 2007 (SI 2007/2204).

Section 52 of the Act also provides for the giving of practice directions by the President of the Court of Protection dealing with practice and procedure in the Court of Protection. These various rules and practice directions further require the use of specific prescribed forms.

The result of this legislative and regulatory medley is a remarkably complex set of documentation. It is unlikely that every part functions as efficiently as it should and a hallmark of this area of law will be the need for constant refinement and change. At the time of publication, the Ministry of Justice is proposing amendments to the Lasting Power of Attorney, Enduring Power of Attorney and Public Guardian Regulations 2007, principally to update the prescribed LPA forms (Consultation Paper CP26/08).

Status of the new Court

2.5   To ensure that the new Court of Protection has the standing and authority it requires, the MCA 2005 establishes the new Court as a superior court of record, which will have the same powers, rights, privileges and authority as the High Court.

As a court of record, decisions can be reported (where permitted by the Court) and used as precedents. Not only will the Court build up a body of precedents for its own use and guidance, but reported decisions will be more widely available for the use of lawyers and others looking to see how the Court makes its decisions.

With the authority of the High Court, the Court of Protection also has greater standing to make and enforce its decisions in practice. However, the main improvement and enhancement of the status of the Court is in its composition: only the judges of the Court of Protection have authority to exercise the Court's powers under the Act.

Judges of the Court of Protection

2.6   Section 46 describes the nominated judges of the Court of Protection. For a judge to be nominated as a judge of the Court of Protection, he must be nominated by the Lord Chief Justice or a person nominated to act on his behalf, who may be the President of the Court of Protection or a judicial office holder (as defined in s 109(4) of the Constitutional Reform Act 2005). A person who may be nominated must be a judge from among the judges listed in s 46(2):

(a)   the President of the Family Division;

(b)   the Vice-Chancellor;

(c)   a puisne judge of the High Court;

(d)   a circuit judge; or

(e)   a district judge.

Subsections (3) and (4) further provide that

- one of the judges in sub-ss (2)(a)–(c) will be appointed President of the Court of Protection;

- one of the judges in sub-ss (2)(a)–(c) will be appointed Vice-President of the Court of Protection; and

- one of the judges in sub-ss (2)(d) or (e) will be appointed Senior Judge of the Court of Protection 'having such administrative functions in relation to the court as the Lord Chief Justice, after consulting the Lord Chancellor, may direct'.

The Act therefore provides for the exercise of the Court's powers at different judicial levels. Unlike other courts therefore, the Court of Protection operates at more than one level as a self-contained court. Only where there is an appeal against a decision of one of the High Court judges is it necessary for a decision to be made outside of the Court of Protection by the Court of Appeal or House of Lords.

President and Vice-President

2.7   By an appointment dated 26 September 2005 made by the Lord Chancellor, Sir Mark Potter and Sir Andrew Morritt (President and Vice President respectively of the Family Division) were appointed President and Vice President of the Court of Protection.

The status of the President and Vice President raises the profile of the Court of Protection, reflecting the equivalent and prestigious roles of President and Vice President of the Family Division. Their experience and standing will also help integrate the Court of Protection into the mainstream court system and ensure continuity with the role of the Family Division, which prior to the implementation of the Act had been responsible for exercising the welfare jurisdiction of the courts.

The President of the Court of Protection also has the authority (delegated to him by the Lord Chief Justice) to exercise the power of nomination of judges to the Court of Protection under s 46 of the Act and must concur with the Lord Chancellor in approving any regulations passed under the Act. Under s 52, he has express power to give directions as to practice and procedure as well as to give guidance as to law or the making of judicial decisions.

Although the current holders of these offices were appointed by the Lord Chancellor, following the passing of the Constitutional Reform Act 2005, any future appointment must be made by the Lord Chief Justice, after consulting the Lord Chancellor.

High Court judges

2.8   On 24 April 2007 the President nominated all the High Court judges of the Family Division and Chancery Division as judges of the Court of Protection to hear Court of Protection cases on a part-time basis. Their role will be to hear complex and contentious first instance cases, principally where end of life decisions are in issue, as well as to hear appeals from decisions made at circuit judge level.

Practice Direction 9E deals with cases to be heard by High Court judges and this and the procedure for appeal are dealt with in more detail in Chapter 3.

Circuit judges

2.9   On 16 April 2007 the President nominated the following Circuit Judges to hear Court of Protection cases:

His Honour Judge Alweis
His Honour Judge Barclay
His Honour Judge Behrens
His Honour Judge Cardinal
Her Honour Judge Darwall Smith
His Honour Judge Hamilton
His Honour Judge Hodge QC
His Honour Judge Kaye TD, QC
Her Honour Judge Marshall QC
Her Honour Judge Moir
His Honour Judge Norris, QC – now a High Court Judge
His Honour Judge Pelling QC
His Honour Judge Price QC

His Honour Judge Purle QC was nominated in place of Judge Norris on 13 November 2007.

Senior Judge

2.10   The former Master of the Court of Protection, Denzil Lush, who held that title under s 93 of the (repealed) Mental Health Act 1983, was appointed Senior Judge for the purposes of s 46(4) of the Mental Capacity Act. As he was not a circuit judge for the purposes of that section, the Mental Capacity Act 2005 (Transitional and Consequential Provisions) Order 2007 (SI 2007/1898), art 4 provided that:

'The person who, immediately before the commencement of Part 2 of the Act, holds the office of Master of the Court of Protection, shall be treated as—

(a)   being a circuit judge nominated under section 46(1) of the Act to exercise the jurisdiction of the Court of Protection; and

(b)   having been appointed the Senior Judge of the Court of Protection under section 46(4) of the Act.'

The Senior Judge is a full-time judge of the Court of Protection and sits at the central registry at Archway, where the Court's full-time judges are based. His main role is to head the central registry and permanent court at Archway, described below at **2.13**.

Although the current holder of this office was appointed by the Lord Chancellor, following the passing of the Constitutional Reform Act 2005, any future appointment must be made by the Lord Chief Justice, after consulting the Lord Chancellor.

District judges

2.11   The workhorses of the new Court are the district judges, who will be responsible for the great majority of day-to-day decisions as well as directions and orders that need to be given during the course of proceedings in the Court of Protection. At the time of writing, the President, Sir Mark Potter, has nominated the following district judges to hear Court of Protection cases:

Date	*District Judge*	*Address*
23.01.2007	District Judge Duncan Adam	Swindon Combined Court, The Law Courts, Islington Street, Swindon SN1 2HG
23.01.2007	District Judge Michael Anson	Walsall Hearing Centre, County Court, Bridge House, Bridge Street, Walsall WS1 1JQ
23.01.2007	District Judge Gordon Ashton	Preston Combined Court Centre, The Law Courts, Ring Way, Preston PR1 2LL
23.01.2007	District Judge Bazley-White	Ipswich County Court, 8 Arcade Street, Ipswich IP1 1EJ
23.01.2007	District Judge John Coffey	Liverpool Civil and Family Court, 35 Vernon Street, Liverpool L2 2BX
17.05.2007	District Judge Penny Cushing	Principal Registry of the Family Division (PRFD), First Avenue House, 42–49 High Holborn, London WC1N 6NP
23.01.2007	District Judge Tony Davies	Birmingham Civil Justice Centre, Priory Courts, 33 Bull Street, Birmingham B4 6DS
23.01.2007	District Judge Richard Dawson	Pontypridd County Court, The Courthouse, Courthouse Street, Pontypridd CF37 1JR

Date	District Judge	Address
12.04.2007	District Judge John Freeman	Poole County Court, Civic Centre, Park Road, Poole, Dorset
23.01.2007	District Judge Margaret Glentworth	Wakefield County Court, Crown House, 127 Kirkgate, Wakefield WF1 1JW
12.04.2007	District Judge Nicholas Goudie	Newcastle Combined Court Centre, The Law Courts, The Quayside, Newcastle-upon-Tyne NE1 3LA
17.05.2007	District Judge Richard Harper	Principal Registry of the Family Division (PRFD), First Avenue House, 42-49 High Holborn, London WC1N 6NP
12.04.2007	District Judge Anthony Harrison	Courts of Justice, Crown Square, Manchester M3 3FL
23.01.2007	District Judge Charles Khan	Manchester County Court, Crown Square, Manchester M60 9DJ
23.01.2007	District Judge Knifton	Birmingham Civil Justice Centre, Priory Courts, 33 Bull Street, Birmingham B4 6DS
23.01.2007	District Judge Gordon Lingard	Bradford Combined Court Centre, Bradford Law Courts, Exchange Square, Drake Street, Bradford BD1 1JA
23.01.2007	District Judge Mainwaring-Taylor	Teesside Combined Court Centre, Russell Street, Middlesbrough TS1 2AE
23.01.2007	District Judge David Millard	Nottingham County Court, 60 Canal Street, Nottingham NG1 7EJ
23.01.2007	District Judge Debbi O'Regan	Birmingham Civil Justice Centre, Priory Courts, 33 Bull Street, Birmingham B4 6DS
23.01.2007	District Judge David Owen	Birmingham Civil Justice Centre, Priory Courts, 33 Bull Street, Birmingham B4 6DS
23.01.2007	District Judge Michael Payne	Oxford Combined Court Centre, St Aldates, Oxford OX1 1TL
23.01.2007	District Judge A B Thomas	Gloucester Family and Civil Courts, Kimbrose Way, Gloucester GL1 2DE
17.05.2007	District Judge Susannah Walker	Principal Registry of the Family Division (PRFD), First Avenue House, 42–49 High Holborn, London WC1N 6NP

Date	District Judge	Address
17.05.2007	Senior District Judge Philip Waller	Principal Registry of the Family Division (PRFD), First Avenue House, 42–49 High Holborn, London WC1N 6NP

All the above judges are already appointed and have existing responsibilities and workloads. They are therefore part-time judges. In view of the need to have dedicated judges in place to deal with the day-to-day work of the Court and provide a level of continuity for the conduct of the Court's business, the following judges have been appointed to sit at Archway:

Date	District Judge
30.01.2007	District Judge Susan Jackson
23.01.2007	District Judge Marc Marin
31.01.2007	District Judge Stephen Rogers
12.09.2007	District Judge Keeley Bishop
02.04.2009	District Judge Alex Ralton

The five judges based at Archway are together with the Senior Judge full time apart from Judge Marin who sits one week in four. Due to the higher than expected workload of the Court, it is likely that additional judges will be appointed in the course of 2010. Until then, more cases are transferred to the other district judges, some of whom are also sitting at Archway from time to time.

Location of the Court

2.12   One of the aims of the MCA 2005 is to widen access to justice by making its judges more widely available than was the case under the Mental Health Act jurisdiction. As is clear from the spread of district judges, most of England and Wales is covered quite thoroughly. However, although s 45(3) allows the Court to sit at any time and at any place, there are at the time of writing, only a limited number of designated venues for the Court of Protection. Apart from the central court at Archway in North London, current designated venues are the central courts in Preston, Manchester, Newcastle, Bristol, Cardiff and Birmingham. The number of venues will expand as the demand increases, although this is less of a practical problem than had been anticipated as nominated judges are also able to organise hearings to be conducted in their own courts.

As the facilities at Archway remain limited, arrangements are in place to use the Brent Magistrates' Court as an extension to Archway where hearings require several parties to attend, especially if solicitors and counsel are also in attendance. It is also understood that the Central London County Court will also be used as a venue for hearings before a circuit judge other than the Senior Judge (who is based at Archway) as well as for appeals against decisions of the district judges. Where the issues before the Court are complex or contentious, the case may also be referred to a puisne judge.

The central registry and court

2.13 Section 45(4) of the MCA 2005 provides for the Court of Protection having a central registry at a place appointed by the Lord Chancellor. Although there is provision for further registries to be designated, there is just the one registry at:

Archway Tower
2 Junction Road
London
N19 5SZ
DX 141150 Archway 2

The central registry provides a single venue for all applications to be processed, regardless of where and at what level those applications are to be held. Although the Court of Protection is a separate organisation, premises are currently shared with the Public Guardian who was initially charged with responsibility for the Court's administration. Both bodies currently share a single helpline number and website:

Phone Number: 0845 330 2900
Website: http://www.hmcourts-service.gov.uk/

It is the role of the Court staff based at Archway to process the extensive paperwork relating to applications and proceedings generally. The district judges (with the dedicated Court staff based at Archway) are therefore able to work with the Senior Judge in order to:

- act with the Senior Judge who has principal responsibility for the allocation of cases, addressing both issues of workload and ensuring that cases are heard by the right level of judge;

- provide a single point of reference for new applications and enabling papers to be transmitted to other courts;

- deal with directions and interim orders that do not require attended hearings, whether or not a final hearing takes place whether in Archway or elsewhere;

- provide a venue for hearing applications that can be dealt with at district judge or (in the case of the Senior Judge) at circuit judge level, especially property and affairs cases or cases that address both personal welfare and financial issues;

- hear cases where there is a review of a decision made without an attended hearing or (in the case of the Senior Judge) deal with appeals from decisions of district judges; and

● deal with references from the Public Guardian relating to issues arising in connection with LPAs, EPAs and the supervision of deputies.

Court administration

2.14   Prior to the implementation of the MCA 2005 on 1 October 2007, applications to the Court of Protection under the Mental Health Act jurisdiction were handled by the Public Guardianship Office. Under the new jurisdiction, the Court of Protection is a separate self-contained body that is responsible for handling its own applications and processes. Especially with an enhanced jurisdiction with cases being heard at different levels and in different locations, the role and efficiency of the central registry at Archway is critical if the new jurisdiction is to operate effectively.

Most applications are expected to follow a logical process as they work their way through from first application to an order being made. The Court administration is therefore divided into sections to reflect this as follows:

Receipt and Issue	deals with all new applications including requests for urgent or interim orders and permissions
Pre-hearing and referrals	deals with pre-hearing procedure including notices and certificates of service and interim directions
Post-hearing and dispatch	deals with settling of orders and their dispatch; also EPA and LPA hearings and referrals from the Office of the Public Guardian
Listings and appeals	deals with Court hearings and appeals including liaising with other courts to arrange hearings

It is likely that with the passage of time, the administration and structure of the Court of Protection will evolve to reflect the demands on the new Court and any lessons earned from early experience. It is already apparent that the new Court has struggled to deal with a new jurisdiction while being dependent on the Office of Public Guardian for its central registry, telephone lines and website. Despite the aim of the MCA 2005 to give the Court a new status and sense of identity, the Court has yet to develop a confident public presence of its own. There is therefore a sense that it will suffer from its structural weaknesses with a central court and registry that have been overshadowed by the Office of Public Guardian while judges who rarely sit as Court of Protection judges are scattered across the rest of the country.

To address these concerns, the administration of the Court of Protection was transferred on 1 April 2009 to Her Majesty's Court Service. The aim of this transfer is to provide 'greater flexibility in judicial and courtroom resources, a closer working relationship between Court of Protection and RCJ listing teams, a shared procedural and legislative framework and a clearer definition for users of the respective responsibilities of the OPG and Court.' (*Reaching Out*, February 2009). This should also raise the profile of the Court of Protection within the Court Service.

Powers of the Court of Protection

Principles the Court must apply

2.15   Before addressing the Court's powers in detail, it is important to address the principles – and therefore the constraints – within which the Court can make decisions. The Court is as bound as any other person making decisions on behalf of a person who lacks capacity: it can only make a decision where a person lacks capacity to make that decision and any decision it makes on behalf of a person who lacks capacity to make that decision must be made in that person's best interests.

These limitations or obligations imposed by the MCA 2005 are considered in more detail in Chapter 2. However, it is important to appreciate that the Court is also bound by them before considering its otherwise widely drafted powers under the Act. The Court must therefore work within the framework of the Act, a fact that is emphasised more than once by the Act in defining the Court's powers:

The Court can only act when P lacks capacity

2.16   It is a fundamental principle of the Act that a person has the right to make such decisions as he is capable of making and that no person or body should take that right away. The Court can therefore only intervene if P lacks capacity. If the proposition is reversed, the Court cannot intervene if P has capacity.

Section 16(1), which sets out the Court's powers to make decisions, provides as follows:

'This section applies if a person ("P") lacks capacity in relation to a matter or matters concerning—

(a)   P's personal welfare, or

(b)   P's property and affairs.'

The same limitation applies to a deputy acting with the Court's authority. Under s 20(1):

'A deputy does not have power to make a decision on behalf of P in relation to a matter if he knows or has reasonable grounds for believing that P has capacity in relation to the matter.'

This principle has a number of important and potentially awkward consequences for the practitioner:

● The Court will generally require medical evidence to establish its authority to act at the relevant time. That evidence will furthermore need to be specific to the matter for which authority is required.

● If a decision is made by the Court (or another person acting with the Court's authority) that decision may well be invalid.

- The Act is aimed at replacing individual decisions. This principle is harder to apply where a person has mixed or fluctuating capacity over a period of time.

- A person acting on behalf of P or indeed a third party dealing with P or his deputy or attorney needs to understand the extent of the authority given by the Court, the matter or matters it relates to and whether an assessment is required to determine whether it applies to the matter being dealt with.

Decisions must be made in P's best interests

2.17   It is not sufficient to establish solely that P lacks capacity. The Court is also bound – as is any other person working under the Act's provisions whether directly or with powers conferred by the Court – to act in P's best interests. Any decision made for a person under the Act, must, under s 1(5), be made in that person's best interests. Best interests are defined by the Act at s 4 and are considered in more detail at **1.19–1.22**.

The Court's decisions should be as limited as possible

2.18   While the Court has a great deal of discretion as to how it may act where P lacks capacity, it is an important principle of the MCA 2005 that P is not defined as someone who lacks capacity indefinitely. Thus, s 1(6) sets out the principle that:

> 'Before the act is done, or the decision is made, regard must be had to whether the purpose for which it is needed can be as effectively achieved in a way that is less restrictive of the person's rights and freedom of action.'

This is reinforced in practice by the guidance contained in s 16(4) when the Court is considering the exercise of its powers to appoint a deputy:

> 'When deciding whether it is in P's best interests to appoint a deputy, the court must have regard (in addition to the matters mentioned in section 4) to the principles that—
>
> (a)   a decision by the court is to be preferred to the appointment of a deputy to make a decision, and
>
> (b)   the powers conferred on a deputy should be as limited in scope and duration as is reasonably practicable in the circumstances.'

Although the Act assumes that the appointment of a deputy is a last resort and when appointed, his powers should be as limited as possible, applying this ideal can lead to a number of difficulties in practice:

- Most persons whose lack of capacity is sufficiently advanced to require the involvement of the Court of Protection in administering their property and affairs will need more than a simple one-off order. They will need an ongoing authority to be conferred on a deputy.

- If the deputy's authority is too restrictive in time or scope, the deputy will need to come back to the Court again in only a short period of time, involving a lengthy and expensive application to the Court of Protection.

- The Court of Protection does not have the resources to provide ongoing support to deputies providing orders as and when needed; neither does the Public Guardian have the authority or ability to provide such a facility.

In practice the Court will provide deputies with as much authority as possible to prevent repeated applications to the Court. However, even if this is the practice, it does not lead to an assumption that a deputy will be appointed on an indefinite basis. Some orders do need to be limited in time and scope, especially where the person concerned is a child or young adult and a large damages award is involved. The Court will in such cases limit the appointment to a period of three years so that the deputy must bring the matter before the Court again in a relatively short time and provide an account of his role and whether its continuance is in the best interests of the person concerned.

Where P is a child

2.19   Section 2(5) of the MCA 2005 imposes a minimum age of 16 for P in order for the Court to have jurisdiction. Other defined acts cannot be performed by or on behalf of a person under 18, such as the making of an LPA (s 9(2)(c)), an advance directive (s 24(1) or a Will (s 18(2)). However, the Court can accept jurisdiction in the case of a child in respect of the child's property and affairs. Under s 18(3) so long as P is under the age of 16, the Court may accept jurisdiction in the matter if it considers it likely that P will still lack capacity to make decisions in respect of the matter in question when P reaches 18.

Proceedings involving a child are normally dealt with under the Children Act 1989. However, a case may have a financial consequence or the child may be over 16 and the decision may have longer term consequences. In such a case, the proceedings should be transferred to the Court of Protection. Conversely, the Court of Protection may believe that a case should more properly be dealt with under the Children Act. Such cases can be transferred from one jurisdiction to another so long as the court transferring the proceedings considers it just and convenient to do so and considers the factors laid out in the Mental Capacity Act 2005 (Transfer of Proceedings) Order 2007 (SI 2007/1899).

Power to make declarations concerning capacity

2.20   Section 15 of the MCA 2005 contains a new power for the Court to make declarations as to:

'(a) whether a person has or lacks capacity to make a decision specified in the declaration;

(b)   whether a person has or lacks capacity to make decisions on such matters as are described in the declaration; or

(c)   the lawfulness or otherwise of any act done, or yet to be done, in relation to that person.'

Whether or not a person or a court can make a decision on behalf of another person depends entirely on whether or not that person lacks capacity. One-off decisions are preferable to ongoing delegation of powers and where possible doctors and carers should work within their common law rights or with the protection afforded by ss 5–8 of the Act. The Act does therefore provide a 'safety valve' for professionals and carers making decisions whose validity might be in doubt, especially if there is uncertainty over the capacity of the person on whose behalf a decision is being made. Thus a doctor may obtain a declaration that he may operate on a patient or that he may or may not ignore the instructions of the patient whose capacity is in doubt.

Although this provision is aimed primarily at carers and medical professionals, there is no reason why it should not be used by deputies and attorneys where financial decisions are in issue. For instance, a solicitor who is unsure whether a client is capable of making a Will (perhaps to avoid future litigation where capacity is in issue or where he already acts as deputy for the client) would be able to obtain a definitive declaration that his client has capacity. Clearly the Court will expect professionals to use their own judgment and obtain expert advice to inform themselves, using the Court as a last resort. The last resort nature of the Court's powers to determine issues of capacity is emphasised by the Code of Practice (para 4.65). However, in contentious and complex cases, this might prove a helpful facility for practitioners. The problem faced by practitioners is that they may be asked to implement major decisions for persons who in other respects appear to lack capacity. It is easier in theory than in practice to explain how a person may be incapable of managing his property and affairs but can make a significant decision such as a will or gift.

In a recent case the donor of a registered EPA recovered sufficient capacity to wish to make some substantial lifetime gifts following the sale of her property. She could not deal with the day-to-day management of her property and affairs and it was in any case unlikely that her condition would improve sufficiently to justify an application to cancel registration of the EPA. The donor's attorneys were concerned that the proposed gifts might give rise to questions on the part of the bank or following the donor's death when the gifts would have to be declared to HMRC Capital Taxes. The Court received sufficient medical evidence to provide a declaration under s 15 of the MCA 2005 that the donor could make the gifts notwithstanding the existence of the registered EPA.

Power to direct reports

2.21   To assist the Court in its core functions or to assist with the protection of P's estate and person, the Court has a new statutory power under s 49 of the MCA 2005 to call for a report from one or more of the following:

- the Public Guardian;

- a Court of Protection Visitor;

- a local authority; or

- an NHS body.

The report must deal with such matters relating to P as the Court may direct and may be made orally or in writing as the Court may direct.

The power to call for reports is an important part of the Court's armoury in determining issues concerning P's capacity and best interests. It is also referred to in Rule 85 of the Court of Protection Rules as the first of the directions that the Court may exercise. When an application has been made to the Court, it may direct a report and then use that report to inform the Court directly as to the manner in which its substantive powers should be exercised.

Although reports are aimed at providing the Court with independent and impartial evidence, reports should be used to assist all the parties to an application. Thus Rule 117 of the Court of Protection Rules requires the Court to send a copy of the report to the parties 'and to such persons as the Court may direct'. Rule 118 also allows the Court to permit a party to submit written questions relevant to the issues to the person preparing the report. For instance if there are concerns about P's capacity or best interests, a party to an application may instead of obtaining his own report, ask the Court Visitor to deal directly with his queries.

Not only is there a saving in cost if only one expert advises all the parties, the person conducting the report for the Court will have a right to access information which would otherwise be confidential or restricted. Under s 49(7) of the Act, the Public Guardian or Court Visitor has a right to examine and take copies of health, social services and care home records. Under s 49(8) the Public Guardian or Court of Protection Visitor also has a right to interview P in private.

The Court's power to call for a report is a separate power for the Court to exercise primarily for its own benefit and thereby for the benefit of all the parties. It is in addition to the Court's general powers of case management and its powers on application by a party to issue a witness summons or direct a party to proceedings to provide information (Rules 106 and 107 of the Court of Protection Rules). It is also separate from the report that a deputy is expected to submit to the Public Guardian under s 19(9) as a condition of being appointed.

The status and role of Court of Protection Visitors is dealt with at **2.45** below.

Powers in relation to P's welfare

Section 17 powers generally

2.22   The Court may exercise various powers in relation to the welfare as well as the property and affairs of a person who lacks capacity either directly as a 'one off' decision or through the appointment of a deputy. The Court's powers are set out in s 17 (personal welfare) and s 18 (property and affairs).

The Court's powers in relation to a person's welfare are new powers provided by the Act, and extend in particular to:

(a) deciding where P is to live;

(b) deciding what contact, if any, P is to have with any specified persons;

(c) making an order prohibiting a named person from having contact with P;

(d) giving or refusing consent to the carrying out or continuation of a treatment by a person providing health care for P;

(e) giving a direction that a person responsible for P's health care allow a different person to take over that responsibility.

The Court's powers are widely drafted, and confer a great deal of power on the Court. A decision refusing consent to a particular treatment may relate to a life-sustaining treatment which when withdrawn will bring about the death of P. However, the Court and any person to whom powers are delegated by the Court must act in accordance with the Act's core principles.

Limits to Court's powers

2.23   Although at first sight the Court's powers appear all-encompassing, they are of course still constrained and governed by the principles described above at **2.16–2.18**. Thus the Court cannot act where a person has capacity, its decisions should be as limited in scope and time as possible and decisions must be made in a person's best interests. There are, furthermore, certain acts that the Court cannot authorise. Sections 27–29 set out a number of decisions that are beyond the scope of the MCA 2005 entirely. These must be dealt with within their own legal frameworks. Thus no power contained in the Act permits any decision to be made by the Court or any other person on behalf of a person who lacks capacity:

Under section 27

(a) consenting to marriage or a civil partnership;

(b) consenting to sexual relations;

(c) consenting to a divorce being granted on the basis of two years' separation;

(d) consenting to a dissolution order being made in relation to a civil partnership based on two years' separation;

(e) consenting to a child being placed for adoption by an adoption agency;

(f) consenting to the making of an adoption order;

(g) discharging parental responsibilities in matters not relating to a child's property; and

(h)   giving a consent under the Human Fertilisation and Embryology Act 1990.

Under section 28

(a)   giving medical treatment for a mental disorder; and

(b)   consenting to a patient being given medical treatment for a mental disorder where the treatment is regulated by the Mental Health Act.

Under section 29 – voting at an election for public office or at a referendum.

The restriction in s 29 applies only to elections for public office or a referendum as defined by s 29(2). The Court is not restricted in its powers where the elections relate to private associations or contractual rights, for instance under a company's articles.

Detention of P and deprivation of liberty

2.24   There has been some uncertainty as to the extent of the Court's powers to authorise the detention of a person who lacks capacity to consent to be detained, following the European Court of Human Rights decision in the 'Bournewood' case of *HL v United Kingdom* (2004) 40 EHRR 761 and the High Court decision of *DE and JE v Surrey County Council* [2006] EWHC 3459. These cases have made it clear that if P is in hospital or a care home and lacks capacity to consent to his own detention, P is still being deprived of his liberty. It is irrelevant that P has no knowledge or understanding of his surroundings or actually wishes to leave his premises. His detention is an objective fact, regardless of his state of mind.

This uncertainty has been clarified by the Mental Health Act 2007 which makes a number of amendments to the MCA 2005 known as the Deprivation of Liberty Safeguards (or DOLS). After much deliberation and delay, these amendments came into force on 1 April 2009. New ss 4A and 4B will provide as follows:

'4A Restriction on deprivation of liberty

(1) This Act does not authorise any person ("D") to deprive any other person ("P") of his liberty.

(2) But that is subject to—

    (a)   the following provisions of this section, and

    (b)   section 4B.

(3) D may deprive P of his liberty if, by doing so, D is giving effect to a relevant decision of the court.

(4) A relevant decision of the court is a decision made by an order under section 16(2)(a) in relation to a matter concerning P's personal welfare.

(5) D may deprive P of his liberty if the deprivation is authorised by Schedule A1 (hospital and care home residents: deprivation of liberty).

4B Deprivation of liberty necessary for life-sustaining treatment etc

(1) If the following conditions are met, D is authorised to deprive P of his liberty while a decision as respects any relevant issue is sought from the court.

(2) The first condition is that there is a question about whether D is authorised to deprive P of his liberty under section 4A.

(3) The second condition is that the deprivation of liberty—

    (a)   is wholly or partly for the purpose of—

        (i)   giving P life-sustaining treatment, or

        (ii)   doing any vital act, or

    (b)   consists wholly or partly of—

        (i)   giving P life-sustaining treatment, or

        (ii)   doing any vital act.

(4) The third condition is that the deprivation of liberty is necessary in order to—

    (a)   give the life-sustaining treatment, or

    (b)   do the vital act.

(5) A vital act is any act which the person doing it reasonably believes to be necessary to prevent a serious deterioration in P's condition.'

Decisions affecting treatment for mental disorder and detention for that purpose remain outside the scope of the MCA 2005, and are dealt with under the separate jurisdiction of the Mental Health Act. However, decisions affecting detention and deprivation of liberty of persons who lack capacity and are not being detained for such treatment, such as elderly persons with dementia in care homes, can be dealt with by an order of the Court of Protection under s 16. However, the legislation does not anticipate the Court of Protection being used as a matter of course in every such situation. Applications to the Court are time consuming and expensive and therefore a last resort. The aim is that in the majority of day-to-day cases detention should be authorised by the non-judicial procedure set out in Sch A1 of MCA 2005. This will also provide for the involvement of P or his representative or independent mental capacity advocate (IMCA). A new s 21A also contains a right of referral to the Court of Protection for a determination, effectively making use of an already established system as a forum for judicial review.

The MCA 2005 furthermore contains its own express prohibitions against detention which amounts to a deprivation of liberty being authorised by a deputy (s 20(7)) or by an attorney acting under an LPA (s 11(1)).

A detailed review of the Deprivation of Liberty Safeguards is outside the scope of this work. Further information is available from the Department of Health at:

http://www.dh.gov.uk/en/SocialCare/Deliveringadultsocialcare/
MentalCapacity/MentalCapacityActDeprivationofLibertySafeguards.

Relevance of welfare deputy and further limits on deputy's powers

2.25   The Court can exercise its powers in respect of P's welfare either directly or by appointing a deputy with powers delegated or 'deputed' by the Court. Section 16(4) of the MCA 2005 which sets outs a preference for making single orders to appointing deputies has already been noted. In welfare cases such a preference may be appropriate. A welfare order may for instance be required for a single procedure, for instance determining whether or not P should be treated or deciding where P should live. It should not then be necessary to make any further orders or authorise a person to go on making decisions in the future at least where P's welfare is concerned. It may for instance be appropriate for the Court to make a welfare order deciding where P should live and then make a separate order appointing a deputy to deal with P's property and affairs. The deputy will need long term authority to sell P's property, invest the proceeds and pay the nursing home; the decision as to where P should live is, however, one that only needs to be taken once.

It is therefore unusual for a welfare deputy to be appointed. A person applying for such an order will need to show that the matter cannot be dealt with in a less restrictive manner, whether by a single order or by using the authority conferred by s 5 of the Act (acts in connection with care and treatment). The appointment of a welfare deputy would only be relevant in cases where there is a clear long term need to provide authority at regular intervals or over an extended period of time. A welfare deputy may therefore need to be appointed in situations where:

- there has been a history or risk of abuse or abduction and a health care provider needs the reassurance of knowing that ongoing authority can be provided;

- P's health needs are complex and frequent medical intervention or treatment is required which does not form part of an established pattern.

Section 20 furthermore sets out additional restrictions appropriate to when a deputy is responsible for welfare matters. Not only must a deputy not act when a person lacks capacity, but the deputy has *no* authority to:

- prohibit a person from having contact with P;

- direct a person responsible for P's health care to allow a different person to take over that responsibility;

- 'refuse consent to the carrying out or continuation of life-sustaining treatment in relation to P.' A life or death decision is therefore reserved to the Court of Protection;

- restrain P unless the five conditions set out in sub-ss 20(8)–(13) are satisfied, that:

  – the deputy is acting within the scope of an express authority;

- P lacks capacity in relation to the matter;

- the deputy reasonably believes that the restraint is necessary to prevent harm to P;

- the restraint is proportionate to the likelihood of P suffering harm and the seriousness of that harm; and

- the act of restraint does not amount to a deprivation of liberty.

Powers in relation to property and affairs

Powers generally

2.26   The principal powers of the Court of Protection are contained in s 18 of the MCA 2005 and are broadly similar to those given to its predecessor by s 96 of the Mental Health Act 1983. The Court's powers to make decisions on P's behalf in respect of property and affairs extend in particular to:

(a)   the control and management of P's property;

(b)   the sale, exchange, charging, gift or other disposition of P's property;

(c)   the acquisition of property in P's name or on P's behalf;

(d)   the carrying on, on P's behalf, of any profession, trade or business;

(e)   the taking of a decision which will have the effect of dissolving a partnership of which P is a member;

(f)   the carrying out of any contract entered into by P;

(g)   the discharge of P's debts and of any of P's obligations, whether legally enforceable or not;

(h)   the settlement of any of P's property, whether for P's benefit or for the benefit of others;

(i)   the execution for P of a will;

(j)   the exercise of any power (including a power to consent) vested in P whether beneficially or as trustee or otherwise;

(k)   the conduct of legal proceedings in P's name or on P's behalf.

There are further administrative powers relating to property and affairs contained in Sch 2 to the Act:

para 5	vesting orders in respect of any settlement made by P or power exercised on behalf of P to appoint trustees or retire as a trustee
para 6	varying a settlement made by virtue of s 18
para 7	vesting stock in a curator appointed outside of England and Wales
para 8	preserving an interest in P's property to take effect as the same interest under a Will or intestacy
para 10	appointing a properly qualified person to exercise P's powers as patron of a benefice

Limits to Court's powers

2.27   Although at first sight the Court's powers appear extremely wide, they are of course still constrained and governed by the principles described at **2.15–2.18** above. However, these principles impose greater difficulties where P's property and affairs are concerned. The Court's authority is limited to making decisions on P's behalf. This is straightforward where a single decision is made, such as the making of a Will. It can be shown that P lacks testamentary capacity and the Court therefore has authority to make a Will on P's behalf. But it is less clear what happens where ongoing authority is required over a period of time, for the management and administration of P's property and affairs. It is often difficult to separate the ability to manage property and affairs from the ability to make specific decisions and this is considered in more detail at **1.5** above. Although in practice it provides a deputy with extensive authority and a discretion as to whether it can be used (see below), the Court will need a detailed medical analysis of what it is that P can and cannot do. This gives the Court four basic options:

1   declaring that the management and administration of property and affairs is in itself a matter that P lacks capacity to do for himself;

2   declaring that P cannot manage his property and affairs apart from those specified matters that are reserved to or retained by P;

3   declaring that P can manage his property and affairs to a limited degree and that certain matters are reserved to or to be dealt with by the Court or deputy; or

4   confirming that P lacks capacity to do various things and placing the onus on the deputy or person dealing with P to ensure that they are acting within the scope of the authority given.

In many cases, these issues will not give rise to any difficulty. If P has advanced dementia and is in a nursing home, issues of capacity do not arise. But what happens if P has some ability to carry out individual acts, but without understanding their wider relevance? Or if P has the ability to do some things but not others, but the day-to-day administration of P's affairs overlaps with matters that P is also able to do for himself? The difficulty faced by the Court, deputies and those providing medical advice is in contrast to the clarity of the previous Mental Health Act jurisdiction. Section 95 gave the Court authority, with respect to the property and affairs of a 'patient' (who by definition could not manage his property and affairs), to do or secure the doing of all such things as appeared necessary or expedient:

(a)   for the maintenance or other benefit of the patient;

(b)   for the maintenance or other benefit of members of the patient's family;

(c)   for making provision for other persons or purposes for whom or which the patient might be expected to provide if he were not mentally disordered; or

(d)   otherwise for administering the patient's affairs.

The MCA 2005 jurisdiction requires greater clarity, thought and therefore effort in determining what authority needs to be conferred and how it should be exercised. Neither is there an explicit authority to maintain P or his family. All acts performed under the MCA 2005 must be authorised by the Court and must be in P's best interests.

Territorial limits to Court's jurisdiction

2.28   The Court's powers under the MCA 2005 extend only to P's property and affairs situated within England and Wales. Section 63 and Sch 2 provide for reciprocal recognition of the equivalent authority in other jurisdictions. These include Scotland, Channel Islands and the Isle of Man. Where other jurisdictions are concerned the authority of the Court of Protection may be recognised or proceedings may have to be brought locally. International aspects of P's estate – foreign property of P or property of a person who lacks capacity and whose habitual residence is in another jurisdiction are dealt with in Chapter 16.

Power to appoint deputies

2.29   As with making welfare decisions for a person who lacks capacity, the Court can, under s 16 of the Act, make decisions or appoint a deputy to make those decisions. Although s 16(4) sets out the aim that a decision of the Court is preferred to the appointment of a deputy, this will not be possible in most cases where authority is needed to deal with the day-to-day management or oversight of P's estate. A single order might, however, be appropriate where other arrangements are already in place for the management of P's property and affairs, for instance under an LPA or EPA or under a settlement.

The procedure for appointing a deputy is dealt with in detail in Chapter 5 and the powers and responsibilities of the deputy are dealt with in Chapter 4.

Restrictions on deputies

2.30   In general, the deputy has powers delegated or deputed to him by the Court to make decisions on P's behalf. The Court may determine the extent of the deputy's authority and has the responsibility of ensuring that the deputy has sufficient authority to carry out his obligations to P's estate consistent with the limitations and constraints imposed by the Act. However, not all the specific powers available to the Court under s 18 can be delegated and where these are not available to the deputy, the deputy must apply to the Court for authority. The aim of the Act is therefore to allow deputies to deal with day-to-day matters but to require deputies to return to the Court for certain decisions to be made.

The following powers are expressly excluded from the powers that can be conferred on a deputy and are therefore reserved to the Court (s 20(4)):

(a)   the settlement of any of P's property, whether for P's benefit or for the benefit of others;

(b)   the execution for P of a Will; or

(c)   the exercise of any power (including a power to consent) vested in P whether beneficially or as a trustee or otherwise.

As already mentioned, a deputy must work within the constraints of the Act. Section 20(6) explicitly states that his authority is subject to the provisions of the Act and in particular ss 1 and 4. It may, however, not always be sufficient for a deputy to comply with the best interests requirements of the Act. A deputy also has fiduciary duties towards P's estate which must not be overlooked, especially where P is acting in a professional role.

Powers in relation to enduring powers of attorney

2.31   The Court of Protection also has the responsibility and jurisdiction for dealing with proceedings relating to EPAs under Sch 4 to the MCA 2005. Subject to the limitations of the EPA itself, and unless the Court intervenes, an attorney who derives his authority from his appointment by the donor generally operates without any further authority or supervision. The Court does, however, have to intervene if there are any disputes over the EPA or the role of the attorney, or if the attorney needs to exceed his authority under the instrument.

EPAs are dealt with in Chapter 14.

Powers in relation to lasting powers of attorney

2.32   The Court of Protection also has the responsibility and jurisdiction for dealing with proceedings relating to LPAs under ss 22 and 23 of and Sch 1 to the MCA 2005. The Public Guardian (whose role is dealt with at **2.36** below) is simply responsible for registering LPAs. If an application to register an instrument as an LPA is correctly made, and there are no objections, then the Public Guardian must register the instrument as an LPA.

If any objection is made to registration of an instrument as an LPA or an application is made to cancel the LPA, then this must be dealt with by the Court of Protection. LPAs are dealt with in more detail in Chapter 15.

Service standards

2.33   A party who is not happy with a judicial decision of the Court of Protection has a right, with permission where it is required, to request an oral hearing where a matter was decided without an oral hearing, or appeal to a judge at a higher level or to the Court of Appeal. These procedural issues are dealt with in more detail in Chapter 3. Decisions of the Public Guardian are also subject to a separate review process (see **3.52**).

Both the Court and the Office of Public Guardian currently have the same general service commitments which are set out in booklet OPG503, available from the OPG Customer Services or website. Although service standards are under review and will be set out separately following the transfer of the Court administration to HM Court Service, both bodies provide (as at 31 March 2009) a commitment to:

- reply to letters, faxes and emails within 15 working days;
- see visitors at the OPG offices within ten minutes, with or without an appointment;
- aim to answer telephones within 60 seconds;
- post application forms or printed advice within one working day of being requested;
- acknowledge a complaint within two working days; and
- within 15 working days of a complaint, provide a full response or an explanation as to why a full response cannot be given and when a full response will be given.

Where the OPG is dealing with the registration of an LPA or EPA, it is committed to:

- registering the instrument within five working days of the end of the relevant waiting period provided there are no objections in relation to the application; and
- if there are any errors in the application, inform the applicant within ten working days of receipt.

The time standards become progressively more generous where the Court of Protection is involved in making decisions:

- where a deputy has been appointed, the OPG will notify the deputy of the type of supervision required;
- where an application is made to the Court, the Court will contact the applicant within 25 working days of receipt of the application;
- where no oral hearing is directed, the Court will give a direction within 21 weeks of receipt of an application; and
- where an oral hearing is directed, the hearing will be set for within 15 weeks of the direction.

The Court's service standards do not indicate when a direction for a hearing will be given where a hearing is appropriate. Clearly it is not always obvious immediately whether a hearing will be necessary and it may take several weeks for the Court to receive responses to an application. Even when a hearing is necessary and a direction is made to that effect, it provides little comfort to realise that this might not take place for a further three months.

Complaints

2.34   It is always good policy for any potential complainant to attempt to resolve an issue before it becomes a complaint. Often a potential complaint can be avoided simply by an explanation of what has happened, an opportunity for a matter to be considered in detail or an apology if there has been an error. As with any professional organisation, the Court of Protection and Office of Public Guardian aim to address complaints and resolve them where possible. Complainants in turn are expected to take their complaints through two stages; first through the person they are dealing with and then, if the complaint cannot be resolved, by way of a formal complaint to the Head of Court Administration (Gabby Bradshaw) or the Public Guardian (Martin John). In practice, such complaints are treated seriously and referred to a senior member of staff to resolve.

If the matter cannot be resolved internally a complaint about the Court of Protection wil be referred to the Area Director of the Court Service; a complaint about the Office of the Public Guardian may be referred to the independent Adjudicator who can be contacted at:

Haymarket House
Haymarket
London
SW1Y 4SP
Tel: 020 7930 2292
Fax: 020 7930 2298
Email: adjudicatorsoffice@gtnet.gov.uk
Website: www.adjudicatorsoffice.gov.uk

The appointment of an Adjudicator does not affect the rights of complainants to refer cases to the Parliamentary Commissioner for Administration (the Ombudsman) or their MP. However, the Parliamentary Commissioner or an MP will expect the internal and official independent procedures to have been used first. Complaints about the Court Service must be referred to the Parliamentary Commissioner's whose details are as follows:

Office of the Parliamentary Commission for Administration
Millbank Tower
Millbank
London
SW1P 4QP
Tel: 0845 015 4033
Fax: 020 7217 4160
Email: phso.enquiries@obudsman.org.uk
Website: www.ombudsman.org.uk

The Public Guardian

Background

2.35   Prior to the implementation of the MCA 2005, the administrative work of the Court was carried out by the Public Guardianship Office, which took on that role from the Public Trust Office in April 2001. As mentioned above at **2.2**, the role and capability of the Public Guardianship Office was regularly criticised by, among others, the National Audit Office in its reports of 1999 (HC 206, 1998–99) and 2005 (HC 27 2005–06) and the Lord Chancellor's Department in its Quinquennial Review of 1999. Generally criticism centred around the performance of this body and its inability to pay its way from fees charged to its customers. There was also an underlying concern that the Public Guardianship Office and Court of Protection were too closely entangled and it was often unclear where responsibility lay for particular tasks. Thus applications were processed by the Public Guardianship Office, even though these were for judicial decisions. Correspondence would come from the Public Guardianship Office requesting information or giving permission for a small gift or major expense; in most cases a decision had been made by a nominated officer authorised to make decisions under the Mental Health Act 1983, but frequently letters of advice or guidance were sent which had no formal authority. Although the Public Guardianship Office was an executive agency within (at the time of its demise) the Ministry of Justice, it had no statutory authority or standing to make decisions. The new legislation would therefore provide a vehicle for the functions of this body to be defined and placed on a statutory footing. This would be combined with the policy of ensuring that these functions would be administrative and supervisory and that judicial decisions would be made by duly appointed judges within the Court of Protection.

Role of Public Guardian

2.36   Section 57 of the Act provides for the creation of a new, statutory office-holder to be known as the Public Guardian. Section 58 confers on the Public Guardian various functions, principally:

- establishing and maintaining registers of LPAs and deputies appointed by the court;

- supervising deputies appointed by the court;

- directing a visit by a Court of Protection Visitor to a deputy, donee or P and the making of reports;

- receiving security from deputies;

- receiving reports from donees of LPAs and from deputies (including accounts);

- reporting to the Court on such matters relating to proceedings as the Court requires;

- dealing with representations and complaints about the conduct of donees and deputies; and

- publishing information.

The Lasting Power of Attorney, Enduring Power of Attorney and Public Guardian Regulations 2007 (SI 2007/1253) extend the Public Guardian's duties and powers, so that the duties include the provision of a register of EPAs.

The Office of the Public Guardian

Nature of OPG

2.37   The Public Guardian is a statutory office holder and this role is currently held by Martin John who is also chief executive of the Office of Public Guardian (OPG), which is an executive agency of the Ministry of Justice.

The OPG provides continuity with the Public Guardianship Office, but the new body emphasises the separation of roles between the OPG and the Court implicit in the Mental Capacity Act. The existence of such a body, to enable the Public Guardian to carry out his statutory duties, was first promoted by the Department for Constitutional Affairs in its submission to the parliamentary joint scrutiny committee after the introduction of the draft Mental Incapacity Bill. This submission (HC1083 MIB 1222) proposed this new body as follows:

'A new Office of the Public Guardian (OPG)

There would be a new Office of the Public Guardian (OPG), replacing the existing Public Guardianship Office. Both the new Court and the Office of the Public Guardian would build on the existing court and office structures. The OPG would liaise and work closely with other agencies in financial, health and welfare areas.

As now the OPG would have partly an administrative function and partly a supervisory function. It would be responsible for registering LPAs and for supporting the Court. Its supervisory function would be mainly focused on financial decision making (see below). However, it would have a role in identifying and tackling possible abuse with other agencies by providing a focus for concerns and fielding them to the appropriate agency.

The new Court and OPG would, as now, set fees to cover costs, with a remissions policy where the criteria were met. …

Under the Bill, the Public Guardian has a supervisory role in monitoring LPAs and Deputies. The OPG's supervisory role would be geared to risk and would intrude as little as possible. The focus would be on supervision of Deputies. Deputies would have a new and unique relationship with the person lacking capacity under the Bill and further work is being undertaken to understand how this will affect the monitoring requirements.

Where there are allegations of possible abuse (of any kind) Office of the Public Guardian would liaise closely with all of the agencies and individuals involved, including social services, the police, voluntary organisations and Adult Protection Committees. The existing Public Guardianship Office is already establishing and developing partnerships with local authorities and other bodies to ensure that any concerns about a person lacking capacity are highlighted and acted upon. Work is also in progress to establish an investigation unit.

The OPG is supported by the currently named Lord Chancellor's Visitors. Visitors would be able to visit attorneys and Deputies if so directed and provide an independent and impartial report on circumstances to the Court.'

The Office of the Public Guardian currently shares the same premises as the Court of Protection at Archway (see **2.13**). However the Public Guardian is in the process of diverting operations to other offices, including central London, Birmingham and Nottingham. While there is no need for the Public Guardian to be in the same location as the Court (and there are policy reasons to separate the two bodies as much as possible) and a regional presence is a worthwhile goal, there are concerns that a small organisation such as this will dilute its operational effectiveness.

Public Guardian Board

2.38   Although the OPG is part of the Ministry of Justice and therefore responsible to the Lord Chancellor and Minister of Justice, it also has a duty to account under s 59 of the MCA 2005 to a Public Guardian Board. Members of the Board are appointed by the Lord Chancellor and s 59(5) requires at least one member of the Board who is a judge and at least four who appear to the Lord Chancellor 'to have appropriate knowledge or experience of the work of the Public Guardian'. Section 59(6) provides for further regulations to be made dealing with the composition of the Board, terms of office and conduct of meetings and these have been enacted as the Public Guardian Board Regulations 2007 (SI 2007/1770). These provide, inter alia, that members are appointed for a fixed term not exceeding four years and may be reappointed for one further term on its expiry.

Under s 49(2), the Public Guardian Board has a duty to:

'... scrutinise and review the way in which the Public Guardian discharges his functions and to make such recommendations to the Lord Chancellor about that matter as it thinks appropriate.'

The Lord Chancellor is required by s 59(3) to 'give due consideration to recommendations made by the Board'. The efficacy of the Public Guardian Board lies entirely in the willingness of its members to hold the OPG to account. Its first annual report, published on 7 October 2008, indicates that as a body it is prepared to evaluate critically the operation of the OPG and the implementation of the MCA 2005. Its first annual report is available from the OPG website at: http://www.publicguardian.gov.uk/docs/pgboard-report

Wider public role of the OPG

2.39   The OPG is not just responsible for dealing with deputies and donors of powers of attorney who lack capacity. One of the Public Guardian's statutory functions under the MCA 2005 is to publish 'in any manner the Public Guardian thinks appropriate, any information he thinks appropriate about the discharge of his functions'. This gives the Public Guardian a 'public relations role' which the OPG website defines as follows:

'The OPG also provides information on mental capacity to the public, legal and health professionals, and researchers. It can provide contacts with other organisations working in the field of mental capacity. The OPG also has responsibility for policy issues relating to the Mental Capacity Act and in relation to mental capacity issues generally.'

Powers of the Public Guardian

Statutory powers

2.40   The core function of the Public Guardian is to deal with the non-judicial aspects of the MCA 2005 jurisdiction relating to powers of attorney and deputies. In practice this is limited to registration of powers of attorney and the supervision of deputies after their appointment by the Court. Where supervision is concerned, the Court will direct a report to be submitted by a deputy to the Public Guardian; the Court may also direct a report from the Public Guardian under s 49 of the Act. The Public Guardian's powers are therefore geared towards enabling him to obtain that report.

The Public Guardian's principal powers are contained in s 58 of the MCA 2005 and the Lasting Power of Attorney, Enduring Power of Attorney and Public Guardian Regulations 2007. The Public Guardian may, for the carrying out of his functions:

- examine and take copies of health records, social services records and care home records;

- interview P in private;

- allow a deputy an extended period of time to submit a report;

- require a deputy to verify or authenticate documents submitted with a report;

- require a deputy to submit a final report on the termination of his appointment;

- require a deputy to provide specified information or produce specified documents;

- direct a Court of Protection Visitor to visit a person; and

- require a donee of an LPA or an attorney under an EPA to provide specified information or documents.

The Public Guardian does have sufficient powers to obtain information from deputies and attorneys, whether at the express direction of the Court, as part of an ongoing obligation to supervise or in response to a query or concern from a relative, friend or healthcare professional. However, if the Public Guardian does have his own concerns as to fraud or misuse of the power, then the Public Guardian may investigate the matter further and see if there is an error or oversight that can be readily corrected. However, if the matter cannot be resolved informally, the Public Guardian must make an application to the Court of Protection. Rule 43 of the Lasting Power of Attorney, Enduring Power of Attorney and Public Guardian Regulations 2007 confers authority on the Public Guardian to make applications to the Court 'in such circumstances as he considers it necessary or appropriate to do so'. In welfare cases, the Public Guardian is furthermore not required to obtain permission before making an application (Rule 51 of the Court of Protection Rules).

Powers of supervision

2.41   To carry out his functions, the Public Guardian does in most cases have control over the way in which deputies are supervised. Only the Court of Protection has authority to order that a report be made to the Public Guardian under s 19(9)(b) or under s 49 of the Act. Rule 39 of the Lasting Power of Attorney, Enduring Power of Attorney and Public Guardian Regulations 2007 states that such a report must contain or be accompanied by specified information. Where the report relates to P's property and affairs then it is for the Public Guardian to specify the information required, subject only to any other direction of the Court and the information being reasonably required by the Public Guardian to exercise his functions under the Act. The Public Guardian also has authority under the Public Guardian (Fees, etc) Regulations 2007 to determine which of the three levels of supervision are appropriate to the case.

The Public Guardian's role in supervising deputies and attorneys is dealt with separately in the chapters dealing with those matters.

Interaction with the Court

2.42   After the MCA 2005 was passed in 2005 and prior to implementation, it was unclear whether the Public Guardian would be responsible for processing applications to the Court of Protection and continue that function of the Public Guardianship Office. As mentioned in the context of the administration of the new Court of Protection (**2.14** above), the Court has been established as a separate body with its own administration, although sharing premises, a website and contact numbers with the Public Guardian. This has proved to be an imperfect arrangement and from 1 April 2009 the Court administration was transferred to HMCS. It is expected that the separate character and function of the two bodies will in due course be further emphasised by their occupying separate premises.

While the separation of powers between the Court and Public Guardian is necessary if the policy required by the MCA 2005 and Human Rights Act is to be followed, it does present some practical difficulties. At first sight, there are two bodies with one address, telephone number and website, working under the same statutory framework for the same people who lack capacity. The OPG website addresses this issue as follows:

'How does the OPG and COP work together?

The OPG works closely with the Court to make sure that the best interests of people who lack mental capacity are served.

If you have not made or registered an LPA for property and affairs or for personal welfare, and you lose capacity to make decisions on these areas for yourself, someone else may apply to the Court for the power to make these decisions for you.

Only the Court is able to decide who is the best person to do this for you and it will give that person whatever powers it believes are necessary for them to act in your best interests.

The Court may appoint a Deputy decision maker, who can be given a wide range of powers or it may make a single order, covering an individual decision.

In coming to its decision, the Court may ask the OPG to obtain a report on an individual case. This report can cover a wide range of issues and may involve the OPG sending a specialist visitor to gather the facts in the case.

Once the Court has made its order, it is up to the OPG to monitor and supervise any Deputies who are appointed. The OPG can decide on the level of supervision each case requires and this will depend on a wide range of factors.

Where a Deputy fails to meet the supervision requirements laid down, the OPG has the power to take the case back to the Court. The case will then be reviewed and the Court may take further action, including terminating the appointment of the Deputy.

Both organisations will complement one another, with the Court providing the decision making functions and the OPG providing regulation and supervision.'

In practice, it is much harder for the two bodies to work effectively together as only the Court of Protection has authority to make decisions. If a decision is required from the Court then a formal application has to be made using the Part 9 or Part 10 procedure (see Chapter 3). Unless the application is made within existing proceedings, the Court will have no record of the management of the case and no prima facie evidence that at the time the application is made and for the matter which is the subject of the application, P lacks capacity. The Court will therefore require evidence of earlier proceedings, the authority and status of the applicant or other party, medical evidence that P lacks capacity and the evidence required to support the application. Although the Public Guardian is not required to pay a fee, any such application still requires a great deal of information and is therefore time-consuming and expensive to prepare.

To ensure that deputies do not need to keep coming back to the Court for routine decisions, the policy of the Court is to provide deputies with as wide an authority as possible. The Court will in most cases make the order appointing a deputy and pass the order to the Public Guardian to deal with security and the supervision of the deputy. The Court has finished its involvement in the case and the Public Guardian has no authority to make any further decision. The Public Guardian cannot therefore give advice in response to a particular query. If an anxious deputy wants to know whether he can spend money on a further holiday for P or arrange extensive repairs to P's property, the Public Guardian cannot advise on the merits of the case lest such advice be treated as a form of consent. The Public Guardian can give general advice as to the jurisdiction, website page, helpsheet or Code of Practice. The decision maker meanwhile must exercise his own judgment or apply to the Court. Likewise, the Public Guardian has limited authority to tackle a defect in the accounts or report presented to him for supervision. As mentioned at **2.40** above, if such a matter cannot be resolved informally, the Public Guardian must also make an application to the Court of Protection.

The new jurisdiction therefore requires a new approach on the part of deputies and their advisers. There is no longer the safety net of the Public Guardian being there in the background approving day-to-day transactions. In effect, the responsibility for making decisions has been outsourced from a public body to the private individual. While this is liberating for many experienced deputies, it does reduce the level of protection available to the person who lacks capacity and increases the burden on the private individual to ensure that he is making the right decision. While it is not the place of this work to take issue with an administrative change that has such wide reaching implications, this is an underlying theme of the work especially where the role of decision makers needs to be addressed.

Service standards and complaints

2.43   Service standards and complaints are dealt with above at **2.33** and **2.34**.

The role of the Official Solicitor

2.44   The Official Solicitor to the Supreme Court is appointed by the Lord Chancellor and acts as a legal representative to persons under disability in legal proceedings in England and Wales. In proceedings before the Court of Protection the Official Solicitor is frequently instructed to act as litigation friend for P, whose interests might otherwise not be adequately represented, especially where there is an actual or potential conflict of interest between P and his deputy. The Official Solicitor thereby supplements the capacity of P during the proceedings in question.

In practice the Official Solicitor will continue to serve the very useful role he has provided under the Mental Health Act 1983 jurisdiction. This was frequently used to provide an independent source of representation, principally in proceedings disposing of P's property or where a Will was being made on behalf of P. Although this important role should not change under the MCA 2005 jurisdiction, and Rule 143 expressly allows the Court to appoint the Official Solicitor, the Court of Protection Rules do not require the Official Solicitor to be appointed litigation friend. The Official Solicitor is described in its website as a 'litigation friend of last resort' and there may be cases where a competent friend, relative or solicitor can act in this role. However, in most cases brought before the Court, the Court will at the directions stage consider whether P should be joined as a party, and if so, whether a litigation friend should be appointed by the Court. The Court will then consider whether the Official Solicitor should be appointed or whether some other person should be appointed.

In contentious welfare cases it is more likely that the Official Solicitor will be appointed, building on his experience in dealing with welfare decisions under the High Court declaratory regime that existed prior to implementation of the Act. Certainly a case should be discussed at an early stage with the Official Solicitor's staff and Practice Direction 9E, which deals with serious medical treatment, states that:

'Members of the Official Solicitor's staff are prepared to discuss applications in relation to serious medical treatment before an application is made. Any enquiries about adult medical and welfare cases should be addressed to a family and medical litigation lawyer at the Office of the Official Solicitor.'

The Practice Direction further states at para 14 that the Court will, at the directions stage:

'if P is to be joined as a party to the proceedings, decide whether the Official Solicitor should be invited to act as a litigation friend or whether some other person should be appointed as a litigation friend.'

The Official Solicitor's staff includes a number of experienced solicitors who specialise in Court of Protection proceedings and whose experience and practical knowledge not only assist the Court and P but also any other party to the proceedings. The Official Solicitor may for instance advise the Court on an aspect of its powers or procedures or liaise with other parties to clarify issues, make suggestions and assist with achieving a consensus between the parties where possible.

Official Solicitor
81 Chancery Lane
London
WC2A 1DD
DX 141150 London/Chancery Lane WC2
Tel: 020 7911 7127
Fax: 020 7911 7105
E-mail: enquiries@offsol.gsi.gov.uk
Website: http://www.officialsolicitor.gov.uk

Court of Protection Visitors

2.45   The concept of the Court having its own panel of experts or visitors is an established one that operated under the Mental Health Act jurisdiction. It would prevent the Court from being isolated in its offices, removed from the actual client whose affairs were being dealt with, and dependent on incomplete or partisan evidence being obtained by the parties.

The Lord Chancellor's Visitors, who were appointed under s 102 of the Mental Health Act 1983, had two principal functions:

•   reporting directly to the Court in response to a particular issue requiring a decision by the Court; and

•   providing a general support and monitoring service, visiting clients in their own homes and generally making sure that the client, carers, Public Guardianship Office and receivers were working effectively.

The role of the Visitors is an important one, especially where there are no relatives or friends who can act as a deputy or report problems to the Court. The importance of this role (which was not managed as well as it should have been) was recognised by the National Audit Office in its 1999 Report, which stated that 'Visitors should act as the eyes and ears of the [Public Guardianship Office], gathering information essential to the patient's welfare and the effective running of their estates' (National Audit Office, *Protecting the Financial Welfare of People with Mental Incapacity* at para 3.1).

The role of visitors has been recognised by the MCA 2005, which provides for two categories of visitors, special and general. The title Lord Chancellor's Visitor is replaced by the title Court of Protection Visitor. Section 61 provides as follows:

'(1) A Court of Protection Visitor is a person who is appointed by the Lord Chancellor to—

    (a)   a panel of Special Visitors, or

    (b)   a panel of General Visitors.

(2) A person is not qualified to be a Special Visitor unless he—

    (a)   is a registered medical practitioner or appears to the Lord Chancellor to have other suitable qualifications or training, and

    (b)   appears to the Lord Chancellor to have special knowledge of and experience in cases of impairment of or disturbance in the functioning of the mind or brain.

(3) A General Visitor need not have a medical qualification.

(4) A Court of Protection Visitor—

    (a)   may be appointed for such term and subject to such conditions, and

    (b)   may be paid such remuneration and allowances,

as the Lord Chancellor may determine.

The power to call for reports is contained in s 49 where the Court directs a report and the Public Guardian also has power to call for reports under s 58(1)(d) and r 44 of the Lasting Power of Attorney, Enduring Power of Attorney and Public Guardian Regulations 2007.

The importance of the Visitors' function is further emphasised by their rights, set out in ss 49 and 61 to access information and interview P in private. A Special Visitor conducting a report for the Court also has a right to carry out a private medical, psychiatric or psychological examination of P's capacity and condition.

As at October 2007, there were nine Special Visitors who are all senior consultant psychiatrists. There were a further 40 General Visitors. All Visitors are self-employed and paid for each visit they undertake. The number of Visitors, their status and relevance does, however, remain subject to constant review. There have been concerns that changing the status of some visitors to employees will limit the number and efficacy of visitors (see for instance the comments of Trevor Lyttleton in the *Law Society Gazette* 31 July 2008 and 11 September 2008). On the one hand, the Visitor 'service' is an important part of the new jurisdiction, protecting and supporting vulnerable adults without being overly intrusive. On the other hand, it is a time-consuming and expensive operation to ensure that several thousand clients can be visited each year, which needs to be covered by the supervision fees recovered by the OPG. It is also likely that as the Court's welfare jurisdiction becomes more widely understood and used, more detailed reports will be needed. These may well be very complex reports addressing issues of capacity, welfare, treatment and best interests. The issues raised may be more extensive than a Special Visitor can deal with and more complex than a General Visitor, who is trying to see a number of clients in the same day for a fixed cost per visit, might be able to provide. It is therefore also possible for the Court to obtain reports under s 49 from other specialists within a local authority or NHS body. For example, the Court may decide that a report from a social worker or case manager is more appropriate.

Independent Mental Capacity Advocates

2.46 The principal role of Court of Protection Visitors is to report directly to the Court or Public Guardian. There will, however, be many instances, especially where welfare decisions are being taken and the person concerned has capacity to understand or participate in decisions being made, where the person also requires advice and assistance.

Sections 35–41 of the MCA 2005 therefore set up a new independent mental capacity advocate (IMCA) service to provide safeguards for people who (Code of Practice, 10.1):

- lack capacity to make a specified decision at the time it needs to be made;

- are facing a decision on a long-term move or about serious medical treatment;

- have nobody else who is willing and able to represent them or be consulted in the process of working out their best interests.

The role of IMCAs is further defined by regulations made pursuant to ss 35 and 36 of the Act, principally:

- the Mental Capacity Act 2005 (Independent Mental Capacity Advocates) (General) Regulations 2006 (SI 2006/1832);

- the Mental Capacity Act 2005 (Independent Mental Capacity Advocates) (Expansion of Role) Regulations 2006 (SI 2006/2883).

The MCA 2005 does not just provide IMCAs as a useful service for use at the Court's discretion. An IMCA must be involved in cases where important welfare decisions are being made on behalf of P by a public body and there is no other independent person who can be consulted for the purposes of determining P's best interests in relation to the decision. In all such cases the relevant NHS body or local authority must instruct an IMCA and take account of any information given or submissions made by the IMCA. Important welfare decisions are:

- the provision of serious medical treatment by a NHS body (s 37). Serious medical treatment is defined as 'treatment which involves providing, withholding or withdrawing treatment of a kind prescribed by regulations made by the appropriate authority';

- the provision of accommodation by a NHS body (s 38). This applies where arrangements are being made to provide accommodation or arrange new accommodation in a hospital or care home, whether or not the accommodation itself is provided by the NHS body;

- the provision of accommodation by a local authority (s 39). This applies where the local authority is arranging residential accommodation or a change of residential accommodation.

The requirement to consult an IMCA does not apply where there is another person to be consulted. Section 40(1) (on amendment by the Mental Health Act 2007) provides that the requirements set out in ss 37–39 do not apply where there is:

'(a)   a person nominated by P (in whatever manner) as a person to be consulted on matters to which that duty relates;

(b)   a donee of a lasting power of attorney created by P who is authorised to make decisions in relation to those matters,

(c)   a deputy appointed by the court for P with power to make decisions in relation to those matters; or

(d)   a donee of an enduring power of attorney (within the meaning of Schedule 4) created by P'.

The role of IMCAs in welfare matters is a new one and will no doubt evolve as the MCA 2005 becomes more widely understood. There are, needless to say, resource issues, as the requirement to appoint an IMCA is not one that can be charged for. The IMCA service must therefore be funded by NHS bodies and local authorities with the conflict over the allocation of scarce resources which this entails. It is also likely that charities in the voluntary sector will be able to provide some additional IMCA services.

Chapter 3

Practice and procedure in the new Court of Protection

Nature of proceedings in the new Court of Protection

3.1 Court of Protection proceedings under the Mental Health Act 1983 jurisdiction were generally regarded as flexible and informal. Applications would often be made by letter, evidence could be accepted in various forms, the Rules were short and flexible and the Court's approach was inquisitorial rather than adversarial. Hearings would be conducted in chambers and the Court would often look to the parties to achieve a consensus or compromise where possible. The Court would see its role as to establish the truth of a given set of circumstances and with a very wide discretion conferred by the Mental Health Act 1983 form a decision as to what was 'for the benefit' of 'the patient' or as to what 'the patient' might do if he had capacity. Although such proceedings were pleasantly different from those in other courts, this was considered inappropriate for the new jurisdiction introduced by the MCA 2005. Not only should the new jurisdiction reflect the legal process required by the European Convention on Human Rights (ECHR), but the new Court must in effect combine two jurisdictions: the statutory rules that governed the Court of Protection in dealing with property and affairs and the formal court process required by the Civil Procedure Rules 1998 (CPR) for the High Court Family Division in welfare and medical cases. Although welfare and medical cases were rare, the issues would generally be more contentious, involving quite literally matters of life and death. Parties to such proceedings would include the Official Solicitor and a health authority or local authority social services department. Detailed medical evidence would need to be addressed and witnesses cross-examined.

The new Court of Protection aims therefore to absorb and combine two very different and almost entirely separate areas of law into a single uniform jurisdiction. This new jurisdiction can therefore operate in respect of any area – whether welfare or financial – within the new Court's jurisdiction and may be exercised by any judge in any part of England and Wales who has been duly nominated under s 46 of the Act.

The Court of Protection Rules

The new Rules and Practice Directions

3.2 To achieve the somewhat ambitious objectives of the MCA 2005, ss 51 and 52 provide for the enactment of Court of Protection Rules and the making of Practice Directions by the President of the Court of Protection. The Court of Protection Rules 2007 (SI 2007 1899) were laid before Parliament on 4 July 2007 and came into force on 1 October 2007. Minor amendments and the introduction of a new practice direction were introduced on 1 April 2009 by the Court of Protection (Amendment) Rules (SI 2009/582).

The Rules can be obtained from the parliamentary website: http://www.opsi.gov.uk/si/si2007/uksi_20071744_en.pdf or from the Office of the Public Guardian website at: http://www.publicguardian.gov.uk/docs/Court_Rules_2007.pdf

The Rules extend to 202 sections and are divided into 23 parts as follows:

Part 1	revokes the Court of Protection Rules 2001 and Court of Protection (Enduring Powers of Attorney) Rules 2001
Part 2	sets out the overriding objective enabling the Court to deal with a case justly, having regard to the principles contained in the Act, when it exercises any power under the Rules, or interprets any rule or practice direction
Part 3	contains provisions for interpreting the Rules, and for the CPR to be applied in default (Rule 9)
Part 4	makes provision as to court documents, including the requirement for certain documents to be verified by a statement of truth (Rule 11)
Part 5	sets out the Court's general case management powers, and includes the power to dispense with the requirement of any rule (Rule 26)
Part 6	deals with the service of documents generally
Part 7	sets out the procedure for notifying P
Part 8	relates to cases where the Court's permission is required before proceedings can be started
Part 9	describes how to start proceedings; how to file an application; the steps to be taken following the issue of an application; responding to an application; and who the parties to the proceedings are
Part 10	deals with applications within proceedings, including the Court's powers to grant interim remedies
Part 11	contains a single rule (Rule 83), which applies whenever anyone seeks to invoke the Human Rights Act 1998
Part 12	sets out how the Court will deal with applications, including the allocation of cases (Rule 86)
Part 13	deals with hearings, including issues of privacy and access
Part 14	sets out the procedure in relation to evidence and witnesses
Part 15	sets out the procedure in relation to experts
Part 16	sets out the procedure in relation to disclosure
Part 17	deals with the appointment of litigation friends
Part 18	deals with change of solicitor
Part 19	deals with costs
Part 20	deals with appeals
Part 21	covers the enforcement of orders

| Part 22 | covers transitory and transitional matters, the detail of most of which will be provided in separate practice directions |
| Part 23 | contains some miscellaneous provisions, including one (Rule 201) relating to objections to the registration of an enduring power of attorney |

The Rules are supplemented by a further 33 practice directions which are numbered by reference to the Part of the Rules to which they relate:

4A	General provisions: Court Documents
4B	General provisions: Statements of Truth
6A	Service of documents
7A	Notifying P
8A	Permission
9A	The application form
9B	Notification of others that an application has been issued
9C	Responding to an application
9D	Applications by currently appointed deputies, attorneys and donees relating to property and affairs
9E	Applications relating to serious medical treatment
9F	Applications relating to statutory wills, codicils, settlements and others dealing with P's property
9G	Applications to appoint or discharge a trustee
9H	Applications relating to the registration of Enduring Powers of Attorney
10A	Applications within proceedings. A further practice direction supplements Parts 10A and deals expressly with Deprivation of Liberty Applications (Rule 82A)
10B	Applications within proceedings: urgent and interim applications
11A	Human rights
12A	Hearings: court's jurisdiction to be exercised by certain judges
12B	Procedure for disputing the court's jurisdiction
13A	Hearings (including reporting restrictions)
14A	Written evidence
14B	Depositions
14C	Fees for examiners in the court
14D	Witness summons
14E	Section 49 reports
15A	Expert evidence
17A	Litigation friend
18A	Change of solicitor

19A	Costs
20A	Appeals
21A	Enforcement- contempt of court
22A	Transitional provisions
22B	Transitory provisions
22C	Appeals under Part 7 of the Mental Health Act
23A	Request for directions where notice of objection prevents public guardian from registering Enduring Power of Attorney
23B	Where P ceases to lack capacity or dies

The Practice Directions are available from the Office of the Public Guardian website at: http://www.publicguardian.gov.uk/forms/practice-directions.htm

The Rules and accompanying Practice Directions are further supplemented by provisions contained in:

- the Lasting Power of Attorney, Enduring Power of Attorney and Public Guardian Regulations 2007 (SI 2007/1253);

- the Mental Capacity Act 2005 (Transfer of Proceedings) Order 2007 (SI 2007/1989); and

- the Civil Procedure (Amendment) Rules 2007 (SI 2007/2204).

The various rules and practice directions further provide for the use of 29 prescribed Court of Protection forms in addition to the prescribed forms of Lasting Power of Attorney (LPA) and the prescribed forms for use in connection with the registration of LPAs and Enduring Powers of Attorney (EPA).

To those familiar with the Mental Health Act jurisdiction, this makes for a daunting contrast. However, it is the function of the Rules to bring the full scope of the Court's jurisdiction into a single body of rules, from an uncontested application to appoint a deputy to a contested hearing concerning life-sustaining treatment. The Rules therefore have to be rigid in terms of providing a proper legal process, while also being flexible enough to deal with simple cases, emergencies and vulnerable parties who may not have the benefit of professional advice.

The Rules must also work within the framework of the Act itself, especially where capacity is in issue. The Court cannot make assumptions about P's capacity or inability to participate in the proceedings. The Rules must therefore also provide for the participation of P where possible or representation of P where this is necessary. Any decision made on behalf of P must be shown to be in P's best interests. And where the Court is evaluating or authorising decisions made by others, those decisions must be made with regard to the Statutory Code of Practice. To achieve all these objectives, the Rules are long and complicated. The role of the practitioner therefore is to navigate the system and find the correct procedure to follow.

Civil Procedure Rules

3.3   The Court of Protection Rules not only reflect the CPR, they also import several provisions of the CPR:

- Rule 9 applies the provisions of the CPR to proceedings in the new Court 'in any case not provided for' by the Court of Protection Rules;

- Rule 25(7) applies rr 25.12–25.15 of the CPR in relation to security for costs;

- Examiners appointed under r 34.15 of the CPR may act as examiners under the Court of Protection Rules (Rule 111);

- Provisions for detailed assessment of costs in Court of Protection proceedings are governed by Part 47 of the CPR (Rules 155 and 160); and

- Rule 184 imports the CPR provisions relating to the Court's powers to make and enforce orders, covering (a) Parts 70 (General Rules about Enforcement of Judgments and Orders), 71 (Orders to Obtain Information from Judgment Debtors), 72 (Third Party Debt Orders) and 73 (Charging Orders, Stop Orders and Stop Notices) of the CPR; and (b) Orders 45 (Enforcement of Judgments and Orders: General), 46 (Writs of Execution: General) and 47 (Writs of Fieri Facias) of the Rules of the Supreme Court.

Terminology

3.4   The MCA 2005 and the Rules introduce a new terminology. The person in respect of whose property or welfare the application is made is known – inelegantly if efficiently – as 'P'. The Rules define P as

> 'any person who lacks or, so far as consistent with the context, is alleged to lack, capacity to make a decision or decisions in relation to any matter that is the subject of an application to the court and references to a person who lacks capacity are to be construed in accordance with the Act'.

Other definitions that we need to be familiar with include:

respondent	Any person other than P who is to be treated as a party to the application
applicant	A person making an application under the Act
notified person	A person given notice of an application but who is not a party (at that stage) to the application
protected party	A party to proceedings (other than P) who lacks capacity to conduct the proceedings
protected beneficiary	A protected party (under the CPR) who also lacks capacity to manage and control money recovered by him or on his behalf or for his benefit in proceedings

litigation friend	A person who can fairly and competently conduct proceedings on behalf of P, a child or a Protected Party
donor	A person who has granted a LPA or an EPA
attorney	A person appointed to act under an EPA
donee	A person appointed to act as an attorney under a LPA
deputy	A person appointed by the Court of Protection to manage a person's property and affairs or make welfare decisions under the MCA 2005, s 16

Role of the Court

3.5   One of the perceived failures of the Mental Health Act 1983 jurisdiction is that the Court would often appear to be a passive bystander. The Court would set a hearing date at some distant point in the future and wait for the parties to conduct a dispute between themselves; only when that process was exhausted, would the case come to Court. The Court would therefore play no part in the conduct of the case between setting a hearing date and the hearing itself. This laid back approach had its merits in terms of allowing parties to resolve as many issues as possible between themselves, so that only intractable cases or issues within cases would come to the Court for a final hearing. This also reduced the pressure on a very small Court, working with limited support.

The MCA 2005 however creates a much wider jurisdiction for a new Court of Protection. Many cases, especially welfare cases, are highly contentious and complex and will be dealt with by lawyers and judges who are familiar with the CPR. The Court of Protection Rules therefore allow the Court to take a more active role in the conduct and management of proceedings. Rule 3 sets out clear principles for the Court to follow. The Rules themselves have the overriding objective of enabling the Court to deal with a case justly, having regard to the principles contained in the Act itself. The Court will give effect to that overriding objective, when under Rule 3(2) it:

(a)   exercises any power under these Rules; or

(b)   interprets any rule or practice direction.

Dealing with a case justly includes, so far as is practicable (under Rule 3(3)):

(a)   ensuring that it is dealt with expeditiously and fairly;

(b)   ensuring that P's interests and position are properly considered;

(c)   dealing with the case in ways which are proportionate to the nature, importance and complexity of the issues;

(d)   ensuring that the parties are on an equal footing;

(e)   saving expense; and

(f)   allotting to it an appropriate share of the court's resources, while taking account of the need to allot resources to other cases.

Rule 25 goes on to provide the Court with active case management powers to:

(a)   extend or shorten the time for compliance with any rule, practice direction, or court order or direction (even if an application for extension is made after the time for compliance has expired);

(b)   adjourn or bring forward a hearing;

(c)   require P, a party's legal representative or litigation friend, or a party, to attend the court;

(d)   hold a hearing and receive evidence by telephone or any other method of direct oral communication;

(e)   stay the whole or part of any proceedings or judgment either generally or until a specified date or event;

(f)   consolidate proceedings;

(g)   hear two or more applications on the same occasion;

(h)   direct a separate hearing of any issue;

(i)   decide the order in which issues are to be heard;

(j)   exclude an issue from consideration;

(k)   dismiss or give judgment on an application after a decision on a preliminary basis;

(l)   direct any party to file and serve an estimate of costs; and

(m)   take any step or give any direction for the purpose of managing the case and furthering the overriding objective.

The Court may furthermore make of its own motion any order within proceedings which it considers appropriate 'even if a party has not sought that order in his application form or application notice' (Rule 27).

The Court may also exercise its powers generally of its own initiative. Coupled with its powers to make directions of its own initiative or at the request of a party under Rule 85, and its powers to control evidence, the Court does have a great deal of autonomy over how proceedings are conducted. While the Rules are extremely detailed and in many instances highly prescriptive – especially where the parties are concerned – the Court can to a large extent do as it pleases.

The problem created by the Court's powers of case management is that activity in a case depends on precise directions being given. Parties must file evidence or carry out specified steps within a defined timescale. This works well where the case progresses smoothly. But it only takes one party to fall behind or require some other direction for the whole process to be held up by a need for further directions. A contested case involving several parties may produce a small collection of orders for directions, which may need to be dealt with at attended hearings.

Permission

3.6   Section 50(2) of the MCA 2005 stipulates a general rule that permission is required from the Court for any application made. However, permission is NOT required under s 50(1) if the Rules so permit or if the application is made:

(a)   by a person who lacks or is alleged to lack capacity;

(b)   if such person is under 18, by anyone with parental responsibility;

(c)   by the donor or donee of a LPA to which the application relates;

(d)   by a deputy appointed by the Court for a person to whom the application relates; or

(e)   by a person named in an existing order of the Court, if the application relates to the order.

The Mental Health Act 2007also introduces a new s 50(1A) which provides that permission is not required for an application by a relevant person's representative for a review under s 21A which relates to P's detention in hospital or a care home.

Rule 51 further stipulates that no permission is required if the application:

(a)   is made by the Official Solicitor;

(b)   is made by the Public Guardian;

(c)   concerns P's property and affairs, unless the application is of a kind specified in Rule 52;

(d)   concerns a LPA which is, or purports to be, created under the Act;

(e)   concerns an instrument which is, or purports to be, an EPA;

(f)   is made within existing proceedings in accordance with Part 10;

(g)   is made under s 21A by the relevant person's representative (for a Deprivation of Liberty application); or

(h)   is made by a person who files an acknowledgment of service or notification for any order proposed that is different to that sought by the applicant.

Rule 52 goes on to require permission in the following situations UNLESS one of the exemptions applies:

●   in an application for the exercise of the jurisdiction of the court under s 54(2) of the Trustee Act 1925, where the application is made by a person other than:

    (a)   a person who has made an application for the appointment of a deputy for which permission has been granted but which has not yet been determined;

    (b)   a continuing trustee; or

    (c)   any other person who, according to the practice of the Chancery Division, would have been entitled to make the application if it had been made in the High Court.

- in an application under s 36(9) of the Trustee Act 1925 for leave to appoint a new trustee in place of P, where the application is made by a person other than:

  (a)   a co-trustee; or

  (b)   another person with the power to appoint a new trustee.

- in an application seeking the exercise of the court's jurisdiction under s 18(1)(b) (where this relates to the making of a gift of P's property), (h) (settlement of property) or (i) (execution of a will) of the Act, where the application is made by a person other than:

  (a)   a person who has made an application for the appointment of a deputy for which permission has been granted but which has not yet been determined;

  (b)   a person who, under any known will of P or under his intestacy, may become entitled to any property of P or any interest in it;

  (c)   a person who is an attorney appointed under an EPA which has been registered in accordance with the Act or the regulations referred to in Sch 4 to the Act;

  (d)   a person who is a donee of a lasting power of attorney which has been registered in accordance with the Act; or

  (e)   a person for whom P might be expected to provide if he had capacity to do so.

- in an application under s 20 of the Trusts of Land and Appointment of Trustees Act 1996, where the application is made by a person other than a beneficiary under the trust or if there is more than one, by both or all of them.

The effect of these rules is to ensure that anyone who has standing as an attorney or deputy or has a material interest in the outcome of an application may make an application. The permission process is largely intended for welfare cases to prevent interfering and vexatious friends and relatives or professional bystanders such as lobby groups or charities from interfering in potentially complex and expensive cases without good cause. However, it also serves to ensure that all other remedies have been explored and exhausted before an application for what may be a serious, contentious and costly matter is brought before the Court. As explained by the Department for Constitutional Affairs in its submission to the parliamentary scrutiny committee which examined the draft Mental Incapacity Bill (HC 1083 MIB 1222):

> 'The Court would operate a permission stage for certain types of applications to ensure that litigation is only brought before the Court when it would be of benefit to the person who lacks capacity and to ensure that all parties have exhausted other methods of reaching consensus before going to court.'

The procedure for applying for permission is dealt with at **3.21** below.

Making an application – beginning proceedings

3.7   The procedure for starting proceedings is set out in Part 9 of the Rules. Almost all applications requiring an order or decision of the Court must be started in this way with their own supporting evidence and information. Only where a matter is very straightforward and a deputy has been appointed or there is a registered EPA or LPA in place is there any relaxation of the considerable burden placed on the applicant. These routine cases are covered by Practice Direction 9D and are dealt with below at **3.43**.

To start proceedings, a person making an application must file with the Court the following documents:

- Court of Protection Application Form (COP1) setting out the order or permission requested. The application form is designed to satisfy Rule 63 which requires the application to state:

  (a)   the matter which the applicant wants the court to decide;

  (b)   the order which the applicant is seeking;

  (c)   the names of the applicant, P, any person (other than P) whom the applicant reasonably believes to have an interest which justifies him being heard in relation to the application (and who are to be named on the application form as a respondent to the proceedings) and any person (other than P) whom the applicant intends to notify; and

  (d)   if the applicant is applying in a representative capacity, what that capacity is.

- If permission is required, an order granting permission OR an application for permission in COP2.

- Assessment of Capacity Form (COP3). If the applicant is unable to complete an assessment of capacity form (for instance where P does not reside with the applicant and the applicant is unable to take P to a doctor, or where P refuses to undergo the assessment), the applicant should file a witness statement with the application form explaining why he has not been able to obtain an assessment of capacity, what attempts (if any) he has made to obtain an assessment of capacity and why he knows or believes that P lacks capacity to make a decision or decisions in relation to any matter that is the subject of the proposed application to the Court.

- Supporting Information Form (COP1A for property and affairs applications and COP1B for welfare applications).

- Depending on the application and the order sought, any other documents required to be submitted (see Practice Direction 9A). For example, a deputy or attorney making an application must submit a copy of the order appointing the deputy or the power of attorney as the case may be.

- Any additional evidence required to support the application. All such evidence must be set out either in a witness statement or must be clearly annexed to the application form (where it is covered by a Statement of Truth contained in that form).

- The prescribed fee (£400).

Proceedings are commenced by the applicant filing an application form in Form COP1. However, proceedings are not formally started until the Court issues the application form (Rule 62).

Who is a party?

Parties to the application

3.8   The Rules make provision for five classes of person to be parties (other than the applicant):

- A person named as a respondent and who files an acknowledgement that he wishes to be joined as a party

- A person notified of an application and who files an acknowledgement stating that he wishes to be joined as a party and whom the Court orders be added as a party

- A person who wishes to be joined as a party and who has applied using Form COP10 and who is subsequently joined as a party by the Court

- P, where he has applied (in his acknowledgement or subsequently) to be a party and he has been joined as a party by the Court

- Any person (including P) whom the Court orders to be added as a party to the proceedings.

It is important to avoid an assumption that someone is a party simply by virtue of having an interest in a case or receiving a form of notice. A person named as a respondent or a notified person must take a formal step within a prescribed time limit if he wishes to be joined as a party. It is essential to respond to an application within 21 days, even if there is only time to submit an acknowledgement form. This can include a request for filing further evidence at a later date.

The Court still retains a wide discretion to add parties and this will be used quite frequently. For instance where P lacks capacity and the application concerns P's welfare or property, the Court can direct that P be added as a party and then direct for P to be represented by the Official Solicitor, the deputy or another person as litigation friend. The Court may also join parties at a later date if they have a material interest and apply to be joined. Frequently a person will be notified of an application and not appreciate the importance of the matter until after he has taken advice or more information has to come to light and the time limit for responding has expired. The Court will generally allow parties to be joined to the proceedings if it is practicable.

Where a person is making an application, it is not always clear initially who is to be a party to the proceedings or simply given notice of proceedings. The Rules therefore provide for two initial classes of interested persons:

- those with a material interest in the outcome (respondents); and

- those with a personal interest in the welfare and interests of P (persons notified).

Respondents

3.9 The Rules do not specify who should be a respondent. Rule 6 defines a respondent as 'a person who is named as a respondent in the application form or notice, as the case may be.' As it is the applicant who fills in the application form, it is clear that the onus is on the applicant in the first instance to name the correct respondents. An applicant who fails to name the correct respondents can create a procedural obstacle for another party and greatly add to the time and expense of the progression of the case.

The respondent's obligation is emphasised by the notes accompanying the application where the applicant is advised as follows:

'You must provide the details of any person who you reasonably believe has an interest which means they ought to be heard by the court in relation to the application. Respondents have the opportunity to be joined as parties to the proceedings if they wish to participate in the hearing. You must serve respondents with copies of all documents relating to your application when the court has issued your application form, in order to allow them the opportunity to support or oppose your application.'

In practice, a respondent is someone with a material interest in the outcome. A respondent will therefore be required to perform an act or cease to perform an act or have a direct financial interest either by having to pay for an act to be performed or who may be less well off as a result of the act being performed. Thus in a personal welfare application, especially if it involves issues of serious medical treatment, a person or body who provides or will provide clinical or caring services to P and who is required to carry out an act will be named as a respondent to the proceedings (assuming that such person is not already the applicant). In an application for a statutory will or gift where a person will receive less by virtue of the application than he would otherwise if no application were made, then he is materially prejudiced and must be joined as a respondent.

Practice Direction 9F makes it clear that this is an absolute requirement and more than a general principle. Thus the applicant must name as a respondent:

(a) any beneficiary under an existing will or codicil who is likely to be materially or adversely affected by the application;

(b) any beneficiary under a proposed will or codicil who is likely to be materially or adversely affected by the application; and

(c) any prospective beneficiary under P's intestacy where P has no existing will.

A named respondent who is served with the papers is not automatically a party to the proceedings. It is not sufficient to be named in the application and served with the application form and copy documents. Rule 73(1) defines parties to the proceedings who include 'any person who is named as a respondent **and** who files an acknowledgement of service in respect of the application form.' A respondent must therefore file an acknowledgement if he wishes to be a party.

Persons given notice

3.10   In most non-contentious cases where no one has a direct material interest in the matter, it is nevertheless appropriate for persons to be given notice in general terms so that they are aware of what is proposed and can intervene if they have sufficient interest, whether to protect the interests of the person concerned or their own interests. It is left to them to make further representations and apply to be joined as a party. This provides an important safeguard for the person concerned. For instance, where a person applies for the appointment of a deputy for P, it is appropriate to notify P's relatives. They have no material interest in the application, but may well have a view about the suitability of the proposed deputy. If it transpires that the notified person wishes to make an objection or has a material interest in the outcome of the case then the Court can join that person as a party under Rule 73 or by way of a direction under Rule 85.

As to who should be given notice of an application, Practice Direction 9B lays down some clear and helpful guidelines:

'The applicant must seek to identify at least three persons who are likely to have an interest in being notified that an application form has been issued.

The applicant should notify them:

(a)   that an application form has been issued;

(b)   whether it relates to the exercise of the court's jurisdiction in relation to P's property and affairs, or his personal welfare, or both; and

(c)   of the order or orders sought.

Members of P's close family are, by virtue of their relationship to P, likely to have an interest in being notified that an application has been made to the court concerning P. It should be presumed, for example that a spouse or civil partner, any other partner, parents and children, where they exist, are likely to have an interest in the application.

This presumption may be displaced where the applicant is aware of circumstances which reasonably indicate that P's family should not be notified, but that others should be notified instead. For example, where the applicant knows that the relative in question has had little or no involvement in P's life and has shown no inclination to do so, he may reasonably conclude that they need not be notified. In some cases, P may be closer to persons who are not relatives and if so, it will be appropriate to notify them instead of close family members.'

Although the Practice Direction allows close friends to be notified in place of blood relatives, it does contain a list of classes of relationship, similar to the prescribed classes of relatives to be notified on registration of an EPA (see **14.22** below). Thus at least three people should be notified in descending order (as appropriate to P's circumstances):

(a)   spouse or civil partner;

(b)   person who is not a spouse or a civil partner but who has been living with P as if they were;

(c)   parent or guardian;

(d)   child;

(e)   brother or sister;

(f)   grandparent or grandchild;

(g)   aunt or uncle;

(h)   child of a person falling within subparagraph (e);

(i)   step-parent; and

(j)   half-brother or half-sister.

If the applicant decides that a person listed in one of the above categories in paragraph 6 ought to be notified, and there are other persons in that category, the applicant should notify all persons falling within that category unless there is a good reason not to do so. For instance, it may not be appropriate to notify a relative who has had little or no involvement in P's life and has shown no inclination to do so. However, if the applicant chooses not to notify such a person, the evidence in support of the applicant form must also set out why that person was not notified.

In addition to the list of relatives, the following persons should also be notified where appropriate:

(a)   where P is under 18, any person with parental responsibility for P within the meaning of the Children Act 1989 should be notified;

(b)   any legal or natural person who is likely to be affected by the outcome of any application should be notified. For example, where P is receiving care or treatment from a local authority or primary care trust (and the application is made by another person) the authority or trust should be notified where the application relates to the provision or withdrawal of medical or other treatment, or accommodation, from P;

(c)   where there is a deputy appointed by the court ('a deputy') or a person appointed under either an EPA or a LPA ('an attorney'), to make decisions on behalf of P in regard to a matter to which the application relates, the deputy or attorney should be notified. For example, where the application relates to P's property, and the deputy has been appointed to make decisions in relation to P's property, the deputy should be notified; and

(d)   where there is any other person not already mentioned whom the applicant reasonably considers has an interest in being notified about matters relating to P's best interests, that person should be notified. For example, P may have a close friend with an interest in being notified because he provides care to P on an informal basis.

Other factors the Court will consider

3.11   The applicant has responsibility initially for determining whether a person should be classed as a respondent or merely given notice. Clearly the applicant will be a party, as will a respondent who has been named as such and who has filed an acknowledgement of service. That does not necessarily mean that the applicant will choose the right parties to notify or the parties notified will understand what they need to do. It may for instance become clear later on in the proceedings that some other person ought to be notified and/or joined as a party. It may also be appropriate for P to be joined as a party. However, apart from the initial parties, it will be for the Court to decide who should be joined as a party. Rule 73 gives the Court power to add and remove parties, whether on their own application or by way of a direction under Rule 85. A person who has not been named as a respondent or who has not been notified also has a right to apply to be joined as a party.

The Court will of course be bound to involve as a party any person with a material interest in the case or where the interests of justice require. The Court will have to be guided by the relevant Practice Direction as well as earlier guidance set out in the case of *Re B (Court of Protection) (Notice of Proceedings)* [1987] 2 All ER 475.

Re B concerned an application for the exercise of a power of appointment in which the applicant requested that notice on the beneficiaries be dispensed with because of the acrimonious nature of their relationship. The Court rejected the submission, Millett J stating clearly that:

'... all persons materially affected should be given every opportunity of putting their cases forward. Of course, there will be exceptional cases in which it will be right to exclude a party from the proceedings, notwithstanding the fact that he is a party interested. Plainly delay, cost, embarrassment and the exacerbation of family dissensions are all relevant matters. But only in the most exceptional circumstances should the considerations to which I have referred be overridden ... In the ordinary case, and in the absence of emergency or need to act with great speed or of some other compelling reason, all persons who may be materially and adversely affected should be notified of the application. Such persons will normally include persons who have been named as beneficiaries in a previous will or who are next of kin in the case of an intestacy where the application is made under s 96(1)(e) and the persons entitled in default of appointment where the application is made under s 96(1)(k).'

Practice Direction 9F refers to any beneficiary under an existing or proposed will or codicil who is likely to be materially or adversely affected by the application (paragraph 9). The applicant must consider someone who is adversely affected but someone who has a material interest in the outcome. A beneficiary whose interest is not affected, for instance if he receives the same benefit under the new will as under the existing will is materially affected and needs to be named as a respondent.

The Court of Protection has traditionally been wary of creating situations where a party is denied a right to present his case. This predates the Human Rights Act 1998 and reflects the unusual and often final jurisdiction of the Court, for once a person has died it is practically impossible to reverse an earlier decision. This approach, combined with Practice Direction 9F, gives an applicant and the Court no apparent leeway to avoid naming as respondents individuals who may in reality have very little interest in the matter. Prior to October 2007, applications had been made under the Mental Health Act jurisdiction for statutory wills where the patient was intestate and over a dozen beneficiaries were entitled on intestacy. Many of those beneficiaries had been unaware of the patient's existence. The estate was not extensive, the patient was terminally ill and many of the beneficiaries lived abroad. The Court allowed notice to be dispensed with on the basis that the majority of the beneficiaries had been notified and taken together as a class, were deemed to have been notified.

It is unclear whether the new Court of Protection would have any discretion to disregard a potential party. This would also give rise to difficulties where the existing beneficiaries under a will are discretionary beneficiaries or charities. It is likely that the robust approach of the Court in *Re Davey dec'd* [1980] 3 All ER 342 where notice was dispensed with in unusual circumstances cannot be followed. This case and the parties to a statutory will application are considered in more detail at **13.41**.

Persons bound as if parties

3.12   Although a person may not take an active part in the proceedings whether as a respondent or a person who wishes to be joined as a party, Rule 74 still provides for the following persons to be bound by any order or direction of the Court in the same way as a party to the proceedings:

- P; and

- any person who has been served with or notified of an application form under the Rules (whether or not that person has acknowledged the application).

Litigation friend

3.13   The underlying assumption within the Rules is that P will not be a party to the proceedings unless he is joined by the Court as a party. There are therefore two separate procedures for P:

- where P is *not* a party, the notification rules in Part 6 apply (see **3.17** below). P may subsequently apply to be joined as a party or the Court may join P as a party. However, so long as P is not a party, P will still be bound by any order or direction of the Court under Rule 74; and

- where P is a party to the proceedings, then so long as P lacks capacity in relation to the matter to which the proceedings relate, P must have a litigation friend (Rule 141(1)).

A protected party (that is a person who lacks capacity other than P) who is a party to the proceedings must also be represented by a litigation friend. There is also a clear presumption that a child should be represented by a litigation friend, but the Court may, in the case of a child, dispense with this requirement and allow the child to conduct his own proceedings.

The requirement for and role of the litigation friend mirror the equivalent provisions in Part 21 of the CPR. Thus a litigation friend may be appointed by the Court directly, or may be any other person who is able and willing to conduct the proceedings.

Litigation friend appointed by Court

3.14   In the majority of cases the Court will appoint a litigation friend, either of its own motion or on an application from the applicant or one of the parties. The Court may appoint the Official Solicitor as litigation friend, but is not bound to do so and may for instance appoint a deputy or another solicitor to act in that role. However, no appointment can be made without the consent of the person appointed. To save time the Court will often appoint a litigation friend 'subject to' consent being filed subsequently.

An application for the appointment of a litigation friend must be made in Form COP9 in accordance with the Part 10 procedure. The application must meet two requirements:

- The application must be supported by evidence (Rule 143(3). Thus where the litigation friend is to be appointed for a protected party, the Court must have medical evidence that the protected party lacks capacity to conduct proceedings; and

- The Court must be satisfied that the person to be appointed satisfies the conditions in Rule 140(1), that:

  (a)   he can fairly and competently conduct proceedings on behalf of P (or child or protected party as the case may be); and

  (b)   he has no interest adverse to the person being represented.

Practice Direction 17A confirms that any evidence in support of an application must satisfy the Court that the proposed litigation friend consents to act and satisfies the conditions laid down in r 140(1).

Where the protected party is not the person to whom the application relates then this last requirement is satisfied by the proposed litigation friend completing a certificate of suitability in form COP22.

Litigation friend without a Court order

3.15   Where there is no Court order appointing a litigation friend in place, then a deputy with the power to conduct proceedings on behalf of a protected party may continue to act as litigation friend in respect of any proceedings to which his power relates, so long as a copy of the order appointing him is served on every other party to the proceedings and every other person who would be served with an application notice on behalf of a protected party under Rule 32 (Rule 142(2)). For example an application is made for a statutory will for a person who lacks capacity (P); the Official Solicitor is appointed to act as litigation friend for P and as P's wife also lacks capacity her deputy is given authority to act as her litigation friend. The wife's deputy may then need to make a further application as litigation friend for the wife. Where there is no one appointed by the Court and no deputy with the power to conduct proceedings, then a person can act as litigation friend provided he files with the Court a certificate of suitability and serves a copy on every other party to the proceedings and every other person who would be served with an application notice on behalf of a protected party under Rule 32 (Rule 142(3)). The certificate of suitability is in Form COP22 which contains a statement of truth. The prospective litigation friend must state that he satisfies the conditions set out in Rule 140(1), namely that:

(a)   he can fairly and competently conduct proceedings on behalf of P (or child or protected party as the case may be); and

(b)   he has no interest adverse to the person being represented.

Practice Direction 17A imposes three further requirements where a certificate of suitability is filed. The prospective litigation friend must also:

(a)   state that he consents to act;

(b)   state that he knows or believes that the child or the protected party lacks capacity to conduct the proceedings himself; and

(c)   state the grounds of his belief and, if his belief is based upon medical opinion, or the opinion of another suitably qualified expert, attach any relevant document to the certificate.

Any medical evidence filed with the certificate of suitability does not, however, need to be copied and served on any other person unless the Court directs otherwise. The prospective litigation friend must however file a certificate of service in respect of every person or party on whom the certificate of suitability has been served.

Notices – respondents and persons to be notified

3.16   As we have seen at **3.7** proceedings are started when the Court issues the application form. The Court will then return the issued application form to the applicant and it is then the responsibility of the applicant, within 21 days of the application form being issued, to:

Serve on a respondent:	Give notification to a person notified:
• a copy of the application form	• a notice that an application has been issued (COP15); and
• copies of any documents submitted; and	• a form for acknowledging service (Form COP5)
• a form for acknowledging service (Form COP5)	

Although the Rules as well as form COP20 distinguish between service on respondents (Rule 66) and the giving of notification to other persons (Rule 70), Practice Direction applies Part 6 of the Rules (service of documents) to both procedures.

Within seven days of serving the above documents on a named respondent, the applicant must file a certificate of service (Form COP20) in respect of each person on whom documents have been served.

Where there are other persons to be notified (who are not respondents), the applicant must in addition and also within 21 days of the application being issued, give notice to such persons that an application has been issued and of the order sought. Notice is given in Form COP15 which sets out the prescribed information, although there is no requirement (at this stage) to provide the notified person with full details of the application and supporting evidence.

Any documents served or given to a person notified must be accompanied by a form for acknowledging service or notification (Form COP5). The applicant must furthermore file a certificate of service or notification (COP20) in respect of every person served or notified.

To those practitioners used to dealing with receivership applications, this imposes a considerable administrative burden. On making an application to appoint a receiver, the applicant would merely state in Form CP5 the names of the persons notified and the dates they were sent a simple Notification Letter. Under the new Rules, the applicant person applying to appoint a deputy must have his application issued and *then* notify the persons to be notified (a two-page form), provide them with a form for acknowledging service (a six-page form) and *then* notify the Court that the notices have been given (a 12-page form).

The applicant's duty to serve the application on a respondent and notify other parties is without prejudice to any subsequent directions of the Court under Rule 85 to join another person as a party. It is then for the applicant to serve the application and any relevant papers on that person within 21 days of the direction being made (or such other period as the Court directs), provide the person served with a form for acknowledgement of service and file a certificate of service with the Court.

Notifying P

Information given to P

3.17   The giving of notice to P is governed by Part 7 of the Rules and the accompanying Practice Direction.

Unless the person concerned is a party to an application, the applicant must under Rule 42(1) notify P that an application has been issued unless service on P is dispensed with under Rule 49. Notice must be given as soon as practicable and in any event within 21 days of the application being issued. The person effecting notification (who may be the applicant, his agent or other person as directed by the Court) must give notice personally to P. Not only must P be provided with a notice in Form COP14, setting out the information that must be given to P, the person effecting notification must also ensure that he explains the specified information to P in a way that is appropriate to P's circumstances (for example, using simple language, visual aids or any other appropriate means).

Part 7 of the Rules expects P to be kept informed and notified at various stages in the proceedings:

Event	*Matters to be explained:*
Application issued	• that an application has been issued; • the date on which any hearing is to be held; • who the applicant is; • that the application raises the question of whether P lacks capacity in relation to a matter or matters, and what that means; • what will happen if the Court makes the order or direction that has been applied for; • where the application contains a proposal for the appointment of a person to make decisions on P's behalf in relation to the matter to which the application relates, details of who that person is; and • that P may seek advice and assistance.
Application withdrawn	• that an application has been withdrawn; • the date on which any hearing is to be held; • the consequences of that withdrawal; and • that P may seek advice and assistance.

Event	*Matters to be explained:*
Appellant's notice issued	• that an appellant's notice has been issued; • the date on which any hearing is to be held; • who the appellant is; • the issues raised by the appeal; • what will happen if the Court makes the order or direction applied for; and • that P may seek advice and assistance.
Appellant's notice withdrawn	• that an appellant's notice has been withdrawn; • the date on which any hearing is to be held; • the consequences of the withdrawal; and • that P may seek advice and assistance.
Final order	• that a final order has been made; • the effect of the order; and • that P may seek advice and assistance.
Other matters as the Court directs	• such matters as may be directed by the Court; and • that P may seek advice and assistance.

In view of the amount of information that must be given to P, it will not always be possible to provide all the information required for each event at the same time. For instance, an application may be issued and the applicant must notify P as soon as practically possible. However, it may not be until a greater period of time has elapsed and directions have been issued setting the case down for a hearing. P should then be notified again of the hearing.

Once P has been notified of any of the matters required by Part 7, the person effecting notification must within seven days of notification, file a certificate of notification/non-notification in Form COP20, certifying that the information shown in COP14 has been given to P or explaining why P could not be notified. The person effecting notification must also certify that he has explained the core details of the application outlined above.

When an application form or appellant's notice has been issued, the person effecting notice must also provide P with an acknowledgement of service Form COP5.

Dispensing with notice

3.18   Rule 40(3), which applies whether P is a party or not, allows the Court of its own motion or on an application to direct that P must not be notified of any matter or document or provided with any document.

Rule 49, which applies so long as P is not a party, also provides the Court with power to make an order dispensing with any of the requirements contained in Part 7 of the Rules. However, this power can only be exercised on a separate application under Part 10.

The clear presumption in practice will always be in favour of complying with the Rules in notifying P. The whole tenor of the Act is in favour of protecting P's rights and dignity by involving P as much as possible. The limited circumstances in which an application for notice to be dispensed with would be appropriate, are illustrated by Practice Direction 7A, which states that:

> 'Such an application would be appropriate where, for example, P is in a permanent vegetative state or a minimally conscious state; or where notification by the applicant is likely to cause significant and disproportionate distress to P.'

The problem with this part of the Rules is that it does not distinguish between a person with some capacity and a person with no capacity. The Rules generally presuppose that P will be as involved as possible, whether by being notified of various events through the course of the case or by being joined as a party directly or through a litigation friend. However, in many cases a deputy will need to be appointed for someone with advanced dementia and a lot of effort (and expense) will be incurred providing notification and explanations to no purpose whatsoever. However, the applicant faces a difficult dilemma. Does he make a separate application in Part 10 to dispense with notification or does he go through the motions and effect notification?

If the applicant wishes to be dispensed with the requirement to notify P, he will need to make a case for notice to be dispensed with. Not only will he need to file an application notice under Part 10, but he will need to provide evidence, to show that:

(a)   P is incapable of benefiting from the requirements of Part 6; or

(b)   P lacks capacity to comprehend the application; or

(c)   the proposed notification is likely to cause significant and disproportionate distress; and

(d)   that P's rights will not be prejudiced as a result.

Notice not required – where P is a party

3.19   In cases where P is a party, then the provisions of Part 7 which relate to notice to P do not apply. Notice can instead be served on the litigation friend. In most cases the Court will aim to direct that P is to be joined as a party when issuing the application. However, in many cases the application may need to be issued before directions are issued. The Court will therefore join P as a party after proceedings have started, in which case P will have to be notified at least once.

Method of service

3.20   Although P must be notified in person, any other person may be served using more conventional means. If a solicitor is acting for a person and the person serving has been informed in writing that the solicitor is acting, then any document can be served on that solicitor.

Where it is not known whether a solicitor is acting on behalf of a person, the document may be served by:

(a)   delivering it to the person personally;

(b)   delivering it at his home address or last known home address; or

(c)   sending it to that address, or last known address, by first class post (or by an alternative method of service which provides for delivery on the next working day).

Only where it appears to the Court that there is a good reason to authorise service by a different method, the Court may direct that service is effected by that method. Such a direction must specify the method of service and the date when the document will be deemed to be served.

As to what is meant by 'an alternative method of service' and 'electronic means' is left to Practice Direction 6A which states that where a document is to be served by electronic means:

'5. …

(a)   the party who is to be served or his legal representative must have previously expressly indicated in writing to the party serving:

(i)   that he is willing to accept service by electronic means; and

(ii)   the fax number, e-mail address, or electronic identification to which it should be sent; and

(b)   the following shall be taken as sufficient written identification for the purposes of the preceding paragraph:

(i)   a fax number set out on the writing paper of the legal representative of the party who is to be served; or

(ii)   a fax number, e-mail address or electronic identification set out on an application form or a response to an application filed with the court.

6.   Where a party seeks to serve a document by electronic means he should first seek to clarify with the party who is to be served whether there are any limitations to the recipient's agreement to accept service by such means, including in relation to the format in which documents are to be sent and the maximum size of attachments that may be received.

7. An address for service given by a party must be within the jurisdiction and any fax number must be at the address for service. Where an email address or electronic identification is given in conjunction with an address for service, the email address or electronic identification will be deemed to be at the address for service.

8. Where a document is served by electronic means, the party serving the document need not in addition send a hard copy by post or document exchange.'

Application for permission

3.21 The requirement to obtain permission to make an application is considered at **3.6** above. Where a person wishes to make an application for which permission is required, the applicant must apply for permission by filing a **permission form** (Form COP2) and must file with it:

(a) any information or documents specified in the relevant practice direction;

(b) a draft of the application form which he seeks permission to have issued; and

(c) an assessment of capacity form, where this is required by the relevant practice direction.

A person applying for permission must therefore file with the Court the following:

- Court of Protection Permission Form (COP2) setting out the applicant's relationship or connection to P; the reasons for making the application; the benefit to P of the order to be made and whether this can be achieved in some other way. The form also contains a statement of truth.

- Court of Protection Application Form (COP1) setting out the substantive order or permission requested. This may be in draft form or as the main application if made alongside the application for permission.

- Assessment of Capacity Form (COP3).

- Supporting Information Form (COP1A for property and affairs applications and COP1B for welfare applications). The Supporting Information Form may, however, be submitted subsequently once Permission has been granted.

- Any other supporting evidence or information that is relevant to the application.

Within 14 days of the Permission Form being filed, the Court will issue the form and make one of the following decisions:

(a) grant the application without a hearing and may give directions in connection with the issue of the application form;

(b) refuse the application without a hearing; or

(c) fix a date for the hearing of the application.

Where the Court fixes a date for a hearing, it will notify the applicant and 'such other persons as it thinks fit', and provide them with any documents submitted with the application and a form for acknowledging notice. It is not clear from the Rules or the Practice Direction who should be notified, but it is assumed that the Court will expect P to be notified where appropriate and also involve any person named as a respondent in the application if this has been submitted in draft form. As evidence served by the Court may be sensitive or confidential, the Court must also consider whether any document is to be provided on an edited basis.

Once the Court has made an order giving or refusing permission, it will serve copies on the applicant and any other notified person who has filed an acknowledgement. If he has not already filed the application, the applicant may then proceed with his substantive application.

Applications within proceedings

When relevant

3.22   Because a formal application is a relatively cumbersome process, Part 10 of the Rules provides for a process known as applications within proceedings. The title is misleading, as it includes:

- matters which are ancillary to an application; or

- an emergency or ex parte application made before the substantive application has been made.

Although the Rules and Practice Directions make frequent reference to applications within proceedings or the Part 10 procedure, they provide limited guidance as to when applications should be made within proceedings and what the extent of their role is. Part 10 of the Rules is a very wide ranging 'catch all provision' that can cover anything from an application to serve a witness statement to an emergency injunction not to withdraw life-sustaining treatment. However, its principal function appears to be to resolve ancillary matters, while the substantive application is in progress. Examples include applications for:

- issue of a witness summons to obtain a document or file from another party (Rule 106);

- the appointment of a litigation friend for P or a protected party (Rule 143 and PD 7A paragraph 13);

- directions to deal with the location the case is to be heard at or the level of judge to hear the case;

- authority to dispense with notice being given to P (Rule 49);

- an order for information to be disclosed with an application to be edited, for reasons of confidentiality (Rule 19);

- a direction that a document is privileged and cannot be disclosed (Rule 138);

- an interim order to obtain access to funds;

- an interim order to sell or purchase a particular property;

- reconsideration of an order made without a hearing or without notice to any person (Rule 89);

- enforcement of an order that a party will not comply with (Rule 185);

- hearing the application in public, waiving reporting restrictions or disclosing information about proceedings (Rules 90–93);

- disputing the Court's jurisdiction to hear an application where the application is made by someone who has not been served with or notified of the application (Rule 87 and PD12B);

- obtaining evidence from a witness by a deposition or from a witness abroad (Rules 108–116); and

- the transfer of P's property under the control or ownership of another person when P regains capacity (Rule 202).

Procedure

3.23   The Part 10 procedure generally assumes that an application has already been made and issued. However, an application notice can be filed at the same time as an application form, for instance where an interim measure or direction is required. An application can also be commenced 'where the exceptional urgency of the matter requires' without filing an application form (PD10B).

Unless the matter is exceptionally urgent, an application within proceedings is commenced by the applicant filing an **application notice** (Form COP9) together with any evidence which he wishes to rely on. The application notice must state what order is required, the grounds being relied on (which should be explained briefly and can be set out in the notice itself or a witness statement) and provide a draft of the order sought.

In most cases, where the Court receives an application notice, the Court will issue the application notice and if there is to be a hearing, give notice of the hearing date. Rule 78(4) is not clear as to whether the Court is responsible for notifying the applicant, as well as any respondent named in the application notice or other party. Rule 78(3) refers to the Court giving notice of a hearing date while Rule 78(4) refers to notice 'being given' without specifying who is to give notice! Clearly any applicant must ensure that parties to the application notice are notified of a hearing date. The applicant must in any event within 21 days of the application notice being issued, serve a copy of the issued application notice on any respondent named in the application notice, any other party to the proceedings and any other person as the Court may direct (Rule 78). In this context, the respondent to the application notice may not be a party to the main application. For instance one party to an application may require a summons for the disclosure of confidential records and the person or body holding the information is named as a respondent in the application notice. Other parties who must be served include the applicant to the main application and P if he has been joined as a party. The applicant must also file a certificate of service (COP20) in respect of each application notice served by him, within seven days of such service being effected. However, the persons notified do need to be provided with a form for acknowledging service.

Where a Part 10 application is to be dealt with at a hearing then this may be by way of a telephone hearing (PD 10A paragraph 17). This at least avoids the effort and expense of several parties to an application attending the Court in person. Although the Court may direct a telephone hearing, it is the responsibility of the applicant to organise the telephone hearing using a special legal conference facility provided by British Telecom.

Emergencies

3.24 Rule 78(5) does allow an application to be made without filing an application if this is permitted by a rule or Practice Direction or if the Court dispenses with this requirement. The Practice Directions do not help a great deal. Practice Direction 10A states that an application may be made without service of an application notice:

'(a) where there is exceptional urgency;

(b) where the overriding objective is best furthered by doing so;

(c) by consent of all parties;

(d) with the permission of the court; or

(e) where a rule or other practice direction permits.'

Practice Direction 10B sets out a procedure to be followed in urgent cases, but does not define what is meant by an emergency. In practice, it will be for the applicant to determine whether an application should be made urgently without an application notice and for the Court to agree with this. It should also be self-evident as to when an application is urgent. If life-sustaining treatment is in issue or there is evidence of financial or physical abuse, then it is likely that the Court will agree to deal with an application as an emergency. Clearly an emergency situation should not arise where a party has delayed making an application so that it becomes urgent as a result. The Practice Direction contains the following warning:

'In some cases, urgent applications arise because applications to the court have not been pursued sufficiently promptly. This is undesirable, and should be avoided. A judge who has concerns that the facility for urgent applications may have been abused may require the applicant or the applicant's representative to attend at a subsequent hearing to provide an explanation for the delay.'

Where the applicant makes an application without service, then the evidence in support of the application must also set out why service was not effected. Where the Court makes an order pursuant to an application without notice, the applicant must as soon as practicable or within such period as the Court directs, serve on the respondent and any other parties to the proceedings a copy of the application notice, the Court order and any evidence filed in support of the application (Rule 81).

Where there is an emergency, Practice Directions 10A and 10B allow for a number of practical measures that can be taken:

- An application can be made orally at a hearing. If the applicant has insufficient time to file an application notice, the application can be made orally, but the applicant should notify the Court and the other parties as soon as he can of the nature of the application and the reason for it. This is a very useful measure and allows a request for a particular order or direction to be made at a hearing.

- Where an application has been made without notice, the applicant should take steps to advise a respondent by telephone, unless justice would be defeated if notice were given.

- A direction that an application be treated as urgent will not normally be given without the consent of every other party entitled to be given notice of the application.

- The Court may direct that the application or part of it be dealt with by way of a telephone hearing.

- The Court may permit the use of video conferencing facilities.

- If an order is made without notice to any other party, the order will ordinarily contain an undertaking by the applicant to the Court to serve the application notice on the respondent and any other party specified as soon as practicable or as directed by the Court, as well as a return date for a further hearing at which other parties can be present.

- A draft order should be filed with the application notice if possible and the draft may be on a disk; if no application notice has been filed, the draft order can be produced at the hearing.

- Even if the Court allows an application without notice on the grounds of 'exceptional urgency' the Court will require an undertaking that the application form in the terms of the oral application be filed on the next working day or as directed by the Court.

- In cases of extreme urgency, application can be made by telephone. Practice Direction 10B refers to the Court of Protection telephone number for applications in office hours and the Royal Courts of Justice security office for applications outside office hours.

Considerations for emergency and interim measures

3.25   In dealing with any emergency measure, the Court will strongly consider the justice of the case and whether any party will be prejudiced by the application. The Court must also consider what medical evidence it requires. Although Part 10 and the accompanying Practice Directions do not refer to medical evidence, it would be inappropriate for the Court to make an order without prima facie evidence that P lacks capacity. The Court's powers under s 16 of the Act are only available if P lacks capacity in relation to a matter or matters. The Court is also bound by the framework of the Act when determining the terms of the order being made. Not only must a decision be made in P's best interests, but the Court must also comply with s 1(6) of the MCA 2005:

> 'Before the act is done, or the decision is made, regard must be had to whether the purpose for which it is needed can be as effectively achieved in a way that is less restrictive of the person's rights and freedom of action.'

The Court must therefore make a declaration or order which is the most limited that can be made to achieve the requirements of the situation. As a result it is likely that most emergency orders will be in the form of interim orders or injunctions which will only last as long as they need to and no later than the date on which a hearing takes place. At the hearing, a substantive order can be made.

Where any order is made without a hearing or without notice to a person affected by the order (and most interim measures will be dealt with outside of a hearing or without notice being given) then unless there is to be a hearing listed to take place within the framework of the proceedings, the Court will need to direct service of the order on P, any party to the proceedings and any other person affected by the order, so as to comply with the requirements of Rule 89. Rule 89 gives any such person a right to apply to the Court for an attended hearing to reconsider the order made.

Interim measures

3.26   On the basis that many cases that need to be dealt with on an application notice can be dealt with by way of interim measures, Rule 82 provides a list of specific interim remedies the Court may apply:

> '(1) The court may grant the following interim remedies—
>
> (a)   an interim injunction;
>
> (b)   an interim declaration; or
>
> (c)   any other interim order it considers appropriate.
>
> (2) Unless the court orders otherwise, a person on whom an application form is served under Part 9, or who is given notice of such an application, may not apply for an interim remedy before he has filed an acknowledgment of service or notification in accordance with Part 9.
>
> (3) This rule does not limit any other power of the court to grant interim relief.

Part 10 of the Rules contains the only references in the Rules to interim measures. Section 48 of the MCA 2005 contains a power under the heading 'interim orders and directions' for the Court to make an order or give directions in respect of any matter 'pending the determination of any matter' provided the matter is within the Court's jurisdiction and the decision is in P's best interests.

There is no specific power for the Court to appoint an interim deputy as there was under r 42 of the Court of Protection Rules 2001. In practice the Court will simply insert a 'sunset clause' in the order appointing the deputy so that the order will expire after a fixed period (see **5.27** below).

Neither the Rules nor the Practice Directions contain any reference to when interim measures are appropriate, the extent of those measures and how long they should last. Section 48 merely states that it must be in P's best interests to make the order. This may appear unhelpfully obvious, but any measure that is not in P's best interests or does not comply with s 1(6) of the Act would be open to challenge and the Court would in practice take the statutory considerations carefully into account. Any such measure will therefore be limited and if made without a hearing or without notice to a party affected by it, will comply with Rule 89.

Responding to an application

3.27   A respondent served with an application or a person given notice of an application has 21 days from service to file an acknowledgement of service or notification in Form COP5. The person completing the form must:

(a)   state whether he opposes the application and if so, set out the grounds for doing so;

(b)   state whether he seeks a different order from that set out in the application form and if so, set out what that order is;

(c)   provide an address for service, which must be within the jurisdiction of the court; and

(d)   be signed by him or his legal representative.

Furthermore, where P or a person is given notice of an application, he must in his acknowledgement:

(a)   indicate whether he wishes to be joined as a party to the proceedings; and

(b)   state his interest in the proceedings.

His response must also be accompanied by a witness statement containing any evidence of his interest in the proceedings and if he opposes the application, any evidence on which he wishes to rely. Clearly there will often be insufficient time to file detailed evidence; however the response should provide some evidence to indicate that the person responding has an interest and requesting an extension of time for further evidence to be filed.

It is then for the Court to serve any acknowledgement of service or notification it receives on the applicant and any other person who files such an acknowledgement.

Subsequent procedure

3.28   Once all the notices have been served within their relevant time limits, the Court must deal with the application. Depending on the nature of the proceedings, whether or not it is opposed and whether it involves any substantial dispute of fact or law, the Court will decide whether it is necessary to hold a hearing. The Court must take one of the following steps:

- make the order sought and dispose of the application without a hearing;
- set a date for a hearing for directions;
- set a date for a hearing;
- specify a date before which the application will be considered without a hearing; or
- give directions in writing.

The very precise requirements laid down by the Rules seem to evaporate at this point. There is no formal requirement for the Court to do anything more within any particular timeframe. It is now left to the Court to consider whether to hold a hearing or to dispose of the matter. However, when the Court does set a hearing date, whether for disposing of the matter or for directions, the Court must give notice to the parties and anyone else the Court directs should be notified.

The Court's wide-ranging powers and discretion more or less reflect the Mental Health Act 1983 jurisdiction where once an application was made, it was then left to the Court to set the pace, decide whether the matter was urgent or not, whether a hearing was required, and what directions should be issued. Thus an application for the sale of a property would be disposed of immediately without a hearing; an application for the appointment of a receiver would be set down for consideration at a future hearing date, at which it would be disposed of without a hearing; if the application might be contested, directions would be issued joining parties and directing service on them. The new Rules are therefore evolutionary rather than radical, setting out in more detail what the Court can do to deal with the application in the most efficient and appropriate way, bearing in mind that the same Rules need to cover every situation from a simple application for a gift to a contested medical emergency.

Directions

3.29   So long as the Court cannot dispose of the matter immediately or without holding a hearing, it can make any of the following directions (Rule 85):

'(a)   require a report under section 49 of the Act and give directions as to any such report;

(b)   give directions as to any requirements contained in these Rules or a practice direction for the giving of notification to any person or for that person to do anything in response to a notification;

(c)   if the court considers that P should be a party to the proceedings, give directions joining him as a party;

(d)   if P is joined as a party to proceedings, give directions as to the appointment of a litigation friend;

(e)   if the court considers that any other person or persons should be a party to the proceedings, give directions joining them as a party;

(f)   if the court considers that any party to the proceedings should not be a party, give directions for that person's removal as a party;

(g)   give directions for the management of the case and set a timetable for the steps to be taken between the giving of directions and the hearing;

(h)   give directions as to the type of judge who is to hear the case;

(i)   give directions as to whether the proceedings or any part of them are to be heard in public, or as to whether any particular person should be permitted to attend the hearing, or as to whether any publication of the proceedings is to be permitted;

(j)   give directions as to the disclosure of documents, service of witness statements and any expert evidence;

(k)   give directions as to the attendance of witnesses and as to whether, and the extent to which, cross-examination will be permitted at any hearing;

(l)   give such other directions as the court thinks fit; and

(m)   unless the court has decided to consider the application without a hearing, fix a date for any hearing or the period within which such hearing is to take place as soon as practicable.'

Directions can be given in writing, at a hearing and at any stage in the proceedings. There is therefore no single 'directions' stage in the proceedings and in a complex and long running case, directions may be give on more than one occasion and in more than one form. Directions may also be given at the request of a party or on the Court's own initiative. The Court's powers to make directions are furthermore in addition to its general case management powers under Rule 25 and described at **3.5** above. Where parties need to be heard on a directions hearing, the hearing may be conducted by telephone (see **3.22** above).

Preparing for the hearing

3.30   Where it is likely that a case will need to be dealt with at an attended hearing the Court will usually issue directions for the serving and exchange of evidence that the parties intend to rely on at the hearing. The applicant will also be directed to provide a paginated set of the orders and evidence that the judge may need to refer to and provide the other parties with a copy of the same set of documents. The parties may also be directed to exchange skeleton arguments.

Although the Rules and Practice Directions make no reference to skeleton arguments except in the context of an appeal (see **3.46** and PD20A), these are often used in first instance hearings as a useful way of summarising the points of law and evidence a party will rely on and therefore shorten the time that the Court would otherwise need to hear these issues addressed at the hearing.

The result of such detailed directions is that attended hearings which are contentious require a great deal more preparation than may have been the case under the Mental Health Act 1983 regime. Cases are more litigious in the way they are conducted and while this provides for a more thorough exchange of legal arguments, there are significant cost implications which need to be borne in mind by anyone contemplating a contested application.

The hearing

Where held

3.31   As part of the directions process, the Court must decide whether a hearing is to take place, at what level and whether it should be in public.

There is no reference in the Rules to the place at which a hearing is to take place. Initially, it must be for the applicant or respondent to request a hearing in a particular place. Otherwise the Court will assume that the application will be heard in London. As the Court is required to give notice of a hearing, it will also specify where the hearing should take place. To some extent, the choice of judge or nature of the case may determine the location, so that an application that is to be heard before a High Court judge will be heard at the Royal Courts of Justice. A contested welfare case before a circuit or district judge may require a large courtroom for lawyers, witnesses and relatives and the case will be heard at the Central London County Court or Brent Magistrates Court. All applications are made to the central registry in London and around half of all attended hearings will also take place at Archway in London. However, some 40 district and circuit judges have also been nominated as judges of the Court of Protection under s 46 of the MCA 2005 and many of these will sit at one of the regional court centres (currently Preston, Manchester, Newcastle, Bristol, Cardiff and Birmingham) or at their own courts (see **2.12** above). As all applications will be processed centrally, it will be for the parties to request in writing that a hearing take place at a location other than London.

The Court must also give careful consideration to the level at which a case should be heard. Generally, property and affairs cases will be dealt with by a district judge, although many cases, including the more complex ones will be heard by the Senior Judge who has the status of a circuit judge. A contentious case such as one involving new points of law or several days of hearing with counsel for more than one party may be referred directly to a High Court judge (see for instance *Re P* [2009] All ER (D) 160 (Feb)).

A more routine application – whether for directions or even a substantive hearing which simply requires the parties to discuss and clarify a matter that is not contentious can also be dealt with by way of a telephone hearing. A telephone hearing is a particularly effective way of liaising with several parties in different locations without the effort and expense of their combined attendance at the Court.

Welfare cases involving appointment of welfare deputies, routine consent and contact issues will be dealt with by a circuit judges. However, the following serious cases are reserved to the President, Vice President and nominated High Court judges (see Practice Direction 9E):

- an application for a declaration as to the lawfulness of the non-therapeutic sterilisation of a person who lacks capacity to consent to such a procedure;

- an application for a declaration as to the lawfulness of the termination of a pregnancy of a person who lacks capacity to consent to such a procedure;

- an application for a declaration as to the lawfulness of a medical procedure to be performed on a person who lacks capacity to consent to it, where that procedure is for the purpose of making a donation to another;

- an application for a declaration as to the lawfulness of a medical procedure or treatment to be carried out on a person who lacks capacity to consent to it, where that procedure or treatment must be carried out using a degree of force to restrain P;

- an application for a declaration as to the lawfulness of experimental or innovative treatment for the benefit of a person who lacks capacity to consent to such treatment;

- an application for a declaration as to the lawfulness of medical research carried out on a person who lacks the capacity to consent to such procedures; and

- an application in which a party seeks to rely on any provision of or right arising under the Human Rights Act 1998 or who seeks a remedy available under that Act.

Privacy of hearing

3.32   The question of whether a hearing takes place in private or public is a controversial one. On the one hand, the custom is that justice is a public matter and the courts should be open to the public who can see that justice is being done. On the other hand, Court of Protection cases are often of a sensitive nature and concern the private affairs of someone who lacks capacity and therefore should be protected. Part 13 of the Court of Protection Rules deals with the issue of privacy of hearings and Rule 90 sets down a general rule that hearings are to be in private. The Rules also restrict the right to attend to the parties, P (whether or not he is a party), legal representatives and court officers. No other person or class of persons may attend without the Court making order authorising their attendance.

The Court may, however, order that a hearing be held in public. If a hearing is held in public and if any information about a hearing (whether private or public) is disclosed, the Court may also impose restrictions on the publication of the identity of any of the parties.

The way in which any hearing is conducted will depend on factors such as the court in which it is held, the attitudes of the parties and the complexity of the facts. However, cases may also vary markedly according to the judge before whom the case is held. Judges from a litigation background may well conduct hearings differently to judges from a civil background or who operated under the Mental Health Act 1983 jurisdiction. However, regardless of the manner in which a hearing is conducted, evidence can only be admitted in accordance with the Rules.

Disclosure

3.33   It is also for the Court to order whether information relating to the proceedings should be published. Publication about any proceedings held in private, without the prior consent of the Court, is otherwise a contempt of court (Rule 91(1) and see **3.54** below).

Notwithstanding the general rule, s 12(2) of the Administration of Justice Act 1960 sets out an exception so that 'the publication of the text or a summary of the whole or part of an order made by a court sitting in private shall not of itself be contempt of court except where the court (having power to do so) expressly prohibits the publication.' As this appears to contradict Rule 91(1) of the Court of Protection Rules, it is advisable for a party who may wish to refer to proceedings to request disclosure in advance. It must also be appropriate, if the Court of Protection is to serve its purpose as a court of record, to consent to publication of information about judgments (without identifying the parties) for the education and guidance of lawyers and others who need to increase their understanding of the Court's procedures and deliberations.

Evidence

3.34   The Court of Protection Rules give the Court a great deal of discretion as to how evidence is to be used in proceedings. Thus the Court may give directions as to the issues on which it requires evidence (for instance the Court may direct a specialist report on P's capacity), the nature of the evidence it requires and the way in which evidence is to be placed before the Court. The Court may also exclude evidence that would otherwise be admissible.

The general rule, contained in Rule 96, is that any evidence which is to be proved by the evidence of a witness, must be proved:

- at a final hearing, by oral evidence; or

- at any other hearing or if there is no hearing, in writing; but

- subject to any order or direction of the Court.

Written evidence

3.35   Where written evidence is submitted, it cannot be relied upon unless it has been filed in accordance with the Rules or a Practice Direction – or the Court gives permission. A written statement must therefore be verified by a statement of truth confirming that the person who makes the statement believes the facts in the document are true. If a document or statement is not verified by a statement of truth, it cannot be relied on as evidence unless the Court directs.

If a person makes a false statement in a verified document, he is in contempt of court.

Any written evidence should be submitted in accordance with the form set out in the Practice Direction. This can either be in one of the prescribed forms (COP1A or COP1B or COP24). Where it is a separate statement in writing or a document exhibited to a witness statement, it must:

• unless the nature of the document renders it impracticable, be on A4 paper of durable quality having a margin not less than 3.5 centimetres wide;

• be fully legible and should normally be typed;

• where possible be bound securely in a manner which would not hamper filing or otherwise each page should be endorsed with the case number;

• have the pages numbered consecutively;

• be divided into numbered paragraphs;

• have all numbers, including dates, expressed as figures; and

• give in the margin the reference of every document mentioned that has already been filed.

Witness statements

3.36   A witness statement is simply a written account of the evidence that a person would be allowed to give orally in relation to an issue of fact, and must contain a statement of truth. The aim of a witness statement is to address issues of fact and belief. However, it is difficult to avoid justifying a particular measure or point of view. However, it is often more appropriate to leave argument over matters of law or procedure to skeleton arguments or the hearing.

Once a witness statement has been filed, it is for the Court to give directions as to service on other parties. However if the matter is urgent there is no reason why parties should not serve witness statements on each other before being required to do so by the Court.

Where the same witness goes on to give oral evidence at a hearing, the witness statement stands as his evidence in chief – unless the Court directs otherwise. The Court may also allow the witness to give further oral evidence to amplify his statement or give evidence on new matters that have arisen since the statement was served on the parties.

Witness summaries

3.37   A party required to file a witness statement for use at a final hearing, but unable to obtain one, may apply, without notice, to be permitted to file a witness summary instead (Rule 101). The Rules define a witness summary as a summary of:

(a)   the evidence, if known, which would otherwise be included in a witness statement; or

(b)   if the evidence is not known, the matters about which the party filing the witness summary proposes to question the witness.

A witness summary is therefore intended for cases where a party wishes to question an expert witness at a hearing and either the witness is unable or unwilling to file a witness statement or the evidence can better be provided at a hearing. The aim of the Rules is to ensure that so far as possible the Court and the parties have advance notice of the evidence or at least the questions the evidence will be used to address.

Summoning witnesses

3.38   Under Rule 106, the Court may allow or direct a witness summons being issued by a party. The witness named in the summons may be required to attend before the Court to give oral evidence or produce any document to the Court. Rule 106 must therefore be used if a party requires disclosure of evidence or documents held by a person who is not a party. For instance a party to an application may require sight of medical records held by a hospital, reports held by a local authority social services department or a will held by a solicitor.

An application for a witness summons must be made as an application within the proceedings (see **3.22** above) by filing an application notice, detailing:

(a)   the name and address of the applicant and of his solicitor, if any;

(b)   the name, address and occupation of the proposed witness;

(c)   particulars of any document which the proposed witness is to be required to produce; and

(d)   the grounds on which the application is made.

Once issued, a witness summons is binding if it is served at least seven days before the date on which the witness is required to attend before the Court. The witness must also be informed of his right to his expenses and any other compensation for loss of time specified in the Practice Direction.

The Court may also direct that a summons is binding even though it is served less than seven days before the hearing.

Depositions

3.39   It may not always be necessary or appropriate for a party or other witness to be compelled to attend and give evidence in person at a hearing. The witness or party may be too ill to attend a hearing in person or may be resident abroad and cannot reasonably be expected to attend a hearing in person.

Rules 108–116, which are modelled on similar provisions in the CPR, therefore provide for evidence being taken in the form of an oral examination outside of a hearing which will serve in the same way as if it had been given at the hearing. Such evidence is defined as a deposition. The Rules also provide for a deposition to be taken outside of the jurisdiction.

A party requiring a deposition from a person must obtain an order from the Court. An application is made as an application within proceedings, explaining why the order is required and providing details of the intended deponent, when and where the deposition should be taken and who should examine the deponent. It will be for the Court to direct whether the examination is conducted before a circuit judge, district judge, examiner of the Court or other person appointed by the Court. Practice Direction 14B implies that the party obtaining an order for examination must subsequently apply for an examiner to be allocated. However, this would require two applications for the use of this facility and, in most cases, it should be possible for the order to be made covering both taking of evidence by examination as well as choosing an examiner.

As well as having the power to issue an order for the examination of the deponent, the Court may also:

- state the time, date and place of examination;

- give directions for the conduct of the examination;

- require the production of any document which the Court considers is necessary for the examination; and

- direct that the party obtaining the order file a witness statement or summary dealing with the evidence to be addressed in the examination.

The examination may take place before a judge, an examiner appointed by the Lord Chancellor or such other person as the Court directs. A person appointed for the purposes of CPR r 38.15 can also act as an examiner. Once the examiner has been allocated, the party requiring the deposition must provide the examiner with copies of all documents in the proceedings necessary to inform the examiner of the issues.

When the examination takes place, then unless the Court directs otherwise, it must be conducted in the same way as if the witness were giving evidence at the final hearing itself. The person giving the evidence – the deponent – will have his evidence recorded in full. A video or audio recording can be taken, but the examination must be transcribed so as to provide an exact written record. That will then be treated as a deposition. If the witness fails to attend the examination, refuses to be sworn or refuses to answer any lawful question, then the examiner must complete a certificate of the refusal or failure to answer questions. A standard form COP23 is provided for this purpose. If the deponent objects to answering a question or where objection is taken to a question then the examiner must also record the objection and give his opinion as to its validity. Once such a certificate has been filed with the Court, the party requiring the deposition may apply without notice to the Court for an order requiring the witness to attend, or to produce any document.

Once the deposition has been completed, the examiner must send copies to the party obtaining the order and to the Court, which may then give directions as to service on other parties. However, if the person who obtained the order for examination wishes to use the deposition in evidence, he must notify the Court and any other party of his intention at least 14 days before the date fixed for the hearing. Notice is given in Form COP31.

Evidence taken abroad

3.40   Where a witness is outside the jurisdiction, then the Court may issue a letter of request to a designated Court if the witness is in a Regulation State or to the judicial authorities if the witness is outside of a Regulation State. A person requiring an order for a deposition to be taken outside of the jurisdiction should file an application notice in COP 9 in accordance with Part 10, together with the documentation prescribed. Rules 115 and 116 provide for a slightly different procedure depending on whether or not the deposition is to take place in a Regulation State:

Rule	*Rule 115*	*Rule 116*
Territory State	*Regulation State*	*Not a Regulation*
	'Regulation State' has the same meaning as 'Member State' in the Taking of Evidence Regulation, that is all Member States of the European Union except Denmark (Council Regulation (EC) No. 1206/2001 of 28 May 2001).	
Documentation	• Draft form of request (using Form A annexed to the Taking of Evidence Regulations) OR Draft Form I if the Court is taking evidence directly.* • A translation unless English is one of the official languages of the country where the examination is to take place. • An undertaking to be responsible for any costs sought by the court taking the evidence.	• Draft letter of request. • Statement of the issues relevant to the proceedings. • A list of questions or the subject matter of questions to be put to the examinee. • A translation unless English is

Rule	Rule 115	Rule 116
Territory State	*Regulation State*	*Not a Regulation*
Documentation – *contd*		one of the official languages of the country where the examination is to take place. • An undertaking to be responsible for any government expenses.
Procedure	• The requested court executes the request in accordance with its own laws. For instance, a request by a foreign court for evidence to be taken in England & Wales is dealt with by the Treasury Solicitor.	• The examination may take place on oath or affirmation in accordance with any procedure permitted in the country in which the examination is to take place. • If the government of that country permits a person to be appointed to conduct the examination, such a 'special examiner' may be the British Consul or Consul-General.
Return of evidence	• Dealt with in the same way as evidence taken by deposition in England & Wales	• Dealt with in the same way as evidence taken by deposition in England & Wales

* Form A is annexed to Practice Direction 14B; Form I (as well as Form A) are annexed to CPR Part 34

Documents

3.41   Difficulties often arise where one party has information which is not available to the other, for instance a testamentary document or medical evidence. Therefore where a party has access to information which is not reasonably available to the other party, the Court may direct that party to prepare and file a document recording the information.

There is however no express provision in the Rules to obtain documentation from a person who is not a party to the proceedings. It is not clear therefore what a party can do if for instance he needs sight of a testamentary document held by a firm of solicitors or financial data held by a bank. The firm of solicitors or bank is not a party to the proceedings. The only way to require such information to be made available is to seek a witness summons requiring the relevant documents to be produced to the Court (Rule 106). An application for such a summons can be made in COP1 in the body of the application or subsequently as an application within the proceedings (COP9) (see **3.36** above).

Other evidence

3.42   Although Part 14 of the Rules (which deals with evidence) is detailed as to how evidence should be submitted, there are further references to the submission of evidence in other parts of the Rules:

- Within its general case management powers, the Court may hold a hearing and receive evidence by telephone or any other method of direct oral communication.

- The Court may allow a witness to give evidence through a video link or by other means.

- A person may be allowed to make a deposition outside of England & Wales. However, there is nothing in the Rules to prevent a witness statement being made by a person outside of England & Wales

- Evidence must be given by affidavit if required by the Court or by the Rules. The only part of the Rules which formally calls for an affidavit in place of a witness statement is in an application for committal.

- The Court may call for a report under s 49 of the MCA 2005 from the Public Guardian, a Court of Protection Visitor, local authority or NHS body.

- Expert evidence may be filed. However, unless filed with the application and addressing specifically the issue of P's best interests and capacity, expert evidence cannot be filed except with the Court's permission, on the basis that such evidence should be for the benefit of the Court and all the parties and not just one party to the proceedings. Expert evidence is therefore addressed to the Court and where possible experts should be jointly instructed by more than one party.

Routine and subsequent applications

3.43   Rule 71 provides for a Practice Direction to govern applications being made in different ways in specified circumstances. It would be clearly inappropriate for a deputy wanting authority for a small gift or authority to buy or sell a property to go through a formal application process each and every time an order is required. Practice Direction 9D does therefore envisage routine applications by existing deputies (as well as attorneys) being able to use a simplified procedure. This will still require an application form (COP1) to be submitted (with an application fee of £400), but without giving notice to P or any other person unless specifically directed to do so by the Court.

PD 9D provides the following list of cases where the 'short procedure' would be appropriate:

(a)   applications for regular payments from P's assets to the deputy in respect of remuneration;

(b)   applications seeking minor variations only as to the expenses that can be paid from P's estate;

(c)   applications to change an accounting period;

(d)   applications to set or change the time by which an annual account may be submitted;

(e)   applications in relation to the sale of property owned by P, where the sale is non-contentious;

(f)   applications for authority to disclose information as to P's assets, state of health or other circumstances;

(g)   applications to make a gift or loan from P's assets, provided that the sum in question is not disproportionately large when compared to the size of P's estate as a whole;

(h)   applications to sell or otherwise deal with P's investments, provided that the sum in question is not disproportionately large when compared to the size of P's estate as a whole;

(i)   applications for the receipt or discharge of a sum due to or by P;

(j)   applications for authority to apply for a grant of probate or representation, where P would be the person entitled to the grant but for his lack of capacity;

(k)   applications relating to the lease or grant of a tenancy in relation to property owned by P;

(l)   applications for release of funds to repair or improve P's property;

(m)   applications to sell P's furniture or effects;

(n)   applications for release of capital to meet expenses required for the care of P;

(o)   applications to arrange an overdraft or bank loan on P's behalf;

(p)   applications to open a bank account on behalf of P or for the purpose of the deputyship at a private bank, a bank that is not located in England

and Wales, or at a bank which has unusual conditions attached to the operation of the account; and

(q)   applications for the variation of an order for security made pursuant to Rule 200.

This process is not to be confused with the transitory provisions set out in Practice Direction 22B operating for the benefit of receivers appointed before 1 October 2007 who could apply using COP9 without payment of a fee for orders such as those listed above. These provisions operated only until 30 June 2008. After that date, an application must be made using the Part 9 procedure. However, the policy of the Court and Public Guardian is to ensure that deputies do not need to come back to the Court and make formal applications unless there is no other choice. In most cases, a new order appointing a deputy will be very widely drawn so that the deputy has in effect the powers of an attorney and acts with the same degree of autonomy. Older, more restrictive, orders appointing receivers have in most cases been 'upgraded' where necessary. Thus in most cases, even quite significant decisions such as the buying or selling of property will fall within the scope of the deputy's autonomy. While this may make for less regulation, effort or expense on the part of the Public Guardian, it will make the deputy's task more difficult and potentially more onerous if he has to make such major decisions alone. The effect in practice is that the principal burden of regulation shifts from the statutory bodies (who are responsible for safeguarding the property and affairs of persons without capacity) to the deputy (and his insurers). The practical difficulties facing a deputy are considered in more detail in Chapter 7.

Reconsideration and appeal

Reconsideration of a decision made without a hearing – Rule 89

3.44   Any party, person affected by an order or P who is aggrieved by an order of the Court, which was made without an attended hearing or without notice being given to any person affected by it, may apply to the Court for reconsideration of the order made. The application must be made within 21 days of the order being served, using the Part 10 procedure (Rule 89(3)). The person applying for the order to be reconsidered may request that the matter be dealt with at a hearing, although the Court may reconsider the order without a hearing. However, if the Court directs that a hearing be held, the Court must fix a date for the matter to be heard and notify the relevant parties of that date. On reconsidering an order, the Court may affirm, set aside or vary its earlier order.

Rule 89 allows only one attempt at a reconsideration. If a person remains aggrieved by the Court's decision, he must use the appeal process described below. It is a simple and often effective way of dealing with routine orders made without a hearing, such as the appointment of a deputy where a provision of the order is inappropriate.

Permission for an appeal

3.45   The procedure for appealing against an order of the Court is set out in Part 20 of the Rules and the accompanying Practice Direction.

A person aggrieved by an order made by the Court at an attended hearing or without an attended hearing but on an application for a reconsideration of a decision under Rule 89 may appeal that decision of the Court. The appellant must file an appellant's notice within 21 days of the decision being appealed or within such period directed or specified by the judge making the order in question. Rule 175(2)(b) confers on the Court discretion to allow a period other than 21 days for use in cases where a decision is made but the written judgment setting out the reasons for the decision is deferred to a later date.

Permission is required in every case except for when the appeal relates to an order for committal to prison. The appellant may seek permission from the 'first instance judge' who is the judge of the Court whose decision he is appealing against or from the appeal judge. In most cases, the first instance judge will be expected to allow leave to appeal as a matter of course where the case has been contested and issues of fact and interpretation have been argued before the Court. Where permission has not been granted, the appellant's notice will include an application for permission, which can be requested from the appeal judge. The Court's discretion to allow an appeal does nevertheless need to be considered objectively and although the interests of justice require that an aggrieved party has a right to appeal, Rule 173 requires the Court to deter vexatious or compulsive litigants. Thus permission shall be granted only where:

(a)   the court considers that the appeal would have a real prospect of success; or

(b)   there is some other compelling reason why the appeal should be heard.

If permission is refused by a district judge, then permission may be requested from a judge of the level of circuit judge or above. If permission is refused by a circuit judge, then permission may only be requested from the President, Vice-President or other nominated High Court judge.

An appeal against a decision of the first instance judge will be heard by a judge of the next level. Thus an appeal against a decision of a district judge will be heard by a circuit judge and an appeal against a decision of a circuit judge will be heard by the President, Vice-President or other nominated High Court judge. An appeal against a decision of a High Court judge lies to the Court of Appeal.

An appellant must also be aware of the limitations to the evidence that he can use to support his appeal (see **3.46** below).

Procedure for appeal

3.46   The appellant must file, within 21 days of the order given by the first instance judge or such other period permitted by the first instance judge under Rule 175(2), an appellant's notice in Form COP36. A fee of £400 is also payable.

This procedure is only for use on an appeal in the Court of Protection; where the appeal is to the Court of Appeal, whether from a High Court judge acting as a first instance judge or by way of a second appeal, the Court of Appeal procedure must be followed.

Practice Direction 20A lays down in more detail the procedure to be followed by the parties to an appeal. Rule 174 requires the parties to the appeal to comply with this.

In addition to the appellant's notice filed with the Court, the appellant must also file with the Court:

(a)   one additional copy of the appellant's notice for the Court;

(b)   one copy of his skeleton argument;

(c)   a sealed copy of the order being appealed;

(d)   a copy of any order giving or refusing permission to appeal, together with a copy of the judge's reasons for allowing or refusing permission to appeal;

(e)   any witness statements or affidavits in support of any application included in the appellant's notice;

(f)   the application form and any application notice or response (where relevant to the subject of the appeal);

(g)   any other documents which the appellant reasonably considers necessary to enable the Court to reach its decision on the hearing of the application or appeal;

(h)   a suitable record of the judgment of the first instance judge; and

(i)   such other documents as the Court may direct.

The Practice Direction has two further expectations of the appellant:

•   the appellant should consider what other information the Court will need. This may include a list of persons who feature in the case or glossaries of technical terms. A chronology of relevant events will be necessary in most appeals (Paragraph 14); and

•   a skeleton argument should be submitted using Form COP37. If the form is insufficient, a more detailed document can be submitted as an attachment to Form COP37. This helps concentrate minds on the relevant issues, requiring the appellant to summarise the arguments he will rely on at the hearing.

A copy of the appellant's notice and the other documents filed with the Court must be served on any other party who is the respondent to the appeal. The appellant must then file, within seven days of service, a certificate of service in respect of each respondent served.

A respondent to the appeal is defined by Rule 170(d) as:

'(i)   a person other than the appellant who was a party to the proceedings before the first instance judge and who is affected by the appeal; or

> (ii)   a person who is permitted or directed by the first instance judge or the
> appeal judge to be a party to the appeal.'

The appellant may also need to request some other remedy. For instance, an injunction may be required to prevent P being moved or treated pending the outcome of the appeal. Such a request can be dealt with in the appellant's notice (at paragraph 6.3) or in a separate application using the Part 10 procedure (in Form COP9). A separate application may be appropriate where for instance a care home is involved but is not a party to the appeal. In any event, the application notice should be filed with the appellant's notice.

Where the appellant is unable to file all of the documents required with his appellant's notice, he must indicate which documents have not yet been filed and the reasons why they are not currently available. The Practice Direction requires the appellant to provide a reasonable estimate of when the missing document or documents can be filed and then file and serve them as soon as reasonably practicable. However, where the skeleton argument is not served with the appellant's notice, this must be filed and served on all the respondents within 21 days.

Extension of time

3.47   The time limit for an appeal may prove demanding, especially in view of the information that needs to be submitted with the appellant's notice. Where the time for filing an appellant's notice has expired, the appellant must include in the appellant's notice an application for an extension of time (paragraph 6.2 of Form COP35). This should state clearly the reason(s) for the delay and the steps taken prior to the application being made.

Respondent's notice

3.48   A respondent who himself needs permission to appeal or wishes to ask the appeal judge to uphold the order of the first instance judge for reasons different from or additional to those given by the first instance judge must file a respondent's notice using Form COP36. The respondent's notice must be filed within such period as the first instance judge directs or where no such direction is given, within 21 days of the earliest of the following events:

- the date on which the respondent is served with the appellant's notice where:

  (i)   permission to appeal was given by the first instance judge; or

  (ii)   permission to appeal is not required;

- the date on which the respondent is served with notification that the appeal judge has given the appellant permission to appeal; or

- the date on which the respondent is served with the notification that the application for permission to appeal and the appeal itself are to be heard together.

The respondent's notice serves a similar purpose and is in a similar form to the appellant's notice. The respondent must therefore address the same issues and provide documentation and evidence in the same form. He must therefore file with his respondent's notice:

(a)   one additional copy of the respondent's notice for the Court;

(b)   one copy of his skeleton argument;

(c)   a sealed copy of the order being appealed;

(d)   a copy of any order giving or refusing permission to appeal, together with a copy of the judge's reasons for allowing or refusing permission to appeal;

(e)   any witness statements or affidavits in support of any application included in the appellant's notice;

(f)   any other documents which the appellant reasonably considers necessary to enable the Court to reach its decision on the hearing of the application or appeal; and

(g)   such other documents as the Court may direct.

The Court will issue a respondent's notice and, unless it orders otherwise, the respondent must serve the respondent's notice on the appellant, any other respondent and on such other parties as the Court may direct, as soon as practicable and in any event within 21 days of the date on which it was issued. The respondent must further file a certificate of service within seven days beginning with the date on which the copy of the respondent's notice was served.

Evidence at hearing

3.49   The Rules are prescriptive as to the use of evidence at an appeal. Clearly an appeal is not to be used as a vehicle for submitting new evidence or argument which should have been made available at the first instance decision. However, if new evidence has subsequently come to light or the interests of justice require its disclosure, then the appeal judge may allow its disclosure. Rule 179(2) lays down a presumption that unless the appeal judge orders otherwise, he will not receive oral evidence or evidence that was not before the first instance judge. Rule 173(2) also allows the Court, when giving permission for an appeal, to consider whether the order should:

(a)   limit the issues to be heard; and

(b)   be made subject to conditions.

Appeal hearing

3.50   It is then for the Court to issue any relevant directions and notify all the parties of the hearing date.

At the hearing, the appeal judge may limit the appeal to a review of the first instance judge unless the appeal judge considers that in the circumstances it would be in the interests of justice to hold a re-hearing.

In hearing the appeal, the appeal judge will in any event review the decision of the first instance judge and may affirm, set aside or vary any order (or any part of such order) made by the first instance judge. The appeal judge may also refer any claim or issue back to the first instance judge, order a new hearing or make a costs order (Rule 178).

Second appeal

3.51   A further appeal against a decision of the appeal judge of the Court of Protection can only be made to the Court of Appeal (Rule 182). However, such an appeal can only be made with the permission of the Court of Appeal and the procedures of the Court of Appeal will apply to such an appeal.

Decisions of the Public Guardian

3.52   The Public Guardian has limited powers to enable him to discharge his functions under s 58 of the MCA 2005. These are set out in the Lasting Power of Attorney, Enduring Power of Attorney and Public Guardian Regulations 2007 and the Public Guardian (Fees, etc) Regulations 2007 and are dealt with in more detail in Chapter 1. For example, the Public Guardian will determine the level of supervision required from a deputy, which the deputy wishes to have reviewed. Rule 42 of the Lasting Power of Attorney, Enduring Power of Attorney and Public Guardian Regulations 2007 allows a deputy to require the Public Guardian to reconsider any decision he has made in relation to the deputy.

The right to a review is exercised by the deputy giving notice within 14 days of notice of the decision being given to the deputy. There is no formal process for a review, but the deputy must, in giving notice of the review, state the grounds on which reconsideration is required, and provide any relevant information or documents. The Public Guardian must in response provide the deputy with written notice of his decision and if the original decision is upheld, a statement of his reasons.

There is no formal mechanism for a further appeal against a decision of the Public Guardian. Except where the MCA 2005 and its regulations provide for a decision to be referred to the Court of Protection, the only redress against a decision of the Public Guardian is by way of judicial review.

Enforcement

Powers of enforcement

3.53   Section 47(1) of the MCA 2005 confers on the Court of Protection 'in connection with its jurisdiction the same powers, rights, privileges and authority as the High Court'. Orders made by the Court of Protection can therefore be made in the same way and with the same powers of enforcement as orders of the High Court. This is confirmed by Rule 184 of the Court of Protection Rules which incorporates the following relevant provisions of the CPR:

'The following provisions apply, as far as they are relevant and with such modifications as may be necessary, to the enforcement of orders made in proceedings under these Rules—

(a)   Parts 70 (General Rules about Enforcement of Judgments and Orders), 71 (Orders to Obtain Information from Judgment Debtors), 72 (Third Party Debt Orders) and 73 (Charging Orders, Stop Orders and Stop Notices) of the Civil Procedure Rules 1998; and

(b)   Orders 45 (Enforcement of Judgments and Orders: General), 46 (Writs of Execution: General) and 47 (Writs of Fieri Facias) of the Rules of the Supreme Court.'

Contempt

3.54   The principle sanction against a person who ignores or disobeys an order of the Court is a committal for contempt of court.

Court of Protection proceedings are as a rule, conducted in private, although the Court can permit the hearing to be held in public or information about a hearing to be disclosed (see Part 13 of the Court of Protection Rules and **3.33** above). It is a contempt of court to publish information about proceedings heard by the Court of Protection in private, without the Court's permission. It is also a contempt of court to make, or cause to make, a false statement in a document verified by a statement of truth. If a person makes or causes to make a false statement without an honest belief in its truth, then proceedings may be brought against him for contempt (Rule 14(1)). Such proceedings can only be brought by the Attorney General or with the permission of the court (Rule 14(2)).

Procedure

3.55   The Court of Protection may, under Rule 194, make an order of enforcement of its own motion where it considers this necessary. A party who wishes to apply for an order for enforcement may do so, using the Part 10 procedure for applications within proceedings (Rule 183(2)). However, the party seeking enforcement must also observe the requirements of Part 21.

An application for committal for contempt must be made in Form COP9 and in accordance with Part 21 of the Court of Protection Rules. The applicant must file the original and one copy of the application notice and the original and one copy of the evidence in support. The evidence in support of the application notice must be contained in an affidavit, setting out the factors listed in Practice Direction 21A:

'(a)   the name and description of the person making the application;

(b)   the name, address and description of the person sought to be committed;

(c)   the grounds on which committal is sought;

(d)   a description of each alleged act of contempt, identifying:

   (i)   each act separately and numerically, and

   (ii)   if known, the date of each act; and

(e)   any additional information required by paragraphs 5 and 6.

[Paragraph 5] Where the allegation of contempt relates to prior proceedings before the court, the affidavit must also state:

(a)   the case number of those prior proceedings;

(b)   the date of the proceedings; and

(c)   the name of P.

[Paragraph 6]   The affidavit must also set out in full any order, judgment or undertaking which it is alleged has been disobeyed or broken by the person sought to be committed. This will apply where the allegation of contempt is made on the grounds that:

(a)   a person is required by a judgment or order to do an act, and has refused or neglected to do it within the time fixed by the judgment or order or any subsequent order;

(b)   a person has disobeyed a judgment or order requiring him to abstain from doing an act; or

(c)   a person has breached the terms of an undertaking which he gave to the court.'

On filing the application notice, the applicant must obtain from the Court a date for the hearing of the committal application. This is provided in Form COP29 (notice of hearing for committal order). Copies of Form COP29, the application notice and affidavit must then be served personally on the person whose committal is sought. Although the Court may dispense with service, a committal order is a serious matter and is usually dealt with at separate hearing for a committal hearing. Practice Direction 21A therefore specifies that the Court may 'at any time give case management directions (including directions for the service of evidence by the person sought to be committed and evidence in reply by the applicant) or may hold a directions hearing'. The Court may, if the committal application is ready to be heard, proceed forthwith to hear it. The Court may therefore give a direction or suspended order to the effect that a person shall comply with a direction or order, failing which he must attend a hearing for committal.

Before the Court can commit a person for failure to comply with an order or judgment, a copy of the order with a penal notice attached to it must be served personally on that person. The penal notice cannot be attached to an order without the Court's direction (Rule 192(2)). The issue of an order in these terms is therefore within the control of the Court. Where a penal notice is attached to an order, it must be shown prominently and be in the following terms:

> 'You must obey this order. If you do not, you may be sent to prison for contempt of court.'

When a committal hearing does take place, the general rule is that the hearing should be in public. This reverses the general rule that Court of Protection proceedings are held in private. Rule 188(2) specifies that the hearing is to be in public unless the Court directs otherwise. At the hearing, no grounds may be relied on except those set out in the application notice unless the Court directs otherwise. The person sought to be committed has a right to give oral evidence at the hearing (in accordance with Rule 187), but he may be cross-examined on that evidence. If the Court decides to hold the hearing in private and determines that a person has committed a contempt, then it must state publicly, the name of the person, the nature of the contempt and any order imposed.

Ending proceedings

Court has no jurisdiction where P has capacity or has died

3.56   Practice Direction 23B deals with the termination of proceedings. It begins by stating the self-explanatory proposition that an order of the Court of Protection will continue until it is discharged or, if made for a specified period, will cease to have effect when that period comes to an end. An order of the Court of Protection will come to an end on the death of P.

The Court of Protection furthermore has no jurisdiction in those matters in respect of which P has capacity. Therefore where P ceases to lack capacity in respect of a matter which is subject to an order of the Court, or if P dies, the order ceases to have any effect. However, steps may need to be taken to finalise the court's involvement in P's affairs.

Application to end proceedings

3.57   Where P ceases to lack capacity in relation to the matter or matters to which the proceedings relate, an application may be made by any of the following to end the proceedings and discharge any orders made in respect of P (Practice Direction 23B para 3):

(a)   P;

(b)   his litigation friend; or

(c)   any other person who is a party to the proceedings.

An application is made by filing Form COP9 in accordance with the Part 10 procedure, together with any evidence in support of the application. The applicant must serve a copy of the application notice on all other parties to the proceedings as soon as practicable and in any event within 21 days of the date on which the application notice was issued. The application must in particular be supported by evidence that P no longer lacks capacity to make decisions in relation to the matter or matters to which the proceedings relate. It must also be made clear whether P ceases to lack capacity only in relation to the proceedings (and continues to lack capacity in relation to other matters).

As an application under the Part 10 procedure is not considered to be a new application, no fee is payable.

Applications where proceedings have concluded

3.58   Where P ceases to lack capacity after proceedings have concluded, an application may be made to the Court to discharge any orders made (including an order appointing a deputy or an order in relation to a security bond) by filing Form COP9 in accordance with the Part 10 procedure, together with any evidence in support of the application. The application should set out details of the order or orders the applicant seeks to have discharged, and must be supported by evidence that P no longer lacks capacity to make decisions in relation to the matter or matters to which the proceedings relate.

If the Court Funds Office is holding funds or assets on behalf of P, it will require an order of the Court to the effect that P no longer lacks capacity to make decisions with regard to the use and disposition of those funds or assets before any funds or assets can be transferred to him (Rule 202).

Procedure to be followed when P dies

3.59   Although the Court has no jurisdiction following the death of P, the Court will still need to issue final directions to discharge a deputy and any orders made, including any security bond in place. An application for final directions following P's death should be made by filing Form COP9 in accordance with the Part 10 procedure. Practice Direction 23B directs that the Part 10 procedure be used even though there are no current proceedings. An application should attach the original or a certified copy of P's death certificate. Where there are funds in Court, then it will be for the personal representatives of the deceased to liaise directly with the Court Funds Office to arrange for such funds to be released.

A security bond taken out by the deputy will remain in force until the end of the period of seven years commencing with the date of P's death, or until it is discharged by the court. The Public Guardian may also require a deputy to submit a final report on P's death. Before it will discharge a security bond, the Court must be satisfied that the Public Guardian either:

(a)   does not require a final report; or

(b)   is satisfied with the final report provided by the deputy.

Personal representatives

3.60   According to the Practice Direction, where there are solicitor's costs outstanding which would be due from P's estate, the personal representative may agree any of these costs without an order from the Court. The Practice Direction is silent on the subject of whether a solicitor who is also the personal representative can agree such costs. However, where these costs cannot be agreed, the personal representative or the solicitor may apply to the Court for a direction that the costs be assessed. Application should be made in Form COP9 in accordance with the Part 10 procedure.

Enduring powers of attorney

Position after 1 October 2007

3.61   Although the Enduring Powers of Attorney Act 1985 has been repealed by the MCA 2005 and no new EPAs can be created, EPAs created before 1 October 2007 remain valid under Sch 4 of the MCA 2005.

EPAs are dealt with in more detail in Chapter 15, but the procedure for registration is summarised in this chapter in the context of Court proceedings generally.

Registration

3.62   Although an EPA may have been created under the Enduring Powers of Attorney Act 1985 prior to 1 October 2007, it ceases to have any validity if the donor is mentally incapable. The attorney must, if he has reason to believe that the donor is becoming or has become mentally incapable of managing his property and affairs, as soon as practicable make an application to register the EPA with the Public Guardian.

The registration process is relatively straightforward if carried out correctly. The attorney or attorneys applying to register the EPA must notify the donor personally and also give notice to at least three relatives or all the members of the prescribed class of relatives (MCA 2005, Sch 4 Part 3 and the Lasting Power of Attorney, Enduring Power of Attorney and Public Guardian Regulations 2007, Part 3).

Any person notified of an intention to register the EPA must be notified in Form EP1G. The relevant rules and application form refer to all notices being 'given' and although there is no reference to any mode of service in the Act, Part 6 of the Rules provides for the service of documents generally. Thus documents may be served by personal delivery or by sending to a person's address by first class post. However, in respect of notice given to the donor, the donor must be notified personally and the attorney must also provide or arrange for the provision of an explanation to the donor of the notice and its effect and why the notice is being brought to his attention. The information provided to the donor must furthermore be provided in a way that is appropriate to the donor's circumstances.

The other persons who must be notified of the intention to register the power are clearly prescribed in para 6 of Sch 4 of the MCA 2005 (see Chapter 15). The notice requirements are therefore more prescriptive than the equivalent requirements for registration of a LPA where named individuals are notified or for notifying a person of an application to the Court of Protection. Although Practice Direction 9B follows a similar logical process in setting out classes of prescribed relatives who should be notified, it also requires the applicant to at least consider:

> 'where there is any other person not already mentioned whom the applicant reasonably considers has an interest in being notified about matters relating to P's best interests, that person should be notified. For example, P may have a close friend with an interest in being notified because he provides care to P on an informal basis.'

The attorney must therefore notify the persons prescribed by the MCA 2005 and cannot depart from this. It may also be inappropriate to follow the spirit of the Practice Direction and go beyond this class for reasons of confidentiality. However, the attorney at least has a discretion under Sch 4 para 6(2) to dispense with notice to a relative to be dispensed with in two situations:

(a)   if his name or address is not known to the attorney and cannot be reasonably ascertained by him; or

(b)   the attorney believes the relative to be under the age of 18 or mentally incapable.

The Court also has a discretion under Sch 4 para 7(2) to dispense with notice being given to the donor or any notifiable relative if:

(a)   it would be undesirable or impracticable for notice to be given, or

(b)   that no useful purpose is likely to be served thereby.

The attorney must make a formal application in Form COP1 using the Part 9 procedure before he can apply to register the EPA. The Court, out of regard for the donor's legal rights and as a matter of public policy, is very unlikely to agree to a donor not being notified of an application.

There is no time limit for serving the notices on the donor and the notifiable relatives. However, the Public Guardian cannot register the EPA under Sch 4 para 13(1) if he receives a valid notice of objection before the end of the period of five weeks beginning with the last date on which a notice was given to the donor and the notifiable relatives.

Application to register the EPA is made to the Public Guardian in Form EP2PG and must be accompanied by the original EPA and the prescribed fee.

Notice of objection

3.63   The Public Guardian deals with registration of enduring powers of attorney and is required to register if the application is made in the prescribed form, no deputy has been appointed and no valid objection is received from a person entitled to notice of the application. If these conditions are not satisfied, then only the Court can register the power. There is therefore a parallel jurisdiction involving the Court and a person applying to object to registration of an EPA must use the Court of Protection procedure and rules.

Notice of objection is given by filing Form COP8 with the Court; the objector must also give notice in writing to the Public Guardian, otherwise there is a danger that the Public Guardian will automatically register the EPA. Although Form COP8 requires the objector to confirm that he has 'notified' the Public Guardian of his application, it may be advisable to serve a copy of COP8 on the Public Guardian to comply with r 25 of the Lasting Power of Attorney, Enduring Power of Attorney and Public Guardian Regulations 2007.

The aim of Form COP8 is to place a significant burden on the objector to state the grounds on which he is objecting, substantiate the nature of his objection and make him aware that his objection may involve court proceedings and that he may be liable for the costs of those proceedings. The form therefore requires additional evidence to be filed with it and contains a statement of truth. The objector must file two copies with the Court which will issue the application form and return it to the objector to serve on the donor and each attorney. Although the form makes no reference to any time limits, Rule 68 requires the application form and a form for acknowledging service to be served on the donor and every attorney as soon as practicable and in any event within 21 days of issue of the application form.

Although Form COP8 anticipates further evidence being filed with it, it may not be possible in practice for a notified relative to assemble the evidence within the short timescale allowed by the registration period. The Public Guardian cannot however register the EPA so long as he receives a 'valid notice of objection' except in accordance with the Court's directions. The objector should therefore ensure that the Public Guardian has a copy of the notice of objection (in Form COP8) which will ensure that the objection is referred to the Court. The Court will then require the objector to file evidence in support of his objection within a defined period.

A person who is not a notified relative and who wishes to object to registration of the EPA must apply in Form COP1, paying an application fee and using the Part 9 procedure.

Further proceedings

3.64   Once an EPA has been registered, any party who wishes to apply to the Court to invoke its post-registration powers under Sch 4 para 16 must apply directly to the Court in Form COP1. Rule 68 applies the Part 9 procedure to an application concerning the exercise of the Court's powers under Sch 4 of the Act. If the applicant knows or has reasonable grounds for believing that the donor lacks capacity, then the procedure for notifying P under Part 7 applies to the donor.

Any person making such an application must proceed on the basis that the Court has no existing record of the case and cannot assume that P lacks capacity. Although the EPA may be registered on the grounds that the donor is mentally incapable and cannot manage his property and affairs, the Court will not have any medical evidence to confirm that the donor lacks capacity for the purposes of the Act. Each application must stand alone and be justified on its own merits and with its own evidence, including medical evidence. Only in very straightforward cases covered by Practice Direction 9D is this procedural burden relaxed.

Lasting powers of attorney

Registration

3.65   Lasting powers of attorney introduced by s 9 of the MCA 2005 are dealt with in more detail in Chapter 15, but the procedures relating to their creation and further operation are summarised here in the context of Court of Protection proceedings.

A LPA cannot be created unless an instrument is completed in a prescribed form and manner and that instrument is registered in accordance with Sch 1 of the Act. The registration process is a straightforward bureaucratic and procedural procedure which validates and brings into operation a LPA.

An application for registration can be made by the donor or by the donee and is made to the Public Guardian. Before making the application, the applicant must give notice in Form LPA001 to any persons named by the donor in the instrument for that purpose. There is therefore no requirement to notify any relatives (unless they have also been named) or other concerned friends such as those described in Practice Direction 9B.

Unlike the procedure for registration of an EPA where the attorney must ensure that the donor is given personal notice, the Public Guardian must give notice to the donor if, as will usually be the case, the application is made by the attorney. The Public Guardian is also responsible for giving notice to the attorneys where the application is made by the donor or to an attorney where the application is made by another attorney. The Public Guardian will give notice by post – after the application for registration has been made – using Form LPA003A (notice to an attorney) or LPA003B (notice to donor). Whether this is an improvement on the Enduring Powers of Attorney Act requirement that the donor be given the notice in person is another matter!

Application for registration is made in a prescribed form, Form LPA002, which must be accompanied by a fee and the original instrument. So long as the procedure is carried out correctly and there are no valid objections within the prescribed notice period, the LPA must be registered by the Public Guardian (Sch 1 para 5).

The prescribed notice period in which an objection can be made is six weeks, commencing on the date on which the Public Guardian gave notice (Rule 12 of the Lasting Power of Attorney, Enduring Power of Attorney and Public Guardian Regulations 2007). A person who wishes to object to registration on one of the technical grounds must do so within five weeks of the notice being given.

The Court may also dispense with notice if satisfied that no useful purpose would be served by giving the notice. However, as with the process for registration of EPAs, this can only be done on a formal application in Form COP1.

Objections to registration

3.66   Although the Public Guardian is the registration authority, the Public Guardian's powers are limited to dealing with any technical or procedural defects in the form or process; only the Court can deal with any objections on the substantive (prescribed) grounds. The grounds on which registration can be refused can therefore be broken down into technical grounds and substantive grounds which will be dealt with by the Public Guardian and the Court of Protection respectively. The grounds for objection are dealt with in detail in Chapter 15, but where the Court is involved there is inevitably some duplication of work on the part of the objector between the two separate bodies. An objection filed with the Court will not be referred to the Public Guardian; it is the responsibility of the objector to ensure that both bodies are duly notified.

A donor who wishes to object to registration of an instrument made by him as a LPA must notify the Public Guardian in Form LPA006.

A person who has been notified of an application and who wishes to object on one of the technical grounds must file an objection with the Public Guardian in Form LPA007.

A person who has been notified of an application and who wishes to object on one of the substantive grounds has a more arduous responsibility. He must, within the prescribed period of five weeks:

- file a formal application for objection in Form COP7; and

- notify the Public Guardian in Form LPA008.

The process for objecting to registration on the substantive grounds mirrors the process for objections to registration of Enduring Powers of Attorney outlined above. Thus Rule 67 mirrors Rule 68, and the objector is required to follow the Part 9 procedure. The application form (COP7) is issued by the Court and must be served on the donor and donees of the power as soon as practicable and in any event within 21 days of issue. Each application form must be accompanied by a form for acknowledging service and a certificate of service must be filed with the Court within seven days of service.

A person who is not a person named for notification and who wishes to object to registration of the LPA must apply in Form COP1, paying an application fee and using the Part 9 procedure.

Further proceedings

3.67   Once a LPA has been created on registration, any party who wishes to apply to the Court to invoke its powers under s 22 or 23 of the Act dealing with the validity and operation of LPAs must apply directly to the Court in Form COP1. An attorney or other party who wishes to apply for an order for a gift or authority for any decision not within the scope of the attorney's authority must use the same formal procedure.

If the applicant knows or has reasonable grounds for believing that the donor lacks capacity, then the procedure for notifying P under Part 7 applies to the donor. Any person making such an application must proceed on the basis that the Court has no existing record of the case and cannot assume that P lacks capacity. Clearly the fact that the LPA is operational does not in any way indicate that the donor lacks capacity. Each application must stand alone and be justified on its own merits and with its own evidence, including medical evidence. Only in very straightforward cases covered by Practice Direction 9D can this procedural burden be relaxed.

Chapter 4

The deputy

When is a deputy required?

4.1 The powers of the Court of Protection under the Mental Capacity Act 2005 (MCA 2005) have been considered in more detail in Chapter 3. It has been noted already that where a person lacks capacity to make a decision or a range of decisions the Court may:

- intervene directly to make a decision on behalf of the person concerned;

- relieve a person dealing with the person concerned from liability by confirming the lawfulness of the third party's decision; or

- appoint a deputy to make decisions on behalf of the person concerned.

It is one of the core principles of the MCA 2005 that where a person lacks capacity, a decision made on his behalf should be the least restrictive possible (s 1(6)). The Act adopts a policy of favouring minimum intervention where possible. Most welfare decisions can be dealt with under s 5 of the Act (acts in connection with care or treatment). If the Court is to consider the appointment of a deputy, then it is bound to consider under s 16(4)(a) of the Act that 'a decision by the court is to be preferred to the appointment of a deputy to make a decision'. Thus if a requirement can be shown and the person's affairs can be dealt with in this way, a single order will be made. This will often be appropriate in welfare cases where a doctor requires a single order authorising him to carry out or withhold a particular course of treatment. However, there are cases where day-to-day decisions need to be made over an extended period and it is impractical for the Court to be involved in each such decision. The Court may therefore delegate authority to an individual person to act as deputy to make welfare decisions for the person concerned. This should, however, be a last resort and a person applying for the appointment of a welfare deputy must provide clear evidence of the need for the appointment and how it will be in the best interests of the person concerned.

Where property and affairs are concerned, and a person lacks capacity to make decisions, a single order may still be appropriate if only a small sum of money is involved. If the estate is a small one and income derives from benefits which can be paid to a named person as an appointee directly by the DWP, then it may be appropriate for the Court to make a single order authorising access to a particular bank account which can be applied for the benefit of the person concerned. However, where regular management and supervision of the person's estate is required and to ensure that decisions can be made, the Court may delegate decision-making powers to an individual or to a trust corporation. Clearly an individual working with the person concerned and his family and carers is going to be in a better position to work with or for the person concerned. The formal and expensive Court process should only be needed in appointing the deputy, setting the deputy's powers, dealing with major decisions and resolving disputes.

Although it may be self-evident in a particular case that a deputy needs to be appointed, the principles of the Act must be followed. A person making an application needs to justify the need for the appointment of the deputy. The applicant needs to identify and explain (with evidence where necessary):

- the matter or matters in respect of which decisions need to be made;

- that the person concerned lacks capacity to make those decisions because of an impairment of, or a disturbance in the functioning of, the mind or brain;

- that there is no other practical alternative to the appointment of a deputy; and

- that the appointment of a deputy and the choice of the person concerned is in the best interests of the person concerned.

What is a deputy?

4.2　　The term 'deputy' is introduced by the MCA 2005 and replaces the former Mental Health Act 1983 term of 'receiver'. The reason for the change in terminology is not just a desire to illustrate the novelty of the new Act; it is to show that a deputy has powers 'deputed' to him and is therefore subordinate to the Court. The deputy is appointed to make decisions on behalf of a person who lacks capacity and is therefore also acting as that person's deputy.

Legal status of deputy

4.3　　A person appointed by a court to deal with the property and affairs of another person who lacks capacity has historically been regarded as the statutory agent of the person for whom he is appointed to make decisions (*Re EG* [1914] 1 Ch 927). This is confirmed by s 19(6) of the MCA 2005 which provides that:

> 'A deputy is to be treated as P's agent in relation to anything done or decided by him within the scope of his appointment and in accordance with this Part.'

Where a person's property and affairs are concerned, a deputy acts in the same way as any other agent, such as an attorney or trustee, with a fiduciary duty towards his principal. The deputy is not therefore liable for the proper debts and expenses of his principal, and legal fees and expenses incurred by him are payable by the principal or his estate. Property in the name of the person concerned does not vest in the deputy but remains in the person's legal ownership. The deputy acts 'as deputy for' the person concerned and not on his own account. For example, bank accounts and shareholdings will show the name of the deputy but always 'as deputy for' the person concerned who retains the legal ownership of the assets.

The concept of agency is necessary and appropriate but sits uneasily with the Act's policy to appoint a deputy to make decisions on behalf of the person concerned. The deputy is protected by his legal status, but is also required by the Act to make decisions on behalf of the person concerned and to act in his best interests. It is possible that the two will come into conflict, where a fiduciary decision on behalf of the estate may not necessarily be the decision that the person concerned would have wanted to make if he had capacity. Where there is such a conflict, the overriding consideration is the 'best interests' of the person concerned. A deputy acting for a person who lacks capacity is not required to make an unwise, irrational or dangerous decision (see *Re P* [2009] EWHC 163 (Ch) which is considered in more detail at **1.23** above)

Who is the client?

4.4   Any legal relationship involving two parties acting together carries with it an inherent conflict of interest. A solicitor or other professional adviser needs to know who his client is. As a deputy is the statutory agent of the person concerned, he will generally provide instructions on behalf of his principal. So long as the deputy is acting within the scope of his authority, a solicitor is acting for the person who lacks capacity as his client, with the deputy making certain decisions on behalf of the client. Thus a solicitor is treated as the solicitor of the person concerned (*Re EG* [1914] 1 Ch 927 at 935).

This principle is displaced in three situations:

- In the course of making an application for the appointment of a deputy, a solicitor is acting for the person making the application. At that stage it should not be assumed that the person concerned lacks capacity, that the applicant will be appointed or that the person concerned will not be joined as a party. However, once a deputy is appointed, the solicitor is the solicitor of the person concerned. In practice the Court treats the solicitor as acting for the person concerned from the time the first application has been made. A solicitor should explain this to the applicant before the application is made to avoid future misunderstandings. It is not uncommon for a conflict of interest to arise and the solicitor will have a duty of confidentiality to the person concerned and the Court even if his instructions in the first instance come from the person making the application.

- If some other person objects to the original application then the solicitor must decide whether he is representing the applicant or the person concerned. If the solicitor decides to continue representing the applicant then it is for the Court to determine whether the person concerned requires separate representation. In that case another solicitor or the Official Solicitor will be instructed to represent his interests (*Practice Direction of AB Macfarlane dated 9 August 1995* [1995] 2 FLR 1036 and *Law Society's Gazette*, 15 November 1995 at page 28).

- Once a deputy has been appointed and a further application is made, there may be a conflict of interest between the deputy and the person concerned. If for instance the deputy instructs a solicitor to apply for a statutory will or gift, the solicitor will, in respect of that particular matter, be acting for the deputy as applicant and the Court will decide whether P should be joined (Court of Protection Rules 2007 (CPR 2007), r 85(2)(c)). The Official Solicitor will generally be instructed to act as litigation friend (CPR 2007, r 143(1)).

Where there is a formal application involving more than one person it is important to identify at an early stage who the parties are and what their interests are. Where two or more solicitors are instructed and might, therefore, be deemed to be acting for the same person, preliminary directions should first be sought from the Court as to which solicitor should be the solicitor in the matter. The applicant or other person may instruct another solicitor and it is in the Court's discretion whether the costs of more than one solicitor shall be paid from the estate (CPR 2007, r 162).

Powers of the deputy – general principles

4.5   The deputy only has such authority as is delegated to him by the Court of Protection. In accordance with the principles of the MCA 2005, not only should the decision made on behalf of a person be the least restrictive, but the powers of the deputy should be as limited in scope and duration as possible (s 16(4)). This is self-evident in welfare matters. A deputy appointed to oversee a course of treatment or a move to new accommodation should not expect to retain his powers indefinitely. There is a greater difficulty where property and affairs are concerned, where for practical purposes a deputy needs as much discretion as possible to deal with the day-to-day administration of the estate without having to come back to the Court on a frequent basis. Each time the deputy applies to the Court a new application needs to be made, generally with a great deal of paperwork and therefore expense, as well as a Court application fee of £400.

Scope of Deputy's authority – property and affairs

4.6   To avoid unnecessary applications to the Court of Protection and the associated costs to the estate as well as to the Court, the Court will in most cases provide a deputy dealing with a person's property and affairs with as widely drawn powers as possible. An unrestricted general order will include the following provisions:

'(a)   The court confers general authority on the deputy to take possession or control of the property and affairs of [P] and to exercise the same powers of management and investment as he has as beneficial owner, subject to the terms and conditions set out in this order.

(b)   The deputy may make provision for the needs of anyone who is related to or connected with [P], if he provided for or might be expected to provide for that person's needs, by doing whatever he did or might reasonably be expected to do to meet those needs.

(c)   The deputy may (without obtaining any further authority from the court) dispose of [P]'s money or property by way of gift to any charity to which he made or might have been expected to make gifts and on customary occasions to persons who are related to or connected with him, provided that the value of each such gift is not unreasonable having regard to all the circumstances and, in particular, the size of his estate.

(d)   For the purpose of giving effect to any decision the deputy may execute or sign any necessary deeds or documents.'

A widely drafted order in these terms will provide the deputy with a great deal of discretion. These powers include authority to arrange investments or buy or sell a property. The deputy is also empowered to maintain another person and to make gifts on behalf of the person concerned. The power of management and control entitles the deputy to enter into a contract and not to be personally liable unless the deputy agrees to such personal liability. However, such wide discretion may be convenient but it also gives rise to two specific problems:

(a)   *Danger of acting outside scope of authority*

The problem for the deputy is that his authority may appear too widely drawn. A deputy must still act in the best interests of the person concerned and has a fiduciary duty to his estate. A deputy may not be certain whether he can carry out a particular decision or may prefer to have some official confirmation that he is acting correctly. A major item of expenditure may be within the scope of the deputy's formal authority, but he may have concerns as to whether the client can afford it even though the client has strong views that he is able to express; or he may feel that the client can afford it but it is not necessarily in his best interests. Prior to October 2007 the Public Guardianship Office would often correspond informally with receivers and provide a letter of guidance to the effect that a particular proposed course of action would not require the Court's approval. Permission was also given regularly by letter. This is no longer possible and any decision of the Court requires a specific order which must be made in response to an application. A deputy who is uncertain as to whether a decision can be made may well be advised to make an application using the short procedure in Practice Direction 9D (see **3.43** above).

(b)   *Lack of accountability*

If the Court confers authority on the deputy to manage the whole of a person's estate, there is invariably a danger that the assets will be inadvertently or deliberately misused. The deputy must account to the Public Guardian, but accounts are not delivered until the end of the accounting period and the supervision provided is far from thorough (see **7.8** below). The Court may therefore restrict the scope of the order in terms of scope and duration. Thus the order may restrict the deputy to spend up to a specified amount in a particular year. The order might also be limited to a three-year period. In either case the deputy must reapply to the Court for permission to extend or renew his authority.

Limitations on deputy – general principles

4.7   A deputy can only make those decisions that are delegated to him by the Court which in turn can only delegate the authority to make decisions which:

- the person concerned lacks capacity to make;

- are within the scope of the Court's authority under the Act; and

- which the Court has authority to delegate to another party.

The scope of the Court's authority to make decisions and in turn delegate decisions as well as the deputy's authority to act are considered at **2.15–2.18** above. However, the practical consequences for the deputy need to be considered in more detail.

Deputy can only act where P lacks capacity

4.8   The Court's power to make decisions and appoint a deputy under s 16(1) applies only 'if a person lacks capacity in relation to a matter or matters.' The Court therefore has no power to appoint a deputy in respect of an individual matter in respect of which P has capacity. A person's ability to manage property and affairs has been considered in more detail at **1.5** above, but it is important to emphasise that even though a deputy has been appointed to act with wide powers, the Court has no power to confer authority and the deputy has no authority to act in respect of any matters that the person concerned has capacity to deal with himself. This crucial limitation is confirmed by s 20(1) of the Act which provides that:

> 'A deputy does not have power to make a decision on behalf of P in relation to a matter if he knows or has reasonable grounds for believing that P has capacity in relation to the matter.'

An order appointing a deputy will generally not make a clear distinction between what a deputy can or cannot do. An order limited to a particular decision or matter may be appropriate in welfare cases, but it will be less frequent in financial cases. For instance a person with a psychiatric disorder who manages his benefits might not be able to deal with the sale of a property or the receipt of an inheritance: an order can be limited to dealing with that particular matter and applying any monies received for the benefit of the person concerned. In most cases however, a widely drawn order will be issued with authority for the deputy to 'make decisions on behalf of [P] that he is unable to make for himself in relation to his property and affairs'.

Whether or not the order is limited to a particular decision or matter, the deputy may still only make 'decisions on behalf of P that he is unable to make for himself.' The onus is therefore on the deputy to exercise his authority appropriately. A third party dealing with the deputy will, unless he has actual notice that the person concerned has capacity, assume from the fact that the order has been made that the person lacks capacity and the deputy is authorised to act. A deputy with authority to act under an order dealing with all of a person's property and affairs where the person has capacity to make certain decisions is in a difficult position. He may find that he is acting outside the scope of his authority. In most cases, the deputy will need to establish a division of responsibility with the person concerned. This is the best solution and fits neatly with the Act's principles. If this cannot be done, the deputy may need to consider:

- ensuring that there is an agreement with or indemnity from the person concerned or even a power of attorney covering his authority to act as the person's agent in respect of those matters; or

- transferring assets to a trust which can be administered by trustees without reference to issues of capacity.

Who may act as a deputy

4.9   Section 19 of the MCA 2005 provides that a deputy must be an individual who has reached the age of 18 or in respect of property and affairs only, a trust corporation. The holder for the time being of a specified office or position can also be appointed. Thus if there is no other suitable person to act, the Official Solicitor or a Director of Adult Social Services can be appointed by reference to the office. No person can be appointed a deputy without his consent.

Where the Court appoints a deputy for a person it is both delegating decision-making powers as well as making a decision on behalf of the person concerned. Any decision made for a person under the Act must be in that person's best interests (s 1(5)) and the Court's powers under s 16, which include the power to appoint deputies, are subject to ss 1 and 4. The Court must therefore consider the choice of deputy carefully having regard to the best interests of the person concerned. In practice therefore, there is a presumption that the deputy will be someone who:

(a)   has the right level of skill and competence, and

(b)   has a close personal connection to the person.

In most cases therefore a relative or close friend will be appointed as someone who knows the person well and can actively promote his interests without putting his estate to unnecessary expense.

There will, however, be cases where an independent or professional deputy will be appointed. There are cases where there are no close relatives or friends or where relatives or friends are unsuitable or unwilling to act. The right or wrong deputy can make an enormous difference to a person's quality of life as well as to the value of the estate.

It is important for any applicant not to make assumptions that a particular person must act or should act as deputy. The final decision as to who should act as deputy rests with the Court, acting in the person's best interests.

Choosing the right deputy – the best interests of P

4.10   In most cases, it is self-evident who should be appointed as deputy. A spouse, parent or child will make an application on the basis that he or she has the closest involvement on a personal and financial level with the person concerned. If there is more than one suitable person, they may agree which one should act. The person who makes the application may also end up being preferred by default, appearing to have done the work and assembled the relevant information. However, where an application is received from two or more persons, or an objection is made to the applicant being appointed, the application will be heard by the Court in an attended hearing.

How the Court resolves a dispute over the choice of deputy is more problematic. The Court must act in the person's best interests and apply the statutory principles set out in s 4 of the MCA 2005. These are considered in general terms at **1.20** above, and apply to the choice of deputy as they apply to any other decision made by the Court. Thus the Court must consider the person's past and present wishes and feelings, beliefs and values, other factors that he would consider and the views of anyone engaged in his welfare. The person concerned may be able to express an opinion on the matter and this must carry a great deal of weight with the Court. He may have had a particular professional relationship with his solicitor or accountant or a history of looking for advice and assistance from a particular person. There may be evidence that the person concerned has entrusted an individual with making decisions – for instance in a letter of wishes, a power of attorney, bank mandate, advance decision or even as an executor in a Will. He may also express a strong dislike for the person managing or attempting to his affairs and, however irrational, if this might have a harmful effect on the person's mental health then the appointment of another competent person may be necessary. But where a person complained to the Court that the deputy was not suitable because he was too short, this was not regarded as an adequate ground to remove an otherwise suitable deputy.

Unless there are no grounds for avoiding a person's known wishes, then the Court should if at all possible give effect to those wishes. As Marshall, J explained in the case of *S v S* 25 November 2008, unreported, (paragraphs 56 and 57) when addressing the weight to be given to the wishes of a couple who could not manage their affairs but who could express their wishes that an independent professional deputy should be appointed:

'The Act does not of course say that P's wishes are to be paramount, nor does it lay down any express presumption in favour of implementing them if they can be ascertained. Indeed the paramount objective is that of P's best interests. However, by giving such prominence to the above matters, the Act does in my judgment recognise that having his views and wishes taken into account and respected is a very significant aspect of P's best interests. Due regard should therefore be paid when doing the weighing exercise of determining what is in P's best interests in all the circumstances of the case.

As to how this will work in practice, in my judgment, where P can and does express a wish or view which is not irrational (in the sense of being a wish which a person of full capacity might reasonably have), is not impractical as far as its physical implementation is concerned, and is not irresponsible having regard to the extent of P's resources (ie whether a responsible person of full capacity who had such resources might reasonably consider it worth using the necessary resources to implement his wish) then that situation carries great weight, and effectively gives rise to a presumption in favour of implementing those wishes, unless there is some potential sufficiently detrimental effect for P of doing so which outweighs this.'

Other considerations

4.11   The courts have generally been reluctant to lay down guidelines that must be considered in the choice of deputy or the relative weight which should be given to the different factors the Court must take into account. A request for guidelines was rejected by the New South Wales Court of Appeal in the case of *Holt v Protective Com* (1993) 31 NSWLR, where the President stated that:

'it is inappropriate that the discretion to appoint or remove the manager of the estate should be confined by rigid rules or even "guidelines" expressed in general terms. This case should not be one for imposing shackles which were denounced by Theobald [on Lunacy]. The only general guideline is that, in any such application, the court is bound, as in exercising any other power of which it is the donee by legislation, to consider all relevant circumstances'.

The principles applied in this case reflect the way the Court still applies its jurisdiction in such cases. Any issue concerning the choice of deputy must take account of the following general considerations:

1   the Court is bound by the legislation (to act in P's best interests');

2   the Court is exercising its discretion;

3   each situation is unique to the individuals concerned and the Court must consider 'all relevant circumstances'.

This approach is emphasised by the Code of Practice which provides at paragraphs 8.32 and 8.33 as follows:

'It is for the court to decide who to appoint as a deputy. Different skills may be required depending on whether the deputy's decisions will be about a person's welfare (including healthcare), their finances or both. The court will decide whether the proposed deputy is reliable and trustworthy and has an appropriate level of skill and competence to carry out the necessary tasks.

In the majority of cases, the deputy is likely to be a family member or someone who knows the person well. But in some cases the court may decide to appoint a deputy who is independent of the family (for example, where the person's affairs or care needs are particularly complicated). This could be, for example, the Director of Adult Services in the relevant local authority (but see paragraph 8.60 below) or a professional deputy. The OPG has a panel of professional deputies (mainly solicitors who specialise in this area of law) who may be appointed to deal with property and affairs if the court decides that would be in the person's best interests.'

The qualities of the proposed deputy

4.12   Acting as a deputy can be onerous. The Public Accounts Committee in its 1994 Report stated, describing the comparable role of a receiver under the Mental Health Act 1983, commented as follows:

> 'for a receivership to be successful it is crucial that the receiver appointed is trustworthy and reliable. It is also important that the receiver is competent to manage the patient's affairs and should take an active interest in the patient's welfare' (*Thirty-Ninth Report of 1993–94* at para 5).

That this was not always achieved in practice was made clear by the the Quinquennial Review of the Public Guardianship Office in November 1999, which expressed concerns that receivers were appointed 'on fairly flimsy evidence about their willingness and ability to undertake what can be an onerous responsibility' and that:

> 'many people are appointed without any appreciation of the amount of work they will be involved in; the degree of administrative competence required to produce annual income and expenditure accounts and the restrictions the Court imposes on the use and investment of the patient's capital . . .' (para 50).

It is arguable that a deputy's responsibilities are more onerous following the implementation of the MCA 2005. A deputy is not just acting as a trustee in a fiduciary role, but also acts in accordance with the principles of the Act. The Deputy's Declaration (see **4.13** below) is aimed at addressing these concerns and ensure that deputies at least know what they were undertaking and to provide the Court with more information about the proposed deputy. The qualities of the proposed deputy are important and the following factors should be considered in each case:

- the ability of the deputy to take on the duties of a deputy (see Chapter 7 below) and to deal with any particular complexities or issues that need to be dealt with (see **4.14** below);

- the degree of contact the proposed deputy has had and continues to have with the client;

- the degree of affection and devotion of the proposed deputy to the client and his relationship generally with the client. Clearly a deputy who cares deeply for the client's welfare and has a good relationship with him is more suited to acting as deputy than someone who does not;

- where the proposed deputy lives. While a deputy does not need to live nearby, a lay deputy who lives locally is likely to be more involved in the welfare of the client and able to assist in an emergency than one who lives some distance away. The Court is reluctant to appoint as a deputy a resident outside England and Wales;

- the occupation of the proposed deputy, and whether the demands of his situation will allow the time necessary to look after the patient's affairs;

- the age or health of the proposed deputy. The Deputy's Declaration asks the question: 'Are there any circumstances (personal or otherwise) which would interfere with your ability to carry out the duties of a deputy effectively? (e.g. ill health or business/family commitments)';

● whether the proposed deputy has acted as a deputy for any other person. An applicant is required to state in the Deputy's Declaration whether he has acted as a deputy before. The proposed deputy may also have relevant experience as an attorney, executor or trustee;

● whether the proposed deputy has any other skills or relevant experience. The Deputy's Declaration asks the applicant to state if he has a 'particular professional skill, life experience or public duty or role' that the applicant thinks may be relevant.

The Deputy's Declaration

4.13   Any person wishing to be appointed a deputy must complete the Deputy's Declaration (Form COP4) as part of the application (see **5.3** below). This is designed to give the Court enough information to identify the appropriate personal qualities outlined above. The form asks 15 questions covering matters such as bankruptcy and criminal offences. The Deputy's Declaration also requires the applicant to give a personal undertaking to comply with a long list of 17 obligations and to state positively why he wishes to be appointed as deputy. There is no point in a person applying to be a deputy without understanding what this involves or applying for the wrong reasons. The Declaration emphasises that receivership carries with it responsibilities and duties and this may help to deter some inappropriate applications.

The size and complexity of the estate

4.14   Where the deputy is appointed to deal with property and affairs then the qualities of the deputy required will be relative to the actual estate. Where the estate is a complex one a close and loving relative may not always be the best candidate to act as deputy. The Australian case of *Holt v Protective Com* (1993) 31 NSWLR 227 and see **4.10** above) concerned an application to remove a receiver and the size and complexity of the estate was held to be an important consideration in determining the choice of receiver:

'. . . in a smaller estate it may often be appropriate to appoint a family member who will be entirely familiar with the assets and liabilities and ready to manage them with greater economy and possibly free of cost to the protected person . . . Different considerations may affect the management of an estate comprised of few liquid assets when contrasted to one which enjoys substantial and regular income.'

Where the estate is a particularly large or complex one, the Court will be more circumspect over the choice of deputy. This is especially the case where substantial sums are recovered in personal injury and clinical negligence cases. Often these awards follow an extremely difficult period for the claimant and the family and their personal distress may well be compounded by the added complication of administering a large estate. There is also a potential conflict of interest between the claimant and the family, who are often themselves financially dependent on the award. It is in the best interests of all concerned to have an independent person providing a degree of objectivity, especially where the Court has conferred a wide discretion on the deputy as to how the award is to be applied and entrusted substantial sums to that discretion. In many such cases an element of detachment is helpful where the claimant and his family have complex personal and emotional issues to address. The difficulties faced by a deputy as well as the risks inherent in the MCA 2005 regime have been considered at **4.6** and the comments of the then Master Lush cited in the case of *Eagle v Chambers* are even more relevant today:

> 'In my view it is not appropriate to say that the court will only appoint professional receivers in damages cases, nor that, if a professional receiver has been initially appointed, a lay receiver should not subsequently be appointed. I consider that the proper approach in general is that a professional receiver is desirable in acquired brain injury cases at least until the first or second year after the award. Such cases are likely to be more complex in the early stages. After this initial period, much will depend on whether there is a family member (or friend) who is both willing and suitable to act. If there is such a person able and suitable to act, he or she may employ a solicitor or accountant to deal with matters reasonably requiring professional assistance. If there is no such person willing to act, then no doubt it will be necessary for a professional receiver to remain in post (in the present case, either the current receiver or a new receiver appointed from the panel)' (cited by Waller LJ at [2005] 1 All ER 136 at 156.

The comments of the former Master of the Court of Protection also emphasise that the Court cannot be prejudiced in favour of an independent professional. It must exercise its discretion and take account of all relevant factors. However, a family member or friend seeking to act as deputy in a large or complex estate must show to the Court that he has the ability to deal with the estate. The Court must also be prepared to act firmly in a person's best interests and appoint a deputy who is better qualified to take on the role even if this is contrary to the past or present wishes of the person concerned.

Conflicts of interest

4.15   The existence of possible conflicts of interest is a relevant factor when considering the appointment of a deputy. However, their existence is not an absolute restriction, as conflicts of interest will arise naturally, for example where the deputy is responsible for funding the care of the person concerned and is also a beneficiary under his Will. In most cases other factors such as the accountability of the deputy to the Court and representation by a litigation friend in proceedings will outweigh a potential conflict of interest. However, a conflict of interest would lead to a presumption against a person being appointed where the proposed deputy is the owner of the care home or property in which the patient resides. This issue is addressed specifically in the Deputy's Declaration, which asks the applicant to answer the following question: 'Are you aware of any matter in which your financial interests may conflict with those of the person to whom the application relates? (e.g. occupation of a property which the person owns, any interest under the terms of their will)?'.

Conflicts with other members of a patient's family should not of themselves prevent a deputy from carrying out his duties unless the conflict is such that it interferes in his ability to manage the patient's affairs. In the case of *Re W* [2002] 1 FLR 832 it was held on the facts of that case that where a sole attorney was in conflict with her siblings, the hostility did not impact adversely on the administration of the donor's affairs. The same principle was applied in *Re E* [2000] 3 WLR 1974, and in *Re F* [2004] 3 All ER 277 However, while the Court must give consideration to the person's wishes, the fact that the conflict between relatives undermines the efficient administration of the estate is not just a factor P 'would be likely to consider if he were able to do so'. It would not be in his best interests to appoint a deputy who cannot function effectively due to family conflict. Where there is a conflict, the Court will generally prefer an independent professional deputy to be appointed.

Convictions and bankruptcy

4.16   It is unlikely that a person with a criminal record, especially one which relates to an offence involving dishonesty, would be appointed deputy to deal with a person's property and affairs. However, an attorney under an Enduring Power of Attorney serving a prison sentence for an unrelated offence has been held not to be an unsuitable person (*Re T*, reported in the *Elderly Client Adviser*, September/October 1997). However, where the Court has a discretion in the matter, it is unlikely that an individual with a court judgment registered against him will be appointed deputy.

A person's bankruptcy is not an automatic bar to acting as a deputy in the same way as it is for an attorney (although a welfare Lasting Power of Attorney is not revoked by bankruptcy). However, there would have to be exceptional grounds to justify the appointment of an individual with a court judgment registered against him or who has been made bankrupt. Nevertheless, prior to the introduction of a Deputy's Declaration in 2001, questions regarding convictions and solvency were not addressed to the applicant and unless disclosed by a personal reference or through an objection from a third party the Court would have been unaware of the applicant's unsuitability on these grounds. With credit checks carried out as a matter of course and a detailed Deputy's Declaration it should be harder for an unsuitable deputy to be appointed.

Costs

4.17   A lay deputy can only recover his out-of-pocket expenses and is generally preferred to a professional deputy who will be entitled to charge a fee for acting. Where two or more applicants are professionals, the one with a long-standing relationship with the patient, knowledge of the patient's affairs and experience in deputyship matters will generally be preferred.

Deputy of last resort

4.18   Prior to October 2007, the Chief Executive of the Public Guardianship Office (and formerly the Public Trustee) would act as a receiver of last resort where there was no one else willing or able to take on this role. The appointment of an official as receiver had been not unusual, but due to the high costs of providing the service (as well as other failings identified by the National Audit Office and the Quinquennial Review of 1999) most 'in house' receiverships were transferred to solicitors and local authorities. By 2007 there were only a handful of cases left, largely ones which were too difficult to handle – often because of a history of violence or public notoriety. These last residual cases were transferred to the Official Solicitor to act as deputy and the Official Solicitor will in exceptional circumstances still accept being appointed as deputy.

Joint and successive appointments

4.19   Although the Mental Health Act regime provided for the appointment of joint receivers, joint appointments were extremely rare. They were often suggested by relatives where they could not agree on who should be appointed. It was felt that such appointments would cause delays and add to the costs involved. In any case a receiver was an individual person accountable personally to the Court.

Despite the scarcity of joint appointments of receivers under the Mental Health Act , s 19 of the MCA 2005 provides expressly for the joint appointments of deputies. It also introduced a power to appoint successive deputies:

   '(4)   The court may appoint two or more deputies to act—

     (a)   jointly,

     (b)   jointly and severally, or

     (c)   jointly in respect of some matters and jointly and severally in respect of others.

  (5)   When appointing a deputy or deputies, the court may at the same time appoint one or more other persons to succeed the existing deputy or those deputies—

     (a)   in such circumstances, or on the happening of such events, as may be specified by the court;

     (b)   for such period as may be so specified.

These provisions set out in the Act have coincided with other changes that make the use of joint and successive appointments more useful. In welfare cases it is often appropriate for more than one person to have authority to make decisions. Parents of a disabled child may need to act separately on different occasions or several children may be required to act jointly in making decisions about their parent's welfare. In financial cases, a more thoughtful look at the best interests criteria means that a loving spouse should not be discounted as a suitable deputy just because of age or ill health. The Act requires a more careful and constructive approach. Thus the spouse may be appointed with a provision for a child to act alongside (jointly and severally) so that he can take over if his parent becomes unable to act or dies. Similarly where two parents are together looking after a severely disabled child, they can share in the responsibilities of acting as deputy.

Where a person's property and affairs are concerned, the Court has become more willing to appoint joint deputies in cases where significant sums of money are involved. This is a consequence of the wide discretion given to deputies and the light supervision provided by the Public Guardian. This in turn makes it harder for lay deputies to obtain indemnity cover (see **5.22**). The only way in which a parent or close relative who wishes to be involved as a deputy can act as such is to be appointed jointly with a professional deputy.

Chapter 5

Application to appoint a deputy

Initial considerations

5.1   Having established that a person lacks capacity to make decisions and that an application to appoint a deputy is required, work can commence on preparing the application. This will inevitably be a time-consuming exercise and will often be a costly exercise. While most applicants will wish for a simpler and cheaper procedure, they need to bear in mind that the Court of Protection knows nothing of the case until it receives the application. Any application involves a fundamental intrusion into a person's life and may have far-reaching consequences over his welfare and property. The Court cannot make assumptions about an order being necessary or the terms of the order required. The Court requires sufficient evidence not just to establish its jurisdiction but also to show:

- sufficient details of the person's situation to enable an appropriate order to be made;

- the decision or decisions that the Court is being asked to make or delegate to a deputy;

- that it is in the person's best interests to make such a decision;

- that there are no alternative or less restrictive ways of achieving the same objective;

- details of any interested relatives or carers and that they are involved;

- the extent to which the person concerned can participate in the decision;

- that the proposed deputy is a suitable person to act and that it is in the best interests of the person concerned for that person to be appointed;

- that relatives or other concerned persons are notified and given an opportunity to participate in the decision being made.

All this information needs to correspond with a standard procedure that complies with the Court of Protection Rules and the administrative requirements of the Court. The result of a properly made application is not just that the Court can process the application smoothly but that the right order will result. If the right person is appointed deputy with the right level of authority, the interests of the person concerned are secured and the deputy can be allowed to carry out his duties with minimal interference from or recourse to the Court of Protection and Public Guardian.

The policy of requiring more information at an early stage to save time and effort at a later stage was adopted by the Public Guardianship Office as part of its efforts to provide receivers with a greater degree of autonomy than had previously been allowed. A formal 'needs-assessment' system was first proposed in *Making Changes: the Way Forward* (December 2000) so that:

> 'each client will be treated according to his or her individual circumstances. More time invested at the outset, as well as through visits and accounts, will help tailor our subsequent involvement to those circumstances.' (at 2.04)

Who makes the application?

5.2   In principle, any person may make an application to the Court of Protection. An application for the appointment of a welfare deputy may require permission (see **3.6** above) but any person may still apply for permission to make an application.

The decision whether to appoint and the choice of deputy are matters for the Court of Protection and if there is any doubt, uncertainty or conflict, it must be left to the Court to resolve this. It is important in practice to separate the application process from the decision to appoint a deputy as well as the final choice of deputy. If there are grounds for believing in good faith that a person lacks capacity to make decisions and that it is in his best interests for a deputy to be appointed, then it is appropriate for an application to be made. The application may also propose that the applicant or another person or (in the case of property and affairs, a trust corporation) is appointed as deputy. The Court is not however bound by the applicant's proposed choice of deputy and may prefer in due course to appoint someone else.

Most applications are uncontentious and it is self-evident who should be appointed. If there is doubt, uncertainty or conflict, one person should bring the application but explain as best he can that the purpose of the application is to bring the application before the Court and any member of the family or any other persons notified can make his own submissions to the Court. An application may be brought by a relative or close friend or a solicitor acting on their behalf; an application may also be brought by a solicitor in his own name, a local authority or the Official Solicitor. A trust company may also apply for a financial deputy and a health authority might also apply for a welfare deputy.

Application procedure

5.3   The application process can be long and for anyone who does not enjoy filling in large numbers of lengthy forms, a painful one. It can take a very long time for the matter to be dealt with: the Court Service Standard requires that if no oral hearing is directed, the Court will give a direction within 21 weeks of receipt of the application. It may take several weeks to prepare an application and a final order may still be incomplete if for instance there is a delay in arranging security. Although most straightforward applications should be dealt with more quickly, an applicant who is concerned that a deputy needs to be appointed has a responsibility to ensure that the application is well made and contains sufficient information to avoid further delays in the process.

The application forms can be obtained free of charge from the Customer Service Unit of the Court of Protection or from the website at: http://www.publicguardian.gov.uk/forms/cop_forms.htm

On a first application, the following documents must be lodged with the Court of Protection at Archway Tower, 2 Junction Road, London N19 5SZ (DX 141150 Archway 2):

(a)   application form (COP1) in duplicate;

(b)   a supporting information form which can be:

    (i)   COP1A for property and affairs applications; or

    (ii)   COP1B for welfare applications;

(c)   application for permission – if required and not already obtained (COP2);

(d)   assessment of capacity form (the medical certificate) (COP3);

(e)   the Deputy's Declaration (COP4);

(f)   any other evidence or information required to support or complete the application;

(g)   cheque for £400 payable to 'the Court of Protection' (unless a fee has already been paid on an application for permission).

The application process is similar to any other application to the Court of Protection made in accordance with Part 9 of the Court of Protection Rules. The Rules do assume that all cases will begin in the same way whether they relate to a small estate with modest sums of money involved or a complex and highly contentious welfare application. The process can, especially if the affairs of the person concerned are relatively straightforward, appear unduly bureaucratic.

Application form – COP1

5.4   In contrast to the procedure under the Mental Health Act 1983 jurisdiction and the 2001 Court of Protection Rules, any application to the Court of Protection is commenced by the applicant filing an application form. Proceedings are then deemed to be started once the Court issues the application form (Rule 62).

A new application is made in a prescribed form, COP1. This sets out the core details of the application:

●   details of the applicant and (if applicable) the applicant's solicitor;

●   the status of the applicant and whether he is the person to whom the application relates, related or connected to that person or applying in a representative capacity;

●   the person who lacks capacity or who is alleged to lack capacity;

- whether permission is required;

- who the respondents are;

- who should be notified;

- the matter the Court is being asked to decide (for instance, that the person concerned lacks capacity to manage his property and affairs);

- the order the Court is being asked to make (for instance, the appointment of a deputy);

- how the application would benefit the person concerned (addressing why it is important to appoint a deputy and confirming that there is no other or less restrictive way of dealing with the matter);

- whether any other applications have been made to the Court;

- whether any special facilities are required to attend a Court hearing.

The form is then signed by the applicant with a statement of truth.

Although the application form is only a short one, it is the most important part of the process. It not only opens or starts the proceedings, but identifies the core issues of the case, and the status of the other parties. It should be used to concentrate the applicant's mind as to what function or decision the person concerned cannot make and why the Court of Protection needs to assist. The applicant should also anticipate the order the Court is likely to provide: will a general order be adequate, or are there any specific matters that need to be dealt with, such as bringing proceedings or obtaining safe custody of a will? Once a final order has been made, if the deputy requires further authority from the Court, a new application will need to be made, with all the expense, effort and delay that it will entail.

The application form will also establish who the initial parties are going to be. It will in particular determine whether someone is served so that he can become a respondent or notified so that he must apply to be joined as a party (see **3.8** above).

Supporting information forms

5.5   The supporting information forms are supplementary to the main application form. There are two forms for property and affairs (COP1A) and for welfare matters (COP1B).

The supporting information forms provide the Court with the practical details it requires to ensure that the right order is made. Although in most cases where a financial deputy is appointed, the deputy will have wide powers to deal with the full extent of the estate, the Court will not assume this at the outset. The details set out in the form will also build up a 'risk profile' of the estate. It will identify particular issues that might give rise to concern or require a specific form of authority, for instance an inheritance, sale of a property or a damages award.

It is therefore essential for the applicant to provide as much accurate and relevant information as possible. Where information cannot be supplied this should be explained and further enquiries may be made. Difficulties may arise in that the only person who can authorise disclosure of personal and confidential information is the person who is incapable of providing that authority. Medical records, financial data or a personal document such as a will cannot be disclosed without authority. Guesses and estimates should therefore be described as such and the applicant will need to show where disclosure of relevant information may be required. The Court may 'take a view' that the application contains sufficient information to enable a deputy to be appointed and it is then for the deputy to deal with the matter directly. If the disclosure of information is critical to the matter that is to be decided, then a separate application may be made using the Part 10 procedure (see **3.23**) for a specific authority for the applicant or some other person to request the information. If the person or body holding the information is uncooperative, then the applicant may apply for a witness summons under Rule 106 requiring a person named in it to produce a document to the Court.

COP1A

5.6   Form COP1A, dealing with property and affairs, is a detailed questionnaire that runs to 17 pages. Unfortunately the form is designed for all types of estate and no distinction is made between the small estate where a simple order may be all that is required and a large and complex estate involving investments, trusts, properties and business interests. The applicant should not be deterred and only needs to address those parts of the form which relate to the P's property and affairs. Although the form is detailed, it is less intrusive (and shorter) than the previous property and information form (form CP5). There is a presumption that the deputy will be given the right authority to get on with the task in hand and that he will carry out his duties correctly. There is therefore no need to provide details of property insurance or how personal effects are to be disposed of; the Court will assume that the deputy will act appropriately to insure the property or deal with personal effects in the person's best interests.

Essential information is still required, and the form is set out in five sections. Section 1 simply sets out the applicant's details. Section 2 asks for details of the personal circumstances and requires information concerning:

- the person concerned – date of birth, address, type of accommodation and marital status;

- how often the applicant visits and who else visits. The persons to be notified have already been named in the application form and the persons to be notified are considered in more detail in Practice Direction 9B and at **3.8** above. The persons who visit may or may not be the same persons who are notified. A family that lives some distance away may be properly notified, but the applicant should provide details of a close friend or neighbour who is a more frequent visitor;

- the care arrangements at home;

- details of a social worker or case manager;

- details of the doctor.

Section 3 covers powers granted or arrangements made. This deals with an existing guardianship order, Enduring Power of Attorney (EPA) or Lasting Power of Attorney (LPA). The applicant also needs to show whether there is a will and provide a copy. If a copy cannot be supplied, then the applicant should show where a copy can be obtained from. The form also asks for the names of the executors. It may seem unnecessary to request this information about the contents of a person's will, but the will is an extremely important document. Not only should its safe custody be addressed, but its contents may have a bearing on the way the estate is dealt with, for instance where there is a specific gift of a property. The persons entrusted with the administration of the estate may also be an indication of whom the person concerned would wish to entrust with the administration of his financial affairs.

Section 4 deals separately with financial matters. The applicant must provide details of:

- the National Insurance number;

- any social security or welfare benefits;

- any pensions;

- interest in a trust;

- interest in a deceased person's estate;

- damages and criminal injuries compensation;

- income from employment;

- miscellaneous income;

- money held in bank accounts (showing account details and balances);

- money held by a third party;

- investments;

- insurance policies;

- land and property, including any jointly owned assets and explaining any proposals to sell;

- personal belongings, showing any individual items of value;

- business interests;

- debts and money owed;

- miscellaneous assets and investments;

- expenditure requirements for personal care and maintenance.

In many cases it may appear unnecessary to provide more than a very basic level of financial information. After all, the Court will provide a widely drafted order covering the whole of the estate, without specifying any particular assets that need to be dealt with (see **5.20** below). However, the detail is important. It enables the Court to assess the nature of the case, whether the proposed deputy is suitable, the level of security that is to be set and whether any restrictions should be placed. If the estate is a large or complex one, the Court may limit the amount that the deputy will be able to spend. The applicant should therefore use this part of the form or a separate schedule to provide a realistic budget showing annual expenditure and allowing for anticipated costs such as legal fees and tax payments.

Section 5 provides space for any other information and in particular background information that may be relevant. Although this part of the form is very general, it is helpful for the Court to have some general information about the person's history, the circumstances giving rise to the application and any other considerations which may assist the Court in making its decisions. It is helpful and appropriate to allow the Court some insight into the personal situation and character of the person concerned. The Court is being asked to act in the best interests of the person concerned and must take account of the individual's circumstances as far as possible.

COP1B

5.7   There is a specific supplementary information form where the application relates to personal welfare, COP1B. The form is, however, the same as COP1A except that it does not contain the same section 4 that deals with financial matters. Section 4 of COP1B is therefore the page for additional information.

Form COP1B is not therefore a complex or demanding form to complete. However, welfare applications are the most difficult and detailed cases that need to be addressed and the essential elements of a welfare application are set out in COP1, the detailed evidence that will accompany it (which should be in the form of a witness statement) and the medical evidence.

The medical certificate – COP3

5.8   Under the former Mental Health Act 1983, the Court's jurisdiction was only exercisable where it was satisfied 'after considering medical evidence' that 'the patient' was 'incapable, by reason of mental disorder, of managing and administering his property and affairs.' The Mental Capacity Act 2005 (MCA 2005) sets out no express demand for medical evidence. But as has already been noted, the Court may only make decisions in respect of those matters which a person lacks capacity to decide. Thus it would be impossible for the Court to exercise its jurisdiction without medical evidence and Practice Direction 9A therefore provides for an application to be made with medical evidence in form COP3.

Submission of medical evidence in the correct form is therefore an integral part of the application as it establishes the Court's jurisdiction and allows the Court to take action or make directions, even if the other papers are incomplete or cannot be submitted. The evidence must also be in sufficient detail to show the Court what decisionsP can or cannot make, as this will determine what the Court can do or authorise the deputy to do. Applications are often delayed because they are submitted without the medical evidence or the applicant has to wait for the medical certificate to be completed when all the other papers are ready. It is therefore advisable to contact P's doctor at the earliest opportunity.

Form COP3 need not necessarily be completed by a medical practitioner, although it must be given by someone professionally qualified and able to give expert evidence in this form. The guidance notes state that the form may be given by:

> 'a registered medical practitioner, psychologist or psychiatrist who has examined and assessed the capacity of the person to whom the application relates. In some circumstances it might be appropriate for a registered therapist, such as a speech therapist or occupational therapist, to complete the form.'

If the person concerned has a particular disability, for instance one that prevents communication, then an applicant may consider submitting two forms dealing separately with capacity and understanding.

While the Court needs to have detailed medical information about P, the medical practitioner completing the form needs to have sufficient information about the issue the Court is being asked to address. The medical practitioner in turn depends on the applicant to explain what information he or she is being asked to provide. The onus therefore is on the applicant to find the right medical practitioner to complete the form and then provide the practitioner with the right information so that the practitioner can determine what it is that P lacks capacity to decide and then provide the evidence to support this. Issues a practitioner must consider in completing a medical assessment – and the difficulties faced – are considered in more detail at **1.17** above.

To guide the medical practitioner through the capacity requirements of the individual case, form COP3 is divided into two parts, for the applicant and the practitioner respectively.

Part A requires the applicant to set out his details and the details of the person concerned. It then follows the same set of questions used in form COP1 to identify the essential issues of the matter. Thus the applicant needs to show:

- the matter the Court is being asked to decide (for instance, that P lacks capacity to manage his property and affairs or is unable to make a will);

- the order the Court is being asked to make (for instance, the appointment of a deputy or the making of a statutory will);

- how the application would benefit P (addressing why it is important to appoint a deputy and there is no other or less restrictive way of dealing with the matter).

The applicant must also confirm his relationship with the person concerned. The form then provides a large box for the applicant to 'provide any further information about the circumstances of the person to whom the application relates that would be useful to the practitioner in assessing his or her capacity to make any decision(s) that is the subject of your application.' Unless the medical practitioner knows the person concerned well and is experienced with the requirements of the MCA 2005, it is the responsibility of the applicant to provide sufficient detail to guide the practitioner through the form.

The medical practitioner must then complete the second part of form COP3. He or she must provide his or her details, relationship with the person concerned and professional qualifications. The form also indicates that the practitioner may send confidential information directly to the Court. The practitioner must then address the assessment of capacity, which follows the logical process set out in ss 2 and 3 of the MCA 2005. Thus the practitioner must confirm:

- that there is an impairment of or disturbance in the functioning of the mind or brain;

- how long this has lasted;

- the matters that the person is unable to decide as a result of the impairment or disturbance;

- that the person concerned cannot understand the relevant information;

- that the relevant information cannot be retained;

- that if information can be understood, it cannot be communicated;

- that the opinion is based on specified evidence.

The practitioner needs to pay careful attention to the questions asked and consider the detail provided by the applicant as well as the guidance notes which accompany the form. It is not sufficient just to confirm that a person lacks capacity and suffers from a particular disability. There must also be evidence to support this. Thus an elderly person who lacks capacity to manage his finances may suffer from dementia which is evidenced by an inability to remember dates and names or a low score on a Mini-Mental State Examination.

The form continues, asking the medical practitioner to assist the Court in making a best interests determination. The form addresses the issues raised by s 4 of the MCA 2005:

- Has the person to whom this application relates made you aware of any views they have in relation to the relevant matter?

- Do you consider there is a prospect that the person to whom the application relates might regain or acquire capacity in the future in respect of the decision to which the application relates?

- Are you aware of anyone who holds a different view regarding the capacity of the person to whom the application relates?

The practitioner is also asked to confirm how long he has acted for the person concerned or from whom he has received a referral, when the last assessment took place, whether he has any financial or other interest in the matter and whether he has any general comments or other recommendations.

The medical certificate is confidential and is prepared for the Court rather than for the person concerned or the applicant. If the practitioner is unwilling to issue a certificate without the consent of his patient (which might not be forthcoming), or if there is no solicitor involved, it can be sent directly to the Court of Protection. Where possible, however, the certificate should accompany all the relevant papers and the practitioner should return it to the solicitor lodging the application.

Where the applicant is unable to obtain medical evidence to support the application then the applicant should file a witness statement with the application explaining why a certificate cannot be obtained and why he believes the person concerned lacks capacity (PD 9A para 14). If there are good reasons why a medical certificate cannot be obtained and there are grounds for believing that the person concerned may lack capacity, the Court may direct one of the Medical Visitors to see the person concerned and prepare a report for the Court.

Medical practitioner's fee

5.9   A medical practitioner is entitled to charge a fee for completing the medical certificate which is a task beyond the scope of his usual professional duties. There is no prescribed fee. Prior to the implementation of the MCA 2005 the British Medical Association would recommend a fee for providing a medical certificate. Unfortunately a COP3 can be a more involved process and in many cases will be referred to a consultant or other specialist to complete. A medical assessment may take more than one meeting and discussions with other professionals, the applicant or family members. There will be a fee payable, but this needs to be seen in context. Medical evidence is a core part of an application that needs to ensure the interests of the person concerned are correctly dealt with.

The Deputy's Declaration – COP4

5.10   The Deputy's Declaration must be completed and signed by the proposed deputy, even if the application is made by someone else. It is perhaps the most important part of the application as the success of the MCA 2005 framework in relation to the life of a person who lacks capacity depends on the skill and integrity of the deputy. The Court cannot and will not provide control, supervision or guidance once a deputy has been appointed and it is all the more important than ever for the right person to be appointed. The Deputy's Declaration should therefore be completed carefully, with consideration given to the questions and additional information provided where necessary. The form should remind a proposed deputy that acting as a deputy is not a right or even an obligation, but an onerous financial and moral responsibility.

The form is set out in five parts to establish:

1   The personal details of the proposed deputy including telephone contact numbers and email and the proposed deputy's connection to the person concerned.

2   The personal circumstances of the proposed deputy. This part of the form contains a list of six questions dealing with the proposed deputy's occupation, whether he has any criminal convictions and whether there are any personal or health reasons that would prevent the proposed deputy from acting. The last question asks whether if the proposed deputy is not appointed, there is any other person who might wish to be considered. This usefully makes the point that the proposed deputy is not automatically going to be appointed and it is for the Court to make the appointment.

3   The financial circumstances of the proposed deputy. This part of the form contains a list of nine questions and deals with matters such as whether the proposed deputy has any outstanding judgment debts, has ever been bankrupt or insolvent, has any criminal convictions or is aware of any conflict of interest.

4   That the proposed deputy is aware of the duties and responsibilities of acting as a deputy. This part of the form consists of a series of 17 undertakings to carry out the duties and responsibilities required of a deputy, including to act in accordance with the principles of the MCA 2005 and have regard to the Code of Practice. The proposed deputy is asked to tick the 'yes' box to give his or her undertaking to 'act in accordance with the relevant duties and responsibilities'. There is also space for comments, for instance to show that the proposed deputy has a particular skill that will be relevant to his role.

5   That the proposed deputy has a positive reason for being appointed. There is no point in a person applying because he feels he ought to or to prevent someone else from applying. The form therefore asks for a 'personal statement to the Court'. This part of the form can also be used to describe any professional skill or other experience which the proposed deputy has, for instance if he or she is an experienced professional deputy.

Form COP4 is concluded by a statement of truth, further emphasising the obligation on the proposed deputy to state that the facts contained in the statement are believed to be true. Thus a statement verified by a statement of truth without an honest belief in its truth is a contempt of court.

Application fee

5.11   A standard application fee of £400 is payable on any first application to the Court of Protection, which includes an application for the appointment of a deputy.

Although the application fee is quite high, the subsequent costs are relatively modest. For applications made prior to October 2007, the fee was £250 but this was followed by a further fee of £330 when a receiver was appointed. Where a deputy is appointed, there is a further set-up fee of £125 (Court of Protection Fees Order 2007 (SI 2007/1745) and Public Guardian (Fees, etc) Regulations 2007 (SI 2007/2051)). Regrettably, the same fee is payable in all cases, regardless of the complexity of the case or the size of the estate. The Court of Protection Fees Order (paragraph 8) does allow for remission of fees, but only if the applicant is in receipt of means-tested benefits. A wealthy applicant who makes an application to recover a small amount of money for a person who is on benefits and lacks capacity does not qualify for remission of the application fee.

Permission

5.12   In the majority of financial cases, no permission is required for an application to the Court of Protection (Rule 51(2)(a)). However, if the application concerns the personal welfare of the person who lacks capacity and the application is not made by a deputy or attorney under a lasting power of attorney, then permission must be obtained to make an application.

The purpose of the permission requirement is twofold: to ensure that welfare applications are only made where an applicant has standing or a genuine interest in the outcome and to ensure that there is a substantive issue that needs to be addressed by the Court. There are many situations where a relative or friend would like to be appointed deputy, but there is no requirement for a deputy to be appointed. Either the welfare decision can be dealt with in a less intrusive way by a single order, or the welfare issues can be addressed by carers under s 5 of the MCA 2005. In such cases, an application for permission is a way of separating cases with a genuine requirement from those that might require a great deal of effort and expense for no purpose.

An application for permission must be made in form COP2, with supporting evidence. It can either be made in advance of the substantive application, with a medical certificate, draft application form and other evidence or at the same time as the application with an application form and further evidence. On the first application that is made, a fee of £400 is payable.

The requirement for permission and the formalities for obtaining permission are covered in more detail at **3.6** and **3.21** respectively.

Subsequent procedure

5.13   On receipt of the papers the Court will ensure that they are in order and allocate a case number. The application form is then issued, which is the point at which proceedings are started (Rule 62(1).

The issue of the application is confirmed by the application form being stamped and endorsed with the issue date. A copy is returned to the applicant with a covering letter confirming who is to be served or notified. It is also the practice of the Court to provide notice forms and certificates of service, whether or not the applicant has access to electronic copies.

Generally an application for the appointment of a deputy is not a contentious one, although it may become contentious at a later stage, once other persons have been notified. Although the vast majority of cases are non-contentious cases, the applicant must still follow the formal procedures laid down the Court of Protection Rules in respect of any application to the Court and these are described in more detail in Chapter 3. Even in a straightforward and non-contentious application for the appointment of a deputy, the applicant must within 21 days of issue of the application arrange for notices in form COP15 to be sent or given within the 21-day period required by Rule 70(1). A person notified has 21 days in which to respond and file an acknowledgement of notification if he or she wishes to oppose the application or apply for some other measure. The applicant meanwhile must file with the Court a certificate of service in form COP20 within seven days of the notification being given. If there is no objection and the application is in order, the Court will proceed to make the order appointing the deputy. In the interests of efficiency, sealed copies of the order may be sent out immediately, but the order will not be effective immediately. The order may not come into effect for a defined period (generally, one month) to enable the applicant to provide security.

Notices are dealt with in more detail at **3.16** and at **5.14–5.17** below. Security is dealt with in more detail at **5.22** below and the form of the order and the scope of the deputy's authority is dealt with at **5.20** below. The nature of the deputy's status and the difficulties faced with acting under the Mental Capacity Act are dealt with at **4.5**.

Notice to P

5.14   It is a fundamental human right of any person to be informed of a legal process that affects that person. The Mental Health Act 1983 procedure for the appointment of a receiver recognised this. The applicant would have to hand the patient a letter from the Public Guardianship Office and then complete a certificate of service. Part 7 of the Court of Protection Rules brings these requirements up to date in the light of the MCA 2005 core principles.

The general principle set out in Rule 42(1) is that the person concerned (P) must be notified that an application form has been issued. If, however, P is a party to the application or if on reviewing the application papers the Court directs that P should be party, then P does not need to be notified on the basis that a litigation friend will be served with the application.

Although the Rules do not refer to a prescribed form of notice, Practice Direction 7A requires notice to be given to P in COP14. However, the Rules go beyond just handing P a piece of paper. Rule 42(2) requires the person effecting notification to explain to P:

● who the applicant is;

● that the application raises the question of whether P lacks capacity in relation to a matter or matters, and what that means;

- what will happen if the court makes the order or direction that has been applied for; and

- where the application contains a proposal for the appointment of a person to make decisions on P's behalf in relation to the matter to which the application relates, details of who that person is.

A detailed verbal explanation leads to some difficulty for the person effecting notification, who may need to go to a great deal of effort to explain these matters, even if there is little prospect of comprehension or the discussion is awkward. The right of P to respond (or not to respond) to the application is a decision that P is entitled to make. Rule 46 therefore requires information to be given 'in a way that is appropriate to P's circumstances (for example, using simple language, visual aids or any other appropriate means'. This merely reflects the Act's core principles, in particular s 1(2) of the Act requires 'all practicable steps' to be taken to help P make the decision and s 3(2) which requires such steps to include an explanation given 'in a way that is appropriate to his circumstances (using simple language, visual aids or any other means).'

P must be notified 'as soon as practicable' and no later than 21 days after the application form was issued (Rule 46(3)).

Dispensing with notice

5.15   The Court may dispense with the requirement to notify P under Rule 49. As has been mentioned above, it is an important right of a person to be notified of such an important matter that concerns him fundamentally. A strong prima facie case therefore needs to be made for notice to be dispensed with. Practice Direction 7A explains that an application to dispense with notification might be made if:

> 'for example, P is in a permanent vegetative state or a minimally conscious state; or where notification by the applicant is likely to cause significant and disproportionate distress to P.'

An application to dispense with notification is made using the Part 10 procedure (see **3.22** above).

Form of notice given to P

5.16   Form COP14, which must be given to P as a record of the matter, is one of the least helpful forms provided by the Court. The form provides spaces for the name and address of the person to whom the application relates, the case number and date of issue, the name of the applicant and then a large blank space headed 'this notice is to tell you that'. It is then for the applicant to fill in the form to explain what the application is about. The guidance notes (Form COP14A) describe the form as one 'which explains the matter for which notification is being provided'. Thus the applicant must show this information in writing as well as ensuring that a personal explanation is given.

Rule 47 further requires that P must be provided with a form for acknowledging notification. This is a standard form COP5. Not only must the applicant fill this in correctly, but P needs to be given a form that will either be wholly incomprehensible or which requires further explanation. It is another form that is less than satisfactory as the same form encompasses persons notified who may apply to be joined as parties as well as respondents who wish to take a part in the proceedings.

Rule 72(2) allows P a period of 21 days in which to apply to the Court to object to the application and be joined as a party. This does not of course prevent P from subsequently asking for an order to be reviewed or applying to be joined as a party; it does however allow the Court to progress the application.

Having drafted forms COP14 and COP15, explained the application to P and handed P the forms, the applicant must then, within seven days of giving notice, file a certificate of notification (COP20) with the Court (Rule 48). Form COP20 is another form that is designed for a variety of parties and the person giving notice to P must complete section 4 of the form to confirm that P has received the information

Notification to friends and relatives

5.17   As soon as practicable and no more than 21 days after an application has been issued, the applicant must notify the persons specified in form COP1 (at section 4.2). The persons to be notified that an application has been issued and whether the application relates to property or welfare matters or both and of the order sought are the persons specified in the relevant Practice Direction (Rule 70(1)). Practice Direction 9B, which complements the rule, identifies the 'persons specified' who should be notified and is covered in detail at **3.10**. The aim of the Practice Direction is to ensure that at least three close relatives are notified of the application.

The Rules are necessarily complicated in that they apply to every type of situation. An application to appoint a deputy should by its nature be necessary and non-contentious and the majority of applications proceed on that basis. There is no need to involve respondents and provide them with full details of the application with all that entails. The notification process is a simple and effective way of ensuring that those close to the person concerned are aware of the application and have an opportunity to raise concerns or make an objection.

Notification is effected by providing the 'persons specified' with a form of notice (COP15). Like Form COP14, the standard form provides room for some very basic details and then requires the applicant to fill in the boxes under the following headings:

- the matter the court has been asked to decide; and

- order(s) the court has been asked to make.

The problem faced by the applicant is that Form COP15 does not explain why the application is being made and what the proposed deputy may or may not do. The Mental Health Act 1983 procedure for the appointment of a receiver required an applicant to send out a Notification Letter to any relatives of a closer degree or anyone else who should be told about the application, because of their close connection. This provided a great deal of information about the role of a receiver. In most cases, it had the effect of making notified persons grateful that the applicant was offering to take on the role of receiver; if it gave rise to objections, they would at least be well informed! It may therefore be necessary for an applicant to go to some effort to involve close family members and other persons who should be notified to explain the process to them or to provide some further information about the role of the deputy and the qualities of the proposed deputy. However, an applicant may also have to exercise discretion over the amount of personal information that should be disclosed.

Service of notification

5.18   Part 6 of the Rules applies to service of documents generally and is dealt with at **3.20** above. The form can be delivered personally, delivered at a person's home address or last known address or sent by first class post to that address (Rule 31). A notified person must also be provided with a form for acknowledging notification. This is a standard form COP5. This provides a period of 21 days in which the person notified can apply to the Court to object to the application and be joined as a party (Rule 72(2)).

The applicant must furthermore within seven days of giving or sending the notice form, file a certificate of notification (COP20) with the Court in respect of each person notified (Rule 48).

Order appointing the deputy

5.19   The Court may also require additional information to complete the order. However, most orders are not tailored to P's circumstances in the same way that an order appointing a receiver used to be. Where a receiver was appointed, the order would usually authorise the closure of specified accounts or the disposal of named assets such as shares or a property. The order would appoint a receiver, who had no authority except to do the things specified in the order.

In contrast, an order appointing a deputy is very widely drafted and will generally not limit the scope of the deputy's authority (notwithstanding the principle set out in s 16(4)(b) of the MCA 2005 that the powers conferred on the deputy should be as limited in scope and duration as is reasonably practicable). The deputy may do everything except what is beyond the scope of his authority, whether by operation of law or by the terms of the order itself. The role is similar to that of an attorney who may do everything he is lawfully permitted to do, subject to any restrictions or conditions contained in the power appointing him. As with an attorney, it is left to the deputy to work within the framework of the Act, a dilemma that is considered in more detail in Chapter 4. The Court's principal concerns are whether a deputy needs to be appointed, and if so, whether the proposed deputy is suitable. Most orders will provide a deputy with authority that is not restricted in time or scope (see **5.20** below). However, if the case is unusual, contentious or complex, the deputy's authority may be restricted by the terms of the order appointing him (see **5.21** below).

The order appointing a deputy cannot be issued until at least 21 days after the last notification has been given by the applicant. If there are no objections or applications in response and there is no need for the Court to issue directions for a hearing or for the service of further evidence, the Court will draw up and issue the order. The order will be made by a judge in chambers without a hearing and will be dated with the date the order was made by the judge. It may take longer for the order to be drawn up, sealed and issued. The issue date will be endorsed on the order. Sealed copies of the order are then sent to the applicant or, where a solicitor is acting, the solicitor.

Where the deputy is appointed to deal with property, the order will also provide for the security to be given by the deputy. In most cases such an order will not be effective until security is in place or there will be a delay of a month before the order can be effective so as to provide time for security to be put in place.

Content and scope of order

5.20   The order appointing a deputy will be headed with the name of the judge making the order, the address of the court in which it was made and an order date. The order will then recite the statutory premises on which it is made:

(a)   that the Court is satisfied that [P] is unable to make various decisions for himself in relation to a matter or matters concerning his property and affairs and/or personal welfare (as the case may be) because of an impairment of, or a disturbance in the functioning of, his mind or brain; and

(b)   the Court is satisfied that the purpose for which the order is needed cannot be as effectively achieved in a way that is less restrictive of his rights and freedom of action.

Most orders will be no more specific than this, referring to 'various decisions' that a person lacks capacity to make. The Court therefore does not need to address the actual decisions a person cannot make, which will be left to the deputy to address in practice.

The order will then confirm the appointment of a named individual or individuals (or in respect of property and affairs, a trust corporation) as deputy 'to make decisions on behalf of [the person concerned] that he is unable to make for himself in relation to his property and affairs subject to any conditions or restrictions set out in this order'. Again, the wording is quite vague: the deputy has authority to make decisions that P is unable to make; what decisions P can make and when, are subject to the deputy knowing when he can or cannot act. However, it is important to note that while the deputy only has authority to make decisions that P lacks capacity to make (MCA

2005, s 20(1)), the deputy is by virtue of his appointment the statutory agent of P (see **4.3**).

In order to avoid any doubt that the deputy is constrained by the MCA 2005 rather than the wording of the order, the order will also state that the deputy 'must apply the principles set out in section 1 of the Mental Capacity Act 2005 and have regard to the guidance in the Code of Practice to the Act'.

Where the order relates to P's property and affairs, it will generally be drafted in a similarly all-encompassing form, conferring authority in the following terms:

1. The court confers general authority on the deputy to take possession or control of the property and affairs of [P] and to exercise the same powers of management and investment as he has as beneficial owner, subject to the terms and conditions set out in this order.

2. The deputy may make provision for the needs of anyone who is related to or connected with [P], if he provided for or might be expected to provide for that person's needs, by doing whatever he did or might reasonably be expected to do to meet those needs.

3. The deputy may (without obtaining any further authority from the court) dispose of [P]'s money or property by way of gift to any charity to which he made or might have been expected to make gifts and on customary occasions to persons who are related to or connected with him, provided that the value of each such gift is not unreasonable having regard to all the circumstances and, in particular, the size of his estate.

4. For the purpose of giving effect to any decision the deputy may execute or sign any necessary deeds or documents.

The deputy's power to take 'possession or control' extends to calling in and receiving any property that P owns or to receive any income P is entitled to. The authority therefore extends to selling investments or property and closing bank accounts. The deputy's power of management and investment is contained in the term 'beneficial owner' which is familiar in trust law and gives the deputy the legal right to deal with and administer assets, even if he holds them in a fiduciary role. The authority to buy and sell property is confirmed by the power to execute or sign deeds and documents.

In most cases a deputy is also authorised to maintain or provide for the needs of others and to make small gifts to charity. These terms are borrowed from the powers allowed to an attorney acting under an EPA under MCA 2005, Sch 4 para 3(2) and 3(3)(b). The deputy does have a great deal of discretion to use this power appropriately.

Small gifts and maintenance are considered in more detail in Chapter 13.

The order will also set out the deputy's responsibility to report to the Public Guardian. A deputy's reporting obligations are considered in more detail at **7.8–7.11** below.

Limitations in order

5.21   Section 16(4) of the MCA 2005 sets out the principle that the powers conferred on a deputy should be 'as limited in scope and duration as is reasonably practicable in the circumstances'. The circumstances usually require the deputy to have the wide discretion set out above, even if that is at odds with the principle set out in s 16(4). The requirements of the judicial process come first and the responsibility of applying the Act's overriding principles are left firmly with the deputy.

The scope of a deputy's authority may however be limited if the circumstances require, in one or more of the following ways:

● by using a sunset clause, limiting the order to a particular period, so that it comes to an end on the expiry of a fixed period of time;

● by restricting the amount the deputy can spend in any one year;

● by appointing a second deputy (for instance where a professional deputy is appointed to act alongside a relative to administer a large estate); or

● by requiring the deputy to make a new application to deal with a further matter that cannot be dealt with immediately.

A welfare deputy may for instance be appointed for a particular purpose, such as a move to a new nursing home. There is no need for the order to continue indefinitely. In financial cases, especially where a large estate or damages award is involved, the Court will in effect make an interim appointment. The family may suddenly have a large sum of money to invest and need to set up a care regime. There may be some uncertainty as to whether a solicitor or a parent should remain as deputy in the long term. The deputy has an opportunity to be tested and to come back to the Court with a new application in perhaps two or three years, providing the Court with an account of his conduct over the period in question or an explanation as to what further authority might be required to deal with the long term management of the award. The Court can review the progress made in setting up the care regime and whether a new deputy should be appointed.

Where expenditure is restricted, the Court will allow expenditure to that level, thus requiring the deputy to make a new application if a larger expense is required. For instance where there is a large damages award, it might not be appropriate for a deputy to have unrestricted access to several million pounds. The annual care costs, tax and household bills might (for example) come to £80,000 a year. The order might provide for a maximum sum of £100,000 that can be withdrawn from the Court Funds Office in any one year. The advantages of this type of order are that it respects the principle of s 16(4), provides the deputy with discretion as to how he spends the money that needs to be spent and protects the capital in the estate. The problem caused by this approach is that the onus is on the applicant to provide a budget for the maximum expenditure required for a year and any anticipated expenses. Thus the applicant must be aware of any special expenses such as the payment of a tax bill, the purchase of a car or a property. Otherwise the applicant must contend with the effort, expense and delay of making a new application to the Court.

Security

5.22   The giving of security is the ultimate safeguard of P's interests and distinguishes the protection available to P where a deputy is appointed from the unregulated status of an attorney acting under a LPA or EPA. Security must also be provided on an ongoing basis, so that the Court of Protection – which has no further interest in the case once the deputy is appointed – is responsible for setting security but then leaves it to the Public Guardian to hold and administer the security.

When the Court makes an order appointing a deputy, the order will specify what security the deputy must give for the discharge of his functions (MCA 2005, s 19(9)(a)). In the past, the level of security would be sufficient to cover approximately 150 per cent of the estimated annual income or if greater, the amount of expenditure anticipated over an 18-month period (for instance where capital was being released to pay care fees). The security bond would pay out immediately on the default of the receiver and with 18 months' income in hand, there would be time to recover any lost or misappropriated assets especially if the receiver carried professional liability insurance. Under the MCA 2005 regime the situation is more complicated, as a deputy has access to significantly greater sums of money under direct control. The level of insurance set by the Court and the consequent cost of providing insurance have increased significantly since October 2007.

Insurance must be arranged with an insurance company approved by the Court or by means of a single master policy with Norwich Union, brokered through HSBC plc. At present, the cost of insurance is not high, so long as the amount secured is reasonable. The cost of insurance at £100,000 is a reasonable £250 per annum; if however a deputy has authority to sell the family home and deal with the investments, assets under his control may amount to £1,000,000 and if security is set at that level, the annual cost is £2,000. Some judges within the Court of Protection have seen the indemnity bond as a means of insuring all the assets under the deputy's control even though the deputy may have his own professional liability cover. For obvious reasons, such large sums of insurance – in direct consequence of orders issued by the Court – have proved controversial. In such cases the estate is either burdened with a huge expense or time and effort (for both applicant and Court staff) need to be spent in having the security reviewed on a reconsideration. The Court has therefore become more careful in drafting appropriate orders, introducing the limitations described above at **5.21**. Where significant sums are involved, for instance if a substantial lump sum is paid in damages, the Court will expect a professional deputy to be appointed either alone or jointly with a family member.

The premium is payable from the estate of the person concerned. On a first application where the applicant pays the premium this may be reimbursed from the estate once the deputy has been appointed and has funds under his control.

The premiums currently payable where security is effected through the Court Master Bond are set according to the following tariff:

Security	Premium	Security	Premium	Security	Premium
£5,000	£25.00	£800,000	£1,600.00	£2,850,000	£5,700.00
£10,000	£35.00	£825,000	£1,650.00	£2,900,000	£5,800.00
£15,000	£45.00	£850,000	£1,700.00	£2,950,000	£5,900.00
£16,000	£80.00	£875,000	£1,750.00	£3,000,000	£6,000.00
£20,000	£60.00	£900,000	£1,800.00	£3,050,000	£6,100.00
£25,000	£70.00	£925,000	£1,850.00	£3,100,000	£6,200.00
£30,000	£80.00	£950,000	£1,900.00	£3,150,000	£6,300.00
£35,000	£90.00	£975,000	£1,950.00	£3,200,000	£6,400.00
£40,000	£100.00	£1,000,000	£2,000.00	£3,250,000	£6,500.00
£50,000	£125.00	£1,050,000	£2,100.00	£3,300,000	£6,600.00
£60,000	£150.00	£1,100,000	£2,200.00	£3,350,000	£6,700.00
£70,000	£175.00	£1,150,000	£2,300.00	£3,400,000	£6,800.00
£80,000	£200.00	£1,200,000	£2,400.00	£3,450,000	£6,900.00
£90,000	£225.00	£1,250,000	£2,500.00	£3,500,000	£7,000.00
£100,000	£250.00	£1,300,000	£2,600.00	£3,550,000	£7,100.00
£110,000	£275.00	£1,350,000	£2,700.00	£3,600,000	£7,200.00
£120,000	£300.00	£1,400,000	£2,800.00	£3,650,000	£7,300.00
£130,000	£325.00	£1,450,000	£2,900.00	£3,700,000	£7,400.00
£140,000	£350.00	£1,500,000	£3,000.00	£3,750,000	£7,500.00
£150,000	£375.00	£1,550,000	£3,100.00	£3,800,000	£7,600.00
£175,000	£420.00	£1,600,000	£3,200.00	£3,850,000	£7,700.00
£200,000	£460.00	£1,650,000	£3,300.00	£3,900,000	£7,800.00
£225,000	£495.00	£1,700,000	£3,400.00	£3,950,000	£7,900.00
£250,000	£525.00	£1,750,000	£3,500.00	£4,000,000	£8,000.00
£275,000	£550.00	£1,800,000	£3,600.00	£4,050,000	£8,100.00
£300,000	£600.00	£1,850,000	£3,700.00	£4,100,000	£8,200.00
£325,000	£650.00	£1,900,000	£3,800.00	£4,150,000	£8,300.00
£350,000	£700.00	£1,950,000	£3,900.00	£4,200,000	£8,400.00
£375,000	£750.00	£2,000,000	£4,000.00	£4,250,000	£8,500.00
£400,000	£800.00	£2,050,000	£4,100.00	£4,300,000	£8,600.00
£425,000	£850.00	£2,100,000	£4,200.00	£4,350,000	£8,700.00
£450,000	£900.00	£2,150,000	£4,300.00	£4,400,000	£8,800.00
£475,000	£950.00	£2,200,000	£4,400.00	£4,450,000	£8,900.00
£500,000	£1,000.00	£2,250,000	£4,500.00	£4,500,000	£9,000.00
£525,000	£1,050.00	£2,300,000	£4,600.00	£4,550,000	£9,100.00
£550,000	£1,100.00	£2,350,000	£4,700.00	£4,600,000	£9,200.00
£575,000	£1,150.00	£2,400,000	£4,800.00	£4,650,000	£9,300.00
£600,000	£1,200.00	£2,450,000	£4,900.00	£4,700,000	£9,400.00
£625,000	£1,250.00	£2,500,000	£5,000.00	£4,750,000	£9,500.00
£650,000	£1,300.00	£2,550,000	£5,100.00	£4,800,000	£9,600.00
£675,000	£1,350.00	£2,600,000	£5,200.00	£4,850,000	£9,700.00
£700,000	£1,400.00	£2,650,000	£5,300.00	£4,900,000	£9,800.00
£725,000	£1,450.00	£2,700,000	£5,400.00	£4,950,000	£9,900.00
£750,000	£1,500.00	£2,750,000	£5,500.00	£5,000,000	£10,000.00
£775,000	£1,550.00	£2,800,000	£5,600.00		

Costs

5.23 The order appointing a deputy will provide the basis for the applicant recovering any legal costs incurred in making the application as well as any ongoing costs for acting as or for the deputy. Thus the order will provide for the reimbursement of out of pocket expenses and where a solicitor has been instructed, for the payment of a solicitor's costs on a fixed costs basis, by agreement with the deputy, or (in default of agreement) by means of detailed assessment. Where the deputy is a solicitor, then costs can be taken by way of fixed costs or by means of detailed assessment.

Costs are dealt with in more detail in Chapter 12.

Notifying P (again)

5.24   As the order appointing a deputy is a final order, P must be notified in accordance with the provisions of Rules 44 and 46.

As soon as practicable and in any event within 21 days of the order being made, the person effecting notification must explain to P the effect of the order and that P may seek advice and assistance in relation to the matter. As with notification of issue of the application (see **5.14** above), the explanation must be made in a way that is appropriate to P's circumstances. But not only must an explanation be given, P must also be provided with a written explanation in COP14, as well as a form for acknowledging service (Form COP5). Form COP14 is unhelpfully short and apart from some basic details, the form contains the words 'this notice is to tell you that' and then leaves a large box for the applicant to complete. The guidance in form COP14A recommends the following wording: 'a final order about you has been made by the Court of Protection'.

Having explained the final order and handed over form COP14 to P, the person effecting notification must then complete – for a second time – a certificate of service in COP20. He must certify in response to the following propositions in paragraph 4.10 as follows:

'Were you notifying the person to whom the application relates of a final order of the court?

If Yes, please confirm that you explained to the person:·

– the effect of the order; and

– that they may seek advice and assistance in relation to the order.'

Form COP20 must be returned to the Court within seven days of the notification being effected (Rule 48).

Reconsideration of order

5.25   It is important for an applicant or, if he is not the applicant, the deputy, to check the order carefully. It is often the case that the applicant or the Court will have overlooked a particular matter for which specific authority is required. The applicant may also be concerned that the security is set at too high a level or that conditions set by the order are inappropriate, for example if it is likely that a budget set by the Court is insufficient or does not take account of a significant expense such as the purchase of a property.

The applicant, as with P or any other party to an application, has a right to apply to the Court for an order made without a hearing to be reconsidered. An application for reconsideration is made in accordance with Rule 89 using the Part 10 procedure and must be made within 21 days of the order being served on the applicant.

Reconsideration of an order and appeals against orders made at a hearing are considered in more detail at **3.44**.

Emergency applications and interim measures

5.26   An application for the appointment of a deputy may take several months to complete. Delays are not uncommon, and it is easy for the applicant to overlook one of the procedural steps outlined above, further delaying the application. The Court's service standards require a direction to be made within 21 weeks of an application being made. There may already have been a significant delay in preparing an application and obtaining necessary medical evidence.

During this lengthy period, steps may need to be taken sooner to protect the estate of the person concerned, for example:

● to obtain access to funds to pay nursing home or care fees or general living expenses;

● to meet a liability under a contract or to pay outstanding care costs;

● to pay for the maintenance of a dependant;

● to obtain custody of relevant documents such as share certificates, title deeds or a will;

● to sell a property or determine a lease;

● to purchase a property;

● to make a claim for benefits;

● to enter into an agreement with a local authority or nursing home for the provision of accommodation;

● to take up a rights issue or share entitlement;

● to issue proceedings to recover assets where there has been fraud, or to comply with a time limit in civil proceedings;

● to apply for a grant of letters of administration;

● to protect assets which may be vulnerable to theft or fraud;

● to obtain further information about the property and affairs of the patient so that a full application can be made in due course; and

● generally where one or more specific matters need to be dealt with immediately.

In welfare applications it may be even more important to determine whether treatment should proceed or not, long before a hearing takes place. However, in any case where interim provision is required, the onus is on the applicant to show why the provision needs to be made and cannot wait until the substantive order is made. The Court does have power under MCA 2005, s 48, so long as there is reason to believe that P lacks capacity in relation to the matter and so long as the provision is within the scope of the Court's authority, to 'make an order or give directions in respect of any matter pending the determination of an application to it'.

There is no simple way of bringing such a matter to the Court's attention. There is no place in the forms for the applicant to use and a simple letter that may have sufficed under the Mental Health Act 1983 jurisdiction is no longer sufficient. If a matter needs to be dealt with urgently or before a substantive order can be made, the applicant must make a separate application within the proceedings using the Part 10 procedure. So long as the procedure is followed and evidence is supplied, a Part 10 application can be made before, after or together with the main application.

While this may appear overly bureaucratic, it is a way of detaching the urgent measure from the mainstream business of the application and bringing it to the front of the queue. Urgent and interim applications are dealt with in more detail at **3.24–3.26** and see also Rule 82 and Practice Direction 9B.

The Court is not obliged to act on an application. The Court has wide powers to make an order of its own motion (Rule 27). This may be necessary where a LPA or EPA has been revoked and a person's affairs have not been administered during the course of a dispute over the validity of the power of attorney or the suitability of the attorney. In such a case a deputy may need to be appointed. The Court may issue a direction authorising the Official Solicitor or another party to make an application while also making an interim order for the release of funds or the protection of assets. If there is no one willing or able to make an application in such circumstances, the Public Guardian does have standing to be an applicant.

Interim deputy

5.27   Under the Mental Health Act 1983 procedure, the Court of Protection would use its powers under r 42(1) of the Court of Protection Rules 2001 to appoint an interim receiver (referred to as a *'receiver ad interim'*). This was done where, for instance, a receiver needed to be appointed urgently to take control of the estate and report to the Court, often where there was a risk of assets being dissipated or being the object of financial abuse or fraud. Under the new procedure, there is no specific reference to an interim deputy, although the MCA 2005, s 48 allows the Court to make interim orders 'pending the determination of an application'. In practice a deputy can be appointed immediately with suitably limited powers, with the appointment being limited to a particular period. Thus a deputy could be appointed for a six-month period which would give time to protect assets, obtain information and carry out any investigations. The order is simply a conventional order limited in time (see **5.22**). The terms of the order may however also include a specific direction to investigate and report to the Public Guardian. If the circumstances then required, the interim deputy would be able to make a further application for a substantive or long-term appointment.

Contested applications

5.28   A first application for the appointment of a deputy will usually be made by one applicant. If another person is given notice and objects to the applicant being appointed he needs to submit Form COP5 showing why a different order should be made and either providing a witness statement setting out the grounds for objection or asking for directions to be issued, which would include a direction for more time to file evidence. A person who is not notified but wishes to oppose an application needs to apply to be joined as a party (Rule 75) using the Part 10 procedure.

Contested applications may arise when a solicitor or local authority makes an application where the interests of a person need to be protected urgently and the close involvement of relatives is not immediately apparent. On notifying relatives one of them may prefer to be appointed deputy. Families are also prone to disagree among themselves as to who should or should not be a deputy and the person concerned may also object to the applicant being appointed. Where one person takes the lead in making the application, the applicant or his solicitor should endeavour to present the application in a non-confrontational manner and explain that any person may make an application and any person notified or with a genuine concern for a person's best interests has a right to object.

Where two or more people cannot agree on who should be appointed they should at least agree on one of them or a solicitor commencing the application. Where one party has already applied there is no need for another party to make a separate application for the appointment of a deputy and the costs of the second application would not be recoverable from the patient's estate. The parties must avoid unnecessary costs being incurred. Rule 162 provides that:

> 'Where two or more persons having the same interest in relation to the matter to be determined attend any hearing by separate legal representatives, they shall not be allowed more than one set of costs of that hearing unless the court certifies that the circumstances justify separate representation.'

While it may be that two opposing prospective deputies do have separate interests, the Court is unlikely to look favourably on an application for costs from both of them if they have used the Court as a forum for a family dispute between themselves or deliberately made the process more complicated than it should have been. This conduct of the parties can be taken into account under Rule 159 if the Court chooses to depart from the general rule (Rule 156) that costs in a property and affairs case will be paid from the estate.

On receiving two or more applications the Court will usually issue directions requiring further witness statements from the parties or direct a report from one of the Medical Visitors or the Public Guardian under MCA 2005, s 49. Directions will usually set a time limit for the submission of evidence and then either set a date for a hearing in the order or provide for a hearing being listed at the first available date after evidence has been filed and served by the parties.

It may be that once evidence has been filed and served, the outcome will be obvious. It may for instance be the case that there is new medical evidence that shows that P has capacity or that his wishes can be ascertained. One party may choose to withdraw or the Court may go ahead and dismiss the objection without a hearing, leaving it open for a party to apply for a reconsideration at an attended hearing. If the matter proceeds to a hearing, the parties may be represented but must have regard to costs which may not necessarily be awarded to all the parties. It was the case under the Mental Health Act 1983 jurisdiction that parties would attend in person simply to ensure that they could air their version of events. It is likely to be more difficult now given the complexity of navigating the Court procedures, the additional fee for a hearing and the risk of a party being represented and one or other parties being at risk of quite significant costs. The Court may appoint whoever it sees fit once it has sufficient evidence to consider the matter fully with regard to all the circumstances and above all, the best interests of the person concerned. Once in a position to appoint a deputy, the Court will proceed with issuing the order. It is likely that if the matter has proved contentious or the medical evidence is unclear or likely to change, the order will be limited in time, requiring the new deputy to apply to be reappointed at a future date.

For where a deputy has already been appointed and a subsequent dispute arises over the appointment, see **6.5** below, and for proceedings generally, see Chapter 3 above.

Chapter 6

Changing and ending the deputyship

Nature of deputy's role

6.1   A deputy is appointed by the Court of Protection and holds his office at the disposal of the Court. The deputy can therefore continue to act so long as the person for whom he is appointed to act is alive and there is a valid order in place authorising him to act. The deputy's authority is of course also limited by the Mental Capacity Act 2005 (MCA 2005). There are limits to the Court's own powers as well as limits to the authority that can be delegated to a deputy (see **2.23** and **2.27**). There are also limits to what a deputy can do (see **4.6**).

The authority of the deputy will, however, continue, unless and until his authority comes to an end in one of the following ways:

- According to the terms of the order. An order appointing a deputy may be limited in time, so that it expires automatically after a fixed period.

- By an order of the Court, removing a deputy, whether or not a new deputy is appointed.

- By the occurrence of an event inconsistent with the operation of the deputyship, principally the death of the deputy or the person concerned or the recovery of the person concerned.

Replacing a deputy

6.2   If the person concerned recovers capacity, then the deputy has no authority to act, although the order appointing the deputy remains in place. Similarly, if the deputy becomes incapable, the order remains in place even though the deputy is unable to act. The bankruptcy of the deputy does not of itself revoke the appointment of a deputy, in contrast to the appointment of an attorney. However, these events may make it appropriate for the deputy to be replaced.

Other circumstances in which a deputy should be replaced include:

- the deputy is unable to carry out his duties and wishes to be replaced;

- a professional deputy wishes to retire from practice;

- the appointment of a deputy has been time limited (see **5.22**);

- a deputy is appointed on a provisional or interim basis, for instance where an elderly spouse is appointed or a solicitor is appointed in a damages case knowing that once the case is settled and a care regime set up, a family member will be appointed;

- there has been a breakdown in the relationship between the person concerned and the deputy;

- the deputy has misappropriated funds under his control, failed to deliver an account or has acted improperly;

- the appointment of the deputy is opposed and a more suitable person should be appointed; or

- there is no requirement for a deputy to act, due to the size of the estate or the nature of the assets, for instance where the assets have been transferred to a trust.

Application to replace a deputy

6.3 An application to appoint a new deputy may be made by the retiring deputy or any other person who would be entitled to apply to be appointed a deputy on a first application. An application is made in the same way as any other first application for the appointment of a deputy (see Chapter 5). The short form application is not appropriate for an application for the removal of a deputy (Practice Direction 9D, paragraph 6). It is not appropriate for the Court to make assumptions about the reasons for the change of deputy and the choice of new deputy. This is a specific decision being made by the Court which must be considered carefully in accordance with the Act's principles.

Thus the applicant must lodge the following documents:

(a) Form COP1 in duplicate;

(b) up-to-date details in Form COP1A (financial) or COP1B (welfare);

(c) up-to-date medical evidence in Form COP3;

(d) a Deputy's Declaration in Form COP4 from the proposed new deputy;

(e) a witness statement in Form COP24 explaining (with evidence) the justification for the change of deputy and addressing the best interests of the person concerned;

(f) cheque for £400 for the application fee.

If the retiring deputy is not making the application then a record of his or her consent to retirement will also need to be provided.

The applicant will need to show in the application who is to be notified or served. An existing deputy must be named as a respondent. The Court will then issue the application in the same way as on a first application for the appointment of a deputy. The persons named in the application must be notified or served as the case may be and the person concerned must also be given notice. It should then be clear whether the application is straightforward and unopposed or complex and opposed, in which case the Court will issue directions for any further evidence that needs to be submitted and an attended hearing.

In determining whether the proposed new deputy is suitable the same considerations will apply as on the first application for the appointment of a receiver (see **4.10**).

Order appointing the new deputy

6.4   The order appointing the new deputy will be in the same form as the first order appointing a deputy (see **5.20**) although the Court may modify the scope or term of the order if for instance the appointment has been contentious and needs to be reviewed again in the near future. Where a financial deputy is appointed, security will also be set in the light of the new deputy's role. The order will also confirm the revocation of the order appointing the former deputy and provide for his or her discharge subject as necessary to the passing of a final account by the Public Guardian.

The person concerned must also be notified of the new order made in accordance with Rule 44 (see **5.24**).

Disputes over the appointment of a new deputy

6.5   An application can be made to appoint a new deputy even though there is an existing deputy already in place, perhaps where another relative believes there is a possibility of fraud or mismanagement of the estate. It is, however, unusual to replace a duly appointed deputy as conflicts over the suitability of the deputy should have come to light in the application and notice procedures. Although the Court must consider such an application, there are no guidelines as to how this particular issue should be addressed. Such a situation was, however, considered in the Australian case of *Holt v Protective Comr* (1993) 31 NSWLR 227 where two brothers of the person concerned applied to be appointed manager in place of the Protective Commissioner of New South Wales. The New South Wales Court of Appeal made the following observations:

(a)   an application for the removal of a manager may be made by any interested person, including the person concerned;

(b)   the burden of proof is on the person seeking the change in the *status quo*;

(c)   it is normally necessary for the person seeking the change to show some reason why the court should remove the existing manager and appoint someone else in his or her place;

(d)   where it is shown that the existing manager is unsuitable to be the manager for the particular person (perhaps because he or she is incompetent, or has acted unlawfully or improperly, or is not acting in the best interests of the person concerned), the court will terminate the appointment and appoint some other suitable person;

(e)   if, however, the unsuitability of the existing manager is not an issue, or if the applicant fails to prove that the existing receiver is unsuitable, it must be shown forensically that the best interests of the person concerned will in some way be advanced or promoted by discharging the existing manager and appointing another receiver in his or her place;

(f)   the standard of proof is the usual civil standard, namely the 'balance of probabilities'. It does not have to be 'clear and convincing' or 'compelling';

(g)   in deciding what is in a person's best interests the court will have regard to all the circumstances.

A person who wishes to remove an existing deputy has a considerable evidential and logistical burden to overcome and must also be aware of the costs involved in making the application, which may not be recovered if the application is unsuccessful. A dispute between family members as to who should take on the role of deputy is immaterial in itself, so long as the deputy is able to carry out his duties and act in the best interests of the person concerned.

Ending the deputyship – P ceases to lack capacity

6.6   The Court's jurisdiction continues only so long as a person lacks capacity and only in respect of those decisions that the person lacks capacity to make. The Court cannot seek to impose its jurisdiction where it is unnecessary and will assist a person in recovering control over his practical ability to make decisions. The Court cannot for instance leave a deputy in place just because it is convenient or safer for the protection of a person's assets.

Where an application is still in hand, the Court should be notified immediately of any improvement in the person's condition which might avoid the need for a deputy to be appointed. Medical evidence must be submitted which should address the medical evidence already before the Court and the prospects of the person's condition improving or deteriorating. If the Court is presented with two conflicting sets of medical evidence, the application may be adjourned while further evidence is obtained from the doctor or a specialist. The Court may also direct a report from one of the Court of Protection Medical Visitors. A Visitor is extremely useful in such circumstances as they are independent and able to review existing evidence objectively in the light of the legal issues involved.

If it is clear that the person's circumstances do not warrant the appointment of a deputy the application will be stayed and no order will be entered.

Where deputy already appointed

6.7   If a deputy has already been appointed, then an application must be made for an order to end the proceedings. Rule 148 specifies that such an application may be made by P, his litigation friend or any other person who is a party to the application. Thus an application may be made by the deputy.

An application to end proceedings is made in Form COP9 (see PD 23B). It is therefore treated as an application within proceedings as it refers back to the original application to appoint the deputy, even though there are no current proceedings before the Court. The benefit of this approach is that the application does not name respondents and no fee is payable on making the application.

The applicant must file his application in Form COP9, setting out the terms of the order being sought. This needs to address whether:

●   the order appointing the deputy be discharged;

●   a final account be passed or dispensed with (if agreed) and any security;

●   the deeds, will, certificates and any other documents or securities be delivered to the applicant or his solicitor;

●   any funds held by the Court Funds Office be transferred; and

●   the costs of the application and any outstanding costs of the applicant be assessed (if not agreed).

The application must be supported by medical evidence. There is no prescribed form of medical evidence, although Form COP3 might be adapted for this purpose. The medical expert should if possible address the original medical certificate (Form COP3) made at the time of the application or at least the earlier diagnosis that the person lacked capacity. The medical evidence must address what it is that the person lacked capacity to decide and that the same person now has capacity.

No further involvement of the Court required

6.8   Once a deputy has been appointed, the Court generally has no further role unless and until a new deputy is appointed. There will therefore be cases where an order is left in place long after it has ceased to be needed, perhaps where the assets have diminished or have been transferred to a trust. There will be cases where a deputy is used to acting in conjunction with a person who makes his own decisions most of the time. The person is currently in good health, the estate is more straightforward or no important decisions need to be made. The deputyship rests in place as a spare or emergency power that can be revived by the deputy if it is needed.

The continued involvement of the Public Guardian depends primarily on the size of the estate or the nature of the decisions being made in a welfare matter. If the estate has reduced through expenditure to below £16,000 in value, the Public Guardian may set supervision at Type 3 (see **7.8**), so that no annual report needs to be submitted. The authority of the deputy may therefore continue for several years, even though there is no formal reporting obligation.

Ending the deputyship – death of P

6.9   As on recovery of a person, the Court no longer has jurisdiction to make decisions or to administer property and affairs after the death of P. No further directions or orders may be given other than to terminate proceedings and deal with outstanding procedural matters such as discharging security, releasing funds or assessing costs.

The deputy's powers also come to an end upon the death of P although the former deputy still has a duty to account for his conduct during the period until the date of death.

As soon as the deputy is informed of the death of the person concerned he should notify the Public Guardian, whose role it is to maintain a register of currently appointed deputies (MCA 2005, s 58(1)(b)). A certified copy of the death certificate must be sent to the Public Guardian as soon as the death has been registered. It is then for the Public Guardian to decide whether a final report is to be submitted. In practice, it appears that the Public Guardian will not always require a final report on the basis that no decisions need to be reported and where assets are involved, the former deputy will account to the deceased's personal representatives.

The former deputy should also make an application in form COP9 to be formally discharged as deputy and for the security bond to be discharged. The application should exhibit a copy of the death certificate and confirmation that the Public Guardian has either passed a final account or does not require a final account (PD 23B paragraph 9).

Costs and remuneration

6.10   The death of the person concerned frequently leaves issues of costs and remuneration outstanding in respect of work carried out prior to the date of death. The Court will expect costs where possible to be agreed with the personal representative, so that there is no need to go to the effort and expense of having costs assessed.

Where costs have been incurred prior to the date of death and no order has yet been made for their payment, an order that such costs be charged on or paid out of the estate may be made within six years of the date of death (Rule 165). Costs are defined at Rule 155(c) as including fees charged on behalf of a party 'in proceedings.' The Court can therefore only award costs after the death of a person in respect of actual proceedings. There is therefore no basis for the recovery of costs if no proceedings had been issued.

Fees owed to Court and Public Guardian

6.11   There is no winding up or closure fee, although an annual administration fee may be due and may be apportioned for the period to date of death. Liability for the payment of any such fee is the responsibility of the estate (Public Guardian (Fees, etc) Regulations 2007 (SI 2007/2051), reg 8). Likewise the estate is liable for payment of any outstanding application or other Court fee.

Further costs incurred after the date of death

6.12   A former deputy acting in a professional capacity must also be aware that as the Court has no authority after the death of the person concerned, it cannot authorise payment for any further work that may be carried out. It is the responsibility of the former deputy to carry out any outstanding obligations to the Court or the Public Guardian, but the deputy must look to the deceased's personal representatives for payment of any costs incurred.

Duties of the personal representative

6.13   It is the responsibility of the personal representative to deal with administration and winding up of the deceased's affairs. The personal representative will need to deal with the following matters:

● if not done by the former deputy, notify the Public Guardian and ensure that a certified copy of the death certificate is supplied;

● separately notify the Court Funds Office and obtain a certificate of the fund in Court as at the date of the death;

● obtain from the former deputy sufficient details of the estate to enable the estate to be duly administered. The deputy no longer has authority over the receivership bank account, which is treated in the same way as any other asset of a deceased person. Therefore, the account is suspended until probate has been granted;

● obtain details of any outstanding debts and expenses such as nursing home fees and the out-of-pocket expenses of the former deputy as these are liabilities of the estate and must be paid by the personal representative;

● settle any outstanding fees due to the Court or the Public Guardian;

● agree the costs of the former deputy's solicitor for work carried out up to the date of death. If costs cannot be agreed then an application can be made in Form COP9 for assessment by the Court. Any such costs are a liability of the estate and will reduce the value of the estate chargeable to inheritance tax;

● obtain the will of the deceased. The will is usually in the safe custody of the deceased's bank or with the deceased's solicitor. The former deputy is expected to have a record of where it is stored. Any undertaking to hold the will to the order of the Public Guardian or the Court (which would be given where a statutory will is made) ceases and the will can be released to the personal representative by the person holding it;

● examine the deceased's will to check for any specific gifts which may have been disposed of on the authority of the Court during the lifetime of the person concerned. The proceeds of sale of such gifts may have been preserved under MCA 2005, Sch 2 para 7.

Release of funds

6.14   Although the fund in Court will not be released without production of the grant of probate (unless the estate is worth less than £5,000) the Court Funds Office will authorise the release of funds to pay inheritance tax which needs to be paid on delivery of the HM Revenue & Customs Account. The personal representative's solicitor will need to request the payment in writing and supply a copy of the HM Revenue & Customs Account. The Court Funds Office will then release sufficient funds to pay the inheritance tax assessed, payment being made to HM Revenue & Customs either directly or via the personal representative's solicitor.

Chapter 7

The duties of a property and affairs deputy

Nature of deputy's role

7.1   A deputy acting for a person under the Mental Capacity Act 2005 (MCA 2005) may have a difficult and complex role to fulfil. Although a deputy is appointed to make decisions concerning a person's 'property and affairs' (MCA 2005, s 16(1)(b)) and may have very wide discretion conferred on him by the Court of Protection, the term 'property and affairs' is not defined. The term was used in Part Vll of the Mental Health Act 1983 and has been construed according to its everyday meaning. In *F v West Berkshire Health Authority,* Lord Brandon referred to the expression 'the affairs of patients' as one that:

> '… cannot properly be construed as having the wider meaning [to encompass the welfare of the patient]. It must rather be construed as including only business matters, legal transactions and other dealings of a similar kind.' ([1989] 2 All ER 545 at 554)

However, while a receiver acting under the Mental Health Act 1983 had no authority to make welfare decisions, he still had to have regard to the welfare of the patient. His principal duty was to safeguard and manage the estate 'for the maintenance or other benefit of the patient. Naturally a conscientious receiver would have regard to the wishes and welfare of the patient. But a receiver's formal obligations seem, with hindsight, to have been delightfully straightforward. A receiver had a fiduciary duty to manage the assets and do whatever was necessary to provide for the needs of the patient. A deputy charged with making decisions in respect of a person's property and affairs under the MCA 2005 also has the same fiduciary duty to the estate and this should not be overlooked. Section 19(6) of MCA 2005 confirms that:

> 'A deputy is to be treated as P's agent in relation to anything done or decided by him within the scope of his appointment and in accordance with this Part [of the MCA 2005]'

The law of principal and agent apply to the relationship between a person and a property and affairs deputy appointed to make decisions, except that the deputy as agent has a duty to account to the Court instead of the person who lacks capacity. Halsbury's Laws (vol 1 para 73) describes the fiduciary relationship as follows:

> The relationship of agency is of a fiduciary nature. In some cases, commonly where property or money has been placed in the hands of the agent for a specific purpose, the agent becomes a trustee for his principal.

In all cases the agent owes duties of a fiduciary character to the principal, for example to keep accounts, to disclose any conflict of interest and not to receive any secret commission or bribe.

A fiduciary also has a duty to act within the scope of his authority, act with due care and skill (in accordance with any professional or other skills that are held out as being relevant) and not to delegate acts of a discretionary nature. A deputy must however also act:

- in accordance with the limitations of the Act, with authority to act only where the person lacks capacity (see **4.7**);

- in the person's best interests, taking account of the Act's principles and the Code of Practice (see **1.21** to **1.23**);

- in accordance with the authority given to him by the Court;

- with regard to the requirements of the Public Guardian; and

- in accordance with any actual wishes or instructions that can be made known.

Maintenance and benefit of P – the first consideration

7.2   The MCA 2005 does not tell a deputy what he must do for the person for whom he is authorised to make decisions. The Court of Protection empowers the deputy to make decisions and those decisions must be made in the best interests of the person concerned. It should go without saying that a deputy must act to the best of his ability to maintain the person concerned. It is a fundamental duty of any agent to act conscientiously to protect the assets in his care and apply them for the benefit of his principal.

However, a deputy cannot simply apply funds to provide the 'best' level of care. In deciding what is in a person's best interests, regard must be had to matters such as past and present wishes and the factors the person would consider if he had capacity. It is for instance not uncommon for a certain type of elderly person to have a long history of avoiding any form of expenditure. A deputy applying the Act's principles must take account of these characteristics and should not assume that a wealthy widow who wishes to live in a hostel might not be happier there than anywhere else. But neither should a deputy neglect the maintenance and benefit of a person who might when he had capacity have resisted such benefits or the expenditure required. As has been mentioned above (see **1.23**), a decision-maker cannot be expected to make an unwise decision. As Lewison J emphasised in *Re P*:

> '… once the decision-making power shifts to a third party (whether carer, deputy or the court) I cannot see that it would be a proper exercise for a third-party decision-maker consciously to make an unwise decision merely because P would have done so. A consciously unwise decision will rarely if ever be in P's best interests.' ([2009] EWHC 163 (Ch) at paragraph 42).

A deputy should also consider the wishes of those concerned for the person's welfare and whether for instance a choice of nursing home is more or less accessible to close relatives who wish to benefit. But where the interests of others relate to their interest in the person's estate as beneficiaries, those interests are very much a secondary consideration. So long as the deputy considers and takes account of the factors set out in MCA 2005, s 4(1) his overriding duty is to whatever it is within his power to do that in the best interests of the person concerned.

Responsibility of the deputy

7.3   The duties of the deputy can appear onerous and should be considered carefully before the role is accepted. In addition to his statutory and fiduciary duties, the deputy must account to the Public Guardian (who is responsible for the supervision of deputies) while being ultimately accountable to the Court for his conduct. There may appear to be several layers of overly onerous responsibilities, but formal accountability is a necessary counterpart to the judicial intervention in a person's autonomy. The aim is to provide a measure of the protection for the person who lacks capacity who is less exposed to risk than a donor of an Enduring Power of Attorney (EPA) or Lasting Power of Attorney (LPA).

A system of accountability should provide the deputy with a corresponding measure of protection. A receiver acting under the Mental Health Act 1983 would generally have a clear understanding of his role and his authority and discretion would have been tightly restricted. The aim of the MCA 2005 regime is to empower and protect a person who lacks capacity, leaving the deputy with the responsibility of deciding if he can act and how he should act. The Court confirms this approach, giving the deputy a practical autonomy to invest money, manage property and make decisions. The effect is to assign responsibility – and liability – to the deputy. A deputy will generally report or account after a decision has been taken, by which time it may be too late to repair the loss caused by an incorrect or inappropriate decision.

It is therefore crucial that deputies have a clear idea of their responsibilities. No deputy should feel obliged to act out of a sense of loyalty or obligation. A good deputy needs to be able to navigate the MCA 2005, while working for and with a person who is vulnerable and dependent on him, and taking responsibility for the management of a person's worldly goods. And while a deputy may obtain professional advice and assistance, he cannot pass over his responsibilities to another person. The Court of Protection should only be involved where a decision is required that may exceed the scope of the deputy's authority or there is real doubt or conflict as to what is in a person's best interests.

Duties of the deputy

7.4   To ensure that a prospective deputy understands the nature and extent of his duties, the Deputy's Declaration (Form COP4) which accompanies an application for the appointment of a deputy sets out 17 personal undertakings which the prospective deputy is required to agree to. These emphasise the core fiduciary duties of the deputy outlined above as well as the deputy's wider duties under the MCA 2005. These should also deter anyone who is not ready to take on the responsibility of acting as a deputy:

'1   I will have regard to the Mental Capacity Act 2005 Code of Practice and I will apply the principles of the Act when making a decision. In particular I will act in the best interests of the person to whom the application relates and I will only make those decisions that the person cannot make themselves.

2   I will act within the scope of the powers conferred on me by the court as set out in the order of appointment and will apply to the court if I feel additional powers are needed.

3   I will act with due care, skill and diligence, as I would do in making my own decisions and conducting my own affairs. Where I undertake my duties as a deputy in the course of my professional work (if relevant), I will abide by professional rules and standards.

4   I will make decisions on behalf of the person to whom the application relates as required under the court order appointing me. I will not delegate any of my powers as a deputy unless this is expressly permitted in the court order appointing me.

5   I will ensure that my personal interests do not conflict with my duties as a deputy, and I will not use my position for any personal benefit.

6   I will act with honesty and integrity, and will take any decisions made by the person to whom the application relates while they still had capacity, into account when determining their best interests.

7   I will keep the person's financial and personal information confidential (unless there is a good reason that requires me to disclose it).

8   I will comply with any directions of the court or reasonable requests made by the Public Guardian, including requests for reports to be submitted.

9   I will visit the person to whom the application relates as regularly as is appropriate and take an interest in their welfare.

10   I will work with the person to whom the application relates and any carer(s) to achieve the best quality of life for him or her within the funds available.

11   I will co-operate with any representative of the court or the Public Guardian who might wish to meet me or the person to whom the application relates to check that the deputyship arrangements are working.

12   I will immediately inform the court and the Public Guardian if I have any reason to believe that the person to whom the application relates no longer lacks capacity and may be able to manage his or her own affairs.

13   I understand that I may be required to provide security for my actions as deputy. If I am required to purchase insurance, such as a guarantee bond, I undertake to pay premiums promptly from the funds of the person to whom the application relates.

14   I will keep accounts of dealings and transactions taken on behalf of the person to whom the application relates.

15   I will keep the money and property of the person to whom the application relates separate from my own.

16   I will ensure so far as is reasonable that the person to whom the application relates receives all benefits and other income to which they are entitled, that their bills are paid and that a tax return for them is completed annually.

17   I will take reasonable steps to maintain the property of the person to whom the application relates (if applicable), for example arranging for insurance, repairs or improvements. If necessary I will arrange and oversee a sale or letting of property with appropriate legal advice.'

Duties of a receiver compared

7.5   As has already been noted, a receiver acting under the former Mental Health Act 1983 regime had similar obligations towards the patient and his estate. In its guidance material for deputies, the Public Guardian's literature explains how and when decisions should be made under the MCA 2005; it does not however provide as much guidance on the day-to-day duties of a property and affairs deputy. The former Public Guardianship Office set out a receiver's duties in greater detail in its booklet 'Duties of a Receiver.' A receiver was expected to:

* act at all times in the best interests of the client;

* safeguard the client's assets;

* open a receivership account at a local bank or building society;

* claim from the Benefits Agency all social security benefits to which the client is entitled;

* take out security and pay any bond premiums as and when required;

* prepare accounts annually or as and when required;

* ensure that the client's funds are being used to provide him or her with the best possible quality of life;

* ensure that all income is collected and bills are paid on time;

* arrange safe keeping of all deeds, documents of title, testamentary documents and other valuable items;

* keep any property in a reasonable state of repair and adequately insured;

- deal with the client's income tax and other tax matters;

- notify the Public Guardianship Office (PGO) of any changes in the client's financial situation, for example, if the client inherits property or money;

- inform the Driver and Vehicle Licensing Authority if the client holds or applies for a driving licence;

- advise the PGO if there is any likelihood of the client getting married, divorced or involved in legal proceedings;

- advise the PGO if the preparation of a will is being considered;

- co-operate with any Lord Chancellor's Visitors;

- obtain the PGO's permission before dealing with any capital monies;

- inform the PGO of the client's recovery or death;

- pay the PGO's fees out of the client's monies as and when requested;

- inform the PGO of any change in the client's address; and

- comply with all directions and orders from the Court of Protection.

Most of these duties remain the same for a deputy, save that a deputy does not need to report to or advise the Public Guardian in advance of decisions being made.

Liability of deputy

7.6   A deputy acts as the agent of the person for whom he has been appointed to act (see s 19(6) of the MCA 2005 and **4.3**). The deputy is not liable for the proper debts or expenses of the person concerned or for contracts entered into on behalf of that person acting within the scope of the authority conferred by the Court of Protection. Neither is he liable for costs incurred on behalf of the person. The decision of the Court of Appeal in *Re EG* relating to the liability of a receiver is still relevant. As Buckley LJ explained:

'[A receiver] is constituted agent by the Court which appoints him ... It is his duty, if so directed, to do many things which will involve the employment of persons such as auctioneers, land agents, valuers and so on. As matter of construction of the [Lunacy] Act it seems to me impossible to say that he is to employ these persons on his own credit and become liable to them. He employs them as agent.' (1914 1 Ch 927 at 935)

This principle does not, however, avoid liability where the deputy acts outside the scope of his authority (for instance where the person has capacity to make a decision) or is negligent. The Office of the Public Guardian publication (COP43) explains the situation as follows:

'If you act outside the terms of your authority or do not carry out your responsibilities properly you will be held accountable for your actions. For example if you fail to claim benefits to which the person is entitled, or spend their money other than for their benefit, the Court will consider that you have caused the person financial loss. Under these circumstances the Court may decide to enforce the security bond or authorise someone to bring an action against you.'

Conflicts of interest

7.7   A deputy may well have a conflict of interest, for instance a child of an elderly parent may be a beneficiary under a will or occupy a property owned by and maintained by the parent. But the duty to account, the duty to act in a person's best interests and the supervision of the Public Guardian do not prevent a deputy from dealing with the day-to-day administration of a person's estate. Thus a professional deputy will be entitled to remuneration, although his costs will be subject to assessment. A deputy who recovers his out of pocket expenses or who is financially dependent will declare the benefits received in his report. . However, the deputy is also a fiduciary and needs to take great care if any decisions are made which might benefit the deputy, especially where this goes beyond the making of small gifts or day to day maintenance. The guidance booklet COP43 explains as follows:

> 'You should not make major decisions where there is a conflict between your personal interests and the interests of the person who lacks capacity. For example if you or a member of your family wishes to purchase a property belonging to the person who lacks capacity, you will need a Court decision about whether the sale should go ahead.'

Where a decision of the Court of Protection is required, then a litigation friend will be appointed to ensure that the person concerned has independent representation.

Supervision of deputy

7.8   The supervision of deputies represents the division of responsibility between the Court and the Public Guardian. Thus the Court may direct a deputy to submit to the Public Guardian 'such reports at such times or at such intervals as the court may direct' (MCA 2005, s 19(9)(b)). The order appointing a deputy will typically provide for the deputy to submit an annual report to the Public Guardian. So although the Court directs that a report be made, it is the Public Guardian who has the statutory responsibility for supervising deputies appointed by the Court (MCA 2005, s 58 and see **2.35** to **2.37**).

Section 58 of the MCA 2005 simply states that the Public Guardian shall have the function of 'supervising deputies'. The actual content of the report may be specified by the Court, but in the absence of any specific direction from the Court, a report shall contain 'specified information or information of a specified description' where what is 'specified' means 'specified in a notice in writing given to the deputy by the Public Guardian' (Lasting Power of Attorney, Enduring Power of Attorney and Public Guardian Regulations 2007

(SI 2007/1253), reg 39). Thus the form of report or the degree of information required from a deputy is determined by the Public Guardian.

Regulation 8 of the Public Guardian (Fees, etc) Regulations 2007 (SI 2007/2051) clarifies the role of the Public Guardian in setting supervision at one of three levels: (a) type I (highest); (b) type II (lower); and (c) type III (minimal). Because of the gap between types I and ll in terms of the level of supervision as well as the cost an intermediate level of supervision, known as type llA was introduced on 1 April 2009.

A fee of £800 is set for type l supervision, £350 for type llA and £175 for type ll supervision. There is no fee for a type lll supervision.

There are no published guidelines as to which case falls in which category. In its consultation paper dated 23 October 2008 (CP26/08) it was confirmed that as at May 2008 only 5% of cases were subjected to type I supervision. The Public Guardian allocates cases to this category in the following circumstances:

- Where there was an objection to the deputy's appointment.

- Where concerns have been reported to the OPG about the deputy's management of P's funds, as a result of which the OPG considers that it needs to monitor the deputy's decision-making.

- Where there is, or will be, a damages award, and there is a need to ensure that the financial arrangements are set up satisfactorily, and are operating effectively.

- Where the sensitivity or complexity of the issues the deputy is managing mean that, at least in the short term, he may require more support.

- Where the deputy has a poor credit history, or outstanding judgment debts, or has in the past been declared bankrupt or entered into an IVA (individual voluntary arrangement), and the OPG considers that there is a need to monitor his decision-making.

- Where the deputy has financial interests that directly conflict with P's: for example, where he lives rent-free in property that P owns.

- Where a report from a Court of Protection Visitor recommends that, for the time being, close supervision is necessary.

The aim is that cases subject to type I supervision would have dedicated case workers who would take a more proactive approach in contacting a deputy and requesting information and reports of progress. Resources, as well as the Visitor service, would be concentrated on these cases.

The great majority of cases were allocated to type ll, with a much lower degree of supervision and support. This lead to concerns, expressed in the consultation paper (CP26/08) and the response that there was inadequate support for the majority of deputies. The Public Guardian proposed that the new type IIA level would provide the following services:

- telephone and letter contact on appointment;

- a letter sent to third parties advising them of the number to call should they have any concerns;

- visits will occur where a client is considered to be more vulnerable, eg usually where the client lives alone or when there was an objection to the appointment;

- letters will be sent to the care providers to gain evidence that the client's needs are being met and wishes taken into account;

- deputies will be required to complete and submit an annual report;

- investigations will be undertaken where appropriate;

- cases will receive at least an annual review of their supervision level.

Type lll 'supervision' is where no supervision is required and the file is closed (see **6.8**).

A deputy who wishes to challenge a level of supervision set by the Public Guardian has 14 days in which to request a reconsideration (Lasting Power of Attorney, Enduring Power of Attorney and Public Guardian Regulations 2007 (SI 2007/1253), reg 42). Although there is no prescribed procedure for challenging a decision of the Public Guardian (see **3.52**), the Public Guardian has confirmed in the response to the consultation paper (CP26(R)/08) published on 11 March 2009 that the level of supervision will be closely monitored and reviewed each year so that cases will move between levels according to perceived need (and risk) rather than remain by default at a particular level. The following observations and commitments were made:

'8.   The new structure for supervision of Deputies will come into effect on 1 April 2009. Most respondents who did offer an opinion agreed that the introduction of type IIA supervision would provide more flexible protection and support and that it would offer a more robust approach. We take the responses received as broad support for the proposals to introduce a new intermediate level of supervision. However, the OPG will periodically test the supervision model and will continue to develop a range of ways to further support Deputies alongside the monitoring and regulatory activities currently undertaken.

9.   There were a number of comments and suggestions received that were outside of the scope of the questions asked in the consultation. We did however note all of these suggestions and the OPG will consider them as part of its wider work on reviewing the implementation of the MCA the best way to work with stakeholders to make improvements. There were a significant number of suggestions made at the workshops, highlighting the importance of balancing "policing" and "supporting" under the banner of supervision.

10. Some common themes emerged in the comments made outside of the direct responses to questions asked. Many who offered ideas were in favour of a more "hands on" approach to supervision and ideas

revolved around more visits to clients/Deputies and more checking of reports. Such routine bureaucracy without clear value was something the OPG was keen to move away from upon its creation. Instead it was considered that a more proportionate approach to supervision, based on an analysis of the level of risk in each case, was required. The additional costs and the effect on fees would need to be weighed in the balance of some of the measures suggested. The most common suggestions revolved around:

● More visits.

● More checking of accounts/reports.

● A requirement upon Deputies to report individual large transactions.

● New requirements around the sale/purchase of property especially if proposed to be in the name of the Deputy.

● Professional Deputies should not be subject to the same supervisory regimes and requirements as lay Deputies.

● Greater transparency on how levels are set and why fee levels are as they are, ie what does the OPG do under each level.

● Broadly speaking the levels should be closer together and type III cases should still be subject to periodic review.'

Annual report

7.9   A fundamental role of a property and affairs deputy is to administer the estate of the person for whom he is acting. A deputy therefore has a fiduciary and an administrative duty to account for any assets he has received or money he has applied. However, the duty to report to the Public Guardian is only a means of checking that the deputy is doing what he should be doing. At the same time, it goes further than a mere financial report. The Public Guardian wants to know what decisions have been made in a reporting period; receipts and payments are just one component of a report. It is not enough that a deputy has been conscientious and economical with the assets; the deputy must show how those assets have been used to benefit the person and what other decisions have been made in the period, whether or not these have a financial implication.

A deputy may also choose to complete an account by reference to the financial year, but, unless the deputy so requests, accounting will be by reference to the first anniversary of the date of his appointment and each subsequent anniversary.

A standard form of account and explanatory factsheet are sent to the deputy by the Public Guardian about a month before the end of the period for which the account is required. The account must be completed and sent to the Public Guardian within eight weeks of the end of the period covered by the account.

Importance of the report

7.10   The report is the primary means by which the Public Guardian carries out his statutory duty to supervise deputies. Even if the report is submitted several weeks after the end of a reporting period, it is in the great majority of cases the only outside or official check there is on the deputy's actions. In the context of receiver's accounts, the National Audit Office described these as a 'basic check to ensure that receivers have accounted for all patients' income received and that payments made in the year were a proper charge against the patients' estate' (*Protecting the Welfare of People with Mental Incapacity*, HC 209 1998–99 at 2.19). Submission of the report is often the only way the Public Guardian is able to check that a deputy is acting appropriately, meeting a person's needs and whether there are grounds for concern. Failure to monitor accounts with sufficient rigour and act on delayed submission of accounts was one of the major criticisms of the National Audit Office in its reports on the Public Trust Office and Public Guardianship Office.

It is too early to tell whether the Public Guardian's supervisory regime is more or less effective. On the one hand, the deputy's report asks a wider range of questions and it may be easier to check the answers to determine whether the deputy is acting in a person's best interests; on the other hand, the financial data required is far more limited. The Public Guardian does not expect detailed accounts or any supporting evidence; neither is there any scrutiny of investment decisions made by the deputy. A more detailed enquiry is made in the rare cases where a closer supervision is set or if the report raises queries that require further investigation.

The report

7.11   The deputy's report is divided into two sections. Section A deals with 'decisions made' and is concerned with demonstrating that the deputy has complied with his obligations to act in a person's best interests. The report makes the following enquiries:

'1.   List the significant decision(s) that you have made as Deputy during the reporting period. (Examples of such decisions might include a change of accommodation or living arrangements, or an alteration in financial arrangements);

2.   Please tell us with whom you consulted in carrying out your role as Deputy, and what form this consultation took. If you did not consult with others, please tell us why this was. (The Code of Practice sets out a number of people you should speak to, if practical and appropriate. See chapter 5 of the Code of Practice for further information).

3.   Where our client was able to participate in decisions that affect them, what was their involvement in any of the decisions you made on their behalf?

4.   Were there any circumstances where you felt it was inappropriate for you to make a decision, or where you felt a decision should, more

>   appropriately, be made by someone else? (Please include any instances where other parties have made decisions about our client without consulting you).

>   5.   Please give details (names, addresses and organisations) of all significant contacts you have had in your role as Deputy. (Note: the Public Guardian may contact third parties for information in some circumstances).'

While it is impressive that the Public Guardian asks for such information and the deputy must address the questions raised, it is not clear how useful this information is. The Public Guardian cannot validate the decisions the deputy has made; all the Public Guardian can do is see that the deputy has considered his duties under the Act and there may be cases where it is obvious from the Report that further enquiries need to be made. The Public Guardian has no power to approve of the decisions recorded.

Section B of the report is less impressive and simply asks for a simple summary of items of income and expenditure, with opening and closing balances. There is no need to show any workings, schedules or even a bank reconciliation. However the fact that such information is not requested does not mean it can be ignored: a deputy still has a responsibility to keep accounts and the Public Guardian may request further information. The report will at the very least provide the Public Guardian with a picture of the estate, an idea of the level of income and expenditure and whether there are any grounds for concern.

The standard report makes no reference to capital or investments and no valuations need to be produced – unless specifically requested. Major changes in investments or reviews of investments might be addressed in section A. Investing money or consulting a fund manager should be shown as 'significant decisions' and someone 'consulted'. However, the basic responsibility remains with the deputy to manage the assets in the best interests of the person concerned.

Given the limited statutory powers of the Public Guardian as well as the limited resources available to his office, the supervision provided by the Public Guardian in all but a tiny fraction of cases is very perfunctory. Supervision provides a basic level of deterrence so that the great majority of deputies will supervise their own conduct. For it to provide a more effective safeguard depends on whistleblowers and complainants bringing cases to the attention of the Public Guardian.

Chapter 8

Managing the property and affairs of P

Acting in the name of P

8.1   A deputy, acting within the scope of his authority, is the statutory agent of the person for whom he has been appointed to act. The deputy acts in the name of the person and not on his own account. As has been noted in the previous chapter, the deputy is therefore not liable under a contract or for any debts incurred unless he has acted negligently or beyond the scope of his authority. As an agent, a deputy has similar duties as an attorney or trustee, who are also fiduciaries. They therefore need to keep trust property separate from their own, to account for any profits and not to benefit from their role, save for reasonable out of pocket expenses. Any property belonging to the person is that person's own property and remains in the person's name even though a deputy has been appointed.

Where a deputy enters into a transaction or makes a decision on behalf of the person concerned, which requires a signature to authorise, he will sign with his own signature followed by the words 'as deputy for [P]'.

Where the deputy executes a deed in the name of the person concerned, the document should recite the name of the person and the name and address of the deputy. The order authorising the deputy to execute the deed should also be recited. He will then generally sign both the person's name and his own name. Thus the recitals and attestation clause of a deed will follow one of two basic forms, depending on whether the deputy is signing pursuant to a specific order:

(a)   Deed entered into pursuant to order

THIS DEED is made the [date of deed] between [name of P (no address)] acting by [name of Deputy] of [address of Deputy] pursuant to an order of the Court of Protection dated [date] of the first part and [name and address of other party] of the other part

(b)   Deed entered into by Deputy acting under general authority contained in order appointing the Deputy

THIS DEED is made the [date of deed] between [name of P (no address)] acting by [name of Deputy] of [address of Deputy] ('the Deputy') of the first part and [name and address of other party] of the other part

WHEREAS the Deputy has been appointed by an order of the Court of Protection dated [date]

(c) Attestation

IN WITNESS whereof …

Signed as a deed by the said [P] acting by the said [Deputy] as aforesaid in the presence of:	Signature in the name of P
	Deputy's signature

Where a deputy or another person executes a will pursuant to an order of the Court of Protection then the method of execution is altered by the Mental Capacity Act 2005 (MCA 2005) (see **13.39**).

Financial management

The deputyship bank account

8.2   A deputy is in a fiduciary role and must therefore keep his own funds separate from those of the person for whom he is acting. He also has a general duty to keep accounts and a statutory duty to report to the Public Guardian. Therefore as soon as the order appointing the deputy has been made, the deputy must open a designated account with a bank or building society which has the following functions:

- it preserves the separate character of the person's money, so that it is not mixed with the deputy's own money;

- it serves as a means of collecting in income and other money coming into the hands of the deputy;

- it enables payments to be made for day-to-day expenses; and

- it assists the deputy with keeping the finances in order and with the completion of the Deputy's Report (see **7.11** above).

Depending on the circumstances and the ability of the person to make decisions, the account may be opened with the person's own bank. This will facilitate the transfer of money from one account to the other. This may work both ways: the deputy may need to close the account and transfer the closing balance to the deputy or money may need to be transferred to the person to manage for himself. In other cases, it may be more convenient to open the account with the deputy's own bank where the deputy is already known to the bank and does not have to provide new identification for compliance and money laundering purposes. Wherever the account is held, the account must be opened in the name of the deputy 'as deputy for [the person]' so that both names appear on the account and on any chequebooks and it is clear that any money in the account is legally the property of the person.

The account should be opened as soon as possible after the appointment of the deputy to avoid delay in receiving assets and applying them to meet expenditure. A prospective deputy may therefore be advised to contact the bank at the earliest stage so that once the appointment has been made, there is as little disruption as possible to the smooth running of the person's finances.

It is the deputy's responsibility to anticipate financial needs and therefore to monitor the account carefully. The deputy should avoid any unnecessary bank or interest charges arising. If the account is likely to become overdrawn the deputy must ensure the account remains in credit. This may be done by selling investments or transferring money from the Court Funds Office or other deposit account. The deputy must allow sufficient time for these arrangements to be carried out, especially if the release of funds or sale of property requires an order of the Court. To avoid frequent requests for the transfer of funds, the deputy should maintain a working balance and have a budget that provides for regular payments to be made to the deputyship bank account.

Money in the control of P

8.3   There should in theory be no need to account for money held by a person directly. If he has capacity to manage an account or other property, then the deputy has no authority to intervene. This may be necessary where the person is living at home and has access to money or wants to have money to hand. There are also cases where a person knows how to spend money, but does not have a grasp of how to manage a budget. In practice therefore, a deputy may have an oversight role, making sure that the person for whom he is acting has sufficient funds to meet an agreed level of expenditure or is spending money within an agreed budget. A deputy may well have to tread tactfully, knowing that his authority is limited while having a wider duty to preserve the estate for the person's long-term benefit.

Successful solutions to this dilemma might involve:

- allowing the person to continue collecting a pension or other benefit so that he has some personal spending money;

- arranging an allowance in cash;

- paying an allowance to a relative, carer or nursing home to hand over on an agreed basis;

- preserving a bank or building society account in the person's own name and making regular transfers of money to that account. The account should be monitored by the deputy who should receive copies of all statements;

- maintaining a joint account with the person or with a third party with a limited budget but which is clearly earmarked for household and personal expenses; and

- allowing the person to keep a credit card with an agreed limit.

Although a deputy should not need to account for money spent by the person concerned, the deputy should be able to show that such money is not under the deputy's control. The deputy should not therefore share the same account. The person concerned should either have his own income (for instance from a pension) or an agreed allowance or subsidy. The deputy need only show what amounts have been paid to the person from funds under his control.

Practical difficulties where money is in the control of P

8.4   While an account in the person's own name may be desirable, administrative problems may arise with banks and financial institutions which are unwilling to allow access to an account to anyone other than the deputy. The problem remains that the appointment of a deputy (or the registration of an Enduring Power of Attorney (EPA)) will indicate an assessment has been made as to whether a person is incapable of managing his property and affairs. Although each case needs to be dealt with on an individual basis, banks and other financial institutions cannot apply the same flexibility as a deputy in assessing each customer's case on its own merits. The local branch manager should not have to make an assessment of capacity which appears to contradict the order appointing a deputy which has been sent to his head office.

In practice, a deputy may need to be persistent with banks, explaining the MCA 2005 principles. There is no consistency in the way in which banks deal with such cases and while frustrating, it is also correct that each case is unique. Banks may accept an account in a person's own name, or may require a separate account in the deputy's name which can be operated by the person (and which may also show his name on the account, so that outwardly it appears to be his own account). It has also been known for deputies simply to leave a person running his own account which remains open, while the deputy operates a separate account elsewhere.

Accounting for day–to-day expenditure

8.5   The Court and Public Guardian generally take a pragmatic view towards the way in which day-to-day expenditure is accounted for. A deputy is not expected to account for every purchase of a newspaper or pint of milk, but is expected to monitor expenditure generally and ensure that money paid to or for a person is consistent with the person's reasonable requirements and is applied for his benefit. The person concerned should not receive too much and so accumulate a surplus of cash, or too little and so be out of pocket. The right level of payment is often achieved through trial and error. The deputy should also ensure that all major expenses such as care costs or repairs and insurance are dealt with directly by the deputy through the deputyship bank account.

In practice, a deputy is not on hand to deal with day-to-day expenses. If the person concerned cannot manage such expenses, then a carer or relative may take responsibility for the day-to-day payments. These can be extensive, especially where the person is living at home and leads an independent life. Food, clothing, transport, activities all need to be paid for. A parent caring for a disabled child may take responsibility for meeting these costs and paying carers. Modest expenses might be reimbursed, but where the expenditure is greater, payments can be paid on account to the carer or relative. It is for the deputy to set the degree of accountability without being overly prescriptive. In most cases where a person is living in his own home, a budget should be set and the carer or relative will only account for increases in the budget. Carers should also keep records and receipts for inspection if required. Where there are extensive household expenses or one carer is arranging payment of wages, then a separate account might be opened so that there is a bank record of payments made.

Out-of-pocket expenses

8.6   The deputy has a right to be reimbursed his out-of-pocket expenses such as travel expenses incurred in visiting the person or the person's property, telephone calls and postage. Prior to October 2007, it was common to contact the Public Guardianship Office to approve large expenses such as hotel expenses or air fares. This is no longer possible, at least without a formal application to the Court. Otherwise a deputy can only take a view as to what is in a person's best interests and be prepared to justify his reasoning if the expenditure is queried.

Where the deputy has spent his own money for the maintenance or benefit of a person, he is entitled to be reimbursed for such expenditure. The deputy is not expected to apply his own funds or to be personally liable for the debts of the person for whom he has been appointed to act. Neither should the deputy be spending his own money where he has authority to access the person's own account. Payments made by a deputy to himself need to be accounted for carefully.

The deputy may also pay the out-of-pocket expenses of friends and carers. In so far as resources allow, the deputy should encourage the positive involvement of relatives and friends and ensure that this is not restricted by their own resources.

Remuneration of the deputy

8.7   Although a deputy is entitled to reimbursement of his expenses, a deputy is not entitled to be paid for his work. This follows from the principle that a fiduciary should not benefit from acting in that capacity, and this applies to an attorney or a trustee in the same way as to a deputy (see **7.1**). However, just as an attorney or trustee may be remunerated if authorised by the power of attorney or trust instrument, a deputy may be remunerated where the Court allows. Rule 167 of the Court of Protection Rules provides expressly for remuneration as follows:

'(1) Where the court orders that a deputy, donee or attorney is entitled to remuneration out of P's estate for discharging his functions as such, the court may make such order as it thinks fit, including an order that—

(a)   he be paid a fixed amount;

(b)   he be paid at a specified rate; or

(c)   the amount of the remuneration shall be determined in accordance with the schedule of fees set out in the relevant practice direction.

(2) Any amount permitted by the court under paragraph (1) shall constitute a debt due from P's estate.'

Remuneration will therefore be allowed to professional deputies for their work, but with the amount of such remuneration in the control of the Court. Generally, the order appointing the deputy will authorise his costs to be paid from the estate either as fixed costs or as assessed by the Court (see Chapter 12).

A lay deputy will only be allowed remuneration in exceptional cases, for instance where the deputyship proves particularly onerous and interferes with the deputy's own work. This may happen where the deputy is self-employed, but generally a deputy who provides such a degree of involvement should be obtaining professional help or is likely to be taking on the role of a carer, which should be remunerated in any event. If the deputy is a carer, dependant or other person for whom the person might be expected to provide, then it may be more appropriate for the deputy to receive a care allowance or gift.

As has been noted at **7.7** where significant payments are made to a deputy, for instance as a carer, then there is likely to be a conflict of interest that cannot be resolved without the express authority of the Court. In practice, a relative providing such a significant degree of support or who is so financially dependent on the person concerned should not be acting as a sole deputy. An independent deputy should be appointed to provide a degree of scrutiny and detachment.

Costs of solicitor or other professional

8.8   A deputy may instruct a solicitor or accountant to act for him. Apart from making the application itself, a lay deputy is expected to carry out the day-to-day administration of the estate. The principle that a fiduciary should not benefit from his role was expressly referred to in the 2001 Court of Protection Rules (r 87(1)) which stated that a receiver, unless authorised by the Court, shall not:

> 'be entitled at the expense of the patient's estate to employ a solicitor or other professional person to do any work not usually requiring professional assistance.'

The principle is not covered by the 2007 Court of Protection Rules. However, a solicitor who acts for a deputy (or any other party) in Court of Protection proceedings is not entitled to remuneration unless there is an order authorising payment of his costs. A lay deputy may also need to engage a solicitor or other professional such as an accountant to deal with day-to-day administrative matters such as completion of accounts or tax returns. He will be responsible for ensuring that the work needs to be done and that any costs incurred are fair and reasonable.

Investments

Existing investments

8.9   Any publication that dealt with the role of a receiver under the Mental Health Act 1983 jurisdiction would contain an entire chapter to itself on dealing with investments and making investments. This need no longer be dealt with in such detail. The Court is no longer exercised with identifying each and every investment that needs to be sold and how assets are to be invested. A deputy is no longer required to call in the assets and invest funds in Court or with panel brokers who had to follow a specified investment policy.

Where investments are held at the time the deputy is appointed, then generally these will fall within the scope of the deputy's authority to deal with the estate (see **5.20**). A deputy with authority to 'take possession or control of the property and affairs of [P]' will have authority to close bank accounts, dispose of shares or sell a property. If the estate is very large the Court may make an order that is limited to (for example) bank and building society accounts, so that the deputy may need to make a new application to sell assets that are excluded from the scope of the order such as the family home or business.

If investments do not need to be called in, then the deputy is still responsible for managing those investments. A share portfolio may already be well managed and tax efficient investments, fixed terms bonds or savings certificates would not be repaid without penalty. Banks, building societies, stockbrokers or company registrars must, however, be contacted and provided with sealed copies of the order appointing the deputy. Those assets will remain in the name of the person concerned but will be administered by the deputy as agent. The deputy will therefore receive statements, dividend vouchers, valuations, share certificates, redemption forms and any other communication.

The circumstances should dictate whether or not investments need to be called in. In some cases it will be obvious that a miscellaneous collection of bank accounts and shares needs to be consolidated in a single account either held by the deputy or with the Court Funds Office, so as to earn a good rate of interest while providing access to cash to pay for care. In other cases, investments are already professionally managed or cannot be realised without a penalty or tax liability. Unless the estate is small or the deputy is consolidating investments, it is vital that professional advice be obtained before investments are disposed of.

Making and managing investments

8.10   Earlier editions of this work contained a lengthy chapter dealing with investments. Under the Mental Health Act 1983 jurisdiction, investments were tightly regulated by the Court and Public Guardianship Office. Where it was appropriate to invest funds, the Court would set an investment policy specifying the balance between equities and cash. Equities would have to be invested by one of the panel brokers appointed by the Court or by a fund manager whose terms would be approved by the Public Guardianship Office Investment Branch. A receiver would be authorised to invest money or the fund manager would receive an investment powers authority from the Court. The performance of the fund managers would also be monitored and measured against market benchmarks.

There were two principal problems with trying to monitor or control investments in this way. The Public Guardianship Office created an administrative burden for itself, while appearing to offer a degree of approval of investment decisions, for which it could not accept responsibility. From October 2007, a deputy with authority to administer a person's property and affairs will generally have 'the same powers of management and investment as he has as beneficial owner' (see **5.20**). The deputy not only has the authority to make suitable investments, but also the responsibility.

A deputy will therefore have prime responsibility for the investments under his control. Generally, once the Court has appointed the deputy, it will have no further interest in the case. Where large personal injury awards are involved, the Court may limit the duration of the order so that a new application will need to be made after a fixed period of usually two or three years. At that point, the deputy will need to provide the Court with details of the investments made.

A deputy will also report to the Public Guardian each year, but the current form of account is perfunctory. It does not require details of investments to be submitted as a matter of course, but only if specifically directed by the Public Guardian. Even if the Public Guardian inspects the accounts in detail and calls for details of the investments carried out, he is not qualified to report on the investments themselves: all the Public Guardian can do is check that the deputy has discharged his responsibilities appropriately.

Responsibility of deputy

8.11   A deputy investing money on behalf of a person is acting as a fiduciary, in a similar role to a trustee. A deputy must therefore account for any commission or profit paid to him. There should in other respects be no practical difference to what is required of a trustee, who must act with a standard duty of care in accordance with the Trustee Act 2000, s 4(1). This is emphasised by the order appointing a deputy which requires a deputy to (a) exercise such skill as in reasonable in the circumstances; (b) have regard to the standard investment criteria, namely the suitability of the investments and the need for diversification in so far as is appropriate to the personal circumstances of P; (c) from time to time review the investments and consider whether they should be varied; and (d) obtain and consider proper advice from a person who is suitably qualified and regulated.Thus a deputy is likewise expected to act with diligence, and manage investments in the same manner as an ordinary prudent man of business would conduct his own affairs. Any deputy must obtain and consider proper advice in the same way as a trustee. The overriding responsibility of a deputy, unless he is professionally qualified to give investment advice, is to obtain suitable advice from an adviser or organisation that is regulated by the Financial Services Authority. A higher standard of care would, however, be expected from a trust corporation, or a professional trustee who neglects to exercise any special care and skill which he professes to have.

A deputy must also have regard to the suitability of the investments to their purpose: an elderly person in a nursing home where fees exceed income has different needs to a brain injured young adult with a damages award that may need to provide for the cost of care over several decades.

Further issues arising under the Mental Capacity Act

8.12   In addition to the above responsibilities, a deputy must also ensure that he is acting within the scope of his authority and in accordance with the principles of the MCA 2005. This could lead to some unintended difficulties where a person has capacity to make investment decisions or could make decisions with adequate professional help. If the person lacks capacity then investment decisions are no different from any other decisions that need to be made in the person's best interests.

The deputy may therefore be expected to consult with the person concerned and take account of his known or likely wishes. In cases where a person has a level of understanding then a deputy should seek to explain and reassure the person as to how his investments are administered. The deputy should also take account of any particular views known to him, for instance where the person had strong ethical views which might influence his likely choice of investments. However these are only factors that must be taken into account. The MCA 2005 also emphasises that any investment decisions must be made in the best interests of the person concerned. As has been mentioned in the previous chapter, the deputy's first consideration is to the maintenance and benefit of the person for whom he is acting. Investments must therefore be focused on meeting the needs of the person, regardless of the claims or interests of prospective beneficiaries.

Compliance

8.13   The compliance issues raised by the Financial Services and Markets Act 2000 and its subordinate legislation are beyond the scope of this book. In general terms the Court of Protection, as a Crown body, is exempt from the legislation. However, any stockbroker, fund manager or financial adviser providing advice in respect of a person's investments will be conducting investment business and must be regulated.

Where the deputy is a solicitor, any dealings by him must be carried out within the scope of his authority and in accordance with advice given by an appropriate regulated adviser. Making arrangements, administering investments and safeguarding investments, which are a necessary part of the main professional service, are not themselves regulated activities that must be supervised by the Financial Services Authority. Such incidental activities are subject to the supervision of the Solicitors Regulation Authority (SRA) and are regarded as exempt regulated activities.

The SRA's requirements are set out in the Solicitors' Financial Services (Scope) Rules 2001 and the 2007 Solicitors' Code of Conduct. The Rules and Code are available from the SRA at www.sra.org.uk/financial-services

Periodical payments

8.14   Where a lump sum may be recovered by way of a damages award or settlement of a personal injury claim, it may be appropriate for part of the sum to be applied towards the purchase of an annuity. From a practical perspective, this will provide the person and his family with reassurance that whatever happens in the future, there will be a secure source of income.

Periodical payments may also provide a better return than investing the equivalent sum in equities or gilts, especially at a time of uncertainty in financial markets. The further advantage of the structured settlement is that the income element of the annuity is free of income tax (Income and Corporation Taxes Act 1988, Part X s 329) which has the effect of increasing the yield of the annuity by up to 40 per cent.

Such settlements have been popular in cases where it has been necessary to enhance a person's income to meet the high costs of care and maintenance, which might not be covered by the return from conventional investments, especially where care costs are expected to increase at a faster rate than more conventional measures of inflation. For a while, such arrangements became less popular due to lower annuity rates and increased damages awards following the decision of the House of Lords in the case of *Wells v Wells* [1999] 1 AC 345. More recently, their importance as a means of protecting a person's assets and guarding against inflation have been recognised especially where a higher inflationary increase is built into the award following the Court of Appeal decision in *Tameside & Glossop Acute Services NHS Trust v Thompstone* [2008] 2 All ER 553, 152 Sol Jo 29. Periodical payments may also be appropriate where the damages award is reduced by contributory negligence or the person receives an offer of a higher return due to his impaired life expectancy.

In any case where a damages award is to be compromised on behalf of a person who lacks capacity then the Court must receive detailed guidance from an expert financial adviser on the merits of periodical payments compared with a lump sum award (see CPR PD 21 para 6.2 and CPR Part 41). Personal injury awards are dealt with in more detail at **10.8**.

Funds in Court

Court Funds Office

8.15   A deputy will need access to funds for day-to-day needs and will be expected to keep a working balance in the deputyship bank account. A deputy may also retain investments in the person's own name if the benefit of retention outweighs the disadvantages of repayment. However, it is expected that the greater part of any available cash will be deposited with the Court Funds Office.

The Court Funds Office provides a banking and investment service for the courts throughout England and Wales, including the High Court. Money deposited with the Court Funds Office is held by the National Investment and Loans Office of the Treasury, whose chief executive holds the post of Accountant General of the Supreme Court. The Court Funds Office is part of the combined Offices of Court Funds, Official Solicitor and Public Trustee which together are an associated office of the Ministry of Justice. The Court Funds Office is situated at:

Court Funds Office
22 Kingsway
London
WC2B 6LE

DX: 149780 Kingsway
Tel: 0845 223 8500
www.courtfunds.gov.uk

Money in Court

8.16   Where cash is held by the Court Funds Office for the benefit of a person who lacks capacity, this may be held in one of three types of account:

- the cash account – this pays no interest and is used like a bank current account to hold funds before they are paid out or transferred to an interest-bearing account;

- the special account – this is the main interest-bearing account and cash belonging to a person who lacks capacity will be held on the special account;

- the basic account – this pays interest at a slightly lower rate than the special account and is only used for funds held on behalf of an adult in County Court and High Court litigation matters. .

Interest is paid gross, twice annually on the last Friday in May and November for the special account and in March and September for the basic account. Interest is paid on these accounts at rates fixed by the Department for Constitutional Affairs with the consent of the Treasury. As of 1 February 2009 the interest rate is currently 3 per cent gross per annum on the special account and 2 per cent gross on the basic account. It is therefore the responsibility of the deputy to ensure that untaxed income is declared in a tax return and that the correct rate of tax is applied and duly paid.

Operating the Special Account

8.17   Prior to October 2007 the Court would authorise lodgement of funds into court and withdrawals had to be authorised by the Court or Public Guardianship Office. From October 2007, a deputy is able to access the Court Funds Office directly.

Where funds are deposited for the first time, the Court Funds Office will require the following documents:

- a sealed copy of the order appointing the deputy;

- a lodgement form (F108);

- an application for authority to access the account (CP22); and

- a cheque for the amount being deposited made payable to the Accountant General of the Supreme Court.

Withdrawal of funds

8.18   Form CP22 will provide details of the deputyship bank account which will receive any monies released from the Court Funds Office account. Monies can be released in one of two ways:

- by regular payments or standing order (using Form F301R); or

- by a single payment (using Form F301P).

When payment to the deputyship bank account is required for the first time, the deputy must also provide the Court Funds Office with a letter or statement from the deputy's bank (which is not more than three months old) showing the account name, account number and sort code.

A payment to a third party will only be made if it is expressly directed by an order of the Court, for example where the Court directs the release of funds to a person who has recovered capacity, or where an order provides for the payment of a debt, settlement of costs or the making of a substantial gift. Payment can also be made to HM Revenue & Customs following a person's death. In such cases, the person authorised to make the withdrawal must use Form F301P.

Where the payment is a gift or charitable donation made within the scope of the deputy's general authority, the deputy should complete Form PG.

Budget set by Court

8.19   The only practical way in which the Court can control expenditure after a deputy has been appointed is to set a budget, specifying a limit on how much can be applied in any one year. For example an order may provide a deputy with wide discretion to spend money, but limit the amount that can be withdrawn in any one year to (say) £100,000. It is then for the Court Funds Office to ensure that withdrawals over the period do not exceed the amount specified. If the deputy needs to exceed the cumulative budget set by the Court, an application needs to be made to the Court for authority.

Statements of account

8.20   The Court Funds Office sends out statements twice a year, in April and October. The April statement is accompanied by tax vouchers showing interest earned in the previous tax year. Statements can be sent out at any other time on request. The deputy may also request a certificate confirming the amount held in the special account or a ledger statement (a transcript) showing all transactions on the account. The transcript is not user-friendly as entries on the cash account and special account are shown on the same statement. The cash account operates like a bank's current account and the statement shows all payments and receipts through the cash account as well as the corresponding transfers from the cash account to the special account (in the case of payments in) or from the special account to the cash account (for payments out). To complicate the statement further, where payments are made from the cash account, accrued interest is applied in priority to capital. Therefore interest accrued on the special account will be transferred to the cash account and the statement will then show a separate transfer of capital required to make up any shortfall.

Insurance policies

8.21   Form COP1A requires the prospective deputy to show whether the person concerned has any life assurance policies. The applicant is asked to provide full details of the policies, the premiums payable and whether it is desired to keep the policies going.

Once appointed, the deputy should send a sealed copy of the order appointing the deputy to every life company with which a policy is held in order to ensure that any arrears, renewals, bonuses or other events affecting the policy are properly dealt with. It is the responsibility of the deputy to ensure that where possible, policies are maintained. Premiums are usually an expense of income, but where large premiums are payable, for instance under a whole of life policy, the deputy must consider carefully whether they are affordable, whether the benefit to a third party outweighs the benefit to the person concerned and whether the Court should be asked to sanction further payments.

Where a policy subsequently becomes fully paid or becomes payable to the incapable policyholder on the occurrence of some other event, such as the death of a life assured where the policy belongs to the person, then the deputy is responsible for making any claim. A widely drafted standard order should include authority to make a claim under a policy. If the order does not extend to this or the life company requires an express form of discharge to be given, then an application must be made to the Court of Protection. Although a formal application would need to be made, this could be dealt with under the short procedure allowed by Practice Direction 9D (see **3.43**).

Interest in a business

8.22   Section 18(1)(d) of the MCA 2005 provides authority for the Court to make decisions in respect of 'the carrying on, on P's behalf, of any profession, trade or business'.

Form COP1A requires the applicant to state whether the person to whom the application relates owns or has an interest in a business and to provide full details of any such business, who is running the business and the interest of the person concerned. The application is no more detailed than this. It is for the applicant to confirm whether the business can be continued, sold to another business partner or wound up and to request the Court to provide sufficient authority to achieve this outcome. The express authority of the Court will be required if the sale of shares or business assets takes place at an undervalue or there is a potential conflict of interest. A widely drafted general order containing powers of management will extend to the continuation of the business in the interim. However, if the business is to be continued, let alone developed, the deputy has to justify this as being in the person's best interests and should only act with suitable professional advice. The deputy should also ensure that the order under which he is acting refers specifically to his authority to carry on the business, if only to avoid confusion when dealing with other parties.

A family business may well expose a conflict between a person's best interests under the Act and material best interests. A person may have had a strong emotional tie to an unprofitable business or to assets which could be sold more profitably. A deputy who has conflicting claims on his authority should seek the sanction of the Court to continue the business.

P is a director of a company

8.23   If the person is a company director the company's articles will usually provide for the removal of the director on the grounds of mental incapacity. Regulation 81 of the articles set out in Table A (Companies (Tables A–F) Regulations 1985, SI 1985/804) provide that the office of a director shall be vacated if an order is made appointing a deputy in respect of the director's property and affairs. The deputy or his professional adviser will need to advise on any financial consequences, such as a director's retirement pension, any other retirement benefits or insurance payments and whether the deputy should apply to be appointed to the board to protect the interests of the person concerned. Although a director who lacks capacity must cease to act as a director, any voting rights he has as a shareholder may be exercised by the deputy.

P is a shareholder

8.24   Consideration should also be given to whether the shares in a company can be sold or should be retained. The deputy will generally have authority to sell shares on the best available terms. If shares are to be sold the deputy must comply with any restrictions on their sale contained in the company's articles or a shareholder agreement.

If shares are to be retained the deputy will have authority to exercise any voting rights, provided the company has evidence of the authority of the deputy to act on the shareholder's behalf (see for instance Table A regulation 56). Where these concern capital transactions affecting the interests of the person concerned, for example the sale of the company or its assets, fixing directors' fees or agreement to the appointment or removal of directors then the deputy must act on detailed impartial advice and if in any doubt, apply for the authority of the Court.

Welfare benefits

Claiming benefits

8.25   It is a basic duty of the deputy to claim all benefits to which the person concerned is entitled. An order that confers authority on the deputy to take possession or control of the property and affairs of a person and to exercise the same powers of management and investment as a beneficial owner, will include all income and benefits to which a person is entitled. On a first application for the appointment of a deputy, an order may not be made until several months after the entitlement to the benefits has arisen. In these circumstances the claim should be made without delay and the situation explained to the Department for Work and Pensions (DWP) when making the claim. If it is likely that there will be an unusually long delay in the application and the benefits are needed to maintain the person, then the Court may issue an interim authority or the applicant can apply to have benefits paid to the prospective deputy (or a relative or carer) as appointee.

The deputy should ensure that, where possible, state benefits are paid directly to the deputyship bank account. However, a person who has capacity to receive and manage his own benefits must be allowed to go on doing so, and the deputy will have no authority to make the claim. The deputy may, however, assist with the claim and ascertain that the person is collecting his benefits and able to go on managing them.

Where a local authority contributes to the cost of care, funding is paid directly to the home. As this is not dependent on the authority deputy, it may be paid to the home before the deputy has been appointed.

Passive indemnity

8.26   Although a deputy is expected to collect all benefits to which a person is entitled, an unusual exception to this principle may arise where the person is in receipt of personal injury compensation that has been awarded specifically to cover the cost of ongoing care. However, the capital is disregarded when claiming means-tested benefits and a deputy could potentially benefit twice over, once from the award and again from the benefits. A defendant – especially where it is a government body – would not expect a claimant to benefit twice in this way and an award may be made on the basis that there will be no such double recovery or that the defendant will be indemnified in respect of any such payments.

The status of an award made on such an assumption has been considered by the Court of Appeal in the case of *Peters v East Midlands Area Health Authority* [2009] EWHC Civ 145. The Court of Appeal accepted that a defendant could not avoid liability on the basis that the claimant's care would be paid from public funds. However, a deputy would be entitled to avoid claiming public funding in such cases. As Dyson LJ, delivering the unanimous verdict of the judges asserted (at paragraph 61):

> 'The scope of the duty of a case manager and Deputy is a question of law. More importantly, neither [the case manager or care expert] was addressing the specific question of the scope of the duty in circumstances where a court has awarded 100% of the care costs that are necessary to meet a claimant's needs. We do not accept that, in such circumstances, there is a duty on the case manager or Deputy to seek full public funding so as to achieve a double recovery. There is no basis in law, fairness or common sense for such a duty.'

The judge went on to consider how a deputy's duty in such a case could be policed to the satisfaction of the defendant. This could be left to the deputy to provide a suitable undertaking to apply to the Court which would in turn provide the defendant with grounds to approach the Court. As the judge explained (at paragraphs 64 and 65):

'[The Deputy] has offered an undertaking to this court in her capacity as Deputy for the claimant that she would (i) notify the senior judge of the Court of Protection of the outcome of these proceedings and supply to him copies of the judgment of this court and that of Butterfield J; and (ii) seek from the Court of Protection (a) a limit on the authority of the claimant's Deputy whereby no application for public funding of the claimant's care under section 21 of the NAA can be made without further order, direction or authority from the Court of Protection and (b) provision for the defendants to be notified of any application to obtain authority to apply for public finding of the claimant's care under section 21 of the NAA and be given the opportunity to make representations in relation thereto.

In our judgment, this is an effective way of dealing with the risk of double recovery in cases where the affairs of the claimant are being administered by the Court of Protection. It places the control over the Deputy's ability to make an application for the provision of a claimant's care and accommodation at public expense in the hands of a court. If a Deputy wishes to apply for public provision even where damages have been awarded on the basis that no public provision will be sought, the requirement that the defendant is to be notified of any such application will enable a defendant who wishes to do so to seek to persuade that the Court of Protection should not allow the application to be made because it is unnecessary and contrary to the intendment of the assessment of damages. The court accordingly accepts the undertaking that has been offered.'

It is not clear from this judgment whether a deputy will be acting within the scope of his general authority to provide an undertaking on such terms and avoid claiming public funding or whether the Court of Protection should sanction this in every case. Common sense suggests that the Court of Protection should not be burdened with applications in every case where there has been a personal injury award. The deputy is acting within the scope of his duty if he does not claim public funding and it should be for the defendant to approach the Court of Protection if there is a perceived breach of this duty. It must also be for the deputy to determine in the first instance what is appropriate for the person concerned and there will be cases where recovery is less than 100 per cent or public provision of assistance is limited where the deputy has a duty to obtain whatever benefits are available.

Means-tested benefits

8.27   Where a person's care is provided or arranged by the local authority, or the person is entitled to means-tested benefits such as the pension credit, the deputy must make a full disclosure so that the correct assessment can be made. The deputy is responsible for checking that the assessment is correct and notifying the local authority or DWP of any changes in the person's circumstances which might increase or decrease the level of funding or benefit to which the person is entitled. The deputy must also supply any financial information requested such as copies of bank statements or a statement of the fund in Court.

The benefit and funding rules are very complicated and a detailed overview is beyond the scope of this work. A great deal more information is readily available from the relevant government departments or bodies such as Age Concern who provide a series of informative and up to date information sheets available at: http://www.ageconcern.org.uk/AgeConcern/factsheets.asp

The deputy must, however, be aware of the main benefits available and how they interact with each other. The deputy's main duty where such benefits are concerned is to provide regular and accurate information to the DWP Pensions Service, Disability Benefits Unit or local authority concerning any of the person's circumstances which might affect his or her entitlement to benefits or funding. The following situations will, for instance, affect the amount of benefit which can be paid:

- as of 6 April 2005, a person may remain in hospital and continue to receive his state pension in full;

- attendance allowance and disability living allowance are not means-tested and can be claimed regardless of resources. These benefits are, however, withheld after the person has been in hospital for 28 days and neither allowance can be claimed while the person is in hospital or in a care home where funding is provided by the local authority;

- attendance allowance and disability living allowance (where the person is under 60) are paid at higher rates if assistance is required with personal care during the night. A person in receipt of means-tested local authority financial support cannot also claim attendance allowance or disability living allowance. If this allowance is already being paid, entitlement ceases 28 days after admission;

- from 27 October 2008 Income Support on incapacity grounds and Incapacity Benefit for claimants under pensionable age have been replaced by the Employment and Support Allowance. A person claiming will be liable to contribute from his capital where it is above £6,000 and below £16,000, this being the amount above which a person is ineligible to claim. As the capital reduces, the Benefits Agency must be notified so that the person's contribution from capital is reduced to the correct amount;

- where the person is in a care home where the care is funded by the local authority, the capital limits for 2009/2010 are £14,000 and £23,000 respectively;

- for both Employment and Support Allowance and means-tested local authority funding, where a person has capital between the lower limit and upper limits, he is deemed to have a weekly income of £1 per £250 of capital;

- for housing benefit and council tax benefit the capital limits are £6,000 and £16,000 respectively;

- if a person is over 60, pension credit is payable in place of income support and the capital limit is £6,000;

- if a person has a property its capital value is ignored by a local authority for 12 weeks, and in certain circumstances care costs paid by a local authority can be repaid (without interest) on the sale of the property (see LAC 2001/25);

- a person who is funding his own care (including care provided on a temporary basis where his home is being sold) is eligible for a contribution to the nursing element of his care costs. A National Framework was introduced on 1 October 2007 with a single level of payment (replacing the three tiers of payment); the rate as at 1 April 2009 is £106.30 per week. However a resident in receipt of the upper rate on 1 October 2007 will continue to be eligible to receive payments at the higher rate, which is £146.30 per week;

- a person who requires medical attention and supervision (for instance after being discharged from hospital) may be entitled to free nursing care at the expense of the local primary care trust. The National Framework which came into operation on 1 October 2007 aims to provide some consistency in the way the strict requirements of eligibility for free care are applied;

- a person who has been detained or treated under Part I of the MHA 1983 is entitled to free after-care services under s 117 of the Mental Health Act 1983 which may include the full cost of continuing care (see LAC 2000/03), the requirements for which should not be unduly restrictive (*R v Manchester CC ex parte Stenett* [2002] UKHL 34).

Compensation for personal injury

8.28   Where a person receives compensation for a personal injury and this is paid directly into court or to a trust for the benefit of that person then the capital is ignored for assessment purposes and he can continue to claim means-tested benefits as though the award had not been made:

- rule 106(2)(b) of the Employment and Support Allowance Regulations 2008 (SI 2008/794);

- rule 42(2) and schedule10 paras 12 and 12A of the Income Support (General) Regulations 1987 (SI 1987/1967); and

- Charging for Residential Accommodation Guidelines 2008, paragraphs 10.025–10.026.

The regulations refer to an award held in trust. The nature of the trust is unimportant; the status of any money is defined by its source. Thus money held by a deputy under the control of the Court of Protection is treated in the same way as a trust and disregarded. The Court of Protection is therefore unlikely to approve the creation of trust funds specifically for the purpose of ensuring entitlement to means-tested benefits (see the Practice Note issued by the Master on 15 November 1996: '*Procedure for the Settlement of Personal Injury Awards to Patients*' and also **13.46**).

Income paid out of a trust to the beneficiary is treated as the person's own income for benefit and tax purposes. Capital may, however, be paid to or for the person provided the capital limits are not exceeded or items are purchased which are personal possessions, for example a wheelchair, furniture or a car.

Caring for P

General considerations

8.29 A property and affairs deputy is not directly responsible for the choice of home and has no authority to determine where a person will live. However, a deputy cannot avoid this issue. Apart from having an ethical and legal duty to maintain the person, he is required to act in the person's best interests, ensuring that a decision to spend a person's money reflects as far as possible the decision the person would have taken but for the want of capacity. The deputy will therefore influence the choice of accommodation, simply by virtue of having access to funding and having authority to enter into a contract with the care provider.

Section 4(1)(7) of the Mental Capacity Act also requires any other person making a best interests determination to consult with and take account of the views of a deputy. In choosing the appropriate accommodation, the deputy will often be one of several parties who together contribute to the decision-making process. The most important party will be the person concerned whose wishes will need to be considered carefully according to his capacity to form his own judgment, and a person may well be capable of deciding where he wants to live long after he has become incapable of managing his property and affairs. Social workers, doctors and relatives will also be involved in varying degrees to ensure that the accommodation is appropriate. Once the choice has been made, the deputy must do all that is within his authority to support the choice that has been made.

In deciding where P is to live, the role of a financial deputy will therefore be an important one. It is hoped that the choice of accommodation will be self-evident and can be determined in the person's best interests. If the person is already in his own home or can participate in the decision, no further decision needs to be made. Only if there is a dispute over where a person should live would it be necessary to apply to the Court to exercise its welfare powers.

Practical duties to P

8.30 The Deputy's Declaration asks the prospective deputy to undertake to 'work with the person … and any carers to achieve the best quality of life for him or her within the funds available'. Even though the deputy is only appointed to deal with property and affairs, he is in a position to make a major contribution to the person's welfare and must do what is in his power to look at the best interests of the person as a whole. Thus the deputy should ensure that subject to his resources the person receives any 'extras' which would benefit his quality of life. For many people small comforts such as their own television, hairdressing, outings, visits from relatives or a favourite drink make a great deal of difference to the quality of their lives. The deputy should also ensure that if possible the person has any photographs and sentimental objects he may wish to have.

To carry out this responsibility the deputy should visit the person or keep in regular contact with the home, or with another relative or friend who is in a position to visit. Where appropriate the deputy should try to encourage expenditure for the person's benefit. While the deputy must obviously have regard to the person's resources, the deputy must give priority to the person's needs and apply those resources accordingly. While this may sound self-evident, a deputy may have a number of competing issues and principles to address:

- the deputy's obligations to manage the estate for the person's long-term benefit;

- the needs and interests of any dependants or future beneficiaries;

- a person's wish to have a particular level of care in a particular location; and

- the provision of a better level of care or in a better location than might be desired or medically necessary.

Thus a deputy may need to spend more than a person can probably afford to maintain a desired level of care, while tying up capital in the family home. While that would be in the person's best interests as defined by the Act, would it be appropriate for a deputy to provide a better and more expensive level of care for a person who cannot appreciate it or who might have been particularly parsimonious in the past?

Duties to the Court and the Public Guardian

8.31 On making an application to be appointed, a prospective deputy must provide the Court with details of the care arrangements and the costs involved. However, this is to provide the Court with a picture of the circumstances, the extent of the authority required and whether the applicant has addressed these requirements. Once appointed, the deputy has primary responsibility for maintaining the person in the chosen environment. The deputy is also responsible for addressing the financial implications, ensuring that any benefits are claimed, that investments are sold and funds are available and that there is an awareness of current and anticipated expenditure. Unless the order appointing the deputy needs to be reviewed, the deputy's general obligation to the Court is a general duty to account and act within the scope of the authority given by the Court. So long as the deputy acts correctly and the order does not need reviewing, a deputy may have no further involvement with the Court.

The formal supervision of the deputy is the responsibility of the Public Guardian and the deputy will, depending on the level of supervision set, need to file an annual report to the Public Guardian. The content of the report, levels of supervision and the efficacy of the supervisory system are considered at **7.8** to **7.11**.

P in a care home

8.32 The choice of a care home may involve a difficult balance between competing principles: on the one hand, the integrity of the estate and the preservation of assets for the future (as well as for beneficiaries); and on the other, the immediate needs of the person concerned. If there is any doubt as to what is appropriate, the best interests of the person must be the overriding consideration. Thus a person who chooses to live beyond his means knowing the consequences might be allowed to do so – so long as the care can be paid for. If he is able to participate in that decision, the deputy may also have the awkward task of taking a longer term view while not upsetting a good working relationship.

To determine what kind of accommodation is appropriate, the deputy will need to consider a wide range of factors:

- What does the person want?

- Is the home within the person's resources and is it appropriate to the person's needs and circumstances?

- What is the person's health and life expectancy?

- What are the implications of the person's needs increasing over a lengthy period of time and can the home meet the increasing need for care?

- Have the appropriate people – anyone named by the person or anyone engaged in his care or interested in his welfare been consulted in making the choice of home?

- How can the person's assets be applied to meet the costs and projected costs? Do assets have to be sold and how should the proceeds be invested to secure the person's maintenance?

- What other benefits are available from the state, on entering the home or in the future?

- What happens if the person's capital becomes exhausted?

- What type and standard of care are provided and what will it cost?

- What extras are provided within the care package and what must the person pay for in addition?

- Is the contract appropriate to the person's needs and sufficiently flexible? Is the person allowed to smoke or keep a pet?

- Does the contract provide a reasonable notice period if the person wishes to move or in the event of his death?

- How will the location affect the family and friends and will they be put to expense in visiting?

Once a suitable home has been selected, the deputy may enter into a contract with the home and should ensure that the correct fees are paid on time.

Maintenance in P's own home

8.33   If a person is able and willing to remain in his own home then the deputy should do everything practicable to facilitate this, even if this leads to a more expensive outcome. As with the choice of a care home, it is not for the deputy to determine where or how the person should live, especially where the person retains capacity to make such decisions for himself. Generally a person who wishes to remain in his own home is expressing a strong desire to do so and has capacity to make that decision. If the person lacks capacity, then past wishes or the views of the carers may influence the decision to remain at home, but a deputy must also be prepared to take an objective view where it is necessary. He should not be required to maintain a property at great expense when there is no material benefit to the person who would in fact be better and more safely cared for in a care home

In determining whether and how the person should be maintained in his own home, the deputy will need to take account of various factors:

- the past and present wishes of the person;
- the views of the person's family and carers;
- the advice of professionals such as doctors, social workers or occupational therapists;
- the level of care and assistance the person will require in his own home;
- whether the home needs to be adapted or repaired and the costs of such adaptations and repairs;
- the cost of nursing care and housekeeping as well as of keeping the property insured and paying utilities;
- the practical and legal obligations towards carers: whether carers are employed or self-employed, that the premises are safe and there is appropriate insurance in place;
- what other expenditure may be required, for example the cost of transport, holidays, furniture or for any additional help in the home (for example, domestic);
- how the home is to be provisioned: who will do the shopping and how will day-to-day expenses be paid for?
- whether the costs of care at home can be afforded;
- whether the expectations of the person are realistic;
- what other benefits and sources of funding are available; and
- the interests of any other family members whether as occupants of the property, co-owners of the property or carers.

Where the person is living in his own home, the deputy must ensure that utilities and household bills are paid. Where possible these should be paid through the deputyship bank account and bills should be sent directly to the deputy for payment. The deputy must also take responsibility for ensuring that the correct level of council tax is paid and that any discount or exemption is applied for. The deputy must also claim housing benefit and council tax benefit where the person is eligible to claim these benefits.

It is the deputy's duty to keep the property secure and in a reasonable state of repair. The deputy is responsible for ensuring that the property is insured to cover its full rebuilding cost and that the contents are insured on a replacement value basis. Policy renewals and schedules must therefore be sent directly to the deputy who is responsible for the maintenance of the policies and payment of premiums through the deputyship bank account. The deputy will also need to ensure that visitors and carers are covered by an appropriate level of insurance.

The deputy as employer

8.34   The deputy must also consider the person's care arrangements and how these will be paid for and administered. Agency carers may be expensive but provide flexible cover and will be employed by the care agency or may be self-employed. A regular carer or domestic help may not be self-employed and will need to be employed directly by the deputy who will be responsible for preparing a contract of employment as well as paying any tax and national insurance contributions. Carers – whether employed or self-employed – have rights that cannot be disregarded. For instance, the Working Time Regulations 1998 govern the maximum number of hours that can be worked without breaks and the National Minimum Wage Act 1998 governs minimum rates of pay. Where a person has ongoing nursing needs or cannot be left alone, more than one carer will need to be employed. The working conditions must also be safe and appropriate and the risk of any activity needs to be assessed.

A deputy is acting within the scope of his authority to employ a person on behalf of the person, who is the legal employer. The deputy is the agent, but is responsible for ensuring that any formalities are complied with. Given the amount of work involved, a deputy may need to involve:

● an occupational therapist to ensure that working conditions are safe;

● an employment lawyer to prepare a suitable contract of employment or to check the terms applied by a care agency;

● a recruitment consultant to find the carer, take references and carry out appropriate vetting with the Criminal Records Bureau;

● a case manager to manage the carers; to make sure that the right amount of care is on hand when needed and that any gaps in care can be covered;

● an accountant or payroll administration to administer the salary, tax and national insurance payments;

● an insurance broker to provide employee liability cover.

Where a person wishes to live at home, those wishes need to be considered carefully. A deputy must, however, consider not just the person's wishes, but a whole range of legal and practical responsibilities. The costs can therefore be considerable, even without taking into account the resources tied up in the property.

Repairs and improvements to home

8.35   General repairs and maintenance can be paid for by the deputy acting under his authority provided the expenditure is in the person's best interests. The deputy would, however, be expected to obtain at least two competitive estimates for the work.

Where substantial repairs are required or a property has to be adapted to cater for the person's physical needs then the costs involved may well be significant. It is likely that specific adaptations will not be matched by an equivalent improvement in the value of the property. The deputy must therefore proceed carefully. The deputy should obtain at least three estimates and where extensive works are required, arrange for a competitive tender to be carried out by an architect who should be experienced in dealing with adaptations for clients with special needs. Depending on the amount of work to be carried out and the costs involved, it may be advisable for the architect to complete a detailed specification in consultation with an occupational therapist before the work is tendered for. The preferred bid may also be checked by a quantity surveyor. Where the costs are considerable or might lead to a reduction in the value of the estate then a deputy would be acting appropriately in asking the Court to approve the contract.

Although the expenditure on the property must be governed primarily by the person's best interests, the deputy must also consider the effect on the provisions of the person's will. If the property is the subject matter of a specific gift, it would be inequitable for major expenditure on the property to be funded by the person's residuary estate, which would thereby diminish in value. In such circumstances, the Court may direct that expenditure carried out for the permanent improvement or benefit of the property be charged against the property (MCA 2005, Sch 2 para 9 – see **8.41** below).

Where an application is made to the Court to authorise significant expenditure on a property, this can be dealt with under the short procedure set out in Practice Direction 9D (paragraph 4(l)).

Sharing a property – benefit to a third party

8.36   Where the property is also the home of a relative or carer then that person may benefit indirectly where the property is being maintained at the expense of the person. For instance a spouse or the parents of a disabled person may occupy the same property. Any benefit to the other party may be:

- incidental to the person's benefit;

- given in return for consideration (where the other party is a co-owner of the property and paying a share of the outgoings);

- necessary for the person's welfare (where the other party is providing a degree of care); or

- it is in the person's best interests to maintain or provide for the needs of another person.

Generally there will be an overlap or even potential conflict between the interests of the person being cared for and the other owner or occupier of the property. These can be resolved, so long as the respective interests are understood and it is in the best interests of the person concerned to provide this benefit. Where there is a benefit to another person, then the deputy also needs to ensure that he is acting within the scope of his authority. A standard form order appointing a deputy (see **5.20** above) will allow the making of provision for such a person. Maintenance and financial provision for dependents is also considered at **13.8** to **13.10**.

However, where the benefit is significant and might prejudice the interests of the person concerned, other family members or potential dependants, then the express consent of the Court should be obtained.

Personal possessions

8.37   The deputy is responsible for safeguarding a person's personal possessions for the benefit of the person and for the person's estate. It is important for the person to have possessions which can be enjoyed or which have sentimental value. The deputy must, therefore, ensure that all such possessions are adequately insured. An inventory of such personal possessions is recommended.

Where it is unsafe for valuable items to be kept by the person or if the person moves to a care home then possessions may be placed in safe custody at the expense of the person's estate. Smaller and more valuable items should be stored at the bank at which the deputyship bank account is held. Arrangements may also be made for items to be held by relatives or by persons who will inherit such items under a will. In these cases the person holding the items must sign an undertaking to the deputy stating that they are held for safe custody only, that they will not be disposed of without the consent of the Court and that they are properly insured.

Unless the order appointing the deputy contains an express authority to make small gifts or the person has capacity to direct the gifts in person, no items can be disposed of by way of gift without the consent of the Court. While it may be attractive for personal effects that are no longer required by a person to be passed on to relatives or beneficiaries, it is usually easier for these to be retained on behalf of the person concerned than to go to the effort and expense of a formal application to the Court.

Where items are to be sold then it is the responsibility of the deputy to obtain the best price and dispose of the items using a clearance firm, dealer or auction house as is appropriate to the items being disposed of. If items are being sold privately then a professional valuation must be obtained beforehand.

The person's will must be checked before any items are disposed of. If a specific legacy is contained in the will, the item referred to in the will may be retained by the legatee (to the order of the person concerned), gifted to the legatee with the approval of the Court or sold. If it is sold, then the proceeds of sale may be preserved in place of the specific legacy under MCA 2005, Sch 2 para 8 (see **8.41** below).

Where an application is made to the Court for the sale or gift of personal effects, this can be dealt with under the short procedure set out in Practice Direction 9D (paragraph 4(g) and (m)). However, the deputy will still need to provide the Court with an explanation for the disposal, a valuation of the items that are to be disposed of and evidence of any interests in those items under a will.

Motor vehicles

8.38   A person's ability to drive is not covered by MCA 2005, although a decision to drive may well fall within the general ambit of the Act in the same way as any other decision a person might make. A deputy must however be concerned for the safety of the person concerned as well as other road users. A person who might suffer from dementia or other disability that might affect his ability to drive safely should not do so without medical advice and if in doubt, a driving licence should be surrendered. It has not been unknown for a deputy to remove a person's car keys.

Further information about medical standards for fitness to drive is available from the DVLA at: http://www.dvla.gov.uk/medical

A person may, however, be the owner of a motor vehicle and the deputy will be responsible for registering the vehicle in the person's name or as deputy for the person (but not in the deputy's own name) and keeping the registration documents in his safe custody. The deputy will also be responsible for ensuring that road tax is paid and the motor vehicle is serviced and fully insured for all drivers who may need to use the vehicle, whether close relatives, named carers or occasional carers who may drive with the permission of the deputy.

Care needs to be taken with any contract arrangements such as Motability to ensure that the restrictions of the contract are complied with and, where Motability is paid through disability living allowance, that any changes in the benefit are notified to Motability.

If a new vehicle is needed for the person's use then the decision will be for the deputy to make, unless the amount the deputy may spend in a year is restricted and an application needs to be made to the Court to release funds. Whether the Court's consent is required, it is for the deputy to select the right car in terms of what is affordable and appropriate to the person's needs. The deputy must, however, take account of the person's wishes which may cause difficulties when an estate car or people carrier which fits a wheelchair would be more appropriate than a sportscar.

Where the main driver is the spouse or close relative, an application may be made to the Court for a gift (see Chapter 13). It may well be more practical and cheaper in terms of insurance for the vehicle to be bought in the carer's name. If the carer is also the main driver, then the Court would not be unsympathetic to such a gift.

Income tax

8.39   One of the duties of the deputy is to deal with a person's 'income tax and other tax matters'. The deputy must therefore ensure that tax returns are completed on time and any overpayments of tax to which the person is entitled must be claimed. Frequently a person becomes liable to self-assessment by virtue of having funds invested in Court where interest is paid gross. A sealed copy of the order appointing the deputy must therefore be lodged with the person's tax district or a new tax reference must be obtained. Tax returns and notices may then be sent to the deputy or his professional agent. The deputy must also keep interest statements, dividend vouchers and contract notes in a safe place.

Where the person's tax affairs are complex, the deputy may engage an accountant or solicitor whose usual fees will be allowed as a proper expense of the estate. Where the deputy is a solicitor, or a solicitor is engaged as part of his retainer to act for the deputy generally, then completion of a tax return should be included within the solicitor's general management fees which will be subject to assessment. Where an accountant is instructed, it will be for the deputy to check that the fees charged are fair and reasonable.

The will

Importance of examining P's will

8.40   The deputy – and any solicitor acting for him – must be aware of the importance of the will, to ensure that no action is taken inadvertently which is contrary to a person's testamentary wishes as set out in the will. Where a testator has already made a will, a copy should be sent to the Court with the application to appoint a deputy (see **5.6** above). If this information is not to hand or the will is held in the custody of a third party then the form must refer to the location of the will. If it is appropriate for the deputy to have sight of the will, then this should be referred to in the order appointing the deputy. The order should either provide for the original to be held in the safe custody of a named firm of solicitors and if they are not the firm acting in the matter, that a copy should be made available to the deputy.

The deputy and his solicitor must also respect the confidential nature of the will and not disclose its contents except as directed by the Court or in proceedings before the Court. Where disclosure is required by Practice Direction 9F and in any proceedings before the Court, the will remains a privileged document.

The contents of the will must be examined carefully, especially to take account of changes in a person's circumstances, where the following matters may need to be considered:

●   the will may have been made years previously and legatees and residuary beneficiaries may have predeceased the testator;

●   an executor appointed by the will may have predeceased the testator or have become unable to act;

- the testator may have planned to dispose of the estate on the basis of a larger estate, perhaps before nursing home fees reduced its value. The estate may not be large enough to pay the residuary beneficiary and individual legacies may need to be abated;

- the testator's estate may have increased in value due to property and investments increasing in value or as a result of an inheritance;

- the existing will might not be appropriate for inheritance tax, for instance where it leaves substantial assets to a non-exempt beneficiary or fails to take advantage of the transferable nil rate band;

- specific gifts referred to in the will may have been disposed of by the testator whether by way of gift or sale. If still held by the testator they may need to be disposed of and MCA 2005, Sch 2 para 8 considered.

If the person concerned is intestate or an existing will is no longer appropriate to his current circumstances then a new will should be considered. If the person lacks capacity to make a new will then a statutory will may be authorised by the Court (see Chapter 13).

Preservation of interest in property – Mental Capacity Act 2005, Sch 2 para 8

8.41 MCA 2005, Sch 2 para 8 restates the provisions of s 101 of the Mental Health Act 1983. This provides that where property is sold or disposed of by virtue of s 18 of the MCA 2005, then any person who would have taken an interest in that property under the will of the person concerned, shall on the death of the person take the same interest representing the property disposed of.

Thus where a will gives a specific legacy of a property which is sold by the deputy with the result that the legacy would otherwise adeem, the Court will direct that the net proceeds of sale (or a replacement property) be set aside so as to represent the original gift in the will. If the property is sold then the net proceeds will be placed in a designated deposit with the Court Funds Office, earmarked to record the identity of the asset. Where a replacement property is bought by the person, then the terms of the will may apply to the replacement property in place of the property referred to in the will. If expenditure is required for the maintenance of such property (or any other property) then the Court may direct that such expenditure be charged on the property for the benefit of the person's estate (MCA 2005, Sch 2 para 9).

Although the Act refers to a property being charged with expenditure, there is no reference to a fund representing the proceeds of sale of a property being used to maintain the person concerned. There is, however, no reason why the Court cannot authorise any fund belonging to a person to be applied for his benefit and Sch 2 para 8(6) allows the Court to 'give such directions as may be necessary or expedient for the purpose of facilitating the operation of sub-paragraphs (1) to (6)'. Unless there are particular reasons for favouring one part of the estate in preference to another part, the designated fund should bear any future expenditure proportionately with the residuary estate. This does of course make for some interesting complications and the provisions of Sch 2 should be treated as no more than a temporary or working presumption that should be reviewed and if necessary displaced by a new will at the earliest opportunity. A new will is in any event preferred by the Court because it gives the testator, deputy or attorney, as well as the Court, an opportunity to review and update the will in the light of current circumstances.

Schedule 2 para 8 only applies to disposals under s 18 of the MCA 2005, thus to sales directed by the Court of Protection or a deputy acting under the Court's authority. The provision does not apply to a disposal by an attorney acting under a registered enduring or lasting power of attorney. The problem facing the attorney in this situation is considered at **8.45** below and at **14.37**.

P making own will

8.42   Capacity is specific to the decision being made (see **1.4**) and the Court has no authority to make a decision which a person is capable of making for himself (see **2.16**). A person may therefore be capable of making a valid will even though a deputy has also been appointed to make decisions on his behalf.

While this is consistent with the provisions of the MCA 2005, it can cause problems in practice. A person for whom a deputy has been appointed to act (or whose enduring power of attorney has been registered) may well be vulnerable or have limited understanding. There may be a *de facto* presumption that he lacks capacity. Prior to October 2007, the Public Guardianship Office was wary of a will being made by a patient under the Mental Health Act 1983 jurisdiction. It was not opposed to the practice, just aware that problems would arise if a will was made casually without proper advice and attention to testamentary capacity. Thus where it was proposed that a will be made for a patient, the Public Guardianship Office expected to be notified in advance and supplied with medical evidence confirming that the patient was capable of making a will. This evidence had to deal specifically with the patient's testamentary capacity. If the evidence was clear that the patient had testamentary capacity evidence, the Public Guardianship Office would authorise the patient's solicitor to take instructions from the patient to prepare a will. The solicitor would be expected to take instructions and make sure that the patient received appropriate advice on the terms and implications of his will and was capable of understanding that advice. The solicitor remained responsible for ensuring that the patient met the legal requirements for making a valid will.

There are no equivalent safeguards for a person for whom a deputy has been appointed to act or who lacks capacity in respect of some decisions, to make his own will. Neither are there any safeguards for a solicitor who wishes to take instructions from such a person. The only choices available to the solicitor are as follows:

- to obtain appropriate medical evidence and take responsibility for ensuring that the client has capacity, without reference to the Court or Public Guardian;

- make a formal application to the Court for a declaration under MCA 2005, s 15 that the client has capacity to make a decision specified in the declaration; or

- make a formal application to the Court for a direction that he may take instructions directly, notwithstanding the appointment of a deputy (or registration of an EPA).

Where a will is made for a person, its safe custody is the responsibility of the person and his solicitor. Clearly it should be kept in a secure place, together with any medical evidence or authority of the Court of Protection relevant to its execution.

Solicitor is acting for P

8.43 If the solicitor preparing the will is also the solicitor of the deputy (or attorney), a conflict of interest may arise. This will not generally prevent the solicitor from acting for the person, especially if there is external and independent medical advice. However, the solicitor must be aware that he is acting for the person concerned and not the deputy or attorney and if there is a potential conflict of interest then the onus is on the solicitor to decline to act for both parties and ensure that an independent solicitor is instructed.

Conflicts of interest are also considered at **7.7** and the identity of the client at **4.4**.

P is incapable of making a new will

8.44 Where the person is incapable of making a new will and a will needs to be made for the person then the Court may authorise a will to be made on behalf of the person under MCA 2005, s 18(1)(i). The Court must make such a will and cannot delegate it to a deputy (s 20(3)(b)). The jurisdiction of the Court to make such a will and the procedures involved are explained in detail in Chapter 13.

Testator is donor of an enduring or lasting power of attorney

8.45 Similar considerations apply where the donor of an EPA or LPA wishes to make a will or where the attorney needs to deal with the donor's estate in the light of the contents of an existing will. However, the attorney will not necessarily be aware of the contents of the donor's will. The will remains a confidential document belonging to the donor and should not be disclosed without the consent of the donor. It should reflect best practice for this issue to be considered at the time the lasting power of attorney is drawn up (or when the enduring power of attorney was drawn up) so that the donor decides if and when the will should be disclosed to the attorney. If appropriate, the power should contain a special condition authorising the attorney to obtain the donor's will. A solicitor acting for a donor should at that stage review the donor's will and address the issue of its safe custody.

If at the relevant time the attorney does not have access to the will of a donor who lacks capacity, the person holding the will may be prepared to release a copy to the attorney but is not obliged to do so. If disclosure cannot be obtained informally, a formal application must be made to the Court for authority to release the will or a copy.

If a proposed disposal of a part of the donor's estate might conflict with the person's will, the attorney may face difficulties. The saving provisions of MCA 2005, Sch 2 para 8 apply only to a disposal under s 18 (where the Court makes the decision or appoints a deputy to make the decision). If property which is the subject of a specific legacy in a will is sold by an attorney, then the gift in the will adeems and falls into residue. This may lead to consequences which are contrary to the wishes of the donor. In such a situation the attorney must consider very carefully the following options:

- applying for a statutory will under MCA 2005, s 18. The attorney under a registered EPA or a LPA is authorised to make such an application (Rules 51(2) and 52(4) of the Court of Protection Rules);

- disclaiming the power of attorney and applying for the appointment of a deputy; or

- applying to the Court of Protection to exercise its jurisdiction under the MCA 2005 without revocation of the power of attorney. 'Switching' between different parts of the Act in such a way is unusual but might be useful if a statutory will application is inappropriate. However, the Court cannot make arrangements for the earmarking of the proceeds of sale by lodging funds in the special account at the Court and would prefer a statutory will application to be made.

Interest in an estate or trust

P has a beneficial interest

8.46   Where a person has a right or interest under a will or intestacy, the Court needs to be informed as part of the application process. This is, however, only to ensure that the Court has a complete picture of the nature of the estate and that the deputy is competent and suitably authorised to deal with an estate of this nature. The Court will then authorise the deputy to give a valid receipt for any monies due to the person concerned and if necessary direct the transfer of funds received from the estate to the Court Funds Office or the deputy.

Where a person becomes a beneficiary after a deputy has been appointed, then the deputy will generally have sufficient authority to act as the person's agent in dealing with the personal representatives. However, the deputy should apply to the Court of Protection for authority to give a receipt. While this will necessitate a formal application and payment of a fee, this can be dealt with under the short procedure set out in Practice Direction 9D (paragraph 4(i)). This will not only allow the Court an opportunity to provide the deputy with authority to receive the funds, but also to check whether the existing authority is too restricted or too wide to administer the sum involved. The Court may also need to review the deputy's security.

Where an application is made to the Court in connection with an interest in an estate, the applicant must provide the Court with:

- a copy of the will or instrument under which the person is to benefit;

- a sealed copy of any grant of probate (if obtained);

- details of the benefits due to the person, and, if the estate has been administered, copies of the accounts; and

- an explanation of the authority required from the Court.

Where the person has a right to income under a life interest, this is payable to the deputy under his general authority to receive the income of the person concerned.

P is a discretionary beneficiary

8.47   Where a person has no fixed entitlement under a will or settlement, the Court has no jurisdiction over payments made at the trustees' discretion or any other voluntary payments made by a third party for the benefit of the person, unless those payments are made directly to the deputy. Often such payments are made directly to a carer or care home or used to purchase items or provide services to the person.

If a deputy does receive a discretionary payment then unless it is substantial it should be paid to the deputyship bank account in the same way as any other income or other money that is paid to the deputy.

P is an executor or personal representative

Non-Contentious Probate Rules 1987

8.48   The status of a person who lacks capacity in relation to a grant of representation is dealt with by r 35 of the Non-Contentious Probate Rules 1987 (SI 1987/2024). This has been updated to reflect the provisions of the Mental Capacity Act and provides as follows:

'35 Grants in case of lack of mental capacity

(1)   Unless a district judge or registrar otherwise directs, no grant shall be made under this rule unless all persons entitled in the same degree as the person who lacks capacity within the meaning of the Mental Capacity Act 2005 referred to in paragraph (2) below have been cleared off.

(2)   Where a district judge or registrar is satisfied that a person entitled to a grant lacks capacity within the meaning of the Mental Capacity Act 2005 to manage his affairs, administration for his use and benefit, limited until further representation be granted or in such other way as the district judge or registrar may direct, may be granted in the following order of priority—

(a)   to the person authorised by the Court of Protection to apply for a grant;

(b) where there is no person so authorised, to the lawful attorney of the person who lacks capacity within the meaning of the Mental Capacity Act 2005 acting under a registered enduring power of attorney;

(c) where there is no such attorney entitled to act, or if the attorney shall renounce administration for the use and benefit of the person who lacks capacity within the meaning of the Mental Capacity Act 2005, to the person entitled to the residuary estate of the deceased.

(3) Where a grant is required to be made to not less than two administrators, and there is only one person competent and willing to take a grant under the foregoing provisions of this rule, administration may, unless a district judge or registrar otherwise directs, be granted to such person jointly with any other person nominated by him.

(4) Notwithstanding the foregoing provisions of this rule, administration for the use and benefit of the person who lacks capacity within the meaning of the Mental Capacity Act 2005 may be granted to such other person as the district judge or registrar may by order direct.

(5) Unless the applicant is the person authorised in paragraph (2)(a) above, notice of an intended application under this rule shall be given to the Court of Protection.'

Application by person authorised

8.49   Where the executor is a person who lacks capacity and no substitute executor is appointed under the will, then the Court will authorise the deputy in the order appointing the deputy or in a separate order to apply for a grant of letters of administration (with the will) for the use and benefit of the person concerned. A standard order appointing a deputy will be insufficient for such purposes. While this will necessitate a formal application and payment of a fee, this can be dealt with under the short procedure set out in Practice Direction 9D (paragraph 4(j)). The applicant will need to provide the Court with a copy of the will and an account of the person's beneficial interest in the estate or if there is no beneficial interest, why there is no one else who can administer the estate.

Where the Court does authorise a person to apply for a grant, a sealed copy of the order must be filed with the Probate Registry. A person so authorised by the Court has priority over any other person to apply for the grant.

Where the person who lacks capacity is a person entitled to apply for a grant of letters of administration of a will or on an intestacy, an authority to apply for the grant will only be issued where there is no other willing and competent person entitled to apply in the same degree.

The effort and expense of an application to the Court can be avoided by an application directly to the Probate Registry under r 35(4). Notice of the application must however be given to the Court of Protection to comply with r 35(5).

Executor acting under an enduring or lasting power of attorney

8.50 A deputy or person authorised by the Court has priority over any other person to apply for a grant of letters of administration. An attorney under a registered EPA may only apply for a grant if no other person has been authorised by the Court to apply for a grant. In such a case the attorney must give written notice to the Court of Protection of his intention to apply for a grant.

Rule 35 of the Non-Contentious Probate Rules 1987 makes no reference to a LPA. A donee of a LPA may therefore act in the same way as any other attorney making an application for the use and benefit of another person under r 31 of the Non-Contentious Probate Rules 1987. However, where the donor lacks capacity, r 31(3) refers the applicant for the grant back to r 35. The donee of a LPA where the donor lacks capacity must therefore either apply to the Court of Protection for authority to apply for a grant or apply to the Probate Registry under r 35(4) with evidence that the donor lacks capacity.

P is a patron of a benefice

8.51 The powers of a person without capacity to exercise a power of appointment to a benefice are no longer reserved to the Lord Chancellor but are exercised by the Court. MCA 2005, Sch 2 para 10 provides as follows:

'(1) Any functions which P has as patron of a benefice may be discharged only by a person ("R") appointed by the court.

(2) R must be an individual capable of appointment under section 8(1)(b) of the 1986 Measure (which provides for an individual able to make a declaration of communicant status, a clerk in Holy Orders, etc. to be appointed to discharge a registered patron's functions).

(3) The 1986 Measure applies to R as it applies to an individual appointed by the registered patron of the benefice under section 8(1)(b) or (3) of that Measure to discharge his functions as patron.

(4) "The 1986 Measure" means the Patronage (Benefices) Measure 1986 (No. 3).'

Chapter 9

Sale and purchase of property

Sale of property

Preliminary matters

9.1　While it may be desirable for a person to go on living in his own home, a time may come when there is no choice but to sell. The decision to sell will be of immense significance, both in terms of the person's future care and the resources of the estate. When considering the sale of a person's property, the following preliminary matters must be considered:

- the proposed sale must be in the person's best interests. Is the decision to sell the property one that the person would make for himself, if he had capacity, or are others such as potential beneficiaries concerned for their own interests? Can the person participate in the decision? If the decision must be made on his behalf, who should be consulted and what factors need to be taken into account?

- if a replacement property is not being acquired, it must be clear that there is no prospect of the person living in the property. This may be clear from the medical evidence or from the facts of the case where the person requires full-time care in a nursing home or has already secured new accommodation.

- the property must be made as secure as possible while it is empty and any valuable contents should be removed;

- insurance cover and essential utilities must be maintained and any conditions imposed by the insurer must be complied with;

- the property must be expertly valued;

- the solicitor acting in the matter must locate the deeds to the property so as to check that the title to the property is good and marketable and suitable for sale by private treaty or by auction;

- the deputy should have sufficient authority to sell the property (see **9.2** below). Even if the deputy has formal authority within the scope of the order appointing him, an application to the Court may still be appropriate if the sale is likely to be contentious or the person's capacity is in issue; and

- the person's will must be checked to make sure that the property is not the subject of a specific gift which would otherwise adeem and which therefore needs to be set aside under s 101 of the Mental Health Act 1983 (see **8.41** above).

Application to sell a property

9.2   Once it is clear that the property can and should be sold, a deputy must ensure that he has sufficient authority to sell the property. A standard general order of the type described at **5.20** will contain sufficient authority to sell a property. If the order does not contain such authority or no deputy has yet been appointed, application may be made in one of the following ways:

● on a first application, using Forms COP1 and COP1A, completed to show that the property needs to be sold;

● if the first application has not yet been determined and an order for sale becomes necessary, application for an interim order may be made in Form COP9. Depending on the timescale and any delays in the substantive appointment of the deputy, the Court will either ensure that authority is provided within the first order or in an interim order;

● if a deputy has already been appointed but the order does not authorise the sale of a property then a new application must be made in Form COP1. If the sale is non-contentious, the short procedure in Practice Direction 9D (paragraph 4(e)) may be used. Whether or not the short procedure is used, the applicant must still pay an application fee of £400 and provide the Court with sufficient evidence of the need for the sale, the value of the property and how the proceeds of sale will affect the estate.

If it is proposed that the property be sold at an undervalue, there is a conflict of interest between the deputy and the seller, or the sale is likely to be contentious, then an application must be made for the Court's consent to the transaction.

If it is in the person's interest to do so, a property can be placed on the market for sale before the order for sale has been issued, and if the property must be sold urgently a deputy may enter into a conditional contract for sale. However, unless a deputy has been appointed, an applicant for an order for sale cannot sign a contract with an estate agent or commission a home information pack. In practice, most agents will wait for these details to be dealt with once the order has been issued so as not to delay the marketing of the property.

Sale by private treaty

9.3   The applicant or deputy will be responsible for negotiating the sale and agree the terms subject to contract and the authority of the Court (if this remains to be provided). It is no longer necessary for the seller to obtain a certificate of value from the selling agent or to obtain the Court's approval of the sale price of the property. The responsibility for determining the price remains firmly with the deputy who must act in the same way as any prudent seller. The deputy should obtain three estimates of the sale price, and if there is a wide discrepancy between the estimates or the property is particularly valuable or unusual, obtain an independent valuation from a qualified surveyor. It is for the deputy to obtain the best price for the property, taking into account the state of the market, the ease of selling the particular property and the buyer's position. The deputy is also responsible for checking the selling agent's terms.

Contract for sale

9.4   Once the order for sale has been issued, the seller's solicitor will need to provide the purchaser with a sealed copy, which the purchaser must file with the Land Registry when registering the transfer.

The Court of Protection is no longer involved in approving the contract or sealing the transfer deed. The seller's solicitor is responsible for drafting the contract for sale and other documents required to sell the property. The contract is entered into by the person concerned acting by the deputy (or other named person as authorised) 'pursuant to an Order of the Court of Protection dated the ... day of ...' No reference should be made to the person's lack of capacity or to his address if it is a residential or nursing home or hospital. The address of the property or the deputy's address should be given instead.

The contract should contain the following special condition:

> 'Copies of the said Order have been supplied to the buyer's solicitors and shall be deemed to be conclusive evidence of the seller's authority to sell. The buyer and [his] [her] solicitors shall not be entitled to raise any requisitions or objections thereto.'

The contract may then be signed by the deputy (or other authorised person) with his own name and with the words 'as deputy for [P]' (see **8.1**). Contracts can then be exchanged in the usual way.

Once contracts have been exchanged, a deputy may allow the buyer access to the property before completion provided that all necessary steps are taken to protect the seller's interests, such as the provision of a 10% deposit. If access is allowed to the property to effect repairs or decorations, the contract or a separate agreement must provide that if the sale does not take place for any reason, the buyer must make good at his own expense any damage done and shall have no claim against the seller in respect of any work done. Clearly such an agreement may be difficult to enforce in practice and should only be considered if it is an unavoidable condition of selling the property at an acceptable price. It is always preferable to expedite completion of the sale rather than incur the risk of unsupervised access to the property.

Prior to completion the deputy must ensure that all utilities and the local authority are notified, meter readings are taken and that vacant possession can be given on completion.

Transfer deed

9.5   As with the contract, it is the seller's solicitor's responsibility to ensure that the transfer is drawn up correctly, even if the transfer document is prepared by the buyer's solicitor. The actual transfer is made by the seller who is the person who lacks capacity, not the deputy, as a conveyance by a deputy is not effective to pass a legal estate. The same covenants for title can therefore be given as if the person were acting in his own right and had capacity to sell the property.

The transfer deed is executed in the same way as any other deed executed by a deputy (see **8.1** above). Thus the seller is described in the transfer as:

'[P] acting by [name of deputy] pursuant to an Order/Direction dated the . . . day of . . . made by the Court of Protection'.

Any express covenants contained in the transfer should be given by '[P] by the [name of deputy] acting as aforesaid'. The attestation clause must also be set out correctly and Form TR1 amended accordingly.

On completion of the sale, the completion monies are paid to the seller's solicitors who will in due course arrange for the funds to be invested or paid into Court with any interest which may be payable.

Sale by public auction

9.6   If the seller is advised by the selling agent that a better price may be obtained by selling the property at auction then the Court will have no objection. The sale may be advertised as being made 'by Order of the Court of Protection'. It is the responsibility of the seller's solicitor to prepare the particulars and conditions of sale. The contract will be in the same form as if the property were being sold by private treaty except that the special condition shall, instead of referring to the buyer having seen the relevant authority, provide that:

'Copies of the said Order will be supplied to the buyer's solicitors on completion and shall be deemed to be conclusive evidence of the seller's authority to sell'.

As with a sale by private treaty, the deputy is responsible for determining the value of the property. The deputy will also be responsible for setting the reserve price before the auction takes place.

Sale where P is a co-owner

9.7   If the property is vested in a person who lacks capacity either solely or jointly as a trustee, the person concerned must be replaced or discharged as a trustee before the legal estate can be dealt with under the trust of land or under the powers vested in the trustees of land, unless the sale is to the other co-owner. An application will therefore have to be made for leave to appoint a new trustee of land under s 36(9) of the Trustee Act 1925 (see Chapter 11 below). The new trustee cannot be the co-owner of the property or an attorney of the co-owner under an EPA. The sale itself will be made by the trustees acting in that capacity, and no further authority for sale will be required.

Sale to co-owner

9.8   Where the person's beneficial interest in the property is being sold to the other co-owner, the sale is no different to any other sale of property. The order appointing the deputy will make it clear whether the deputy is acting within the scope of his authority. However, in most such cases there will be a conflict of interest between co-owners or a restriction on the title preventing a sale without the consent of the Court of Protection. In such cases an application will need to be made to the Court of Protection for the deputy to release to a joint tenant or assign to a tenant in common the beneficial interest in the property.

Purchase of property

Application to purchase a property

9.9   As with the sale of a property, a deputy with a standard general authority will have the Court's authority under MCA 2005, s 18(1)(c) of the Act to purchase a property so long as the purchase is in the best interests of the person who also lacks capacity to make that decision. The deputy is responsible for ensuring that not only is the property appropriate in terms of price, title and condition but that it also meets the person's wishes and other personal requirements.

A formal application for a purchase may also be avoided where the purchase is made pursuant to an interim payment by a defendant in a personal injury claim. The court in which the claim is made may authorise the release of funds to a solicitor to apply towards the purchase.

Otherwise, a formal application for the purchase of a property will have to be made where:

● no deputy has been appointed;

● the deputy's authority is limited and does not extend to the purchase of property;

● there is a conflict of interest between buyer and seller or between buyers where more than one purchaser is involved;

● significant expenditure or borrowing from a lender is required;

● the purchase might prove contentious, for instance if it involves spending more than would be objectively appropriate or there is a dispute as to where the person should be cared for; or

● the purchase is outside of England and Wales.

Where an application to purchase needs to be made, this follows the usual formal process. The short procedure described in Practice Direction 9D does not refer to a purchase of a property. Where such a significant step is proposed, the applicant should file a witness statement explaining with evidence why the proposed purchase is in the person's best interests. The witness statement should provide as much information about the property as possible, and show the reason for the purchase, why the property is appropriate to the person's needs, what other options are available to the person and how the purchase – as well as any future expenditure and outgoings – will be funded. The Court will also expect details of any other occupier of the property and proposals for his or her own maintenance or contribution to the purchase price or maintenance costs. The issues a deputy must address are dealt with in more detail at **8.33** to **8.35** above. The Court will therefore require as much detail as possible about the new property and the deputy will need to consider providing:

(a)   a copy of the agent's particulars;

(b)   a surveyor's report. The surveyor's report must deal with the structure of the property, any repairs or adaptations which will be required and state that the purchase price is a fair market value for the type and location of the property. The surveyor's report (or other specialist report) must also address the suitability of the property to any special needs of the person;

(c)   if extensive improvements or adaptations are required, an architect should provide a detailed report for this purpose, supported by a report from a quantity surveyor if significant expenditure is required;

(d)   some other evidence of the suitability of the property for the person's needs from a person qualified for such a purpose, such as a social worker or occupational therapist;

(e)   a completion statement or detailed budget showing the cost of the purchase and incidental costs, including conveyancing fees and stamp duty land tax.

(f)   any other financial data showing how the property, any repairs and upkeep are to be paid for and that this expenditure will not prejudice the person's financial security;

(g)   details of any consequential expenditure such as the provision of care in the home; and

(h)   details of any shared interest or contribution from family members, including a draft declaration of trust setting out the beneficial interests and other rights and obligations of the co-purchasers.

Completion of purchase

9.10   Generally the surveyor's report or other evidence will be adequate evidence of the value of the property. The onus rests with the deputy to act in the buyer's best interests, whether or not an application to the Court needs to be made.

Depending on when the property is purchased, authority will be provided in the standard general order or a specific order made by the Court. A specific order will need to deal with provision of the purchase money and the release of funds from Court, as well as for the safe custody of the title deeds to the property. The buyer's solicitor is then responsible for approving the contract and transfer. Once in a position to exchange contracts, the contract is signed under hand. If the person who lacks capacity is a party to the transfer and entering into covenants with the seller, the incapable buyer is described in the transfer deed as '[P] acting by [name of deputy] pursuant to an Order/ Direction dated the ... day of ... made by the Court of Protection'. The attestation clause must also be amended in the same way as on a sale (see **9.5** above) and likewise no reference should be made to the buyer's lack of capacity or his address if it is a care home or hospital. The transfer deed is then executed in the same way as any other deed executed pursuant to an order of the Court of Protection (see **8.1** above).

Purchase of beneficial interest in a property

9.11   It may be necessary for the person to acquire a beneficial interest in a property which is being acquired jointly with another person. This may happen, for instance, where the person who lacks capacity is cared for by a spouse or a parent who wishes to buy a new property jointly and the resources of both parties are required to fund the purchase. Where a personal injury award is aimed at providing for a home for a claimant who is a child or young adult, parents will often join together to buy a larger property, using the equity from their own property or their past care award towards the purchase price.

In such a case, a purchaser of a beneficial interest would expect to be a trustee of the trust of land, but this is not appropriate for a person who lacks capacity. The person's beneficial interest can be protected by the property being vested in the names of at least two trustees who may be the other co-owner and a solicitor. The ownership of the property and the beneficial interests will be set out in a declaration of trust.

The party who lacks capacity is not a party to the declaration and should be referred to in the deed by his own name. The declaration will also need to recite the fact that the purchase in the names of the trustees has been approved by the Court of Protection or is made within the scope of the deputy's authority. To safeguard the interests of the incapable party, the declaration of trust must set out the restriction to be entered on the title to the effect that:

> 'no sale of the property shall be made and no disposition shall be registered except with the approval of the Court of Protection and that in the event of a sale the proceeds of the sale of [P's] beneficial interest must be paid to the deputy or as directed by the Court of Protection and that no sale by a survivor of joint proprietors be registered except by an order of the Court or of the Registrar.'

Whether the Court needs to approve the purchase and terms of the declaration of trust depends on the extent of the deputy's authority. A court approving a payment by a defendant can also approve the release of funds for such a purpose without further approval of the Court of Protection. Otherwise a formal application for the purchase must be made in the same way as any other purchase of a property (see **9.9** above). And whether or not a formal authority is required, the deputy must consider carefully the best interests of the person concerned and the benefits to any other co-owner or occupier (see **8.36** above). The other purchasers must also consider their interests separately and in any such joint purchase, independent advice from different solicitors is essential.

Care needs to be taken where the property is already owned and a share is to be acquired on behalf of the person who lacks capacity. The purchase of a beneficial interest will be liable to stamp duty land tax and depending on the sums involved, it may be more advantageous for the existing owners to borrow money by way of a secured loan,

Other dealings with land

9.12   The Court's powers extend beyond the sale or purchase of a property. A deputy acting under a standard general order has authority to manage the person's property and collect any rents due in respect of such property.

Other property issues that a deputy may need to deal with include:

* the granting of a lease or tenancy by the person concerned;

* the granting of a licence, covenant or easement;

* the surrender of a lease or tenancy;

* the acceptance of the surrender of a lease or tenancy;

* the assignment of a lease;

* the exercise of any powers of the patient as tenant for life under the Settled Land Act 1925;

* the mortgaging of the property;

* the discharge of a mortgage belonging;

* the loan of money secured on a property of another person; and

* expenditure on the property (see also **8.35** above).

Where a person's estate consists of tenanted properties, then it is essential for the deputy to have a widely drafted general order that will provide authority for such transactions. Where a formal authority is required from the Court of Protection, the deputy must make a formal application using Form COP1 and paying an application fee of £400. In almost all such cases the short form procedure allowed by Practice Direction 9D (see **3.43**) should be followed in the first instance. This must still be supported by an explanation of why the Court's authority is required and information to enable the appropriate form of authority to be drawn up. If the application is complex or involves a benefit to a third party (for instance a loan on favourable terms) then it will be for the Court to request further evidence or direct that other parties be notified or joined as respondents.

Chapter 10

Litigation

Capacity to conduct proceedings

Background

10.1 The conduct of proceedings is a specific matter that a person may or may not have capacity to decide. It is therefore like any other matter that requires capacity for it to be determined, and must be considered in its own context, regardless of whether a deputy has been appointed to act for a person.

The Mental Capacity Act 2005 (MCA 2005) replaces the presumption in practice that a person who lacked capacity to administer his property and affairs could not conduct proceedings in his own name. Thus a person who was a 'patient' for the purpose of Part VII of the Mental Health Act 1983 could not under the Civil Procedure Rules 1998 (CPR) conduct proceedings without a litigation friend. This presumption was, however, displaced in those cases where a person had not yet been deemed a 'patient' and where the Court of Protection was not yet involved. This issue arose in the case of *White v Fell* (12 November 1987, unreported). It was alleged that the plaintiff – who had suffered a serious brain injury – should be a patient and as someone who had no standing to compromise a claim, thereby allowing a new claim to be made out of time. Although the case dealt with whether the claimant could manage her property and affairs, the ability to conduct and compromise proceedings was integral to her property and affairs. Although the case was unreported, it was cited by Wright J in the first instance decision in the subsequent case *of Masterman-Lister v Jewell* [2002] EWHC 417 (QB) (at paragraph 23):

> 'The expression "incapable of managing her own affairs and property" must be construed in a common sense way as a whole. It does not call for proof of complete incapacity. On the other hand, it is not enough to prove the plaintiff is now substantially less capable of managing her own affairs and property than she would have been had the accident not occurred. I have no doubt that the plaintiff is now quite incapable of managing unaided a large sum of money such as the sort of sum that would be appropriate compensation for her injuries. That, however, is not conclusive. Few people have the capacity to manage all their affairs unaided. In matters of law, particularly litigation, medicine, and given sufficient resources, finance professional advice is almost universally needed and sought. For instance, if the plaintiff succeeds in her claim for compensation, as almost inevitably she will, then she will need to take, consider and act upon appropriate advice. Even without the accident, all that would have been necessary if her property and affairs were to be sensibly managed. It may be that she would have chosen, and would choose now, not to take advice, but that is not the

question. The question is: is she capable of doing so? To have that capacity she requires first the insight and understanding of the fact that she has a problem in respect of which she needs advice. Experience indicates that she has such insight. For instance, when at home some physical task is beyond her, and when she cannot herself find a solution, she calls on her very good neighbour Mrs. W. When she is faced with personal problems such as, for instance, her desire to divorce her husband, she consults her parents, and with them a solicitor. The evidence is that she realises the extent of her disabilities and that she has a very substantial claim for compensation. She recognises the need for advice in administering a large sum which she is likely to receive.

Secondly, having identified the problem, it will be necessary for her to seek an appropriate adviser and to instruct him with sufficient clarity to enable him to understand the problem and to advise her appropriately. Here she will be inhibited by her difficulty in communication and her defective memory. Certainly it will take her longer to communicate than it would have done but for the accident. On the other hand, she has shown herself capable of instructing solicitors; she has shown a determination to overcome her defective memory, and she has apparently succeeded. It may not be without significance that in neither her divorce proceedings, nor in the first action commenced against the defendant was a guardian or next friend appointed.

Finally, she needs sufficient mental capacity to understand and to make decisions based upon, or otherwise give effect to, such advice as she may receive. I accept that she may not understand all the intricacies of litigation, or of a settlement, or of a wise investment policy. As Dr Evans put it, she would not know the difference between long and short term investments. I am sure he is right. But if that were the appropriate test then quite a substantial proportion of the adult population might be regarded as under disability. What seems to me important is that she has demonstrated her capacity to understand and to make decisions in her matrimonial affairs. Perhaps of greater importance is that she had made those decisions for appropriate reasons.'

The decision in *White v Fell* still depended on whether the plaintiff had capacity to manage her property and affairs. In *Masterman-Lister*, a similar issue arose over liability where it was alleged that the claimant had lacked capacity to bring and then compromise proceedings. As the claimant was subsequently a patient for the purposes of the Mental Health Act 1983 it seemed a reasonable assumption that he could not have brought a claim in the first place. Both Wright J and the Court of Appeal rejected this approach. Capacity to conduct proceedings was an entirely separate matter to managing property and affairs. Capacity to bring and then compromise the claim could be dealt with in isolation. Chadwick LJ concluded his judgment ([2003] 3 All ER 162 at 190) by rejecting:

'... the submission that a person who would be incapable of taking investment decisions in relation to a large sum received as compensation [ie a patient under the Mental Health Act 1983] is to be held, for that reason, to be incapable of pursuing a claim for that compensation. I accept that capacity to pursue a claim requires capacity to take a decision to compromise that claim; and that capacity to compromise requires an understanding of what the effects of a compromise will be – in particular, an understanding that it will be necessary to deal with the compensation monies in a way which will provide for the future. But that does not, as it seems to me, require an understanding as to how that will be done . . .'

Thus the fact that the claimant could not manage his property and affairs in the future and knew that this was likely to happen, did not prevent him from making the separate decision to bring and then compromise the claim. That was a specific decision that had to be made in its own time and context. And although these cases anticipated the flexible approach adopted by the MCA 2005, the CPR still assumed that someone who was already a patient was thereby incapable of bringing or defending proceedings.

Civil Procedure Rules

10.2   The conduct of proceedings in the civil courts, including the Civil Division of the Court of Appeal, is governed by the CPR and the accompanying Practice Directions. These have been updated to take account of the MCA 2005.

A person who lacks capacity for the purposes of the CPR is a protected party and as such, must have a litigation friend to conduct proceedings (CPR r 21.2). Capacity for the purposes of the CPR is defined as 'capacity within the meaning of the [Mental Capacity] Act' (CPR r 21.1). Thus it is irrelevant whether a deputy has been appointed or the party is the donor of a registered Enduring Power of Attorney (EPA). The only relevant question is; does the person have capacity to conduct the particular proceedings?

Litigation and the Mental Capacity Act 2005

10.3   In determining whether a person has capacity to conduct proceedings, MCA 2005, s 2 is critical. The person must be able to:

- *Understand the information relevant to the decision (which includes information about the reasonably foreseeable consequences of (a) deciding one way or another, or (b) failing to make the decision:* Does the person understand the nature of the claim, the value of the claim and its purpose? Does the person understand the risks of losing and the costs implications? All practicable steps must also be taken to assist in providing and communicating the information on which the decision is based.

- *Retain that information*: Can the person retain the information for sufficiently long to be able to make and communicate an informed decision?

- *Use or weigh that information as part of the process of making the decision*: Can the person use the information, consider the advantages and disadvantages of the claim and the risks involved and make a decision?

Although both *White v Fell* and *Masterman-Lister v Jewell* both found that the claimant had capacity to conduct and compromise proceedings, both cases reflect the approach taken by s 2 of the MCA 2005 and place a great deal of reliance on the ability of the legal advisers to assist and provide advice that could be acted on. They should not however be used as a way of underestimating the complexity of litigation and the corresponding degree of capacity required to make decisions. Although the case of *Lindsay v Wood* [2006] EWHC 2895 (QB); [2006] All ER (D) 204 (Nov) was decided before the MCA 2005 came into force, the judge, Stanley Burnton J considered both the earlier cases and applied a similar approach, taking account of the actual decision being made in the light of the actual evidence of the case:

> *[paragraph 46]* 'The first matter I have to address is the degree of complexity of the affairs of the Claimant. There are two areas of his affairs to be considered for these purposes. The first is the litigation. There are likely to be offers of settlement, which will require consideration by the Claimant or someone on his behalf. The Claimant can of course be guided by legal and other professional advice; but he should be able to understand and weigh that advice. Doubtless there is a theoretical possibility of an offer so generous that its acceptability is obvious. It is, however, more likely that a lump sum offer will be less than the optimistic estimates of the Claimant's advisers. They should be able to advise the Claimant of the risks of his rejecting the offer, and the risks of his accepting it: in what areas of anticipated costs there may be shortfalls, and what would happen if the award proves inadequate. There may be an offer of periodical payments, or more likely an offer of a lump sum plus periodical payments. And thirdly, there may be more than one form of settlement offered at the same time. The decisions to be made may not be straightforward, and may not admit of unequivocal advice, of the "In my view you should do this" kind. The Claimant may have to weigh up the advantages and risks of one course as against the other.
>
> The evidence of Mrs Lindsay indicates that the Claimant would be unable to manage any complex decisions of this nature. His lack of concentration, his distractibility, the fact that when out he easily becomes lost, his need to be reminded where he is going, his inability to carry out a work task, evidence this. In a structured setting, free from distractions, he can listen and accept advice as to his financial affairs … But the advice he may receive for the purposes of this litigation may be considerably more complex than the relatively straightforward advice that in view of his condition it would be prudent to place the moneys in trust. In addition, it cannot be excluded that he will receive conflicting advice from other persons with whom he may be in contact, advice that would not necessarily be disinterested. He would be unable to weigh the merits of such advice as against that of his professional advisers.'

The litigation friend

10.4   A person who is appointed to act as a deputy has no right thereby to act as a litigation friend. Likewise, an attorney acting under a registered EPA has no such right (*Gregory & Anor v Turner & Anor* [2003] 2 All ER 1114). A litigation friend must be appointed for the purposes of the proceedings and this can be done in one of two ways:

- without a court order – where either a deputy has authority from the Court of Protection or a person makes a claim or enters the proceedings and serves a certificate of suitability on all the other parties; or

- by a court order – where any party including the proposed litigation friend applies directly to the court for an order appointing the litigation friend.

Court of Protection and litigation friend

10.5   Where a person is a protected party and either a deputy has been appointed or an application is being made in the Court of Protection, then the Court of Protection can exercise its own powers to a person to conduct proceedings in the name of or on behalf of the protected party under MCA 2005, s 18(1)(k). This will generally be done by the Court authorising the deputy or some other suitable person to act and provide a sealed order confirming this.

A deputy or person who has applied to be appointed deputy and who wishes to act for a protected party must apply to the Court of Protection for authority to act as litigation friend. This will require a specific application to the Court of Protection. If no application is pending then a detailed application must be made in Form COP1. Given the serious implications inherent in any litigation, applications relating to litigation are not suitable for the short procedure (Court of Protection Rules, Practice Direction 9D, para 6(b)).

An application must be accompanied by supporting evidence to persuade the Court that the person lacks capacity to act in person, that the appointment of a litigation friend is in his best interests and that the deputy has no adverse interest. The application will also need to address the person's liability as to costs and the prospects of success. Unless the claim is routine or the deputy has no choice (for instance where a claim has already been brought against the person) the deputy should provide an opinion from counsel as to the merits of the claim.

The right to conduct proceedings on behalf of the person concerned extends to claims for personal injury and professional negligence, matrimonial proceedings, claims under contract or against employers and claims under the Inheritance (Provision for Family and Dependants) Act 1975. The person may also have to defend proceedings for contractual or professional liability arising before the onset of incapacity. In addition the person may be personally liable for civil damages notwithstanding his incapacity – for example, if he is responsible for a car accident.

Other person acting as litigation friend

10.6   Not every claim will involve a deputy. Often a claim is brought long before a deputy is appointed. Most personal injury claims are brought by parents or close relatives, and a deputy is only appointed subsequently, once liability has been determined and it is clear that there will be assets that need to be managed by a deputy. The claim can therefore be brought under CPR r 21.5(3) without reference to the Court of Protection provided the proposed litigation friend files with the court a certificate of suitability confirming:

(a)   that he consents to act;

(b)   that he knows or believes the claimant/defendant lacks capacity to conduct proceedings;

(c)   the grounds of his belief and, if his belief is based upon medical opinion or the opinion of another suitably qualified expert, attaching any relevant document to the certificate;

(d)   that he can fairly and competently conduct proceedings on behalf of the protected party;

(e)   that he has no interest adverse to that of the protected party; and

(f)   where the protected party is a claimant, that he undertakes to pay any costs which the protected party may be ordered to pay in relation to the proceedings, subject to any right he may have to be repaid from the assets of the protected party.

The certificate of suitability must also be served on any other person on whom details of the claim must be served and a certificate of service confirming that this has been done must be filed with the court in which the proceedings are being conducted (CPR r 21.5(4)). However, the medical evidence does not have to be served on the other parties (CPR PD 21 para 2.4).

Litigation friend appointed by court

10.7   The court in which the proceedings are being conducted may also appoint a litigation friend or replace an existing litigation friend on an application by another person provided that the court is satisfied that the proposed litigation friend meets the requirements set out in a certificate of suitability filed by that person.

Settlements and awards

Civil Procedure Rules

10.8   No action may be compromised or settled on behalf of a protected party without the consent of the court in which the proceedings are being conducted (CPR r 21.10(1)). Even if no proceedings have been issued, an application must still be made for the approval of the settlement (CPR r 21.10(2)). The court will want to ensure that any proposals for the compromise or settlement of the proceedings are in the interests of the protected party and that where the claim relates to personal injuries and consequential care costs, these have been reflected within the proposed settlement.

The procedure for approval of awards in cases involving a protected party are dealt with at paragraph 5 (where no proceedings have been issued) and paragraph 6 (where proceedings have been issued) of CPR PD 21 which provides as follows:

'Settlement or compromise by or on behalf of a child or protected party before the issue of proceedings

5.1 Where a claim by or on behalf of a child or protected party has been dealt with by agreement before the issue of proceedings and only the approval of the court to the agreement is sought, the claim must, in addition to containing the details of the claim and satisfying the requirements of rule 21.10(2), include the following –

(1)   subject to paragraph 5.3, the terms of the settlement or compromise or have attached to it a draft consent order in Practice Form N292;

(2)   details of whether and to what extent the defendant admits liability;

(3)   the age and occupation (if any) of the child or protected party;

(4)   the litigation friend's approval of the proposed settlement or compromise,

(5)   a copy of any financial advice relating to the proposed settlement; and

(6)   in a personal injury case arising from an accident –

    (a)   details of the circumstances of the accident,

    (b)   any medical reports,

    (c)   where appropriate, a schedule of any past and future expenses and losses claimed and any other relevant information relating to the personal injury as set out in the practice direction which supplements Part 16 (statements of case), and

    (d)   where considerations of liability are raised –

        (i)   any evidence or reports in any criminal proceedings or in an inquest, and

        (ii)   details of any prosecution brought.

5.2

(1)   An opinion on the merits of the settlement or compromise given by counsel or solicitor acting for the child or protected party must, except in very clear cases, be obtained.

(2)   A copy of the opinion and, unless the instructions on which it was given are sufficiently set out in it, a copy of the instructions, must be supplied to the court.

5.3 Where in any personal injury case a claim for damages for future pecuniary loss is settled, the provisions in paragraphs 5.4 and 5.5 must in addition be complied with.

5.4 The court must be satisfied that the parties have considered whether the damages should wholly or partly take the form of periodical payments.

5.5 Where the settlement includes provision for periodical payments, the claim must –

(1)   set out the terms of the settlement or compromise; or

(2)   have attached to it a draft consent order,

which must satisfy the requirements of rules 41.8 and 41.9 as appropriate.

5.6 Applications for the approval of a settlement or compromise will normally be heard by –

(1)   a Master or a district judge in proceedings involving a child; and

(2)   a Master, designated civil judge or his nominee in proceedings involving a protected party.

Settlement or compromise by or on behalf of a child or protected party after proceedings have been issued

6.1 Where in any personal injury case a claim for damages for future pecuniary loss, by or on behalf of a child or protected party, is dealt with by agreement after proceedings have been issued, an application must be made for the court's approval of the agreement.

6.2 The court must be satisfied that the parties have considered whether the damages should wholly or partly take the form of periodical payments.

6.3 Where the settlement includes provision for periodical payments, an application under paragraph 6.1 must –

(1)   set out the terms of the settlement or compromise; or

(2)   have attached to it a draft consent order,

which must satisfy the requirements of rules 41.8 and 41.9 as appropriate.

6.4 The court must be supplied with –

(1)   an opinion on the merits of the settlement or compromise given by counsel or solicitor acting for the child or protected party, except in very clear cases; and

(2)   a copy of any financial advice.

6.5 Applications for the approval of a settlement or compromise, except at the trial, will normally be heard by –

(1)   a Master or a district judge in proceedings involving a child; and

(2)   a Master, designated civil judge or his nominee in proceedings involving a protected party.'

Role of Court of Protection

10.9   The consent of the Court of Protection is no longer required by the CPR. Prior to October 2007 the court in which the proceedings were conducted would by convention and of its own motion require the approval of the Court of Protection to a financial award made in favour of a person who lacked capacity. This practice was based on the decision of the Court of Appeal in *Re E (Mental Health Patient)* [1985] 1 All ER 609 which stated that if a person's affairs are within the jurisdiction of the Court of Protection, the approval of the Court of Protection should be sought in relation to anything affecting that person's property or affairs.

The CPR make no reference to the Court of Protection except in relation to the transfer or carry over of an award to the Court of Protection (CPR PD 21 para 10). The procedures for approval of the award described above and the treatment of the protected party as a protected beneficiary provide adequate protection for a protected party and do not delay the outcome of the case with a further procedure involving another court.

Protected beneficiary

10.10   Where money is recovered on behalf of a protected party, the party is defined as a protected beneficiary in respect of the further administration of that fund (CPR r 21.11). It is for the court making or approving the order disposing of the fund to address where it should be paid to.

Who can receive funds on behalf of a protected beneficiary is dealt with by CPR PD 21 para 10.2 which provides that:

'Where the sum to be administered for the benefit of the protected beneficiary is –

(1) £30,000 or more, unless a person with authority as –

(a) the attorney under a registered enduring power of attorney;

(b) the donee of a lasting power of attorney; or

(c) the deputy appointed by the Court of Protection,

to administer or manage the protected beneficiary's financial affairs has been appointed, the order approving the settlement will contain a direction to the litigation friend to apply to the Court of Protection for the appointment of a deputy, after which the fund will be dealt with as directed by the Court of Protection; or

(2) under £30,000, it may be retained in court and invested in the same way as the fund of a child.'

The Practice Direction makes no reference to a person with equivalent authority in a foreign jurisdiction. Where the protected party lives in or plans to move to another jurisdiction, it appears that a deputy will need to be appointed to receive the award before it can be transferred.

A fund of less than £30,000 may also be held in court, although it is not clear how useful such a facility will be as any use of that money will require the authority of the court. Otherwise the fund must be transferred to the Court of Protection pending the appointment of a deputy.

Interim payments

10.11 Litigation is usually a complex and lengthy process. Often liability will be determined at an early stage, with quantum left to a later date, especially where the long-term consequences of an injury need time to be determined. And even where a case has been determined, there may be a further delay while an application to appoint a deputy is made. All the time, the protected party has immediate care needs that need to be provided for. The CPR therefore provide for the making of interim payments (CPR Part 25), as well as for making other directions before the fund is transferred to the Court of Protection.

Any money recovered on behalf of a protected party, whether as an interim payment or on a final award, is subject to the control of the court (CPR r 21.11). Pending the appointment of a deputy the court may authorise any payment to the litigation friend or his legal representative (CPR PD 21 para 8.1).

Extent of court's powers prior to transfer

10.12 The CPR are in this area unhelpful and contradictory. CPR r 21.11 gives the court a wide discretion as to how it is to apply money recovered on behalf of a protected party. The court must, however, consider whether the party is a protected beneficiary, who is dealt with in more detail by the relevant Practice Direction. Paragraph 8.1 provides as follows:

'When giving directions under rule 21.11, the court –

(1) may direct the money to be paid into court for investment,

(2) may direct that certain sums be paid direct to the child or protected beneficiary, his litigation friend or his legal representative for the immediate benefit of the child or protected beneficiary or for expenses incurred on his behalf, and

(3) may direct that the application in respect of the investment of the money be transferred to a local district registry.'

Paragraph 8.1 appears to give a very wide leeway as to how money is applied in favour of a litigation friend or his legal representative, in contrast to CPR PD 21 para 10.2 which appears mandatory as to the transfer of funds to the Court of Protection. It has therefore been suggested that the court could for instance authorise the payment of funds to a trust or to purchase a property.

The correct interpretation of the CPR must be somewhere between these two provisions. Paragraph 8.1 may refer to monies being paid to the litigation friend or legal representative but qualifies this as that the payment must be 'for the immediate benefit … of the protected party or for expenses incurred on his behalf.' If therefore there is a genuine and immediate need, such as the payment of care costs or even the purchase of a property, the court can release funds for this purpose either as an interim payment or as part of the final order. The remainder of the fund, which will be held for the long-term needs of the protected party, must however be transferred to the Court of Protection. If it is in the best interests of the protected party for the damages award to be held in a private trust, then that is a matter for the Court of Protection to determine under the MCA 2005 acting in the long-term best interests of the party.

Transfer to Court of Protection where party is a protected beneficiary

10.13   Once the case has been determined or settled and if no deputy has yet been appointed, an application for the appointment of a deputy should be commenced as soon as possible. Where a case is determined as to liability then an application should be made at that early stage so that the deputy will be appointed before the case is finally determined.

If there is a delay in appointing a deputy, then an immediate need can be dealt with by an interim payment. But that should only be a temporary or provisional measure. It is advisable to have damages placed under the control of the Court of Protection as soon as possible so that they can be applied as necessary while also being protected. As mentioned, CPR PD 21 para 10.2 provides that:

> 'the order approving the settlement will contain a direction to the litigation friend to apply to the Court of Protection for the appointment of a deputy, after which the fund will be dealt with as directed by the Court of Protection.'

To facilitate the smooth transfer of money the judgment or order should use the form set out in practice Form N292 or similar wording. The order should follow the wording based on the Practice Direction dated 7 September 1990 and made jointly by the Master of the Court of Protection and the Senior Master of the Queen's Bench Division ([1991] 1 All ER 436; [1991] 1 WLR 2):

> 'that the defendant do within [. . .] days pay the said sum of £[. . .] into Court to be placed to and accumulated in a Special Account pending an application by the [litigation friend] to the Court of Protection for the appointment of a [deputy] for the [claimant] and that upon such appointment being made the said sum of £[. . .] together with interest thereon [subject to a first charge under the Access to Justice Act 1999] be transferred to the Court of Protection [there to be dealt with as a fund of a protected beneficiary] as the Court of Protection thinks fit.'

Carry over of funds

10.14   To transfer funds from the court in which the action has been determined to the Court of Protection the claimant's solicitor must lodge a payment schedule in the court marked 'Transfer to Court of Protection credit' and showing the full name and address of the patient. Where the action has been determined in the High Court, Form 200 needs to be completed and lodged in the District Registry or Action Department of the Central Office. From there it will be forwarded to the Court Funds Office to carry over the award to the control of the Court of Protection.

For details of the procedure required see CPR PD 21 paras 10.3–10.7.

Statutory charge

10.15 Where the action has been publicly funded, the damages are effectively frozen because of the statutory charge that cannot be released until costs have been assessed and any shortfall due to the Legal Services Commission repaid. So as not to delay the availability of the damages for the protected party, the claimant can leave a reserve to cover any shortfall and the bulk of the award can be carried over without delay to the Court of Protection. The claimant's solicitors must, however, complete an undertaking to the Legal Services Commission to cover the reserve, which must exceed the full extent of the claim on the legal aid fund. The reserve also needs to take account of costs and disbursements incurred, or to be incurred, less any legal aid contributions paid by the claimant and any costs recovered from the defendant. On receipt of the undertaking, the Legal Services Commission will notify the Court Funds Office of the amount to be released to the order of the Legal Services Commission. When lodging the payment schedule the claimant's solicitor must show the figure representing the reserve for costs and the net balance being transferred.

Chapter 11

Trusts and trustees

The incapable trustee

11.1   Capacity in relation to a trustee's functions is specific to the matter or matters being determined, in the same way as any other matter in relation to which a decision is made under the Mental Capacity Act 2005 (MCA 2005). A trustee cannot be replaced just because he is finding it harder to act and requires assistance in making decisions. The formal capacity of the trustee to go on acting is a separate matter from whether the trustee is unable to carry out his duties effectively and in the interests of the trust as a whole.

In most cases, the lack of capacity of a trustee will allow the trustee to be replaced. However, if the trustee's authority is required for a decision, then a decision made on behalf of that trustee must be made in the trustee's best interests. Trustees also have fiduciary duties to manage the trust assets and the best interests of the trustee must encompass the interests of the trust. It should be taken for granted that the trustee will wish to do the best he can for the trust. However, the trustee may also be the settlor or a beneficiary, or have a close personal relationship with the settlor or beneficiaries. He may have wishes as to how the trust should be distributed or who should replace him. These are all relevant factors that need to be taken into account.

Replacing the incapable trustee

11.2   The lack of capacity of a person does not of itself discharge that person from the office of trustee. However, unless he has delegated his trustee functions to an attorney and this survives the incapacity, the effective management of the trust requires the trustee who lacks capacity to be discharged from the trust and replaced by a new trustee. Where possible, this should be dealt with by the other trustees or the person authorised by the trust instrument. If there is no such other person, then the Court of Protection may exercise its powers under s 18(1)(j) of the MCA 2005 to direct or authorise the exercise of any power vested in a person as trustee.

P a trustee of land

11.3   Where a person is a trustee of land and lacks capacity to act as a trustee, the incapable trustee must be discharged from the trust and where necessary replaced by a new trustee to enable the legal estate to be dealt with. Section 22 of the Law of Property Act 1925 (as amended by the Trustee Delegation Act 1999 and the MCA 2005) provides as follows:

'(1) Where a legal estate in land (whether settled or not) is vested, either solely or jointly with any other person or persons, in a person lacking capacity (within the meaning of the Mental Capacity Act 2005) to convey or create a legal estate, a deputy appointed for him by the Court of Protection or (if no deputy is appointed for him) any person authorised in that behalf shall, under an order of the Court of Protection, or of the court, or under any statutory power, make or concur in making all requisite dispositions for conveying or creating a legal estate in his name and on his behalf.

(2) If land subject to a trust of land is vested, either solely or jointly with any other person or persons, in a person who lacks capacity (within the meaning of that Act) to exercise his functions as trustee, a new trustee shall be appointed in the place of that person, or he shall be otherwise discharged from the trust, before the legal estate is dealt with by the trustees.

(3) Subsection (2) of this section does not prevent a legal estate being dealt with without the appointment of a new trustee, or the discharge of the incapable trustee, at a time when the donee of an enduring power of attorney or lasting power of attorney (within the meaning of the 2005 Act) is entitled to act for the trustee who lacks capacity in relation to the dealing.'

The procedure for appointing a new trustee is different according to whether the person lacking capacity has a beneficial interest in the land of which he is a trustee and whether there is another competent trustee.

P has beneficial interest and there is another trustee

Trustee Act 1925, s 36

11.4   Where the person lacking capacity has a beneficial interest in the trust assets *and* there is another competent trustee, the competent trustee can appoint a new trustee with the leave of the Court of Protection under s 36(9) of the Trustee Act 1925 (Trustee Act).

Section 36(1) of the Trustee Act specifies who can appoint a new trustee where a trustee has died or wishes to retire and in other situations such as where the trustee is incapable of acting. The appointment may be made by:

'(a)   the person or persons nominated for the purpose of appointing new trustees by the instrument, if any, creating the trust; or

(b)   if there is no such person, or no such person able and willing to act, then the surviving or continuing trustees or trustee for the time being, or the personal representatives of the last surviving or continuing trustee.'

The requirement that the appointment is subject to the consent of the Court of Protection is provided by s 36(9) of the Trustee Act which states:

'Where a trustee lacks capacity to exercise his functions as trustee and is also entitled in possession to some beneficial interest in the trust property, no appointment of a new trustee in his place shall be made by virtue of paragraph (b) of subsection (1) of this section unless leave to make the appointment has been given by the Court of Protection.'

Section 36(9) only serves to benefit a co-trustee, or other person with power to appoint a new trustee. The Court cannot confer on a deputy (even if the deputy is the other trustee) the authority to exercise a trustee function (MCA 2005, s 20(3)(c)).

Rule 52(3) of the Court of Protection Rules further provides that an application to appoint a new trustee under s 36(9) can only be made without the permission of the Court of Protection if it is made by a co-trustee, or other person with power to appoint a new trustee.

Application to appoint a new trustee under s 36(9)

11.5   Where a deputy has been appointed or an application for a deputy is pending, application for leave to appoint a new trustee is relatively straightforward in that the Court will at least have medical evidence to refer to. However, the application must still be made as a new or substantive application using Form COP1. Detailed supporting evidence must be provided and a fee must also be paid, even if the application relates only to the sale of a property.

Leave to appoint a new trustee is given by the Court of Protection by way of a certificate issued under seal. The applicant is then authorised to execute a deed of appointment or transfer document where the new trustee is being appointed to sell land.

Where a deed of appointment is required, this should recite the trust, the property contained in it, and the fact that the trustee being replaced or retired is one of the trustees (although the lack of capacity should not be referred to). The deed should further recite that the retiring trustee 'has become incapable of acting in the trusts of the said trust', that the appointor 'wishes to appoint the new trustee in place of the retiring trustee' and that 'pursuant to section 36(9) of the Trustee Act 1925 leave to make such appointment was given on the [date] by the Court of Protection'.

The traditional form of testimonium may be in the following form:

'NOW THIS DEED WITNESSES that the appointor in exercise of the power for this purpose by the statute in that behalf given to him now appoints the said [name of new trustee] to be a trustee in the place of the said [P] (to act jointly with the said [name of continuing trustee]) for all the purposes of the said trusts or such of the same as are still subsisting and capable of taking effect.'

Evidence in support of an application

11.6   An application must be supported by the information required by Practice Direction 9G. In addition to the material expressly referred to, the Practice Direction refers to Form COP1 'and its annexes' without specifying what those annexes are. The assumption is that the application will be accompanied by an application for permission (if this is necessary) and medical evidence (if an application for the appointment of a deputy is not being made at the same time). If no application is made to appoint a deputy, the Court may also require a Form COP1A to be completed on the basis that P's interest in the trust assets should be dealt with by the Court in the wider context of P's property and affairs.

The information should be set out briefly in a standard witness statement, using Form COP24, with additional evidence exhibited to it. The witness statement should be used to provide a brief narrative of the trust's history and the information that does not require further documentary evidence such as the names and addresses of the present trustees. The following information must, where relevant, be provided:

(a)   a copy of the existing trust document;

(b)   where relevant, a copy of any original conveyance, transfer, lease, assignment, settlement trust or will trust;

(c)   the names and addresses of any present trustees and details of any beneficial interest they have in the trust property. If the present trustees are not the original trustees, an explanation should be provided as to how they became trustees and copies of any deeds of appointment and retirement should be provided;

(d)   the full name, address and date of birth of any person proposed to replace P as a trustee, and details of his relationship to P;

(e)   confirmation that the trust is not under an order for administration in the Chancery Division;

(f)   if there is only one continuing trustee, the applicant must confirm that both the trustee and the proposed new trustee have not made an enduring power of attorney or a lasting power of attorney in favour of the other party;

(g)   if an enduring power of attorney or a lasting power of attorney has been executed by a continuing trustee, a certified copy of that document must be provided. If the power has not been registered, the applicant must confirm that the trustee is still capable of carrying out his duties as a trustee;

(h)   the full name and address of any person who has an interest in any trust property as the beneficiary of a will, and whether any of them are children or persons who lack capacity;

(i)   if the proposed new trustee is not a solicitor or a trust corporation (for example, a bank) and has not been appointed as a deputy for the trustee lacking capacity, the applicant must provide a witness statement from a person independent of the applicant, who has no interest in the trust property, attesting to the applicant's fitness to be appointed as trustee [which should also be in Form COP24];

(j)   if the application relates to a transfer of assets in a will trust or similar settlement into the names of new trustees, accurate details of the trust assets must be provided (including full details of any stocks and shares held);

(k)   a copy of any notice of severance and evidence of service;

(l)   a copy of the will and grant of probate to the deceased's estate (where relevant);

(m)   confirmation of all relevant consents; and

(n)   a copy of a signed trustee's special undertaking [Form COP12]: the new trustee is required to undertake that while P continues to lack capacity, the statutory power of appointing new trustees will not be exercised except with the prior approval of the Court and that in the event of land being sold, the Court's approval will first be obtained and that the proceeds of any such sale will only be dealt with as directed by the Court.

If a witness statement attesting to a person's fitness to act is required, this must be given by an independent party who is not the applicant's solicitor. The person giving the certificate must show how long he has known the applicant and give details of the applicant's occupation. The certificate should contain the following statements:

'(i)   during my acquaintance with the applicant I have had many opportunities of forming an opinion upon his [her] capability and integrity, and

(ii)   in my judgment and opinion the said applicant is a fit and proper person to be appointed a new trustee of the said conveyance/assent/trust;'

Where the application relates to real property, the applicant must also provide details of:

(a)   the address of the property concerned, and whether it is freehold or leasehold;

(b)   the title number of the property and a copy of its entry in the Land Registry (if registered land). If the land is unregistered, the applicant should provide evidence of the root of title and; and

(c)   if the property is leasehold the applicant should advise the court as to whether he has a licence or consent to the assignment, and provide a copy of the same (or advise if a licence or consent is not necessary and the reason why it is not needed).

P has beneficial interest in the land and there is no other trustee or there are other trust assets

Problem caused by Trustee Act 1925, s 40

11.7   Where there is no continuing trustee who can apply for leave to appoint a new trustee or there are assets in the trust which require an order of the Court to vest them in a new trustee, an application must be made requesting the Court to exercise its statutory powers to appoint a new trustee and to vest any trust property in the new trustees. The provisions of s 36 – which allow another trustee to appoint the replacement trustee – only apply to vest property covered by s 40:

'(1) Where by a deed a new trustee is appointed to perform any trust, then—

(a)   if the deed contains a declaration by the appointor to the effect that any estate or interest in any land subject to the trust, or in any chattel so subject, or right to recover or receive any debt or other thing in action so subject, shall vest in the persons who by virtue of the deed become or are the trustees for performing the trust, the deed shall operate, without any conveyance or assignment, to vest in those persons as joint tenants and for the purposes of the trust the estate interest or right to which the declaration relates; and ...

(3) An express vesting declaration, whether made before or after the commencement of this Act, shall, notwithstanding that the estate, interest or right to be vested is not expressly referred to, and provided that the other statutory requirements were or are complied with, operate and be deemed always to have operated (but without prejudice to any express provision to the contrary contained in the deed of appointment or discharge) to vest in the persons respectively referred to in subsections (1) ... of this section, as the case may require, such estates, interests and rights as are capable of being and ought to be vested in those persons.

(4) This section does not extend—

(a)   to land conveyed by way of mortgage for securing money subject to the trust, except land conveyed on trust for securing debentures or debenture stock;

(b)   to land held under a lease which contains any covenant, condition or agreement against assignment or disposing of the land without licence or consent, unless, prior to the execution of the deed containing expressly or impliedly the vesting declaration, the requisite licence or consent has been obtained, or unless, by virtue of any statute or rule of law, the vesting declaration, express or implied, would not operate as a breach of covenant or give rise to a forfeiture;

(c)   to any share, stock, annuity or property which is only transferable in books kept by a company or other body, or in manner directed by or under an Act of Parliament.'

Thus, where the trust consists of shares, then the mere appointment of new trustees does not of itself vest the property in the new trustees.

A further difficulty arises in that ss 36 and 40 of the Trustee Act make no provision for a trust where the person who lacks capacity is the sole trustee and there is no other person authorised by the trust instrument to appoint a new trustee.

Trustee Act 1925, ss 41 and 54

11.8   Additional powers, reserved jointly to the Chancery Division of the High Court and the Court of Protection are set out in s 41 and s 54 of the Trustee Act:

'41(1)   The court may, whenever it is expedient to appoint a new trustee or new trustees, and it is found inexpedient difficult or impracticable so to do without the assistance of the court, make an order appointing a new trustee or new trustees either in substitution for or in addition to any existing trustee or trustees, or although there is no existing trustee.

(2) In particular and without prejudice to the generality of the foregoing provision, the court may make an order appointing a new trustee in substitution for a trustee who . . . lacks capacity to exercise his functions as trustee, or is a bankrupt, or is a corporation which is in liquidation or has been dissolved.'

'54(1)   Subject to subsection (2), the Court of Protection may not make an order, or give a direction or authority, in relation to a person who lacks capacity to exercise his functions as trustee, if the High Court may make an order to that effect under this Act.

(2)   Where a person lacks capacity to exercise his functions as a trustee and a deputy is appointed for him by the Court of Protection or an application for the appointment of a deputy has been made but not determined, then, except as respects a trust which is subject to an order for administration made by the High Court, the Court of Protection shall have concurrent jurisdiction with the High Court in relation to—

(a)   mortgaged property of which the person concerned has become a trustee merely by reason of the mortgage having been paid off;

(b)   matters consequent on the making of provision by the Court of Protection for the exercise of a power of appointing trustees or retiring from a trust;

(c)   matters consequent on the making of provision by the Court of Protection for the carrying out of any contract entered into by the person concerned;

(d)   property to some interest in which the person concerned is beneficially entitled but which, or some interest in which, is held by the person concerned under an express, implied or constructive trust.'

Thus the Court of Protection can – by virtue of s 54 of the Trustee Act – exercise its own powers under MCA 2005, s 18(1)(j) and Sch 2, para 5 for the benefit of the trust. These powers may however only be exercised if:

● a deputy has been appointed or an application to appoint a deputy has been made;

● no order for administration has been made in the High Court; and

● the application is made by the deputy, a person who has made an application for the appointment of a deputy, a continuing trustee or any other person who, according to the practice of the Chancery Division, would have been entitled to make the application if it had been made to the High Court.

Rule 52(2) of the Court of Protection Rules further provides that an application by any other person to appoint a new trustee under s 54(2) of the Trustee Act requires the permission of the Court.

Form of application

11.9   The application to appoint a new trustee must be made using the general form of application (COP1) and accompanied by the same supporting evidence as an application under s 36(9) of the Trustee Act (see **11.6** above and Practice Direction 9G paragraph 2(c)). The applicant must take care, however, to describe the assets in the trust accurately, and submit evidence of those assets. Vesting of trust assets will be by virtue of the order only, so it is essential that the assets are correctly described.

No deed of appointment is required. The order of the Court of Protection makes the appointment of the new trustee and vests the trust assets in the new trustees (MCA 2005, Sch 2, para 5).

The Practice Direction makes no reference to persons who are to be notified. The requirement under the Mental Health Act 1983 jurisdiction was that if the application was made by a person who was not the receiver, notice had to be given to the receiver and to any other person who would have to be served with notice if the application had been made in the High Court. Under the Court of Protection Rules, the usual notice provisions (Rules 66–70) would apply to such an application.

Where P is sole beneficiary

11.10   Where the person who lacks capacity is the sole beneficiary and the trust can be brought to an end, then an application may be made under s 54 of the Trustee Act to appoint new trustees and vest trust property in the beneficiary. If assets are registered in the trustee's name but are payable to the beneficiary (even if they are one and the same person), a direction to pay the assets to the deputy will be sufficient.

Where, however, the trust consists of a property where the person lacking capacity is the surviving trustee and entitled to the deceased co-owner's share then the beneficial interest can be dealt with in a number of ways:

(a)   the deputy may apply under s 54 of the Trustee Act for new trustees to be appointed; the trustees can then sell the property. No order for sale is required;

(b)   the deceased co-owner's personal representative may join in the conveyance or transfer to sell the property; or

(c)   the deceased co-owner's personal representative may vest the beneficial title in the estate of the person concerned by completing an assent of the beneficial interest or a statutory declaration so that the person concerned is registered as sole beneficial owner. The property can then be sold by the deputy in the usual way.

P is a trustee without a beneficial interest

Other trustee available

11.11   If the trustee lacking capacity has no beneficial interest in the trust and there is another trustee who is competent, the other trustee can appoint a new trustee under s 36(1) of the Trustee Act (see **11.4** above). The requirement of s 36(9) of the Trustee Act for leave of the Court to be obtained does not apply.

No other trustee available

11.12   The procedure to be followed where the trustee has no beneficial interest and there is no other trustee capable or willing to appoint a new trustee depends on whether the beneficiaries are of full age and capacity.

Application under s 20(2) of the Trusts of Land and Appointment of Trustees Act 1996

11.13   Where the beneficiaries are of full age and capacity and (taken together) absolutely entitled to the property under the trust, the beneficiaries may give a written direction to appoint a person to be a new trustee in place of the incapable trustee. The direction may be given to the deputy of the person concerned, the attorney acting under a registered enduring power of attorney or lasting power of attorney or a person authorised for this purpose by the Court of Protection.

Where there is no deputy or attorney under a registered power of attorney or they are unwilling to appoint a new trustee, an application may be made directly to the Court of Protection for a person to be authorised to make the appointment. The application must be in Form COP1 and accompanied by the same supporting evidence as an application under s 36(9) of the TA 1925 (see **11.6** above and Practice Direction 9G paragraph 2(d)).

The aim of s 20 of the Trusts of Land and Appointment of Trustees Act 1966 is to empower beneficiaries to remove a trustee where they are absolutely entitled. Thus any beneficiary can make an application. Permission is only required under Rule 52(5) 'where the application is made by a person other than a beneficiary under the trust or, if there is more than one, by both or all of them'.

Retirement as a trustee

11.14   Where a trustee lacks capacity, it may be unnecessary for a new trustee to be appointed if there are at least two continuing trustees, the other trustee is a trust corporation or the trust is practically at an end. If it is impractical for the trust to continue without the retirement of the trustee who lacks capacity, an application must be made to the Court of Protection under MCA 2005, s 18(1)(j) to authorise the deputy to exercise the right of the incapable trustee to retire and to be discharged from the trusts under s 39 of the Trustee Act.

Application must be made in the general form (Form COP1) requesting that 'the deputy be authorised in the name and on behalf of P to exercise the power vested in P of retiring from the trusts [as described] and for such purpose to execute such deeds as may be necessary'. Practice Direction 9G is headed applications to 'appoint or discharge a trustee' and while it assumes that a retiring trustee will be replaced by another, the same procedure information must be provided to remove a trustee, save for any references to the proposed new trustee. The application will therefore need to be accompanied by a witness statement and supporting evidence as for the appointment of a new trustee suitably adapted as no new trustees will be appointed (see **11.6**). The order will also provide for any consequential vesting of property subject to the trust in the continuing trustees.

Costs

Solicitor's costs

11.15 A solicitor's costs can be dealt with in accordance with the Practice Direction issued by the President of the Court of Protection (see **15.2**). Category II allows fixed costs of £360 to cover an application under s 36(9) or 54 of the Trustee Act or s 20 of the Trusts of Land and Appointment of Trustees Act 1996 for the appointment of a new trustee in the place of 'P'and applications under MCA 2005, s 18(1)(j) for authority to exercise any power vested in P, whether beneficially, or as trustee, or otherwise.

In view of the considerable amount of work involved, it is likely that in all but the most straightforward of cases, a solicitor will wish to have costs assessed.

Court fee

11.16 There is a single application fee of £400. This is payable in respect of any application, even if it is made in conjunction with another application and the issues and parties are similar. For example where a property is vested in trustees and P is the surviving trustee, applications need to be made to appoint a deputy and to replace P as a trustee of land. These are dealt with as two separate applications.

Delegation of powers by an attorney

11.17 The Court's power to intervene in the exercise of a trustee's powers need not be exercised where the trustee has previously delegated his authority to another person and that authority survives the onset of incapacity. However, a trustee's power to delegate in such circumstances has been restricted by the Trustee Delegation Act 1999 (TDA 1999) and where an attorney cannot make use of the restricted powers contained in this Act, he is in the same position as a deputy and must act within the framework of the Trustee Act and MCA 2005, s 18(1)(j).

Enduring power of attorney registered prior to 1 March 2001

11.18   Where the enduring power of attorney was created before 1 March 2000 and an application to register the power was made before 1 March 2001, the attorney can benefit from the wide-ranging powers set out in s 3(3) of the Enduring Powers of Attorney Act 1985, even though this was repealed by the TDA 1999. Section 3(3) – which is preserved for these purposes by MCA 2005, Sch 5, para 14(2) provided as follows:

> 'Subject to any condition or restrictions contained in the instrument, an attorney under an enduring power of attorney, whether general or limited, may (without obtaining any consent) execute or exercise all or any of the trusts, powers or discretions vested in the donor as trustee and may (without the concurrence of any other person) give a valid receipt for capital or other money paid.'

Thus trustee powers could be delegated without limitation and for an unlimited period and in respect of land an attorney could give a valid receipt for capital monies even if the attorney was also the other beneficial owner. The provisions of this section therefore conflict with the limited delegation powers contained in s 25 of the Trustee Act and the rule that at least two trustees can give a valid receipt for capital monies contained in s 27 of the Law of Property Act 1925.

These powers remain available to attorneys of enduring powers of attorney created before 1 March 2000 and registered before 1 March 2001 so that an attorney could still sell a jointly owned property as attorney for the incapable trustee and as trustee in his own right (TDA 1999, s 7(3)).

Enduring power of attorney registered after 1 March 2001

11.19   Although the provisions of the TDA 1999 have restricted the wide powers which were contained in s 3(3) of the Enduring Powers of Attorney Act 1985, the TDA permits a trustee to delegate his powers to an attorney in certain limited situations. The most important concession, and the one which has the greatest practical benefit to the majority of cases where both enduring and lasting powers of attorney are relevant, relates to land in which the donor has a beneficial interest. An attorney's power to deal with land in such circumstances is subject to two conditions:

- the attorney provides evidence in favour of the purchaser that the donor has a beneficial interest in the land. Section 2 of the TDA 1999 provides that a purchaser will have conclusive evidence if the attorney makes an 'appropriate statement' at the time of the sale or up to three months afterwards. This can be done very easily in the case of registered land by incorporating a statement in Form TR1 stating that the attorney confirms 'that the donor has a beneficial interest in the property at the date hereof' (see also Land Registry Practice Leaflet 32 *Powers of Attorney*); and

- where there are two trustees, the sale must be made by two people whether jointly in the same capacity or in different capacities (TDA 1999, s 7). Thus an attorney cannot sell as attorney and trustee, and if both trustees are incapable, the same attorney cannot sell as attorney for each trustee.

Appointment of second trustee by donee of lasting or enduring power of attorney

11.20   It is advisable therefore for donors of enduring and lasting powers of attorney to appoint more than one attorney if the first attorney is a co-trustee. However, if there is no other attorney who can act, s 8 of the TDA 1999 amends s 36 of the Trustee Act to provide a convenient mechanism for an additional attorney to be appointed. Provided the appointment is for the purpose of exercising a trustee function relating to land, the attorney, acting under a registered lasting or enduring power of attorney may appoint a new trustee solely for this purpose. The appointment can most easily be made in the conveyance or transfer document.

The fact that land is being dealt with on behalf of an incapable trustee would be contrary to the provisions of s 22(2) of the Law of Property Act 1925 which provides that the incapable trustee must be discharged before the land can be dealt with. To avoid a conflict with this provision, s 9 of the TDA 1999 inserted a new subsection (3) into s 22 of the Law of Property Act 1925:

'Subsection (2) of this section does not prevent a legal estate being dealt with without the appointment of a new trustee, or the discharge of the incapable trustee, at a time when the donee of an enduring power of attorney or lasting power of attorney (within the meaning of the [Mental Capacity Act 2005] is entitled to act for the trustee who lacks capacity in relation to the dealing.'

Chapter 12

Costs

Funding of the Court of Protection and Public Guardian

12.1   The work of the Court of Protection and the Office of the Public Guardian is financed by fees collected from patients or their estates, thus without public subsidy. The Mental Capacity Act 2005 makes no change to the pre-existing arrangements, despite the increased demands on the jurisdiction caused by the new legislation. The only concession appears to be that the Court of Protection, as a judicial body, is not required to recover all its costs. Instead, the Court is only required to recover 63 per cent of its costs (*Annual Report and Accounts 2007–2008*).

Prior to September 2000, the main source of revenue had been the annual administration fee which was levied on a scale basis according to the annual income of a person whose affairs were under the control of the Court. The effect was a levy amounting to approximately 5 per cent of a person's income, and the larger the income the greater the expense to the estate which often bore no relation to the cost, let alone the quality, of the service provided. By contrast, certain procedures which were very time consuming for the Court to deal with were charged only at nominal cost or no costs at all. For instance, the fee on a statutory will application would be £100 and no fees were charged for applications made under the Enduring Powers of Attorney Act 1985.

In an attempt to make the charging structure more equitable, new fees were introduced in September 2000. Scale fees were abolished and replaced with a modest fixed annual fee while transaction fees, which arose when additional action was required from the Court, were increased. It was hoped that the reduction of in-house receivership work, increasing the autonomy available to receivers and other efficiency improvements would enable the Court and the Public Guardianship Office to work within its new budgets. However, the reduction in fees collected was not matched by other savings and led to a significant drop in revenue. In an attempt to stem the losses, significant fee increases were introduced in 2002. Since 2000, fees have gone up and down in each year in an attempt to raise the maximum revenue as discreetly as possible. The services offered are often dictated by budgets, and the cost of operating the Court and its jurisdiction has actually gone down over the last decade, as the following figures illustrate:

12.1 *Costs*

Year	1996–97 £000 (1)	2002–03 £000 (1)	2007–08 £000 (2)
Fee income	19,278	9,896	17,686
Other income		581	
Subsidy		2,507	774
Expenditure	−19,274	25,188	−20,844
Deficit	£4	−12,204	−2,384

(1)   National Audit Office, *Protecting the Financial Welfare of People with Mental Incapacity* at page 61

(2)   Based on the half-year figures provided in the *Annual Report and Accounts 2007–2008*, at page 75

Court of Protection fees

12.2   On the implementation of the Mental Capacity Act 2005 (MCA 2005), new fees were introduced to reflect the separation of the Court process from the administrative work of the Public Guardian. These fees also served to emphasise the principle that any matter requiring a determination by the Court is made on a formal application, for which a fee is payable. There is also a separate fee for a hearing. Taken together, the fees also serve to deter applicants from making applications unnecessarily.

The fees charged by the Court as at 1 April 2009 are set out in the Schedule to the Court of Protection Fees Order 2007 (SI 2007/1745) as amended by the Court of Protection Fees (Amendment) Order 2009 (SI 2009/513):

Application fee (art 4)	£400.00
Appeal fee (art 5)	£400.00
Hearing fees (art 6)	£500.00
Copy of a document fee (art 7(1))	£5.00

References in this chapter to article numbers are, except where indicated, to those set out in of the Court of Protection Fees Order 2007.

When is fee payable?

12.3   An application fee of £400 is payable on the making of any application under Part 9 of the Court of Protection Rules 2007. Thus all applications are treated in the same way, whether made by deputies, attorneys, donees or other persons. An application fee is also payable on an application for permission, although if permission is given, it is not payable again on the making of the application.

A separate hearing fee of £500 is payable when the Court has 'held a hearing', after the hearing has taken place and a final order, decision or declaration has been made. However, a hearing fee is only payable when an actual hearing has taken place, and not on a telephone hearing.

An application fee of £400 is also payable on filing an appellant's notice and a further hearing fee is payable when an appeal is heard. It seems particularly harsh that a person who appeals against a decision of the Court of Protection must pay again to have an appeal heard, even if the appeal has the result of reversing a decision of a first instance judge. It is of course possible for the appeal judge to award costs (which include Court fees) against a party, but the onus remains on the appellant to make payment up front and bear a risk that costs will not be recovered.

No fee payable

12.4   No fee is payable on the following applications:

- where an application is made within the proceedings on an application notice;

- on a first application where an application for permission has been made and permission has been granted (art 4(2));

- where an application is made under r 67 of the Court of Protection Rules 2007 by the donee or a person named in a lasting power of attorney (LPA) and the and is solely in respect of an objection to the registration of the LPA;

- where an application is made under r 68 of the Court of Protection Rules by a donor, attorney or notified person and is solely in respect of an objection to registration of the enduring power of attorney (EPA);

- where the application is made by the Public Guardian; and

- where P dies within 5 days of an application being made (art 4(5)).

Multiple applications

12.5   There is some confusion as to what an application consists of. The Fees Order refers to 'an application' in the singular, so that if more than one application is made, a separate fee is payable in respect of each application. This can cause a degree of unfairness. A person who needs to have a welfare deputy appointed as well as a financial deputy and also has an interest in a property so that new trustees must be appointed will end up bearing the cost of three applications. However, a single application may ask for a number of orders. For instance, an application for gifts under s 18(1)(b) may provide for several recipients in different amounts with separate gifts made out of income and capital. As a simple rule of thumb, an application made under the same statutory provision which involves the same parties may be treated as a single application even if more than one order is made in consequence. If the application involves different statutory provisions and different parties or the same parties with different interests, then a separate application will need to be made, even if the applications are subsequently joined and dealt with at the same hearing.

Who pays the fee?

12.6   It is clear from the Fees Order that Court fees are payable by the applicant or appellant. It is therefore the responsibility of the applicant to fund the application. Although an applicant should be entitled to recover his costs, there is no guarantee that the application will be completed or that the Court will authorise the payment of costs from the estate.

Exemption from fees

12.7   Because the fee is levied on the applicant, any means-tested exemption is based on the assets of the applicant and not those of the person concerned. Thus art 8(1) provides that 'no fee shall be payable under this Order by a person who, at the time when a fee would otherwise become payable, is in receipt of any qualifying benefit' where a 'qualifying benefit' is a means-tested benefit such as income support or housing benefit. Article 8(2) ignores this concession where the applicant has an award for damages in excess of £16,000 which would otherwise be disallowed in assessing eligibility to means-tested benefits.

Remission of fees

12.8   An exemption from fees based on the applicant's means alone could cause some obvious injustice. If the estate of the person concerned is a small one, or only a minor matter needs to be dealt with, the cost to the estate, when reimbursing the applicant, is disproportionate. There is no clear basis for addressing this injustice. Article 9 requires each such situation to be looked at on its own merits:

> 'Where it appears to the Lord Chancellor that the payment of any fee prescribed by this Order would, owing to the exceptional circumstances of the particular case, involve undue hardship, he may reduce or remit the fee in that case'

To address this potential unfairness, the Court of Protection has from 1 April 2009 introduced a remission policy so that the applicant and P are treated in the same way. If P is entitled to a 'qualifying benefit' (except where P is also entitled to a personal injury award) then the fee payable is remitted in full. The Court of Protection remission policy is also extended to cases where P's income is not in receipt of a 'qualifying benefit' but has a gross income below £16,500. Depending on the level of P's income, fees may be remitted in whole or in part as follows:

Income	Percentage of fee remitted
Up to £12,000	No fee payable
£12,001 to £13,500	75% remission
£13,501 to £15,000	50% remission
£15,001 to £16,500	25% remission
Over £16,500	No remission – the full fee is payable

The Court may also exercise its discretion within the scope of art 9 to remit fees where payment may cause P – whose estate must bear the cost – undue hardship.

An application for exemption or remission is made using form COP44A which is available from www.hmcourts-service.gov.uk

Public Guardian fees

12.9   Fees charged by the Public Guardian for the carrying out of his duties to register powers of attorney and supervise deputies are set out in the Schedule to the Public Guardian (Fees, etc) Regulations 2007 (SI 2007/2051) as amended by the Public Guardian (Fees, etc) (Amendment) Regulations 2009 (SI 2009/514):

Enduring power of attorney registration (regulation 4)	£120.00
Enduring power of attorney office copy (regulation 4A)	£25.00
Lasting power of attorney registration (regulation 5)	£120.00
Lasting power of attorney office copy (regulation 5A)	£25.00
Application to search the registers (regulation 6)	£25.00
Appointment of deputy (regulation 7)	£125.00
Type I (highest) supervision (regulation 8)	£800.00 per annum
Type II (lower) supervision (regulation 8)	£175.00 per annum
Type llA (intermediate) supervision (introduced from 1 April 2009)	£350.00 per annum
Type III (minimal) supervision (regulation 8)	No fee

Exemptions and remission

12.10   Regulation 9 of the Public Guardian (Fees, etc) Regulations provides for the exemption of fees on a similar basis to the Fees Order, thus using eligibility for means-tested benefits as the sole criterion for exemption. However, the eligibility applies to the 'relevant person' who is the donor of the LPA or EPA or where the fee relates to the supervision of the deputy, 'P'. Thus a person who has a small estate can claim exemption from supervision fees, even though the deputy has ample means of his own. The Public Guardian also has power to reduce or remit a fee where it appears to the Public Guardian that payment of a prescribed fee, would, owing to the exceptional circumstances of the case, cause undue hardship.

An application for exemption or remission must be made to the Office of the Public Guardian using Form OPG506A.

Solicitors' costs

Costs in proceedings

12.11   Costs incurred in any proceedings are governed by Part 19 of the Court of Protection Rules in addition to Parts 44, 47 and 48 of the Civil Procedure Rules.

The traditional practice was that costs were paid from the estate of the person concerned, unlike in civil proceedings where costs follow the event. The principle applied by the Court of Protection was that where an application was made in good faith, supported by medical evidence, in the interests of the person concerned and without an improper motive then the applicant is entitled to his costs from the estate even if he is unsuccessful (*Re Cathcart* [1892] 1 Ch 549). The Court of Protection Rules follow this principle, where the proceedings concern a person's property and affairs. Thus Rule 156 sets out the following general rule:

> 'Where the proceedings concern P's property and affairs the general rule is that the costs of the proceedings or of that part of the proceedings that concerns P's property and affairs, shall be paid by P or charged to his estate.'

Personal welfare applications

12.12   The principle followed by *Re Cathcart* and Rule 156 is reversed where the matter concerns a person's personal welfare. The rationale for this is that such cases do not generally involve property and there is no assumption that there are assets that can be both disputed and bear the cost of proceedings. Parties to such cases may be local authorities or health authorities; other individuals should be deterred from making welfare applications unless they have a very strong and compelling case. Rule 157 provides as follows:

> 'Where the proceedings concern P's personal welfare the general rule is that there will be no order as to the costs of the proceedings or of that part of the proceedings that concerns P's personal welfare.'

The problem with this rule is that a financial deputy, especially if he is acting in a professional role, will be deterred from making a worthwhile welfare application. A deputy concerned for the welfare of a person for whom he has been appointed to act cannot assume that costs will be charged to the estate. A deputy in such a position will have to include a direction dealing with professional fees either in his application or as a separate application.

Apportioning costs

12.13   Where the case concerns both property and welfare issues, then the Court may apportion costs between the respective issues (Rule 158).

Departing from the general rule

12.14   The general rule is not inflexible and can be avoided by the Court. Rule 159 provides the Court with power to depart from the general rule 'if the circumstances so justify'. The Court must have regard to all the circumstances, including the conduct of the parties, whether a party has succeeded on part of his case, even if he has not been wholly successful; and the role of any public body involved in the proceedings. Rule 159(2) defines conduct of the parties as including:

(a)   conduct before, as well as during, the proceedings;

(b)   whether it was reasonable for a party to raise, pursue or contest a particular issue;

(c)   the manner in which a party has made or responded to an application or a particular issue; and

(d)   whether a party who has succeeded in his application or response to an application, in whole or in part, exaggerated any matter contained in his application or response.

To depart from the general rule does therefore involve an allocation of blame which the Court of Protection tries to avoid. If costs are in issue, it will involve further argument, with parties making further representations and having a right to be heard. It is therefore often taken for granted that in financial cases costs are payable from the estate as a matter of course. However, exceptions to the general rule do arise from time to time and can be illustrated by the following examples:

●   An application was made by a receiver for a deed of variation redirecting the estate of the patient's deceased husband to his son (the patient's stepson). The stepson was a party to the proceedings and the main beneficiary of the variation which was approved by the Court. He was ordered to pay half of the applicant's costs in the proceedings.

●   An attorney applied to register his mother's EPA but both his mother and the co-attorney objected to the registration on the ground that registration was premature and the donor had capacity. Despite clear evidence of capacity from the donor's doctor that she retained capacity, the son persisted with his application. The Court awarded the costs of the other parties against the son and directed that he pay his own costs.

●   In a statutory will application, one party produced a home-made will which she claimed was P's last will and which should be upheld by the Court. The Court would not make a finding on the validity of this earlier will, but the party had caused delays in producing the will and was evasive and inconsistent in cross-examination. No order for costs was made in favour of that party.

Solicitor's costs must be justified

12.15   The Court of Protection Rules make no reference for the need to justify the involvement of a solicitor as deputy or in acting for a party. This is in contrast to the 2001 Rules which contained a presumption that a receiver was not entitled – without the approval of the court – to employ at the expense of the person concerned a solicitor or other professional person to do any work which would not normally require professional assistance. This does not, however, allow a deputy to employ professional help as a matter of course. A financial deputy is still a fiduciary who is expected – within reason – to deal personally with the day-to-day administration and prevent unnecessary cost to the estate.

Where a solicitor is employed or acts as deputy, then the solicitor must generally take fixed costs or have his costs assessed. However, where a solicitor is employed on an application to appoint a deputy, the Court will generally allow the deputy to agree costs with the solicitor. The order will, however, also provide for costs to be assessed in default of agreement. The same approach will apply where a deputy cannot deal with a matter in person and needs advice and assistance from a solicitor (see also **8.8**).

Solicitors' fixed costs

12.16   Fixed costs were introduced in 1983 as a way of fixing the amount which could be charged for particular types of work. Thus a Court order would allow a solicitor to charge fixed costs for a particular activity. Fixed costs are simple to understand and can be collected quickly and easily without the delay and expense of detailed assessment. Prior to 1 October 2007, the amounts allowed by way of fixed costs for defined areas of work were set out each January by the Master of the Court of Protection in a practice note. Rule 167 of the Court of Protection Rules provides for fixed costs to be set by a practice direction. A new practice direction was issued on 1 April 2008 providing for fixed costs for a limited number of categories as follows:

Category I	Work up to and including the date upon which the court makes an order appointing a deputy for property and affairs.	Amount £800 (plus VAT)
Category II	Applications under s 36 (9) or 54 of the Trustee Act 1925 or s 20 of the Trusts of Land and Appointment of Trustees Act 1996 for the appointment of a new trustee in the place of 'P' and applications under s 18(1)(j) of the Mental Capacity Act 2005 for authority to exercise any power vested in P, whether beneficially, or as trustee, or otherwise.	Amount £360 (plus VAT)
Category III (where a solicitor acts as a deputy)	Annual management fee where the court appoints a professional deputy for property and affairs, payable on the anniversary of the court order	a. For the first year: Amount £1,400 (plus VAT)
		b. For the second and subsequent years: Amount £1,110 (plus VAT)
		Provided that, where the net assets of P are below £16,000, the professional deputy for property and affairs may take an annual management fee not exceeding 4.5 per cent of P's net assets on the anniversary of the court order appointing the professional as deputy.

Category IV	Where the court appoints a professional deputy for health and welfare.	The deputy may take an annual management fee not exceeding 2.5 per cent of P's net assets on the anniversary of the court order appointing the professional as deputy for health and welfare up to a maximum of £500.
Category V	Preparation and lodgement of the annual report or annual account to the Public Guardian.	Amount £220 (plus VAT)
Category VI	Preparation of an HMRC income tax return on behalf of P.	Amount £220 (plus VAT)

At the time of publication details of fixed costs for 2009/10 were still awaited. It is expected that costs will be increased in line with the Retail Price Index.

Detailed assessment of costs

Assessment procedure

12.17   For most types of work, fixed costs will be inadequate, especially given the complexities of dealing with the MCA 2005 and the Court of Protection Rules 2007. Under Rule 160 of the Court of Protection Rules, Parts 43, 44, 47 and 48 of the Civil Procedure Rules apply to costs incurred in relation to proceedings in the Court of Protection. These rules govern the assessment of solicitors' costs which is the usual way of determining the proper costs payable to a solicitor in legal proceedings.

If a party is allowed costs on an application, then the order determining the application or a separate order dealing with costs will provide for costs to be assessed if fixed costs or agreed costs are not applicable. Costs are usually awarded on the standard basis and are payable from the estate.

The procedure for obtaining a detailed assessment of costs is straightforward if followed correctly:

(a)   a draft bill should be prepared following the format and using the item numbers used in the model form A bill annexed to the practice direction accompanying Part 48 of the Civil Procedure Rules. Items in the bill should be typed but page and summary totals should be written in pencil;

(b)   the draft bill should be endorsed on the back with the title and reference of the matter, and the details and reference of the firm;

(c)   the draft should commence by reciting the order, direction or letter giving authority to apply for assessed costs and provide a brief statement detailing the period covered by the bill, nature of the work covered by the bill or what the matter relates to, the status of the fee-earners involved in the matter and their hourly rates and whether there were any exceptional circumstances such as complexity or urgency which may be relevant to the level of fee-earner involvement;

(d) the draft bill must be checked carefully by the solicitor lodging it and endorsed with a certificate that all disbursements of under £500 have been paid. It should then be lodged with: Supreme Court Costs Office (Court of Protection section), Cliffords Inn, Fetter Lane, London EC4A 1DQ (DX 44454 Strand);

(e) a draft bill must be accompanied by all supporting documents including the solicitor's correspondence file, attendance records, instructions to counsel, opinions, pleadings, affidavits, orders, any conveyancing or trust documents or the completed statutory will as the case may be, and receipts for any disbursements incurred. The bill must be supported by the evidence and, where time has been spent in attendance or drafting, this must be recorded in the correspondence file or on attendance notes. Computer time records are not regarded as evidence of the time spent.

(f) a copy of the authority for the assessment of the solicitor's costs must also be lodged;

(g) the court fee of £200 is payable on lodgement of the application (unless the amount claimed is less than £3,000 and the short form of assessment is used, where the fee is £100);

(h) the draft bill will be provisionally assessed and returned to the solicitor submitting it. If more than one party is involved, the provisionally assessed bill must be served on the other parties. Form N253 can be used for this purpose. If the provisionally assessed bill is not accepted by the solicitor (or any other party), an appointment for a detailed assessment hearing may be requested within 14 days. If the draft bill is accepted, the summaries on the draft bill, less any amount assessed off the bill, should be completed in ink or typed. The summaries should be completed to show the total costs payable with VAT, disbursements and the assessment fee and certified by the solicitor as being correct. The completed bill should then be returned to the Costs Office;

(i) on receipt of the completed bill, the Costs Office will issue a certificate of assessed costs which is sent to the solicitor. This provides authority for a deputy to arrange payment of the amount on the costs certificate.

Further guidance as to form and content of a bill are set out in the Supreme Court Costs Office Guide which is available from the SCCO website at: http://www.hmcourts-service.gov.uk/infoabout/scco/index.htm

Basis of assessment

12.18 Part 19 of the Court of Protection Rules and Practice Direction make no reference to the basis on which costs are to be assessed. This is a matter for the Court to decide in each case, but the Court will continue to apply the presumption set out in the Practice Note of Master Lush of 2 March 2005, that costs will be awarded on the standard basis. Thus the Court will only allow costs which are proportionate to the matters in issue and will resolve any doubt which it may have as to whether costs were reasonably incurred or reasonable and proportionate in amount in favour of the paying party (CPR r 44.4(2)).

Short form bills

12.19   In June 2004 the Court of Protection authorised a new short form assessment procedure for use in cases where the costs claimed, excluding VAT and disbursements, do not exceed £3,000. The procedure enables costs to be submitted for assessment by firms without having to prepare a professionally drafted bill of costs. As with an application for detailed assessment, the same papers are sent to the Costs Office but instead of a detailed draft bill, a short form summary is submitted showing the time claimed and the hourly rates applied. A short form bill should be submitted in form A-10 which is exhibited to the Supreme Court Costs Office Guide.

A reduced fee of £100 is also payable.

Amounts charged

12.20   Where costs are payable pursuant to an order of the Court, then the amount that can be charged is in accordance with the Court's guidelines. The amount that can be charged must for instance take account of the factors listed in CPR r 44.5(3):

- the amount or value of any money or property involved;

- the importance of the matter to all the parties;

- the particular complexity of the matter, or the difficulty or novelty of questions raised;

- the skill, effort, specialised knowledge and responsibility involved.

The rates at which work can be charged for are also prescribed for all work involving civil proceedings. Guideline rates apply to work carried out in four different categories of fee earner as follows:

A.   Solicitors with over eight years' post qualification experience including at least eight years' litigation experience.

B.   Solicitors and legal executives with over four years' post qualification experience including at least four years' litigation experience.

C.   Other solicitors and legal executives and fee earners of equivalent experience.

D.   Trainee solicitors, para legals and other fee earners.

For 2008 the rates (showing the relevant localities) were as follows:

BAND	Rate	Locality
ONE	A £203 B £180 C £151 D £110	Aldershot, Farnham, Bournemouth (including Poole), Birmingham Inner, Bristol, Cambridge City, Harlow, Canterbury, Maidstone, Medway & Tunbridge Wells, Cardiff (Inner), Chelmsford South, Essex & East Suffolk, Chester, Fareham, Winchester, Hampshire, Dorset, Wiltshire, Isle of Wight, Kingston, Guildford, Reigate, Epsom, Leeds Inner (within 2km radius of the City Art Gallery), Lewes, Liverpool, Birkenhead, Manchester Central, Newcastle – City Centre (within a two-mile, radius of St Nicholas Cathedral), Norwich City, Nottingham City, Oxford, Thames Valley, Southampton, Portsmouth, Swindon, Basingstoke, Watford
TWO	A £191 B £168 C £139 D £105	Bath, Cheltenham and Gloucester, Taunton, Yeovil, Bury, Chelmsford North, Cambridge County, Peterborough, Bury St E, Norfolk, Lowestoft, Cheshire & North Wales, Coventry, Rugby, Nuneaton, Stratford and Warwick, Exeter, Plymouth, Hull (City), Leeds Outer, Wakefield & Pontefract, Leigh, Lincoln, Luton, Bedford, St Albans, Hitchin, Hertford, Manchester Outer, Oldham, Bolton, Tameside, Newcastle (other than City Centre), Nottingham & Derbyshire, Sheffield, Doncaster and South Yorkshire, Southport, St Helens, Stockport, Altrincham, Salford, Swansea, Newport, Cardiff (Outer), Wigan, Wolverhampton, Walsall, Dudley & Stourbridge, York, Harrogate
THREE	A £174 B £156 C £133 D £99	Birmingham Outer, Bradford (Dewsbury, Halifax, Huddersfield, Keighley & Skipton), Cumbria, Devon, Cornwall, Grimsby, Skegness, Hull Outer, Kidderminster, Northampton & Leicester, Preston, Lancaster, Blackpool, Chorley, Accrington, Burnley, Blackburn, Rawtenstall & Nelson, Scarborough & Ripon, Stafford, Stoke, Tamworth, Teesside, Worcester, Hereford, Evesham, and Redditch, Shrewsbury, Telford, Ludlow, Oswestry, South & West Wales
LONDON	A £396 B £285 C £219 D £134	City of London: EC1, EC2, EC3, EC4
LONDON	A £304 B £231 C £189 D £121	Central London: W1, WC1, WC2, SW1
LONDON	A £219–256 B £165–219 C £158 D £116	Outer London: (All other London post codes: W, NW, N, E, SE, SW and Bromley, Croydon, Dartford, Gravesend and Uxbridge)

For work carried out after 1 January 2009, the rates are as follows:

	Band A	Band B	Band C	Band D
London 1	£402	£291	£222	£136
London 2	£312	£238	£193	£124
London 3	£225–£263	£169–£225	£162	£119
National 1	£213	£189	£158	£116
National 2/3	£198	£174	£144	£109

Specific problems on assessment

12.21   It is not possible for a solicitor to run up as many hours as he chooses to complete particular work. It is the role of the Costs Office to ensure that the time spent and the rate at which the work is charged is appropriate to the matter. Recent reported cases also emphasise the following considerations:

- Inter-office communication between fee-earners is generally not an appropriate expense of time (*In the matter of Leighanne Radcliffe, 20 December 2004* (Case No L211/1))

- Work needs to be carried out at the appropriate fee-earner level (*In the matter of Michael Ashton* [2006] EWHC 90060 (Costs))

- The guideline rates should be applied and treated as a starting-point when assessing a solicitor's costs *Smith & Ors* [2007] EWHC 80088 (Costs))

- A solicitor can only recover from the estate of the person concerned the amount that has been allowed on assessment. A solicitor acting for another party in Court of Protection proceedings can agree different terms with his own client. However, the solicitor is responsible for ensuring that the client is fully aware of the terms. The Practice Direction to CPR r 48.8 reminds a solicitor (at para 54.1):

  'A client and his solicitor may agree whatever terms they consider appropriate about the payment of the solicitor's charges for his services. If however, the costs are of an unusual nature (either in amount or in the type of costs incurred) those costs will be presumed to have been unreasonably incurred unless the solicitor satisfies the court that he informed the client that they were unusual and, where the costs relate to litigation, that he informed the client they might not be allowed on an assessment of costs between the parties. That information must have been given to the client before the costs were incurred.'

It is incumbent on a solicitor with conduct of a case, especially a professional deputy, to ensure that work is carried out at the right level. As the costs judge, Master Haworth, pointed out in the case of *Smith & Ors* (concerning the rates claimed by a receiver):

'I also find that substantial elements of day to day general management work are mundane and routine, once the receiver has provided overall direction as to the issues which are to be dealt with. In that respect it is incumbent on the receiver to pass that work down to a lower but relevant level or grade of fee earner to be implemented. In relation to that work the receiver cannot expect to be remunerated at anything like the level of his or her own expertise. Mr Bacon accepted and I find that it is entirely possible for a receiver to reclassify and downgrade (where appropriate) his or her own staff within the bands provided in Appendix 2 to the Guide to Summary Assessment in order that general management work is dealt with with the utmost economy and expedition by the appropriate level of fee earner in individual cases. The issue as to the appropriate status or grade of fee earner for the work in question will always be a matter for discretion when Costs Officers and/or Costs Judges are assessing a receiver's general management costs.'

Chapter 13

Gifts and other dispositions of property

Legal basis

13.1   The principal role of those concerned with the property of a person who lacks capacity is to ensure that such property is safeguarded and applied for that person's benefit. However, it is often necessary to look beyond the immediate material needs of a person. There may be others who are involved in and contribute to the person's welfare and who need to be supported in return. A wife looks after her elderly husband, a mother looks after her disabled child or a grandparent helps with school fees. These are immediate and real obligations, although in practice it is often difficult to measure them. It is harder still to project these obligations into the future, when making a will for someone which may not come into effect for several years.

Before 1926, the judges who exercised the jurisdiction in lunacy had limited powers, within the scope of Crown's prerogative to manage a patient's affairs, to authorise voluntary payments from an incapable person's income. Such payments had to be based on a strong presumption that the person would undoubtedly have made them if mentally capable. Typical examples were subscriptions to local charities which a local landowner would have been expected to make, or educating the heir to his estate. The Law of Property Act 1925 introduced a new power, as a result of which a settlement could be created (usually a revocable life interest) which allowed for the estate to devolve on the person's death under the terms of the settlement. These powers were replaced by similar powers under the Mental Health Act 1959. It was not until this Act was amended by the Administration of Justice Act 1969 that the courts acquired a right to make a will on behalf of a person who lacks capacity.

Mental Health Act 1983

13.2   The statutory framework was replicated by the (now repealed) ss 95 and 96 of the Mental Health Act 1983 and ss 3 and 8 of the Enduring Powers of Attorney Act 1985. Section 95 of the Mental Health Act 1983 sets out some wide ranging and positive principles. . Section 95(1) provided as follows:

'(1)   The judge may, with respect to the property and affairs of a patient, do or secure the doing of all such things as appear necessary or expedient —

(a)   for the maintenance or other benefit of the patient;

(b)   for the maintenance or other benefit of members of the patient's family,

263

(c)   for making provision for other persons or purposes for whom or which the patient might be expected to provide if he were not mentally disordered . . .'

Although the Mental Health Act 1983 appeared widely drafted, there were important limitations where there was a benefit to another person. The benefit had to be either for maintenance, where there was a clearly measurable need such as a spouse's nursing home fees or a child's school fees or a provision which the patient might be expected to make. And where provision was being made for another person, the provision had to be such that the patient might be expected to provide. The decision-maker was exercising a substituted judgment, and was limited to doing what the patient would have wanted to do.

Enduring Powers of Attorney Act 1985

13.3   Although the Enduring Powers of Attorney Act 1985 has been repealed, the same powers are conferred on an attorney under an enduring power of attorney (EPA) by Sch 4 of the Mental Capacity Act 2005 (MCA 2005). These provisions give an attorney a statutory basis for making dispositions in favour of a third party and need to be considered carefully for the following reasons:

- they apply to attorneys acting under an enduring power of attorney made before 1 October 2007;

- the Court of Protection uses similar wording in the authority it confers on a deputy; and

- there are no equivalent provisions in the MCA 2005 for an attorney acting under a lasting power of attorney (LPA).

MCA 2005, Sch 4 para 3(2) provides as follows:

'(2)   Subject to any conditions or restrictions contained in the instrument, an attorney under an enduring power of attorney, whether general or limited, may (without obtaining any consent) act under the power so as to benefit himself or other persons than the donor to the following extent but no further, that is to say —

(a)   he may so act in relation to himself or in relation to any other person if the donor might be expected to provide for his or that person's needs respectively; and

(b)   he may do whatever the donor might be expected to do to meet those needs.'

The approach adopted in respect of EPAs is still limited by reference to identifying a person's needs and then doing what the donor might be expected to do to meet those needs. As with the approach of the Mental Health Act 1983, the attorney is applying a subjective test in identifying needs and then exercising the donor's judgment on his behalf. The attorney therefore has less discretion than the Court or a deputy appointed by the Court making acting in the best interests of the person concerned.

An attorney also has limited authority to make small gifts under Sch 4 para 3(3). A decision to make such gifts must be made in the donor's best interests and is considered at **13.5** below.

Mental Capacity Act 2005

13.4   Although the provisions of the Mental Health Act 1983 (and Sch 4 to the MCA 2005) may be open to improvement, they do at least provide a statutory basis for making gifts to another party. The MCA 2005 takes a different approach. A decision made on behalf of a person who lacks capacity must be made in accordance with the Act's general principles and specifically, according to s 4, in the person's best interests. However, s 4 explains how a decision should be arrived at; it does not provide a basis on which the decision itself is made.

The formal authority for making certain decisions, whether these are made by the Court or another person, is contained in the following provisions:

'Section 1 – the principles

...

(5)   An act done, or decision made, under this Act for or on behalf of a person who lacks capacity must be done, or made in his best interests.'

'Section 12 – scope of lasting powers of attorney: gifts

(1)   Where a lasting power of attorney confers authority to make decisions about P's property and affairs, it does not authorise a donee (or, if more than one, any of them) to dispose of the donor's property by making gifts except to the extent permitted by subsection (2).

(2)   The donee may make gifts —

    (a)   on customary occasions to persons (including himself) who are related to or connected with the donor, or

    (b)   to any charity to whom the donor made or might have been expected to make gifts,

if the value of each such gift is not unreasonable having regard to all the circumstances and, in particular, the size of the donor's estate.

(3)   "Customary occasion" means —

    (a)   the occasion or anniversary of a birth, a marriage or the formation of a civil partnership, or

    (b)   any other occasion on which presents are customarily given within families or among friends or associates.

(4)   Subsection (2) is subject to any conditions or restrictions in the instrument.'

'Section 16 – powers to make decisions and appoint deputies: general

(1)   This section applies if a person ("P") lacks capacity in relation to a matter or matters concerning —

    (a)   P's personal welfare, or

    (b)   P's property and affairs.

(2)   The court may —

    (a)   by making an order, make the decision or decisions on P's behalf in relation to the matter or matters, or

    (b)   appoint a person (a "deputy") to make decisions on P's behalf in relation to the matter or matters.

(3)   The powers of the court under this section are subject to the provisions of this Act and, in particular, to sections 1 (the principles) and 4 (best interests).'

'Section 18 – section 16 powers: property and affairs

(1)   The powers under section 16 as respects P's property and affairs extend in particular to —

    (a)   the control and management of P's property;

    (b)   the sale, exchange, charging, gift or other disposition of P's property;

    (c)   the acquisition of property in P's name or on P's behalf;

    (d)   the carrying on, on P's behalf, of any profession, trade or business;

    (e)   the taking of a decision which will have the effect of dissolving a partnership of which P is a member;

    (f)   the carrying out of any contract entered into by P;

    (g)   the discharge of P's debts and of any of P's obligations, whether legally enforceable or not;

    (h)   the settlement of any of P's property, whether for P's benefit or for the benefit of others;

    (i)   the execution for P of a will;

    (j)   the exercise of any power (including a power to consent) vested in P whether beneficially or as trustee or otherwise;

    (k)   the conduct of legal proceedings in P's name or on P's behalf.

(2)   No will may be made under subsection (1)(i) at a time when P has not reached 18.

(3)   The powers under section 16 as respects any other matter relating to P's property and affairs may be exercised even though P has not reached 16, if the court considers it likely that P will still lack

capacity to make decisions in respect of that matter when he reaches 18.'

'Section 20 – restriction on deputies

(1)   A deputy does not have power to make a decision on behalf of P in relation to a matter if he knows or has reasonable grounds for believing that P has capacity in relation to the matter.

...

(3)   A deputy may not be given powers with respect to —

(a)   the settlement of any of P's property, whether for P's benefit or for the benefit of others,

(b)   the execution for P of a will, or

(c)   the exercise of any power (including a power to consent) vested in P whether beneficially or as trustee or otherwise.

(4)   A deputy may not be given power to make a decision on behalf of P which is inconsistent with a decision made, within the scope of his authority and in accordance with this Act, by the donee of a lasting power of attorney granted by P (or, if there is more than one donee, by any of them).'

'Schedule 2 paragraph 2

The will [made pursuant to section 18] may make any provision (whether by disposing of property or exercising a power or otherwise) which could be made by a will executed by P if he had capacity to make it.'

'Schedule 4 paragraph 3

(3)   Without prejudice to sub-paragraph (2), but subject to any conditions or restrictions contained in the instrument, an attorney under an enduring power, whether general or limited, may (without obtaining any consent) dispose of the property of the donor by way of gift to the following extent but no further, that is to say —

(a)   he may make gifts of a seasonal nature or at a time, or on an anniversary, of a birth or marriage, to persons (including himself) who are related or connected with the donor, and

(b)   he may make gifts to any charity to whom the donor made or might be expected to make gifts,

provided that the value of each such gift is not unreasonable having regard to all the circumstances and in particular the size of the donor's estate.'

The Act therefore requires a decision-maker to apply a two part process. The Court, or in the case of an LPA, the donee, authorises the decision, such as the making of a gift. The Court or the person with the authority to make the decision must then decide whether the person concerned can or should make the gift, who the recipient should be and how much the gift should be for. The principle measure of the gift is therefore the 'best interests' of the person concerned.

The requirement that the decision is in a person's best interests is simple, flexible and practical. The decision-maker must take into account the factors set out in s 4. He must therefore consider the past and present wishes of the person, the views of carers and relatives and the factors that he would consider (the persons he might be expected to provide for). He can also take into account the prudence or suitability of the decision. Can it be afforded, how will it affect the beneficiaries, what are the tax implications? Or to put it simply: is it, or is it not, in the person's best interests?

Small gifts – without reference to the Court

By attorney under an enduring power of attorney

13.5   Where an EPA is in place, it is for the attorney, acting under Sch 4 to the Act and subject to the terms of the instrument to exercise his judgement. Subject to any restrictions in the instrument, the attorney's discretion is further restrained:

- a recipient who is not a charity must be 'related or connected' with the donor;

- gifts must be of a seasonal or anniversary nature;

- a charity must be one the donor might be expected to make gifts to;

- the size of the gift must not be unreasonable.

Whether or not the attorney exercises that judgment and the manner in which it is exercised depends on the attorney. And although the statutory provision distinguishes between charities and individuals, this does not imply that there is a wider latitude to making gifts to individuals. The making of the gift is a decision that must be taken in the donor's best interests: for instance, the choice of recipient is at the very least a factor that the donor would be expected to consider if he were able to do so.

As for what is 'unreasonable' the attorney has the onerous responsibility of making this decision. Generally the Court would expect the attorney to apply the same considerations as the Court would and apply the 'best interests' criteria laid down by s 4 with a large measure of common sense. Thus the gift should be made from surplus income or to use the wording of Practice Direction 9D 'should not be 'disproportionately large when compared to the size of the estate as a whole'. The gift should not prejudice the donor's financial security and should not be contentious. Although each case depends on its own merits and no gift can be made to coincide with a tax period, the writer's view is that where the donor's estate is close to the inheritance tax threshold, gifts within the course of any one tax year should not exceed the inheritance tax allowance of £3,000 or £250 to any one individual. In the case of *Re W*, gifts of £20,000 to each of the three residuary beneficiaries from an estate worth around £260,000 were held to be excessive (see the first instance decision of Jules Sher QC at [2000] 1 All ER 175). If the estate is substantial, then gifts to individuals should not exceed those amounts unless the individuals are residuary beneficiaries in which case a higher threshold of £10–20,000 might be appropriate.

No formalities apply to the making of the gift although the attorney should keep clear records of the date and the amount both in the context of his duty to keep accounts and to assess any potential tax issues arising at the time of the gift or in the future.

If the gift does not qualify as a 'small gift', or is payable to an individual not 'related to or connected with the donor' or is not of a seasonal or anniversary nature, then the attorney must apply to the Court for authority to make the gift under s 18(1)(b) or Sch 4 para 16(2)(e).

By a donee of a lasting power of attorney

13.6   The authority of a donee of an LPA to make gifts is similar to that of an attorney acting under an EPA. MCA 2005, s 12 mirrors Sch 4 para 3, save that the reference to when gifts can be made is to 'customary occasions'. These are defined at s 12(3) to reflect a wider variety of social norms and encompass 'the occasion or anniversary of a birth, a marriage or the formation of a civil partnership, or any other occasion on which presents are customarily given within families or among friends or associates'. If the gifts are beyond the scope of the donee's authority then a formal application must be made to the Court to exercise its powers under s 18(1)(b) or s 23(4).

By a deputy appointed by the Court of Protection

13.7   Most deputies have widely drawn powers and these may include a provision to make small gifts to charities or individuals that the person might be expected to provide for (see **5.20** above). Usually the Court will set an upper limit on the amount that can be gifted in each year. If the person concerned is wealthy or has a history of making lifetime gifts a person applying to be appointed deputy should make it clear in his application that such a provision is necessary, affordable and in the best interests of the person concerned.

Where a deputy has power to make gifts, this must be by reference not only to the statutory powers of the Court but also the statutory requirement to act in P's best interests. If making an order, the Court is authorising the 'gift or other disposition of P's property' under s 18(1)(b). The Court may then appoint a deputy to make those decisions on P's behalf, who in turn must ensure that the final decision to make the gift is in the best interests of the person concerned.

Maintenance and provision

Statutory basis

13.8   Only Sch 4 to the Act refers explicitly to making provision for the needs of another person. As we have seen (see **13.3** above), an attorney acting under an EPA has express authority to provide for the needs of another person.

However, orders appointing a deputy will contain similar wording such as the following:

> 'The deputy may make provision for the needs of anyone who is related to or connected with [P], if he provided for or might be expected to provide for that person's needs, by doing whatever he did or might reasonably be expected to do to meet those needs.'

The power of a deputy to maintain or provide for the needs of another party must be by reference to the statutory powers of the Court. If making such an order, the Court is effectively exercising its power to authorise the 'gift or other disposition of P's property' under s 18(1)(b). The Court may then appoint a deputy to make those decisions on P's behalf.

The powers contained in s 18(1)(b) are exercisable by the Court either directly or through delegation to a deputy. The donee of an LPA is therefore neglected. The donee does not have a power to maintain and cannot exercise the provisions of s 18(1)(b). Therefore a donee who wishes to maintain a third party and believes it to be in the best interests of the donor, will need to apply to the Court for a decision.

Extent of benefit

13.9   The amount which may be paid by an attorney or a deputy with a suitably worded authority by way of maintenance is not defined and may greatly exceed the amount which could be gifted by an attorney. This can give a very wide discretion. For instance, an attorney acting under a registered EPA has been able to create a settlement for the education of a grandchild of the donor (see *Re the estate of Marjorie Langdon Cameron dec'd* [1999] Ch 386, [1999] 2 All ER 924).

Most persons who require maintenance are carers: spouses looking after an elderly husband or wife, a child looking after an elderly parent or parents looking after a disabled child. Often they will have reduced resources of their own. Not only are they people who might be provided for if there were no issues of capacity or disability, but they often provide care that would be extremely costly to replace. The courts have historically been sympathetic to the needs of such people. The MCA 2005 provides a further source of assistance in that the 'best interests' of the person concerned must extend to the needs and interests of those dependent on him or caring for him.

The benefit to a dependant or carer may be direct or indirect. For instance a disabled child or husband will have assets and income and be the main source of family income. He may own the family home or invest in buying a bigger home, taking responsibility for the cost of household bills, repairs and maintenance. He may pay for holidays and outings, from trips abroad to visits to the seaside. The case of *Re B (deceased)* [2000] Ch 662 involved a claim under the Inheritance (Provision for Family and Dependants) Act 1975 where a mother had given up her job to look after her severely disabled child. The Court of Appeal held that while the daughter's needs had priority, they encompassed the needs of the mother. The needs of one were the needs of the other and the child should therefore provide for the mother.

Allowances

13.10   In cases such as that of a mother looking after a disabled child, an incidental benefit to the carer is insufficient recompense for someone who has a full-time job caring for a child or parent who has complex physical and emotional needs. There is no adequate reward for the quiet devotion of many carers who remain attentive, compassionate and responsible. The Court as well as HM Revenue & Customs accept that it is inappropriate to treat such carers as paid employees. They can, however, receive an allowance for the gratuitous care provided. The amount that is often 'allowed' to a carer is the equivalent of a net wage (thus without tax and national insurance) that would be paid to a professional carer working an equivalent number of hours (up to the legal maximum). A deputy who is responsible for providing this level of care should be able to act within the scope of his authority to make such an arrangement on the basis that if the deputy were not paying an allowance, there would be a corresponding or even greater cost to the estate.

Larger gifts and disposition – general considerations

13.11   Substantial gifts, settlements and wills are more serious matters that must be dealt with by the Court. Thus MCA 2005, s 20(3) provides that the following powers may not be delegated to a deputy and can only be exercised by the Court:

(a)   the settlement of any of P's property, whether for P's benefit or for the benefit of others,

(b)   the execution for P of a will, or

(c)   the exercise of any power (including a power to consent) vested in P whether beneficially or as trustee or otherwise.

Any disposal of a person's property without that person's consent or understanding involves an interference with the individual's right to the enjoyment of his own property as well as the making of subjective judgements about that person's wishes. The judgement of the person who lacks capacity is substituted by a skilled but impersonal body. The MCA 2005 encourages a cautious approach. Decisions made in advance by a person while he had capacity should be respected. Thus an advance decision should not be overridden and an attorney appointed by an LPA is the person preferred to make decisions if the donor lacks capacity. By analogy, a will made by someone of sound mind should be assumed to be the last word on the subject.

With this in mind, no application to the Court which interferes with the arrangements made by a person when he or she had capacity, should be made without a careful consideration of the statutory framework and the guidance given by the courts.

Statutory and judicial framework

13.12   The statutory basis for determining such issues has been considered at **13.4** above. The Court's powers to make decisions are set out briefly in s 18 of the Act. How the Court makes such decisions is more complicated. The decisions must be in the best interests of the person concerned and follow the statutory framework laid down by s 4 of the MCA 2005. Although s 4 is couched in general terms, it provides an essential and logical process that must be followed in reaching a decision. As has already been mentioned, it also allows the decision-maker more flexibility in making a decision. This represents a subtle but significant change in the basis on which decisions are made. The decision-maker is no longer concerned with a substitute decision, trying to justify a decision that the person would have made. Under the MCA 2005, this is a consideration, but it is not the only one (see *Re P* [2009] EWHC 163 (Ch), [2009] All ER (D) 160 and **13.14** below).

Although s 4 of the MCA 2005 is the main measure for making a decision on behalf of another, the courts have provided some helpful guidance in developing this jurisdiction.

It is often quite simple to determine whether most day-to-day decisions are in the best interests of a person. If they make the person more comfortable or his life more congenial then they can be said to be for his benefit. It is also easy to see the merits of maintaining a person's financial and moral obligations, to provide for a spouse or a child with special needs or someone who lives with and cares for the person. But to go beyond this and decide what a person who cannot make decisions might do is a difficult task. How do we know what a person would do, or indeed whether they would do anything at all? Is it possible to avoid a subjective interpretation of what a person ought to do? It is essential to look at what the courts have decided over the years to see what guidelines to follow and presumptions to apply before even beginning to try to demonstrate what another person would wish to do. Whether such decisions deal specifically with wills or settlements, the principles applied by the courts in making decisions on behalf of an incapable person apply to all aspects of this element of the Court of Protection's jurisdiction.

Unfortunately, wills and settlements are not common and most cases which do reach the Court of Protection are uncontroversial. More complex cases and appeals which reach the High Court, let alone the Court of Appeal, are rare. In the few cases which have been reported, the underlying principle is that any disposition should be one which the person concerned would make or might be expected to make if momentarily restored to full capacity. This has been qualified by the decision of Lewison J in *Re P* which to date is the only statutory will made by a High Court judge under the MCA 2005 to be reported. In a considered review of earlier decisions made under the MHA 1983 jurisdiction, the judge qualified the earlier approach in the light of the new Act. While the Court would aim to give effect to the testator's likely wishes, it was not bound to replicate (in so far as it could) the decision which the testator would have made. The earlier decisions, especially the decision of Megarry V-C in *Re D(J)* [1982] Ch 237, [1982] 2 All ER 37 contain 'a good deal of wisdom and wisdom can always be applied'. However, the guidance given could not 'be directly applied to the structured decision making process required by the 2005 Act.' (paragraph 45)

The position before MCA 2005: Re D(J) and the five propositions

13.13   Prior to the decision in *Re P* the leading authority on wills authorised by the Court of Protection (known as 'statutory wills') was the case of *Re D(J)* [1982] Ch 237, [1982] 2 All ER 37. The case concerned Mrs D who in 1962 made a will leaving her house and its contents to her daughter, A, who had lived with her in her house for the previous five years and continued to do so until 1972 when A remarried and left the house to live with her new husband. The residue was left to D's five children in equal shares. Soon afterwards, D began to show signs of dementia. After a visit to A, she insisted on staying with her. The house was sold for £13,500, with the result that the legacy under the 1962 will adeemed, with A simply taking an equal share of the residue. From the proceeds of sale, D bought a new house which was eventually sold for £22,000. Sadly D was unable to live there and continued to live with her daughter. In 1979, A applied for a statutory will giving her a legacy of £22,000 with the residue being divided equally between the five children. The whole estate was worth £50,000. The application was initially dealt with by the Deputy Master of the Court of Protection who authorised a will giving a legacy of £10,000 to A. She appealed and, in the High Court, Sir Robert Megarry V-C authorised a will giving her £15,000 with the residue being left in the same way among all the children equally. In his judgment, the Vice-Chancellor set out five principles, factors or propositions to be considered when the court makes a will for the patient. Because of their importance and continued use as guidance by the Court of Protection, they are set out here in full ([1982] Ch 243 [1982] 2 All ER at 43):

'The first of the principles or factors which I think it is possible to discern is that it is to be assumed that the patient is having a brief lucid interval at the time the will is made. The second is that during the lucid interval the patient has a full knowledge of the past, and a full realisation that as soon as the will is executed he or she will relapse into the actual mental state that previously existed, with the prognosis as it actually is. These propositions emerge, I think, from the judgment of Cross J in *Re WJGL* [1965] 3 All ER 865 at 871–872; [1966] Ch 135 at 144–145 . . .

The third proposition is that it is the actual patient who has to be considered and not a hypothetical patient on the Clapham omnibus. I say that because the will is being made by the court, and so by an impartial entity skilled in the law, rather than the actual patient, whose views while still of a sound disposing mind might be idiosyncratic and far from impartial. In *Re Davey* (dec'd) [1980] 3 All ER 342 at 348, [1981] 1 WLR 164 at 171 Fox J is reported as saying, in relation to a will made by the Court of Protection, that the essential question was "what if anything would be reasonable provision in all the circumstances for the various contestants", and it could be said that this indicates an objective approach made with the wisdom of the court rather than the approach likely to be made by the patient if restored to full mental capacity. I very much doubt if the judge meant to indicate thus, and in any case I do not think it is right. The whole approach of Cross J in *Re WJGL* [1965] 3 All ER 865, [1966] Ch 135 was that of considering the particular patient, momentarily restored to full mental capacity, as being the

273

settlor. Further, in s 102(1)(c) [now s 95(1)(c) MHA 1983], the question is one of making provision for persons or purposes "for whom or for which the patient might be expected to provide if he were not mentally disordered"; and I think that this provision governs the making of a will for the patient, and contemplated the particular patient: and see *Re CMG*. Before losing testamentary capacity the patient may have been a person with strong antipathies or deep affections for particular persons or causes, or with vigorous religious or political views; and of course the patient was then able to give effect to those views when making a will. I think that the court must take the patient as he or she was before losing testamentary capacity. No doubt allowance may be made for the passage of years since the patient was of full capacity, for sometimes strong feelings mellow into indifference, and even family feuds evaporate. Furthermore, I do not think that the court should give effect to antipathies or affections of the patient which are beyond reason. But subject to all due allowances, I think the court must seek to make the will which the actual patient, acting reasonably, would have made if notionally restored to full mental capacity, memory and foresight. If I may adopt Dr Johnson's words, used for another purpose, the court is to do for the patient what the patient would fairly do for himself, if he could.

Fourth, I think that during the hypothetical lucid interval the patient is to be envisaged as being advised by competent solicitors. The court will in fact be making the will, of course, and the court should not make a will on the assumption that the terms of the will are to be framed by someone who, for instance, knows nothing about lapse and ademption. Furthermore, as the court will be surveying the past and the future, the hypothetically lucid patient should be assumed to have a skilled solicitor to draw his or her attention to matters which a testator should bear in mind. In *Re DML* [1965] 2 All ER 129 at 133, [1965] Ch 1133 at 1139, a case on a proposed purchase of an annuity in order to save estate duty, Cross J put a lucid explanation of the proposal into the mouth of a hypothetical legal adviser to the hypothetically lucid patient. In any case, I cannot imagine Parliament intended the court to match the sort of home-made will that some testators make. I do not, of course, say that one must treat the patient as being bound to accept the imaginary legal advice that is given to him: but the patient is to be treated as doing what he does either because of the advice or in spite of it, and not without having had it.

Fifth, in all normal cases the patient is to be envisaged as taking a broad brush to the claims on his bounty, rather than an accountant's pen. There will be nothing like a balance sheet or profit and loss account. There may be many to whom the patient feels morally indebted; and some of the moral indebtedness may be readily expressible in terms of money, and some of it may not. But when giving legacies or shares of residue few testators are likely to reckon up in terms of cash the value of the hospitality and gifts that he has received from his friends and relations, and then seek to make some form of testamentary repayment, even if his estate is large enough for this. Instead, there is likely to be some general recognition of outstanding kindness by some gift which in quantum may bear very little relation to the cost or value of those kindnesses.'

The counter-factual assumption

13.14   The difficulty faced by the courts in exercising the MHA 1983 jurisdiction was that in attempting to decide what a person would do if he had capacity, some curious assumptions would have to be made. The most difficult was the assumption that a person who lacks capacity suddenly and momentarily has a 'lucid moment'. Further assumptions would need to be made, such as imputing legal advice and assistance to the person. This counter-factual assumption made by the courts was described by Lewison J in *Re P* [2009] EWHC 163 (Ch) where (at paragraph 13) he considered the earlier decision of Cross J in the case of *Re WJGL* [1965] 3 All ER 865:

> '. . . Cross J was considering the power to direct the making of a settlement. He held that the particular provisions under consideration were not for the benefit of the patient or his family. Thus the only power he had was the power given by section 102 (1) (c) [of the Mental Health Act 1959]. It follows that the question he was considering was what "the patient might be expected to provide if he were not mentally disordered". Accordingly the Act itself required the court to make the counter-factual assumption that the patient was not mentally disordered, and then to ask itself what, on that hypothesis, the patient might be expected to do. Cross J made it clear that the conclusions that he reached were conclusions reached as a matter of construction of section 102 (1) (c). In essence, the question was: given the counter-factual assumption that the Act required to be made, were there any further assumptions that were necessarily inherent in that assumption? Cross J held (in effect) that there were not and that apart from assuming that the patient was not mentally disordered, he had to be taken as he was. In that case the patient was friendless and cared for at the expense of the state with no opportunity to spend his money, and no prospect of marrying and having a family. Cross J said:
>
>> "It seems to me, therefore, that I must assume that the patient becomes a sane man for a sufficient time to review the situation but knows that after a brief interval of sanity he will once more be as he was before."'

This approach might have worked well where it was clear what the patient would have wished to do. Most cases would be straightforward, with clear evidence from the person concerned or the documents of what he would have wanted to do. However, other cases would require a complex series of hypotheses to reach a sensible outcome, especially where there was no evidence of the person's likely wishes or those wishes were irrational or objectionable.

After MCA 2005: the case of Re P

13.15   This complex approach followed by the courts under the MHA 1983 jurisdiction and its relevance to the new Act was first addressed judicially by Lewison J in the case of *Re P* [2009] EWHC 163 (Ch). Unfortunately the fascinating facts of the case have not been reported. The judgment is limited to the principles that were to be applied in making a statutory will for a person who lacked capacity and where the known wishes of the testator were irrational. In considering whether he was required to exercise a substituted judgment in line with earlier cases, he confirmed that this was not the same as making a decision in a person's best interests (at paragraph 38):

'I agree. It follows from this, in my judgment, that the guidance given under the Mental Health Acts 1959 and 1983 about the making of settlements or wills can no longer be directly applied to a decision being made under the 2005 Act. I say this for a number of reasons:

(i)   The 2005 Act does not require the counter-factual assumption that P is not mentally disordered. The facts must be taken as they are. It is not therefore necessary to go through the mental gymnastics of imagining that P has a brief lucid interval and then relapses into his former state.

(ii)   The goal of the enquiry is not what P "might be expected" to have done; but what is in P's best interests. This is more akin to the "balance sheet" approach than to the "substituted judgment" approach. The code of practice makes this clear in that it points out that the test of best interests was one that was worked out by the courts mainly in decisions relating to the provision of medical care (para 5.1).

(iii)   The previous guidance was concerned with deciding what P would have wanted if he were not mentally disordered. But the 2005 Act requires the decision maker to consider P's present wishes and feelings, which ex hypothesi are wishes and feelings entertained by a person who lacks mental capacity in relation to the decision being made on his behalf.

(iv)   The same structured decision-making process applies to all decisions to be made on P's behalf, whether great or small, whereas the previous guidance was specific to the making of a will, gift or settlement. Moreover, it is a decision-making process which must be followed, not only by the court, but by anyone who takes decisions on P's behalf.

(v)   In making his decision the decision-maker must consider "all relevant circumstances".

(vi)   The Act expressly directs the decision-maker to take a number of steps before reaching a decision. These include encouraging P to participate in the decision. He must also "consider" P's past and present wishes, and his beliefs and values and must "take into account" the views of third parties as to what would be in P's best interests.'

Ascertaining the wishes of P

13.16   Under the MHA 1983 jurisdiction, the wishes or likely wishes of the patient were the most important factor in making a decision on behalf of a patient. The Court was only able to make such provisions as the patient might have made for himself if capable. As was clear from the third of Sir Robert Megarry's five propositions in the case of *Re D(J)*, the Court would look subjectively at the actual person and attempt to form a judgment as to that person's likely wishes if he were restored to full capacity. The person's family circumstances or testamentary history would therefore indicate whom he would wish to provide for. In some cases the person may be able to express his own feelings and views, while in more difficult cases the Court would have to perform an elaborate exercise constructing a set of wishes for a person whose wishes were in fact completely unknown.

The approach adopted by the MCA 2005 is different in that a person's wishes, beliefs and values are only some of the factors that must be taken into account. This does not lessen their importance. Just because a person technically lacks testamentary capacity, this does not mean that his ability to express views and opinions should be ignored. It is often appropriate for an application to be made to the Court where the views of the person are quite clear but there is no legal basis for the person to make the decision personally or because any decision made may be open to challenge and therefore the subject of future litigation. An applicant must therefore show the Court what steps have been taken to consult directly with the person concerned and to ascertain his past and present wishes, beliefs and values. These factors are important and must be respected. But they are not the only criteria affecting the decision. The decision-maker can take account of other considerations, whether or not the decision-maker would or would not have considered then for himself. For instance the person concerned might not be aware of changes in circumstances, tax legislation, the needs of beneficiaries or the wider consequences of his decision. He might not appreciate the impracticality or folly of a particular decision. He may well have been able to make an unwise decision when he had capacity, but there is no obligation on the decision-maker to make an unwise decision on behalf of a person who now lacks capacity. As Lewison J explained in *Re P* [2009] EWHC 163 (Ch) (at paragraph 42):

'I would add that although the fact that P makes an unwise decision does not on its own give rise to any inference of incapacity (section 1 (4) [of the MCA 2005]), once the decision-making power shifts to a third party (whether carer, deputy or the court) I cannot see that it would be a proper exercise for a third party decision-maker consciously to make an unwise decision merely because P would have done so. A consciously unwise decision will rarely if ever be made in P's best interests.'

However, where a person's wishes, values and beliefs are ascertainable and appropriate then they should be implemented if at all possible.

The case of *Re S v S* (25 November 2008, unreported, although a full transcript is available at www.publicguardian.gov.uk/forms/other-orders-cop.htm concerned two sisters who had been appointed to act jointly as attorneys under an EPA for their elderly parents. When the sisters failed to co-operate, the EPA failed and the Court appointed one of the sisters as deputy. On an appeal by the other sister, the judge, Hazel Marshall QC directed that an independent deputy be appointed. The parents had wanted both daughters to act together or not at all, and were capable of giving evidence to this effect. Although the case concerned an EPA and the appointment of a deputy, it is an important decision concerning the weight to be given to a person's wishes under the MCA 2005. The Court was not bound by those wishes, but if they were not irrational or might cause some other intended prejudice, they should be followed if at all possible. As the judge observed (at paragraph 87):

> 'They [their wishes] are not irresponsible in the sense of being an inappropriately disproportionate application of their resources ... there is no other sufficiently countervailing consideration, in terms of consequences which might be detrimental to Mr and Mrs S, which might, in my judgment, mean that implementing their wishes would not be in their best interests. Furthermore, doing so has the obvious merit of conferring on Mr and Mrs S the dignity of having those wishes respected, with the likely effects of that on their well-being.'

Where P's wishes cannot be ascertained

13.17   Where a person has a record of expressing wishes or is capable of expressing wishes, the Court has evidence on which it can determine his best interests. It is more difficult to make a decision on behalf of a person who perhaps has no family, has never had a will or has been incapable for so long that there is no evidence of his personality and circumstances which might influence his likely wishes.

This difficulty was considered by Cross J in the case of *Re WJGL* [1965] 3 All ER 865. L was 68 and had been mentally incapable from about the age of 17. By inheritance and accumulations of income he had acquired a sizeable estate worth some £130,000 which was more than would be required for his maintenance for the remainder of his life. An application was made for lifetime gifts and settlements for a family servant who had helped look after the patient and for the relatives who would in due course inherit on the patient's intestacy. The judge held that it was proper for the court to consider settlements, the object of which was simply to avoid death duties and to accelerate the interests of beneficiaries presumptively entitled under the patient's will or intestacy. The court had to balance the prior requirements of the person with the needs of the relatives, but it could be flexible in accepting the reality that individuals would benefit on the person's death and that immediate gifts would lead to a considerable tax saving:

> 'It must be exasperating to see family money tied up in the Court of Protection for the benefit of none but the Revenue. On the other hand, it is not the function of the court to give away the patient's property to those presumptively entitled to it on his death simply because he will, in all probability, or even certainly, never need it himself.'

The judge allowed a fund of £40,000 to be retained for the patient, the balance of his estate being disposed of in the form of lifetime gifts and settlements.

The subsequent case of *Re C* [1991] 3 All ER 866 concerned a 75-year-old spinster who had been born with severe brain damage and had lived in the same hospital near London since the age of ten. She was the only child of a mother who died in 1918 and a father who died in 1953 leaving her with an estate worth some £1.6 million. She had little memory, understanding or capacity to communicate and few, if any, of her distant cousins knew of her existence. The only person to take an interest in her welfare, apart from the staff and other patients at the hospital, was a voluntary worker who worked for an organisation which befriended mental patients. C was, however, able to enjoy her surroundings and outings and coach trips provided by the hospital. As the estate was sizeable and was the first case to concern a patient who had never had testamentary capacity the case was referred to the nominated judge. The judge, Hoffmann J, authorised an immediate gift of £100,000 to the hospital and £400,000 to C's family to be divided according to the intestacy rules. As part of the same application, a statutory will was approved, giving a legacy of £10,000 to the carer, £15,000 to a grandchild of a cousin who suffered from Down's Syndrome, with the residue being divided between the hospital and the family in the same proportions as the lifetime gift. The judge recognised the difficulty of forming a view about what would be expected from a person who had never enjoyed a rational mind. That the court could form a view was explained as follows (at 870):

'. . . the court must assume that she [Miss C] would have been a normal decent person, acting in accordance with contemporary standards of morality. In the absence of evidence to the contrary, no less should be assumed of any person and in this case there is nothing to displace such an assumption. A person in the position of Miss C would in my view have been influenced by two principal considerations. First, that she had spent the whole of her life in the care of the community. . . . Secondly, that she had derived her fortune from being a child of a family. She would therefore in my view have felt moral obligations to show recognition to the community and to her family. Once one has arrived at the conclusion that the disposition of her property would have been guided by these principles, I do not think it is necessary for the court to be satisfied that the patient would definitely have chosen one particular way of giving effect to them rather than another. A distribution which can be rationally justified as a way of giving effect to these principles would in my view be a provision which the patient "might be expected to provide", even though a somewhat different distribution could also be described. The court cannot of course indulge its own whims in these matters . . . . But I observe that the statute, recognising the difficulty of arriving at any certainty in these matters, says "might" rather than "would be expected to provide". In matters of detail, there must be a range of choices which would be equally valid.'

Although Hoffmann J was bound to do on behalf of Miss C what he felt she would do if she had capacity, he was also making a value judgment on her behalf. The approach allowed by the MCA 2005 encourages a similar approach without necessarily having to impute a particular set of hypothetical wishes to the person. The question for the decision-maker is simple: is the proposed disposition in the person's best interests? This question may well invite the response that a person's best interests are irrelevant when dead and we have no right to impute virtue or generosity to a person when there is no

279

evidence of those qualities. This point was addressed in *Re P* [2009] EWHC 163 (Ch) (at paragraph 44):

> 'There is one other aspect of the "best interests" test that I must consider. In deciding what provision should be made in a will to be executed on P's behalf and which, ex hypothesi, will only have effect after he is dead, what are P's best interests? Mr Boyle stressed the principle of adult autonomy; and said that P's best interests would be served simply by giving effect to his wishes. That is, I think, part of the overall picture, and an important one at that. But what will live on after P's death is his memory; and for many people it is in their best interests that they be remembered with affection by their family and as having done "the right thing" by their will. In my judgment the decision-maker is entitled to take into account, in assessing what is in P's best interests, how he will be remembered after his death.'

Re S and Re R – burden is on the person proving the change

13.18   No court should readily interfere with a person's earlier stated wishes. A person's wishes can equally be an absence of wishes, a desire not to benefit a person or to leave matters to chance or to the predetermined choice of the intestacy rules. Where a person's wishes were ascertained clearly at a particular time prior to the onset of incapacity, there is a presumption that the person would not want to alter those wishes. A person who makes a will must be assumed to want it to come into effect as drafted, even if the will is made several years before his death. The testator should also know that unless the will is altered while he is alive and has capacity, its provisions will remain exactly as he had left them. The beneficiaries of the existing will (or those who take on an intestacy) are also affected by the application and are therefore the respondents to the application (see Practice Direction 9E and **13.33** below). If it is for the applicant to propose changes, then it is for the respondents to oppose those changes and argue for the preservation of the original provision.

Not only does an earlier will or disposition set out a person's wishes, it also defines the parties to the application. The Court must therefore be persuaded that the earlier provisions should be altered. They are in that sense more important than a 'relevant written statement' which s 4(6)(a) of the MCA 2005 requires the Court to consider. The burden is therefore on the applicant to persuade the Court that it is in the person's best wishes to alter those provisions.

In the case of *Re S* [1997] 1 FLR 96, the 'starting point' was the intestacy of Miss S. Ferris J emphasised the presumption of starting with the intestacy rules as reflecting her likely wishes and that the court must be satisfied that the person would have wished to depart from those wishes ([1997] 1 FLR 96 at 99:

> 'It seems to me that I ought not to authorise the making of dispositions to charity except to the extent that I have a reasonable degree of confidence that not only is it objectively reasonable but that it is something which the patient herself would have wished to be done if she were of full capacity and aware of the circumstances.'

The Court must therefore have a 'reasonable degree of confidence' that the important decision it is taking is the right one by reference both to objective reasonableness as well as the subjective presumed wishes of the person.

The case of *Re R* (11 December 1998, [2003] WTLR 1051) also came before Ferris J, on an appeal from a decision of the Master of the Court of Protection. Miss R had made a will in 1992 leaving her estate equally between her two nephews. Shortly afterwards she gave a substantial sum of money to one of her nephews, M, equivalent to half the value of her estate. The other nephew, A, was her attorney under an EPA and despite registering the power in 1993 and becoming aware of the gift, took no action to reverse this until 1998 when Miss R was terminally ill. The Master authorised a statutory will bringing the gift to M into hotchpot. M appealed to the nominated judge, Ferris J, who held that the gift to A did not of itself overturn the presumption that the 1992 gift was valid. He found that the evidence before him was insufficient to show that she would have changed her mind. The judge warned that:

> 'the court needs to have a fair degree of assurance that what it proposes to do does indeed represent the wishes of the patient and that it is what she would decide for herself if she were temporarily to recover her capacity and to receive proper advice as to her position.'

While the Court on need no longer do what the person concerned would have wished to be done, it must still have a reasonable degree of confidence that the decision it is making is in the person's best interests.

Displacing the status quo

13.19 The cases of *Re S* and *Re R* have often been cited in favour of preserving the existing dispositions of a will against those arguing for changes. It was therefore often difficult for an applicant to show that a person who lacked capacity would want to make a will in the first place. The MCA 2005 jurisdiction requires an applicant to show why changes to an existing disposition are necessary, but there is no longer such a heavy burden to show that the person would want to make a will or make a particular disposition.

As we have seen in the case of *Re WJGL* [1965] 3 All ER 865, in the absence of contrary wishes, the Court is not unsympathetic to tax planning considerations. And where there are no relatives who might benefit from an intestacy there is at least a presumption that a person would prefer to die testate than leave his estate *bona vacantia* (*Re Freeman* [1927] 1 Ch 479). As to whether a person would want to make will, the Court is entitled to assume – in the absence of contrary evidence – that he would wish to be well remembered (*Re P* 2009] EWHC 163 (Ch) (at paragraph 44).

However, where there was evidence of a pre-existing intention, the Court would still require a strong argument to show that a person would want to make a new disposition. The MCA 2005 makes it easier to displace such earlier intention. It is simply one factor that needs to be considered as part of an overall assessment of a person's best interests. This does not mean that earlier wishes can be readily overridden. They must be respected and carefully taken into account. But the Court can take account of all other relevant factors without feeling itself bound as a hostage to some earlier wishes.

Re S – each case to be decided on its own merits

13.20   The problem remains that each case is different as it reflects the character and history of the actual patient concerned. The case of *Re S* [1997] 1 FLR 96 was decided on similar facts to those in *Re C*, except that the contribution to S's care by charity was smaller and the contact with her family was greater. The judge, Ferris J, was asked to follow the approach taken by Hoffmann J in *Re C*. The judge made a point of distinguishing that case, as each case must be decided on its own merits:

> 'That this is not an area in which judicial precedent really has any weight and it seems to me that there is as much scope for somewhat differing results to be arrived at in different cases as there is for different individuals who are of full capacity but in similar personal and economic circumstances to make substantially different dispositions of their estate'.

In this case the judge authorised a lifetime gift and a statutory will with in each case 75 per cent of the gift being in favour of the family according to the intestacy rules and 25 per cent to charity. Although the proportion given to charity was more generous than that in *Re S*, it was less than the equal share the Official Solicitor had asked for.

Other considerations – changes in circumstances

13.21   Most applications are made due to changes in circumstances which the person concerned had not anticipated when making a will or when having sufficient capacity to understand (whether explicitly or implicitly) the consequences of an intestacy. The applicant therefore has a clear starting point in the existing will, intestacy or general disposition and should begin by asking whether the existing dispositions are reasonable or just. If not, then the applicant must show how circumstances have changed and how it is in the best interests of the person concerned to respond to those changes.

These considerations may be illustrated by the following situations:

- the estate has increased considerably in value due to inheritance or a personal injury award;

- the nature of the estate has changed due to increasing property prices, falling stock markets or the cost of nursing care;

- the existing dispositions are out of date where the person has remarried thus revoking an earlier will, a property has been sold causing a gift in a will to adeem or a principal beneficiary has died. One of the most common situations justifying an application for a statutory will is the simple (usually home-made) will where everything is left to the surviving spouse who has since died; or

- relationships have changed: either strong feelings have mellowed into indifference or a new moral obligation has been entered into. An earlier will was made in different times, of robust independence and good health. Several years later, the person has received loving care from someone which is not recognised in the earlier will.

A number of recent cases considered by the Court demonstrate how these considerations are applied in practice:

- FS had, while capable, made a new will very deliberately cutting out a close relative and a long-standing accountant. As she became more dependent on those people as well as a new friend, relations improved but by then she lacked testamentary capacity to make a new will. A statutory will was made reflecting these changes in circumstances.

- MK was a young adult who was awarded a substantial damages award in respect of a brain injury suffered at birth. His parents split up soon after the birth and there has been no involvement with the father. His mother remarried and the step-father has played a full and equal role in caring for MK over many years. As MK was intestate, a statutory will was made to provide for the step-father.

- Mr & Mrs W were a proud and independent couple. They had no children and left their estates to each other and on the second death to charities. Over many years, as their health deteriorated, Mrs W's sister and nephew spent more and more time visiting Mr and Mrs W and helping them. The Court authorised new wills sharing the estates (on the second death) between the sister and the charities.

- Mrs B had been an only child and had no issue of her own. In over 50 years she had not had any contact with her 'next of kin' who included cousins in Australia who were unaware of her existence. She spent her entire life with her husband and his family, for many years sharing a home with her sister-in-law and niece. The Court allowed a will in favour of the late husband's siblings and their issue

- KM was an elderly bachelor who formed a relationship with a much younger companion. He provided entirely for the companion's needs. Following a debilitating stroke the companion became a full-time carer. A statutory will was made to provide a home and an income for the companion.

- JH was the beneficiary of a family trust with a power of appointment in favour of his nearest relatives who were his sisters. He had refused to exercise the power, so that the trust would pass to distant relatives on his death. However, the refusal to exercise the power was irrational in that it was based on a delusional belief that the trust had already been brought to an end. The Court agreed a will which would exercise the power of appointment in favour of the nearest relatives.

Tax planning considerations

13.22   Following the reasoning adopted by Cross J in *Re WJGL*, the Court is sympathetic to applications for gifts and settlements which are tax effective, whether as potentially exempt transfers or deeds of variation. There is a presumption in these cases that a person would prefer to see his estate suffer as little tax as possible. On this basis, the Court has been sympathetic to applications for deeds of variation where the person is the main beneficiary under a will. In any such case the applicant must demonstrate that the person's interests are not prejudiced and that he is left with sufficient funds to maintain his standard of living and care for the rest of his life, and allowing for all foreseeable increases in expenditure.

It is, however, essential that the desirability of tax planning is not the only objective measure that can be applied. The Court is still being asked to make the decision in the person's best interests. The tax benefit is a factor that the person might have considered, but it is only one factor. In the case of T, the Court authorised gifts of income to residuary beneficiaries of a will but did not agree to gifts of capital as there was no evidence that T would have wished to make large lifetime gifts. She had been keen to reduce the tax burden of her estate in the past, but she had also been keen to preserve her assets for her own maintenance and allow her beneficiaries to inherit on her death.

The interests of beneficiaries

13.23 In a case decided by the Court under the MHA 1983, Mrs C had left a share of her estate to her great-grandchildren living at her death. It appeared that she was struck by her only two great-granddaughters while they were on a visit from Australia. She did not approve of the lifestyle of some of her other grandchildren and made a will which was capricious but was nevertheless a valid expression of her testamentary wishes. By the time she lost testamentary capacity two years later, it was clear that the will would cause a great deal of conflict between her grandchildren and made no provision for any other great-grandchildren who might be born in the future. All the grandchildren supported an application for a new statutory will and the Master held that the patient could be assumed to act reasonably with the knowledge of the likely effects of her actions on her family. Furthermore, the benefits to the family as a whole outweighed the detriment suffered by the great-grandchildren in being deprived of a share of the estate.

The MCA 2005 makes it easier for the Court to take account of the wishes and interests of beneficiaries. Their views are factors that a person would consider if he had capacity. Section 4(7)(b) also requires the Court to take account of the views of anyone engaged in caring for P or interested in his welfare. Although the Court must take great care in considering the views of persons who have a material interest in the outcome, their wishes and interests are factors that can considered. The Court must also distinguish between fact and opinion. A beneficiary may well have an opinion as to what is in P's best interests; the beneficiary's personal circumstances, hardship or dependency on P are a matter of fact that can be subjected to scrutiny.

The resources of the parties

13.24 It goes without saying that a person's interests must have priority and no disposition will be countenanced by the Court if it might in any way compromise the person's interests. Any application therefore needs to be supported by clear evidence of the assets and income, outgoings and potential liability, addressing a 'worst case scenario'. Thus in the case of *Re WJGL*, L had been cared for at public expense and was likely to go on being cared for at public expense. But Cross J assumed that L was a prudent man who when considering the proposed dispositions 'might well envisage the possibility that the state might some day require him to pay something towards his maintenance' ([1965] 3 All ER 865 at 872).

For similar reasons the Court will assume that the testator is acting honestly as well as prudently. A person who had clearly wanted to dispose of a property to avoid care home fees or to avoid tax regardless of all other considerations would not be allowed to dispose of his assets for such purposes. A consideration of the patient's resources is also relevant in considering the detail of the proposed disposition. Thus the provisions of a will such as the amounts of the legacies and the number of beneficiaries, need to take account of current and future resources.

Applications – who may apply

13.25   Section 50 sets out a general rule that permission is required to make an application to the Court of Protection unless it is made:

- by a person who lacks or is alleged to lack capacity;

- if such person is under 18, by anyone with parental responsibility;

- by the donor or donee of an LPA to which the application relates;

- by a deputy appointed by the Court for a person to whom the application relates; or

- by a person named in an existing order of the Court, if the application relates to the order.

Rule 51 of the Court of Protection Rules goes on to provide further exemptions to the general rule. Thus permission is not required if the application:

- is made by the Official Solicitor;

- is made by the Public Guardian;

- concerns P's property and affairs, unless the application is of a kind specified in Rule 52;

- concerns an LPA which is, or purports to be, created under the Act;

- concerns an instrument which is, or purports to be, an EPA;

- is made within existing proceedings in accordance with Part 10; or

- where a person files an acknowledgment of service or notification for any order proposed that is different to that sought by the applicant.

Rule 51(2)(a) extends the exemption to any case involving a person's property and affairs. There are, however, exemptions to the exemption so that applications made under Rule 52 do require permission unless one of the further exemptions applies. Rule 52(4) therefore provides that in an application seeking the exercise of the Court's jurisdiction under s 18(1)(b) (the making of a gift of P's property), (h) (settlement of property) or (i) (execution of a will) of the Act, permission is required for an application made by a person other than:

- a person who has made an application for the appointment of a deputy for which permission has been granted but which has not yet been determined;

- a person who, under any known will of P or under his intestacy, may become entitled to any property of P or any interest in it;

- a person who is an attorney appointed under an EPA which has been registered in accordance with the Act or the regulations referred to in Sch 4 to the Act;

- a person who is a donee of an LPA which has been registered in accordance with the Act; or

- a person for whom P might be expected to provide if he had capacity to do so.

In practice, there is little impediment to someone making an application so long as he or she has legal standing or a basis on which to make a claim. The only circumstance where permission may be in issue is that an existing deputy cannot or will not make an application. A solicitor or a disinterested friend or relative may need to make an application to bring the matter before the Court. For example, in a recent application, it was proposed that a new will be made for Mrs W. The application was made by the deputy. Mrs W's husband was a respondent, but as he lacked capacity, a litigation friend was appointed to represent his interests. In response to the application, a new will had to be made for Mr W. As the original applicant was also his deputy, it was more appropriate and convenient for the Court to appoint a litigation friend for Mr W to make a new application in the matter of his own will, thus avoiding the requirement to apply for permission.

Applications – procedure

Application forms

13.26   Any application for a statutory will, settlement or gift (that cannot be made by a deputy or attorney without reference to the Court) must be dealt with as a formal application to the Court of Protection. A formal application must be made using the procedure under Part 9 of the Court of Protection Rules.

The application forms can be obtained free of charge from the Customer Service Unit of the Office of the Public Guardian or from the website at: http://www.publicguardian.gov.uk/forms/cop_forms.htm

On an application, the following documents, which must be lodged with the Court of Protection at Archway Tower, 2 Junction Road, London N19 5SZ (DX 141150 Archway 2):

(a)   Application form (COP1) in duplicate.

(b)   Application for permission – if required and not already obtained (COP2).

(c)   Assessment of capacity form (the medical certificate) (COP3).

(d)   A witness statement exhibiting any other evidence or information required to support or complete the application and providing the information required by Practice Direction 9F (see **13.28** below).

(e)   Cheque for £400 payable to 'Public Guardianship Office' (unless a fee has already been paid on an application for permission).

The application form

13.27   A new application is made in the prescribed general application form, COP1. This sets out the core details of the application:

● details of the applicant and (if applicable) the applicant's solicitor;

● the status of the applicant and his standing to make the application for the purposes of Rules 51 and 52;

● the person concerned;

● whether permission is required;

● who the respondents are;

● who should be notified;

● the matter the Court is being asked to decide (for instance, that the person concerned lacks capacity to manage a will);

● the order the Court is being asked to make (for instance, the approval of a statutory will);

● how the application would benefit the person concerned (addressing for instance why it is important to make a will giving effect to the person's likely wishes and moral obligations that he would have expected to address if he had capacity);

● whether any other applications have been made to the Court;

● whether any special facilities are required to attend a Court hearing.

The form is then signed by the applicant with a statement of truth.

Although the application form is a short one, it is the most important part of the process. As mentioned at **5.4** in the context of a first application to appoint a deputy, it not only opens or starts the proceedings, but identifies the core issues of the case. It can be used to concentrate the applicant's mind to the actual decision the person concerned cannot make and why the Court of Protection needs to assist.

Evidence in support – Practice Direction 9F

13.28   Practice Direction 9F sets out the information required by the Court in support of an application. Paragraph 6 provides as follows:

'In addition to the application form COP1 (and its annexes) and any information or documents required to be provided by the Rules or another practice direction, the following information must be provided (in the form of a witness statement, attaching documents as exhibits where necessary) for any application to which this practice direction applies:

(a)   where the application is for the execution of a statutory will or codicil, a copy of the draft will or codicil, plus one copy. A draft must be exhibited to the affidavit [it is the responsibility of the applicant to ensure that the document is accurate, professionally drafted and that a will takes account of the statutory requirements particular to it being executed under the Mental Capacity Act];

(b)   a copy of any existing will or codicil;

(c)   any consents to act by proposed executors;

(d)   details of P's family, preferably in the form of a family tree, including details of the full name and date of birth of each person included in the family tree;

(e)   a schedule showing details of P's current assets, with up to date valuations;

(f)   a schedule showing the estimated net yearly income and spending of P;

(g)   a statement showing P's needs, both current and future estimates, and his general circumstances;

(h)   if P is living in National Health Service accommodation, information on whether he may be discharged to local authority accommodation, to other fee-paying accommodation or to his own home;

(i)   if the applicant considers it relevant, full details of the resources of any proposed beneficiary, and details of any likely changes if the application is successful;

(j)   details of any capital gains tax, inheritance tax or income tax which may be chargeable in respect of the subject matter of the application;

(k)   an explanation of the effect, if any, that the proposed changes will have on P's circumstances, preferably in the form of a "before and after" schedule of assets and income;

(l)   if appropriate, a statement of whether any land would be affected by the proposed will or settlement and if so, details of its location and title number, if applicable;

(m)   where the application is for a settlement of property or for the variation of an existing settlement or trust, a draft of the proposed deed, plus one copy;

(n)   a copy of any registered enduring power of attorney or lasting power of attorney;

(o)   confirmation that P is a resident of England or Wales; and

(p)   an up to date report of P's present medical condition, life expectancy, likelihood of requiring increased expenditure in the foreseeable future, and testamentary capacity.'

Further evidence in support

13.29   Any applicant must be aware at this stage that the Court will have no prior knowledge of the case, even if a deputy has been appointed and there have been previous applications to the Court. Likewise, other parties to the application should be assumed to have no prior knowledge. Existing orders or dealings with the Court must be explained afresh, adding to the administrative burden on the applicant. The applicant should therefore include and address the following matters:

● Paragraph 6 of Practice Direction 9F refers to 'form COP1 and its annexes'. Practice Direction 9A describes the annexes as including, inter alia: form COP1A (where an order relating to P's property and affairs is sought), an order appointing a deputy (where the application relates to or is made by a deputy) and an order appointing a litigation friend (where the application is made by, or where the application relates to the appointment of, a litigation friend). An up-to-date copy of form COP1A should be provided, especially if the application is made by an attorney and an existing copy is not available.

● An explanation of why the application is made and why the applicant believes the proposed disposition is in the person's best interests. Great care should be taken to address the nature of the Court's jurisdiction and the considerations laid down in *Re D(J)*. The Court should have information about the nature or character of the person, referring to his occupation, interests, hobbies, associations, religious practice and charitable activities. Was he generous or frugal, solitary or gregarious, eccentric or sensible, friendly or argumentative, easy going or passionate?

● Where the applicant is showing the nature of personal relationships and their bearing on the proposed will, evidence should be provided. Individuals should be asked to submit witness statements describing what they have done for the person or what interest the person has taken. Letters, Christmas cards or even photographs may be exhibited. In one recent case it was alleged by the applicant that the person had shown very little interest in the family; family members were able to show the Court copies of letters expressing interest and affection as well as photographs showing the person enjoying their company.

● If there is no previous will the applicant must show what efforts have been made to trace a will and why it should be assumed that the person is intestate. The devolution of the estate on an intestacy needs to be described.

- Details of any lifetime gifts made in the past, to provide evidence of persons whom the person has benefited in the past as well as to address any issues of inheritance tax liability.

- The current wishes of the person if these can be ascertained or any earlier wishes that have been recorded. Even if they cannot be ascertained, the applicant should show what steps have been taken to explain the application to the person and to obtain a response. Any evidence of earlier wishes should be supplied, such as attendance notes or a statement from someone who heard the person say he was going to leave a particular object to someone.

The applicant should also bear in mind the words of Megarry V-C in *Re D(J)* [1982] Ch 237 at 252, [1982] 2 All ER 37 at 49, where, in an application for a statutory will, he commented on the evidence before him:

> 'I hope that in future cases ... more attention will be paid to setting out what may be called the hard facts of the case. Those who seek to have a will made for a patient should at least provide detailed information as to the size of the estate, the income, and the expenses of maintaining the patient. A person making a will, whether for himself or anyone else, ought to have a reasonable knowledge of what there is, and what there is likely to be, for disposal under the will. The financial and other circumstances of all those who claim to receive benefits under a will ought also to be made clear. Many a testator will discriminate between those who are well provided for and those who are needy. Some idea should also be given of the nature of the patient while still of testamentary capacity.'

Medical evidence

13.30   Where the application is for a statutory will, the application must be supported by medical evidence addressing itself specifically to the patient's lack of capacity to make a valid will. This is despite the fact that the Court may already have evidence in Form COP3 confirming that the person is incapable of managing his property and affairs. The application before the Court is in respect of a particular decision and must therefore address the person's lack of capacity to make a valid will.

Likewise an application for a gift or settlement, should address the person's lack of capacity to make those particular decisions.

In addition, the medical evidence should deal with the person's prospects of life as this may have a bearing on the size of the estate and hence the suitability of the proposed dispositions. The original evidence must be supplied.

If the applicant is not the deputy, or if no application has been made to appoint a deputy, the medical evidence should also address the person's capacity in general terms, showing the nature of the impairment or disturbance of the functioning of the mind or brain.

Subsequent procedure

13.31 On receipt of the papers the Court will ensure that they are in order and allocate a case number. The application form is then issued, which is the point at which proceedings are started (Rule 62(1). The issue of the application is confirmed by the application form being stamped and endorsed with the issue date. A copy is returned to the applicant with a covering letter confirming who is to be served or notified. It is also the practice of the Court to provide notice forms and certificates of service, whether or not the applicant has access to electronic copies.

Parties to the application

13.32 It is the role of the applicant to show in COP1 who is a respondent and who is a person to be notified. The distinction between the two categories of persons interested in the matter is dealt with in more detail at **3.8**. .Practice Direction 9F provides the following direction at paragraphs 9 and 10:

'9   The applicant must name as a respondent:

(a)   any beneficiary under an existing will or codicil who is likely to be materially or adversely affected by the application;

(b)   any beneficiary under a proposed will or codicil who is likely to be materially or adversely affected by the application; and

(c)   any prospective beneficiary under P's intestacy where P has no existing will. (Practice direction B accompanying Part 9 sets out the procedure for notifying others of an application.)

10.   The court will consider at the earliest opportunity whether P should be joined as a party to the proceedings and, if he is so joined, the court will consider whether the Official Solicitor should be invited to act as a litigation friend, or whether some other person should be appointed as a litigation friend. Procedure on execution of a will'

The Practice Direction is unfortunately quite specific. It refers to 'any beneficiary' and not just a beneficiary who is 'adversely affected' but to one who is 'materially affected.' Thus a beneficiary who receives a small share of an estate which will not be disturbed by a proposed statutory will must still be named as a respondent. Although it may seem unnecessarily onerous to treat every person with the smallest interest in the estate as a respondent, the Court has traditionally been anxious to ensure that anyone affected by an application is given an opportunity to respond (see *Re B (Court of Protection) (Notice of Proceedings)* [1987] 2 All ER 475). This principle has in the past been avoided by exceptional circumstances as in the case of *Re Davey dec'd* [1980] 3 All ER 342 where it was felt that the service of notice would delay an urgent application and the rights of the frustrated respondent could be protected by an appeal if the patient survived or by a claim under the Inheritance (Provision for Family and Dependants) Act 1975 if the patient died. It is less likely that the Court will avoid the rights of a respondent in an application made under the MCA 2005.

Persons 'materially and adversely affected' will also include persons entitled in default of appointment' (*Re B (Court of Protection) (Notice of Proceedings)* [1987] 2 All ER 475 at 480). It is not clear whether a person with a contingent interest should be a respondent. However, a person who is likely to inherit should at the very least and as a matter of good practice, receive notice of an application. For instance, an elderly wife may consent to receive less under her husband's will. This may in turn prejudice the interests of those who would inherit if she predeceases her husband, who may be charities or the children of an earlier marriage.

Where a charitable purpose or a discretionary provision in favour of a class of charities is adversely affected by a proposed disposition, notice of the application must be served on the Attorney-General. Where the person is intestate and has no known beneficiaries who may take on his intestacy so that the estate would pass as *bona vacantia*, the Treasury Solicitor should be notified.

Once a person is a named respondent, there is an absolute obligation to serve the application form (Rule 66(1)). However, such a person does not become a party unless and until he files an acknowledgement of service (Rule 73(1)(b)).

Service on parties

13.33   As soon as practicable and no more than 21 days after an application has been issued, the applicant must serve a copy of the application form on any person who is named as a respondent in the application form, together with copies of any documents filed in accordance with Rule 64 and a form for acknowledging service (Rule 66(1)). The documents filed in accordance with Rule 64 include 'the evidence upon which he intends to rely, an assessment of capacity form as well as 'any other information or material as may be set out in a practice direction'. In effect, every respondent must receive the complete application with supporting evidence.

Part 6 of the Court of Protection Rules applies to service of documents generally, so that the forms can be delivered personally, delivered at a person's home address or last know address or sent by first class post to that address (Rule 31). A respondent must also be provided with a form for acknowledging notification. This is a standard form COP5. This provides a period of 21 days in which the person notified can apply to the Court to object to the application and be joined as a party (Rule 72(2)).

The applicant must furthermore within seven days of service, file a certificate of service (COP20) with the Court in respect of each person notified (Rule 66(2)).

The role of P

13.34   The Court will in most cases direct that the P be joined as a party and appoint the Official Solicitor as litigation friend. If there is a conflict of interest preventing the Official Solicitor from acting, then another solicitor will need to act as litigation friend for P. The role of the Official Solicitor generally is considered in more detail at **2.44** and the appointment of a litigation friend in proceedings is dealt with at **3.13–3.15**. The application and all supporting evidence must be served as soon as possible on the Official Solicitor, in the same way as any other party to the application.

Where dispositions of a person's estate are being considered, the Official Solicitor plays a vital role in ensuring that a person who lacks capacity is separately represented and the Court has the benefit of his impartial advice. A litigation friend has an obligation to ascertain the extent to which P's past and present wishes and feelings can be determined. Where possible, the litigation friend should meet with P in private. Even if P lacks capacity, a meeting may still enable the litigation friend to find out something of P's character, his surroundings, how and by whom he is cared for, who visits him and generally that his welfare is being considered by those who wish to benefit from his estate.

Where the Official Solicitor is acting as litigation friend, his office will consider the application carefully and may make recommendations on the form and merit of the application. The Official Solicitor may also make enquiries independently and correspond with for example former solicitors, carers, a care home or with other parties who might have objections to, or concerns about, the proposed dispositions. Although the Official Solicitor may be just one party among many, his advice as an independent and impartial litigation friend with a great deal of practical experience in the jurisdiction does carry considerable weight.

Subsequent procedure prior to hearing

13.35   The Court will list the application for hearing before a judge of the Court of Protection. Unless the hearing is urgent and depending on the volume of applications before the Court at the time, the hearing will usually be listed to take place within 21 weeks of the application being issued.

This procedural delay gives the Court and the Official Solicitor time to raise preliminary enquiries arising out of the application, for example to request additional information which may not have been supplied in the application or to suggest amendments to the documentation. The Court will also want to know who will be attending the hearing and whether solicitors will be instructing agents. If the case is to be heard out of London, it is for the parties to make their representations directly to the Listings and Appeals section of the Court of Protection.

To save the time and expense of an attended hearing, the parties are expected to attempt to settle the papers or, where agreement cannot be reached, to establish the level of consensus that can be achieved. Negotiations may be conducted through the Official Solicitor who will advise the Court of the results. If the application is unopposed and is not contentious, the terms of the proposed disposition may be agreed with the Official Solicitor. The Official Solicitor will then write to the Court with details of the consents obtained and giving his own consent. The Court will then determine the application on the papers, if necessary before the application had been listed for hearing. The order is then prepared and sealed without an attended hearing.

Where additional evidence is supplied to the Court this must be in the form of a witness statement. If evidence is required from other parties, then it may be necessary to apply (using the Part 10 procedure) for a witness summons to obtain disclosure of information. Depending on the complexity of the case and the issues raised, the Court may issue a directions order or hold a directions hearing (which may be conducted before a judge or by telephone).

If the case is a complex one and likely to proceed to an attended hearing, the directions order may require an applicant to file and serve complete trial bundles and the parties to circulate skeleton arguments.

The hearing

13.36   Where the application proceeds to a hearing this will be heard in chambers before a judge. The choice of venue and the way in which cases are allocated and heard is considered at **3.31**. Most cases that are to be heard in London are heard by the district judges or senior judge at Archway. The Official Solicitor will also be represented if appointed to act as litigation friend for P. Unless judgment is reserved or the hearing is adjourned, the judge will make the order at the hearing which will authorise the applicant or some other person to execute the settlement, deed or statutory will in the form approved by the Court. If a final document needs to be completed to give effect to the order, the judge may decide the main provisions and then ask the parties to submit an agreed draft for approval.

Whether or not the order is made at the hearing, it will also provide for the costs of the applicant, the Official Solicitor and any other party who was legally represented to be assessed and paid from the person's estate and for the safe custody of any documents.

After the order has been made, it will be drawn up, sealed and entered. Sealed copies will be sent to all the parties to the application. However, the order is effective immediately it is made. In an emergency a statutory will can be engrossed and executed immediately after the order has been made and before the order has been drawn up and sealed.

Emergency applications

13.37   Where the application relates to a statutory will and the person concerned is in danger of dying before the application can be heard, the Court will try to assist especially in view of the time it takes to prepare an application and the time then taken for the application to be dealt with. The applicant should in the first instance contact the Court by telephone to explain the circumstances. The Court will arrange for the application to be expedited provided that it receives unequivocal medical evidence showing that the person is terminally ill and giving an indication of his life expectancy. The application (if it has not yet been filed) should be filed immediately and a copy served on the Official Solicitor and any other person whom the Court would normally expect to be served, so as to save time. The applicant must also explain to the Court why the application could not have been made earlier and whether anyone will be prejudiced by the application being dealt with urgently. In extreme cases the application may be heard within a matter of days and the Court will authorise the applicant's solicitor or the Official Solicitor to execute the statutory will so that this can be done immediately after the order has been made. The order is effective immediately it is made and there is no need to wait for a sealed copy to be issued.

The Court does not, however, favour urgent applications. These are procedurally weighted in favour of the applicant and do not allow the Official Solicitor sufficient time to make enquiries. Neither do they allow anyone adversely affected sufficient time to obtain legal advice and make representations. The case of *Re R* (11 December 1998, [2003] WTLR 1051) concerned an appeal to the nominated judge (Ferris J) following an emergency application for a statutory will determined by the Master of the Court of Protection. The judge felt that the emergency did not allow the Court enough time to consider the application fully especially in view of the 'procedural prejudice' suffered by the adversely affected party. However, the judge gave a further warning that:

> 'the making of this application was in [A's] hands and it is his responsibility that the application was made at what in retrospect now seems to be a desperately late stage. I appreciate, of course, the urgency of the matter may not have been fully apparent to him and his advisers at an earlier stage, but in a case of this kind risks resulting from delay must, I think, inevitably fall upon the party who has been guilty of the delay.'

Where there is a genuine risk that the person concerned will die before the matter can be determined substantively, the Court will perform a delicate balancing act. It will weigh the prejudice to one party if no will is made against the prejudice to the other if a will is made. Depending on the complexity of the matter, the Court may:

- authorise a 'holding' will to be executed and set a date for a further substantive hearing;

- leave the provisions of an existing will or intestacy in place and adjourn the hearing to a later date; or

- authorise a statutory will to be executed as a final will. If a party remains dissatisfied with the order, he is entitled to appeal.

Where a 'holding will' is authorised, its provisions should represent as modest a departure as possible from the provisions of the existing will or intestacy. Potential beneficiaries may receive legacies so that some acknowledgement is made of their interest, without significantly damaging the interests of the existing beneficiaries. The holding will can also ensure that appropriate executors are appointed, especially if there is a history of conflict in the family.

In such cases a discretionary trust is often proposed as a compromise solution which would allow the claims of all beneficiaries to be protected. However, the Court will rarely allow a discretionary trust which would have the effect of allowing trustees to choose the beneficiaries after the death of the person concerned, in effect supplanting the decision-making jurisdiction of the Court.

Reconsideration and appeal

13.38   A party dissatisfied with a decision made without a hearing can request a reconsideration under Rule 89. An appeal against a decision made on a reconsideration or at an attended hearing is made to the next level of judge using the appeal procedure in Part 20 of the Court of Protection Rules. This is dealt with in more detail at **3.44**. The appeal judge exercises the same jurisdiction as the first instance judge and is not bound in any way by the decision of that judge. He will effectively hear the appeal as a new application. However, no new evidence may be submitted without leave of the court (Rule 179(2)).

Statutory wills

Form of the statutory will

13.39   The order authorising the execution of a statutory will authorises the applicant or other named person to execute the will approved by the Court by reference to a draft initialled by the judge. It is the responsibility of the applicant's solicitor to make any amendments to the draft will to conform to the terms of the draft will approved by the Court. The final engrossment must furthermore contain a certificate by the solicitor stating that the will is a true copy of the draft approved by the Court.

Once a statutory will has been approved by the Court, the applicant or other person authorised by the Court must execute the will in accordance with Sch 2 para 3 of the MCA 2005 which provides as follows:

'(1)   Sub-paragraph (2) applies if under section 16 the court makes an order or gives directions requiring or authorising a person ("the authorised person") to execute a will on behalf of P.

(2)   Any will executed in pursuance of the order or direction —

    (a)   must state that it is signed by P acting by the authorised person,

    (b)   must be signed by the authorised person with the name of P and his own name, in the presence of two or more witnesses present at the same time,

    (c)   must be attested and subscribed by those witnesses in the presence of the authorised person, and

    (d)   must be sealed with the official seal of the court.'

To comply with the statutory requirements, Practice Direction 9F provides a draft or model testimonium and attestation clause for a will:

'This is the last will of me AB [the person who lacks capacity] of _____ acting by CD the person authorised in that behalf by an order dated the _____ day of _____ 20____ made under the Mental Capacity Act 2005.

I revoke all my former wills and codicils and declare this to be my last will.

1.   I appoint EF and GH to be executors and trustees of this my will.

2.   I give _____

In witness of which this will is signed by me AB acting by CD under the order mentioned above on (date).

SIGNED by the said AB [the person who lacks capacity]	[Signed by:] AB [person who lacks capacity]
by the said CD [authorised person]	CD [authorised person]

and by the said CD with his (or her) own

name pursuant to the said order in our presence
and attested by us in the presence of the said CD.

[Signed by:]

[Names and addresses of witnesses]

Sealed with the official seal of the Court of Protection the _____ day of _____ 20___ '

The statutory will therefore needs to be signed twice by the authorised person, first with P's own name and then with his own name. Any will thus executed shall have the same effect for all purposes as if P were capable of making a valid will and the will had been executed by him as required by the Wills Act 1837. The statutory will is executed by the authorised person on behalf of P and, not being a witness, he may be a beneficiary under the will. No other beneficiary or spouse of a beneficiary should act as a witness as they would be barred from benefiting from the will under s 15 of the Wills Act 1837.

In all other respects, the statutory will is made in the same manner as a will made by a competent testator who is properly advised by a solicitor. It is therefore the responsibility of the solicitor drafting the statutory will to ensure that it is correctly drafted. The statutory will should cover matters such as ademption where the testator's estate might fall in value and substitutional provisions where beneficiaries and executors might predecease the testator. It should have up-to-date and flexible administrative clauses which are appropriate to the size and complexity of the patient's estate.

Finally, in the words of Megarry V-C in *Re D(J)* [1982] Ch 237 at 252, [1982] 2 All ER at 49: 'if the Court of Protection directs a will to be executed, that will ought to look well drafted'.

Safe custody of statutory will

13.40   Once the statutory will has been executed and certified, the original will must be sent to the Court of Protection with two certified copies and the draft will approved by the judge. The Court staff will check that the statutory will has been correctly executed and that the executed will conforms to the terms of the draft approved by the Court. The statutory will is then sealed with the seal of the Court of Protection and sent to the person authorised to hold the will. A copy of the order should be retained with the original statutory will for safe custody.

Where the will has been prepared by solicitors, it is the practice to allow them to retain it for safe custody. In other cases the will may be held in the safe custody of the deputy's bank. The statutory will is the same as the will of any other client: it is a confidential document and must not be disclosed without the consent of the Court during the lifetime of the client. If the client were to recover capacity, then the Court will direct the release of the will to the client.

If there is a previous will, then this should not be destroyed, but remain in safe custody. The envelope containing the old will should be endorsed with a note that a new will has been executed and stating the date on which it was executed.

Status of the will

13.41   The order authorising execution of the statutory will is effective immediately it is made. However, the order has no dispositive effect at all. The statutory will is only effective once it has been executed as P's own will pursuant to the order and the provisions of the MCA 2005. If P dies before the statutory will is executed, the will has no effect and hence, in an emergency, a statutory will may be executed immediately after the order has been pronounced.

Once P has died, the jurisdiction of the Court of Protection over P's affairs and property comes to an end and the Court therefore has no power to correct the statutory will. The case of *Re Davey dec'd* concerned an appeal against a statutory will, the appeal being made after the person had died. The appeal had no basis, for as Fox J pointed out ([1980] 3 All ER 342 at 349, [1981] 1 WLR 164 at 172):

> 'One cannot . . . in this case, get rid of the will simply by attacking the order. The order had no dispositive effect at all. If the patient had died after the order [but before the will was executed] the patient would have died intestate just as a person of full capacity who gave instructions for a will had died before executing it would die intestate assuming he left no other will'.

Even if there are grounds for an appeal against the order authorising the statutory will, once the will has been executed in accordance with Sch 2 para 3 of the MCA 2005, it remains the person's last valid will. Paragraph 4 goes on to state that the statutory will shall have effect 'as if it were signed by P by his own hand' and for all purposes as if 'P had the capacity to make a valid will and the will had been executed by him in the manner required by the Wills Act 1837'.

Effect of sealing

13.42   The fact that the will has not been sealed by the court does not, however, prevent it from being a valid will despite the death of the testator occurring between the time when the will was executed and when it was sealed with the seal of the Court of Protection. The seal does not affect the validity of

the statutory will but provides confirmation by the Court that the statutory will
has been executed correctly in accordance with Sch 3 para 3 of the MCA 2005
(see *Re Hughes dec'd,* Times, 8 January 1999 which addressed the equivalent
provisions in s 97(1) of the Mental Health Act 1983).

Scope of a statutory will

13.43   A statutory will may be made on behalf of any person pursuant to
s 18(1)(i) of the MCA 2005 provided that the person is not a minor (s 18(2))
and the Court is satisfied that the person lacks capacity to make that particular
decision.

The statutory will may dispose of all the person's estate apart from immovable
property outside England and Wales as the capacity to make a valid will
affecting immovable property in another jurisdiction is determined by the *lex
situs* of the other jurisdiction. The territorial scope of a statutory will is
covered by Sch 2 para 4(4) and (5) of the MCA 2005 which provide as
follows:

> '(4)   but sub-paragraph (3) [the will shall have effect for all purposes as if
> P had had capacity …] does not have effect in relation to the will —
>
> > (a)   in so far as it disposes of immovable property outside England
> > and Wales, or
> >
> > (b)   in so far as it relates to any other property or matter if, when the
> > will is executed —
> >
> > > (i)   P is domiciled outside England and Wales, and
> > >
> > > (ii)   the condition in sub-paragraph (5) is met.
>
> (5)   The condition is that, under the law of P's domicile, any question of
> his testamentary capacity would fall to be determined in accordance
> with the law of a place outside England and Wales.'

Thus the statutory will may cover movable property outside England and
Wales if this is governed by the law of domicile of the other country. If,
however, the person were domiciled outside England and Wales, the will
would be ineffective in dealing with his immovable property unless the law of
domicile in his jurisdiction allowed questions of capacity to be determined in
accordance with the law of England and Wales. There remains some
uncertainty as to the meaning of the words 'other property or matter' and
whether it would for instance cover a right to exercise a power of appointment
or to bar an entail.

Subject to these provisos, the statutory will may cover any matters which may
be dealt with by a will made by a testator with full capacity.

Large gifts

13.44   Where the proposed gift is not one which can be made as a 'small
gift' by an attorney within the scope of his authority under the LPA or EPA or

a deputy within the scope of his authority, the application must be dealt with as a formal application to the Court of Protection. A deputy, attorney or other person entitled to apply under Rule 52 must apply using form COP1 and the Part 9 procedure described above (see **13.27** and Practice Direction 9F). However, the short form procedure (see Practice Direction 9D and **3.43**) may be appropriate where

- 'the applicant reasonably considers that the order sought is not likely to be significant to P's estate or to any other of P's interests';

- 'the applicant knows, or reasonably believes, that there are unlikely to be any objections to the application he proposes to make'; and

- the sum in question is not disproportionately large when compared to the size of P's estate as a whole.

Whatever the nature or extent of the proposed gift, the applicant must consider and address the following factors:

- that the proposed gift is within the Court's jurisdiction (see **13.4** above and s 18(1)(b) of the MCA 2005). A gift is not just a transfer of money or property but might include a sale at an undervalue to a deputy or family member or an interest free loan;

- that the proposed gift is consistent with the donor's likely wishes and in his best interests;

- the resources and needs of the beneficiaries;

- the consequences of the gift in terms of inheritance tax and capital gains tax;

- the consequences of the gift in terms of the provisions of a will or intestacy;

- the consequences of the gift in terms of the estate generally and the loss of capital and income available for the person's maintenance;

- whether the donor's interests can be better protected in some other way, for instance through the creation of a settlement or a statutory will that do not lead to an immediate reduction in his resources;

- whether any further documents or actions need to be approved. An order making a gift is effective to authorise the payment of money, but a deed of variation or loan agreement may require the approval of a document and if a gift is of shares, the order will need to authorise the applicant to execute the transfers; and

- how the gift should be made and whether payment may be made from the fund in Court or from other assets which must be realised to effect the payment.

A deed of variation of an interest in a will or a deed of release of an interest in a trust involves a gift by the incapable beneficiary in favour of the persons taking under the proposed variation or release. A draft deed must accompany the application and will need to be approved by the Court. The deed should recite the order and will be executed pursuant to it, but it does not need to be sealed by the Court subsequently.

Settlements

When created

13.45   The Court has jurisdiction to approve a settlement under s 18(1)(h) of the MCA 2005. While a straightforward gift may appear to be a simpler matter to deal with, a settlement may be preferable in a number of instances:

- where an *inter vivos* gift to an individual is inappropriate but a transfer of property from the person's estate should still be made, for example where the proposed beneficiary is a minor or has special needs;

- where the person is a beneficiary under an existing will but may not require an absolute interest or interest in possession which will be charged to inheritance tax on his or her death. However, the person's needs may change and it may give greater protection to vary the will to create a new settlement on discretionary trusts which includes the person as a discretionary beneficiary;

- where property needs to be settled on a person during his or her lifetime. Such settlements were created before statutory wills became available (see **13.1** above) to provide for the disposition of the estate on death. Such settlements are now mostly made by the Court of Protection where the person has suffered a personal injury and received damages, which if placed in trust, would not be treated as the patient's capital for the purposes of assessing the person's entitlement to welfare benefits (Income Support (General) Regulations 1987 (SI 1987/1967), reg 51(1)(a) and Sch 10 para 12) (see **13.46**).

- where the person is a minor and cannot make a statutory will (MCA 2005, s 18(2)), and provision needs to be made for the assets in the event of the person's death. Such an application would be very rare but would be considered where the person has received a personal injury award, may not survive to 18 and the consequences of an intestacy may be inappropriate due to the conduct or circumstances of the parents;

- where the person is a beneficiary of an existing settlement which needs to be varied. If the beneficiaries of the settlement are not all of full age then the matter must also be dealt with under the Variation of Trusts Act 1958.

Special needs trusts

13.46   Trusts for a beneficiary who lacks capacity as an alternative to involving the Court of Protection are less common now, in that money derived from a personal injury and held under the control of the Court of Protection are treated in the same way as a separate trust (*Decision of Social Security Commissioner M Heald, 31 August 1995* (CIS/368/94) [1996] 3 JSSL D136).

The same treatment applies to income from a structured settlement (Social Security Amendment (Personal Injury Payments) Regulations 2002 (SI 2002/2442). As deputies now have a great deal of autonomy and the supervision costs are modest, a strong case needs to be made to persuade the Court to remove the protection it can offer. The disadvantages of such a trust need to be addressed carefully:

- the costs of professional trustees will not be scrutinised and their conduct cannot be called to account by the Court or Public Guardian;

- income and capital gains may be charged at a higher rate;

- unless the trust complies with s 89 of the Inheritance Tax Act 1984, there could be significant tax consequences (see *Phelps v Stewarts and Andrew Dinsmore* [2007] EWHC 1561;

- a deputy will still be needed to act as statutory agent for the person concerned and deal with financial matters that cannot be dealt with by trustees.

A trust may however still be appropriate, especially if the practices of the Court alter in future. For instance if security is set at extortionate rates, then trusts become more cost-effective than a deputyship (see **5.22**). Trusts have also been approved where:

- the person's affairs are under the control of an attorney and a private trust will provide a greater degree of protection;

- the award is a small one and the money can be more conveniently and cost-effectively administered by the family for the benefit of the person concerned;

- the family are the main carers and feel that they have more autonomy or flexibility with a trust and their hostility to the Court impacts on the welfare of the person concerned;

- the person concerned has uncertain or fluctuating capacity and a trust provides a greater degree of protection; or

- the person concerned is likely to recover capacity or believes he may recover capacity (see for instance *Re C* [1960] 1 All ER 393 in which the beneficiary was allowed a power of appointment subject to the agreement of a trustee, exercisable if he had capacity). A bare trust will allow him to be involved as a trustee or feel that he could call for his own assets without going through the Court.

Practical considerations

13.47   As with an application for a gift, a deputy or other person entitled to apply under Rule 52 of the Court of Protection Rules must apply using the general application form COP1, with the supporting evidence referred to above (see **13.27** and Practice Direction 9F). The applicant is responsible for drafting the appropriate trust deed and ensuring that this is appropriate to the person's needs. The applicant must also address the following issues:

- why a settlement is appropriate in the light of the person's wishes and circumstances but having regard to the alternatives, principally leaving assets under the control of the Court or the deputy or making an outright gift and that it is in his best interests;

- if the patient is a beneficiary, what happens to the assets on death;

- the tax implications of the settlement. Care should be taken to avoid an immediate charge to inheritance tax if assets are settled on a relevant property trust;

- any consequential tax implications as a result of assets being disposed of or transferred to the settlement;

- the costs of creating and administering the settlement. In most cases, especially where the beneficiary is a minor or a large damages award is involved, a professional trustee will need to be appointed; and

- the extent to which the person or the Court will retain any rights to vary the terms of the settlement or direct the appointment of new trustees.

Variation of trusts

13.48   Where it is desired on behalf of a person to vary an existing settlement where there are beneficiaries who are not of full age or *sui juris*, the High Court has jurisdiction under the Variation of Trusts Act 1958. However, s 1(3) of the Variation of Trusts Act 1958 provides that the question whether the proposed arrangement would be for the benefit of the person concerned is to be determined by order of the Court of Protection. The application is therefore commenced in the High Court and a copy of the claim form should be exhibited to a separate application to the Court of Protection which will be made in the same way as an application for approval of a settlement. The Court of Protection will then make an order stating whether the proposed arrangement would be for the patient's benefit which will be considered by the High Court when determining the main action under the 1958 Act.

Chapter 14

Enduring powers of attorney and the Court of Protection

Nature of an enduring power of attorney

Status of enduring powers of attorney after commencement of Mental Capacity Act

14.1   Section 66(1)(b) of the Mental Capacity Act 2005 (MCA 2005) repeals the Enduring Powers of Attorney Act 1985 (EPAA 1985) and by virtue of s 66(2) no new enduring power of attorney (EPA) can be created after 1 October 2007. However, there are tens if not hundreds of thousands of EPAs in place and the MCA 2005 therefore provides for EPAs created before 1 October 2007 to remain effective. Schedule 4 of the MCA 2005 serves to govern the operation of EPAs. Although EPAs operate within the framework of the MCA 2005, they operate under the same principles which governed their creation by earlier legislation. They are therefore an anomaly, in that different principles apply to when and how attorneys act under an EPA compared to a lasting power of attorney (LPA); at the same time, an attorney acting for a donor who lacks capacity must also act in the donor's best interests and is bound by the Act and Code of Practice in the same way as any other person who makes a decision under the Act.

What is an enduring power of attorney?

14.2   An EPA is simply a mechanism contrived by statute to enable a person to delegate decision-making powers through a power of attorney which are effective after the onset of incapacity. Any competent adult ('the donor') may grant a power of attorney to another person ('the attorney') to carry out one or more functions on behalf of the donor. However, such a power of attorney is revoked by operation of law in the event of the supervening incapacity of the donor.

The EPAA 1985 introduced the EPA thereby allowing the donor to select the person who will manage his property and affairs in the event of the donor becoming mentally incapable of so doing. Without an EPA, the property and affairs of an incapable person would have to be dealt with under the Mental Health Act 1983 regime, generally with the appointment of a receiver. Because the donor has selected his own attorney, the degree of supervision and accountability required of an attorney is significantly less than that which is required from a receiver (or deputy) appointed by the Court of Protection. However, an attorney has similar fiduciary duties with regard to the property and affairs of the donor, as a receiver (or deputy), and the Court of Protection has overall responsibility for the EPA jurisdiction. This includes dealing with disputes and making decisions which are beyond the scope of the attorney's authority under the EPA.

As will be seen in Chapter 15, the MCA 2005 adopts a similar approach with LPAs which replace EPAs.

Enduring Powers of Attorney and the Mental Capacity Act 2005

14.3   The EPA jurisdiction cannot be understood without reference to the remaining provisions of the MCA 2005 with which it is closely connected. The principle influences of the Act can be summarised as follows:

- the Court of Protection retains jurisdiction to make decisions for persons who lack capacity and to supervise and interpret EPAs and the conduct of attorneys;

- the Public Guardian is responsible for administering the registration of EPAs;

- registration forms and the powers of the Public Guardian in respect of EPAs are set out in the Lasting Power of Attorney, Enduring Power of Attorney and Public Guardian Regulations 2007 (SI 2007/1253);

- an attorney who makes a decision on behalf of a donor who lacks capacity must act in the donor's best interests and have regard to the Code of Practice;

- the Court of Protection Rules 2007 (SI 2007/1744) apply to applications made by attorneys to the Court of Protection;

- another person with standing in a matter may wish to apply to the Court to use its powers, because the attorney cannot or will not exercise his powers under the EPA, or the powers of the attorney do not extend to the particular decision;

- there is a presumption that the Public Guardian will not register an EPA if a deputy has been appointed (Sch 4 para 11(2));

- the Court of Protection may revoke an EPA and exercise any of its powers under the MCA 2005, for instance to replace an attorney with a deputy.

Form of an enduring power of attorney

14.4   For an EPA to be valid, it must be created using the prescribed form (Sch 4 para 2(1)). The form which must be used in respect of EPAs created after 31 July 1990 was as set out in the Enduring Powers of Attorney (Prescribed Form) Regulations 1990 (SI 1990/376). A Welsh language equivalent was also prescribed in March 2000.

The EPA form is set out in three parts:

(a)   Part A contains the explanatory notes which explain the operation of the EPA and the options available to the donor when completing the form.

The notes must be read by or read to the donor. Part A concludes with the pronouncement: 'You can cancel this power at any time before it has to be registered'.

(b) Part B contains the operative part of the EPA, and is set out in three sections. The first section sets out the donor's name, address and date of birth and the names and addresses of the attorneys. The second section contains a number of options for the donor to complete and, where more than one option is shown, the option not required must be clearly crossed out:

- where more than one attorney is appointed, whether the attorneys may act 'jointly' or 'jointly and severally';

- whether the EPA is to confer 'general authority to act on my behalf' or authority to 'do the following on my behalf' so that the EPA can be restricted to the performance of a specific act;

- whether the EPA is to operate in relation to 'all my property and affairs' or 'the following property and affairs' so that the EPA can be restricted to dealing with specific assets or aspects of the donor's property affairs;

- any restriction or condition which the donor wishes to impose (see **14.8** below).

The final part of Part B contains two essential declarations on the part of the donor:

'I intend that this power shall continue even if I become mentally incapable'; and

'I have read or have had read to me the notes in Part A which are part of, and explain, this form'.

The EPA is then signed by the donor as a deed in the presence of an independent witness. If the attorney is incapable of signing for himself, the EPA may be signed at his direction but there must be two witnesses – the prescribed form provides space for two witnesses to cover this eventuality.

(c) Part C is for completion by the attorney(s) and must likewise be signed as a deed in the presence of an independent witness. This part of the form must be completed after the donor has completed Part B – for the power to be an 'enduring power' it must be executed by both the donor and the attorney(s). As a result, if it has not been completed by the attorney, it is not an 'enduring power' in respect of that attorney for the purposes of Sch 4 para 2(1).

Content of the enduring power of attorney

The attorney

14.5 A donor could appoint any person or a trust corporation to act as his attorney provided that, at the time the power was executed by the attorney, the attorney was not a minor or a bankrupt. An EPA could therefore be created before the attorney's 18th birthday provided the attorney then executes the power after his 18th birthday, while the donor had capacity, and before 1 October 2007.

More than one attorney appointed

14.6 An EPA may have been created many years ahead of when it would need to be used and it is impossible to guarantee that an attorney will still be able and willing to act as an attorney. If the attorney disclaims the power, becomes bankrupt or has died after the donor has lost capacity, the EPA is terminated and is of no further use. The EPAA 1985 therefore allowed a donor to appoint more than one attorney provided that the attorneys were appointed to act 'jointly' or 'jointly and severally':

- *Attorneys appointed jointly:* Where attorneys are appointed jointly, both attorneys must act together in any act carried out under the EPA. Thus a cheque drawn on the donor's bank account must be signed by both attorneys. This has the advantage of ensuring that the attorneys co-operate with each other and neither can act without the other's notice which provides the donor with some degree of protection. The disadvantages are that the EPA may be cumbersome to operate in practice and that the EPA is terminated if it can no longer be operated by both attorneys jointly. Thus if one attorney dies or becomes bankrupt, the EPA is terminated.

- *Attorneys appointed jointly and severally:* Where the attorneys are appointed jointly and severally, each attorney may act independently of the other. Such an appointment is more common where more than one attorney is appointed, especially where the attorneys are close and work together with a clear division of responsibility between them. Frequently one attorney will act alone as the main attorney while the other attorney takes a passive role, but is kept informed and available to act if necessary. However, an EPA where two attorneys are acting independently of each other with even the smallest element of mistrust between them makes effective operation of the EPA very difficult. If the attorneys cannot work together then this may well interfere with the proper administration of the donor's affairs and lead to a contested application to the Court of Protection to resolve the issue. The Court must then limit the EPA to one of the attorneys or revoke the EPA (on the grounds of the unsuitability of the attorneys) and direct that a deputy be appointed (see **14.28** and **14.35** below).

Care must also be taken when dealing with an EPA that appoints more than one attorney to ensure that the appointment is expressly 'joint' or 'joint and several'. In the case of *Re E* [2000] 3 All ER 1004) the donor inadvertently created a hybrid power where her three daughters were appointed to act jointly and the appointment was followed by the words 'save that any two of my attorneys may sign'. The application to register the EPA was rejected as such an instrument could not take effect as a valid EPA under s 11(1) of the EPAA 1985 (now contained in Sch 4 para 20(1)) which explicitly states that where more than one attorney is appointed, the instrument cannot create an EPA unless the 'attorneys are appointed jointly or jointly and severally'. Although the appeal to the High Court in the case of *Re E* did not deal with this point (it was not in issue), the case illustrates the problems which joint appointments can create (see also **14.32** below).

Successive appointments

14.7   The appointment of an attorney is personal to the individual and a power which gives an attorney a right to appoint a successor or substitute cannot be an EPA (Sch 4 para 6). However, a donor could create successive appointments either in the same instrument or in separate instruments where one appointment takes effect only on the failure of the prior appointment. Thus a donor might appoint his wife to act under the first EPA. In the second EPA he might appoint his children or his solicitor, but subject to the condition that the appointment of his wife in the first EPA has terminated as a result of her death, incapacity or disclaimer.

The drawback of using separate instruments to create successive appointments is that registration of the second EPA will require evidence being supplied of the failure of the first EPA which may cause some confusion and inconvenience. This does however provide for clarity in that each EPA must be registered separately and it is clear from the registered instrument who is authorised to act as an attorney. It also provides the donor with the protection of the registration system when notification is given by the successor attorneys.

Because of the complexity of drafting separate instruments to achieve a clear objective, EPAs have also been drafted to provide successive appointments in the same instrument. This would mirror the practice common in will drafting, where (for instance) a spouse is appointed as sole executor but if she dies or is unable or unwilling to act as executor, her children are appointed in her place. The practice of the Court of Protection prior to 1 October 2007 was to register such instruments, although the Public Guardian has since expressed concerns that a successive appointment of attorneys is inconsistent with Sch 4 para 20(1) which provides that an instrument which appoints more than one attorney cannot be an EPA unless the attorneys are appointed jointly or jointly and severally.

This has now been considered by the High Court. In the case of *Re J (Enduring Power of Attorney)* [2009] EWHC 436 (Ch), Lewison J confirmed that a successive appointment was effective and that the restriction in Sch 4 para 20(1) only applied in favour of the attorneys who were actually exercising the power. The judge felt that there was no reason why what could be done by two pieces of papers could not be done by one piece of paper and that there were strong policy grounds in favour of registering an instrument containing a successive appointment.

Special conditions on the power

14.8   Although an attorney cannot exclude any provisions contained within the prescribed form of an EPA, the form could be adapted to include 'such additions (including paragraph numbers) or restrictions as the donor may decide' (Enduring Powers of Attorney (Prescribed Form) Regulations 1990 (SI 1990/1376), reg 2(1)).

Similar restrictions and conditions are often used by donors of LPAs and are considered in detail at **15.14**.

Granting the enduring power of attorney

Who could give an enduring power of attorney

14.9   An EPA could be granted by an individual (ie, thus not by a group of individuals or a trust corporation) who was over 18 and who had sufficient mental capacity to create the power. The EPA, however, was a deceptive document. Superficially, it appeared simple, quick to create and cheap to implement. On closer inspection, it still gives rise to far-reaching consequences in terms of what the attorney can do in relation to the donor's property and affairs which may not be appreciated at the time the EPA is made.

Capacity to grant an EPA

14.10   For an EPA to be valid, it must be made by an individual using the prescribed form, and having sufficient capacity to understand the nature and effect of the instrument. The EPAA 1985 did not define the precise degree of capacity required, but as a matter of law a person's capacity to perform a particular legal act is specific to the nature of the act being performed. This has been confirmed by the MCA 2005. Thus a person might be 'becoming incapable' of managing his property and affairs to the extent that his EPA should be registered. At the same time, that person may be capable of making a single decision such as making a will or granting an EPA. This apparent paradox was considered by Hoffmann J in the case of *Re K, Re F* [1988] 1 All ER 358 where registration of an EPA was objected to on the grounds that the EPA had been made immediately before being registered. The judge upheld the validity of the EPA and accepted four basic requirements as to what the donor should understand (at 363):

> 'first, if such be the terms of the power, that the attorney will be able to assume complete authority over the donor's affairs; second, if such be the terms of the power, that the attorney will in general be able to do anything with the donor's property which the donor could have done; third, that the authority will continue if the donor should be or become mentally incapable; fourth, that if he should be or become mentally incapable, the power will be irrevocable without confirmation by the court.'

The judge went on to state that the evidence should show that the donor has understood this. That further requirement was, however, rejected by the Court of Appeal in the case of *Re W* [2001] 1 FLR 832 when it was held that the burden of proof in objecting to the validity of an EPA rested on the objectors. According to this case, the Court would be bound to register the EPA as a valid instrument unless the objectors can satisfy the Court that the instrument is invalid.

Powers and duties of the attorney

Generally

14.11   An EPA made under the EPAA 1985 allowed a donor, when granting an EPA, to confer on the attorney either:

- a general power in relation to all of the donor's property and affairs; or

- a limited power in relation to a specified part of the donor's property and affairs or to do specified things on the donor's behalf.

Where the donor confers on the attorney a general authority, this is defined by MCA 2005, Sch 4 para 3(1) as follows:

> 'If the instrument which creates an enduring power of attorney is expressed to confer general authority on the attorney, the instrument operates to confer, subject to (a) the restriction [as to making gifts] imposed by sub-paragraph (3), and (b) any conditions or restrictions contained in the instrument, authority to do on behalf of the donor anything which the donor could lawfully do by an attorney at the time when the donor executed the instrument.'

The aim of the EPA jurisdiction was therefore to give the attorney the widest powers possible and then leave the donor to restrict those powers as he sees fit. However, an EPA can only apply in relation to the 'property and affairs of the donor'. Unlike an attorney acting under a welfare LPA, an attorney has no authority to direct or provide authority for medical treatment or residence and the attorney's powers are limited in the same way as those of a property and affairs deputy. Subject to these general limitations, an attorney can lawfully do most things subject to three important exceptions (*Clauss v Pir* [1988] Ch 267):

(a)   where statute requires evidence of a signature – thus an attorney cannot sign a will or witness a deed;

(b)   where the donor's competency to do the act arises by virtue of holding some office, public or otherwise – thus an attorney of a Member of Parliament cannot sit as an MP or an attorney of a priest could not administer a sacrament; or

(c)   where the donor's own authority or duty to do the act is of a personal nature, requiring skill or discretion in its exercise – thus an attorney could not vote in an election, sit an exam or drive a car in the name of the donor.

The powers of an attorney are also limited by statute and regulations for instance as to the making of gifts (see **14.12**) below. An attorney cannot also act as a litigation friend in civil proceedings (see **10.4** above).

Power to make gifts and maintain others

14.12   An attorney's powers, as a fiduciaryy, relate to his principal role of maintaining the donor. However, Sch 4 para 3 extends the attorney's powers significantly to the making of gifts and providing for the needs of others. These powers arise whether or not the EPA has been registered, although an attorney who exercised them without the consent of a capable donor would be acting improperly. The more extensive powers of the Court to make decisions to authorise gifts and other dispositions on behalf of the donor do not arise until the donor lacks capacity to make those decisions. The scope of an attorney's authority to make gifts and maintain others is considered in more detail in Chapter 13. An attorney also has certain powers to delegate trustee functions – these are considered in more detail in Chapter 11.

Duties of the attorney generally

14.13   There is, surprisingly, no general duty for an attorney to act. The attorney is not obliged to take on the role of attorney and may disclaim the power at any time he wishes. The only exception to this rule is that once the attorney has executed Part C of the EPA, then, unless he disclaims the power, he has a duty to register the EPA with the Public Guardian when the donor is becoming or has become mentally incapable. And once an attorney starts to act as an attorney, he does assume a number of duties and will be accountable for his conduct until such time as his authority is terminated.

An attorney, when acting as such, has a fiduciary duty towards the donor and the donor's estate and should act at all times in the best interests of the donor to maintain the donor and prevent loss to the donor's estate. When making decisions on behalf of a donor who lacks capacity then he is also required to act in accordance with ss 1 and 4 of the MCA 2005 and act in the best interests of the donor.

The attorney's main duties can be summarised as follows:

- to act within the scope of the MCA 2005 and Code of Practice;

- to act within the scope of the authority given by the power and, in particular, any restrictions or conditions within it;

- to exercise a duty of care in carrying out functions as an attorney, commensurate with any skills he has or holds himself out as possessing, especially if the attorney is a professional attorney who receives remuneration for acting;

- not to delegate save for routine or specialist tasks which the donor would not expect him to carry out personally or where delegation has been authorised expressly by the donor. The general principle is that the attorney is appointed personally to take on the role of attorney and should not avoid his responsibilities by delegating them unnecessarily;

- to keep accounts. While there is no statutory requirement to keep accounts, an attorney is expected to keep an account of his dealings as an attorney. Once an EPA has been registered, the Court may give directions for the production or inspection of accounts;

- not to benefit from his position. As a fiduciary, the attorney should not make a profit at the expense of the donor or benefit materially from his position. Where there is a conflict of interest in respect of a registered EPA and where the attorney may be a beneficiary of a will or gift, the approval of the Court will satisfy this duty. The attorney, however, may benefit personally if he needs to be maintained by the donor or as a recipient of a small gift (Sch 4 para 3(2) and (3));

- to preserve the separate character of the donor's property. As with a deputy, an attorney must keep the attorney's money separate from his own;

- to apply for registration of the EPA if the donor is becoming or has become mentally incapable of managing his property and affairs;

- to comply with any directions of the Court and, where the EPA has been registered, to notify the Court of any disclaimer and to notify the Public Guardian of the death of the donor.

Practical duties of the attorney

14.14 The legal duties of an attorney appear quite general in their nature. However, where an attorney's conduct under a registered EPA might be called to account, the Court of Protection is entitled to have regard to the duties imposed on a deputy which are set out at **7.4** above. While the attorney may not be expected to submit accounts or lodge security, he would be expected, for instance, to collect all state benefits to which the donor is entitled, pay any bills and ensure that any property is maintained and insured.

Duties of the attorney on the donor becoming incapable

14.15 So long as the donor has capacity, the EPA operates as an ordinary power of attorney. The donor may cancel it any time and may direct the attorney's operation of the EPA as he wishes. Whereas an ordinary power of attorney is automatically revoked on the incapacity of the donor, Sch 4 para 1(1) of the EPAA 1985 clearly states that an EPA shall not be revoked by any subsequent incapacity of the donor, provided that:

'(b) upon such incapacity supervening, the donee of the power may not do anything under the authority of the power except as provided by sub-paragraph (2) below unless or until the instrument creating the power is registered under paragraph 13.'

Once the attorney 'has reason to believe that the donor is or is becoming mentally incapable … the attorney shall, as soon as practicable, make an application to the Public Guardian for the registration of the instrument creating the power' (Sch 4 para 4(1) and 4(2)). The criterion for registration is the fact of the donor being 'mentally incapable'. This term is defined as meaning in relation to any person, that he is 'incapable by reason of mental disorder of managing and administering his property and affairs' (Sch 4 para 23(1)). 'Mental disorder' is defined by reference to the Mental Health Act 1983 as meaning 'any disorder or disability of the mind'. Thus for an EPA to be registered, the donor must satisfy two separate conditions:

- he is unable to manage and administer his property and affairs;

- due to a mental disorder.

Thus where EPAs are concerned, different definitions of capacity apply. In contrast, the capacity to make any other decision under the MCA 2005 is relative to the decision itself at the time it is made. The approach followed by the MCA 2005 and the problems this gives rise to where a person's 'property and affairs' are involved is considered in more detail at **1.5** above. Similar difficulties are faced by deputies where the person concerned may lack capacity to manage and administer his or her property and affairs in general, but still has capacity to make specific decisions (see **4.6** above). These complications are avoided by EPAs which deal with 'property and affairs' in general terms. But this in turn gives rise to its own difficulty (which the MCA 2005 seeks to avoid where LPAs are concerned). The problem facing the attorney and donor EPA is that the fact of registration has the effect of creating a presumption that the donor lacks capacity due to the mental disorder which may in practice cause difficulties for the donor (and the attorney) especially when dealing with third parties such as banks or other financial institutions.

The attorney is therefore responsible for making the difficult decision to register. He must register the EPA as soon as he 'has reason to believe' that the need to register arises. The aim of the legislation is therefore to encourage registration at the earliest opportunity. This can give rise to some difficulties. The donor may be 'becoming' incapable and therefore have some understanding of the attorney's conduct. The donor may not be entirely happy with the thought of having his EPA registered. The donor may also have capacity to make specific or limited decisions. Good relations between a donor and an attorney have been known to evaporate as a result of too early an application to register. Most attorneys will instinctively delay registration for as long as possible. However, this instinct may not always be right. The donor may be the object of financial abuse or in danger of dissipating his estate. Many donors deliberately or inadvertently avoid registration until after the donor has become incapable, potentially making their actions voidable, while depriving the donor of the protection of the registration process. It was to avoid these issues that LPAs must be registered before they can be used.

Interim relief

14.16 Because of the potential difficulties faced by the attorney in determining when and whether to register an EPA and because the attorney's powers may be restricted or even void during this period, some assistance is provided by the legislation.

Determining validity of EPA

14.17   Under Sch 4 para 4(5) an attorney may, before applying for
registration, refer to the Court of Protection for its determination any question
as to the validity of the power. If the attorney is uncertain that the EPA was
properly granted or suspects that objections may be made on the ground that
the EPA is not valid or may have been revoked, this issue may be referred to
the Court. Although this provision may appear useful, especially in resolving
potentially contentious issues, it has rarely been used in practice. Use of this
provision may involve considerable delay, especially as it will involve a formal
application to the Court and payment of an application fee of £400 (Court of
Protection Rules 2007, Rule 68(1)). It may be more practicable for the attorney
to apply to register the EPA. The EPA can at least be operated by the attorney
while being registered and any disputes can be addressed during the
registration process.

Assistance of the Court prior to registration

14.18   Section 5 of the EPAA 1985 gave the Court authority to exercise its
general powers under the Act so long as the Court had reason to believe that
the donor may be, or may be becoming, mentally incapable. It was unusual for
these powers to be invoked before an application to register had been made,
and this provision has not been enacted in Sch 4 of the MCA 2005. It is no
longer appropriate in that if a donor lacks capacity and a decision is required
from the Court, the attorney or any other person may make an application to
the Court for relief. There are several situations where such relief might be
required:

(a)   no application to register the EPA has been made, but a friend or relative
or other concerned party wishes to bring the actions (or inactions) of the
attorney to the attention of the Court, so as to ensure the Court's
intervention. The Court can arrange for a Visitor to see the person
concerned and direct further enquiries or revoke the EPA;

(b)   the attorney is himself unable to register due to a temporary illness or is
not yet able to complete the registration application and some urgent
provision is required for the maintenance of the donor, which cannot be
met by s 5 of the MCA 2005;

(c)   the registration has been delayed due to an objection and the attorney
needs to dispose of an asset or perform some other act which would
otherwise require the consent of the donor or which is subject to some
other restriction; or

(d)   the attorney wishes to commence an application for a gift or settlement
which is beyond the scope of his limited authority to make gifts (see
13.5 above); the attorney may not wish to wait for the EPA to be
registered, especially where registration has been delayed or where
registration will be a mere formality and time is of the essence.

Powers of the attorney during registration period

14.19   Once the need to register the EPA arises, the supervening incapacity of the donor renders the EPA invalid for all purposes until it is registered with the Public Guardian. Because registration may take some weeks or even months to complete, so long as an application to register the EPA has been made, the attorney may until such time as the instrument is registered take action under Sch 4 para 1(2) for the following two purposes:

- to maintain the donor or prevent loss to his estate; or

- to maintain himself or other persons in so far as para 3(2) permits him to do so.

These are therefore holding powers which allow the attorney to do what is essential while the EPA is being registered. Thus the attorney can continue to pay nursing home fees, carry out repairs to a property or pay maintenance to a relative or carer who is financially dependent on the donor. The 'prevention of loss' to the estate could also justify the sale of investments which might fall in value or a property which might otherwise not be sold at such a good price.

If these temporary powers are inadequate, the attorney must wait for the EPA to be registered or so long as the donor lacks capacity to make the decision in question, apply to the Court to exercise its powers under the MCA 2005.

There is no equivalent provision for the donee of a LPA.

Registration of an enduring power of attorney

Making the application – Procedure

14.20   Registration of an EPA is a simple procedure provided it is carried out using the prescribed form in the right sequence and the right persons are notified. The procedure is as follows:

- the attorney applying for registration must give notice in Form EP1PG to the donor, any other attorney (who is not applying for registration) and the relatives who must be notified;

- having served the notices, the attorney applying for registration must complete Form EP2PG and send this to the Public Guardian together with the original EPA and a cheque for the registration fee of £120.

The prescribed application form and notice which must be used in all applications made after 1 October 2007 is set out in the Lasting Power of Attorney, Enduring Power of Attorney and Public Guardian Regulations 2007 (SI 2007/1253).

Notice to donor

14.21   The donor must be served personally with Form EP1PG, although notice need not be given personally by the attorney. However, the person notifying the donor must comply with the provisions of reg 23(2) and 23(3) of the Lasting Power of Attorney, Enduring Power of Attorney and Public Guardian Regulations 2007 which provides as follows:

'(2)   In the case of the notice to be given to the donor, the attorney must also provide (or arrange for the provision of) an explanation to the donor of—

(a)   the notice and what the effect of it is; and

(b)   why it is being brought to his attention.

(3)   The information provided under paragraph (2) must be provided—

(a)   to the donor personally; and

(b)   in a way that is appropriate to the donor's circumstances (for example using simple language, visual aids or other appropriate means).'

Curiously, there is no requirement for the person notifying the donor to record or prove that these regulations have been complied with (as there is for instance where P is notified under Part 7 of the Court of Protection Rules). In applying to register the EPA the donor merely certifies in form EP2PG that 'I have given notice of the application to register in the prescribed form (EP1PG) to the donor personally'.

Notices to other relatives

14.22   Notices to anyone else must be 'given' although only the notice to the donor must be given personally. Other notices may therefore be given personally, but may also be sent by first class post, or through a document exchange, or by fax or other means described in Rule 31 of the Court of Protection Rules and Practice Direction 6.

At least three relatives must be notified. Unlike an LPA the donor cannot predetermine the persons to be registered; neither can the attorney select which relatives he wishes to notify. The attorney must give notice to those relatives falling within the classes specified in Sch 4 para 6(1), taking each class in turn until at least three relatives have been notified. Every member of a class must be notified, even if this means that more than three relatives are notified. The classes, in the order in which their members must be notified, are as follows:

- the donor's spouse or civil partner;
- the donor's children (no distinction is made between legitimate or illegitimate children);
- the donor's parents;
- the donor's brothers and sisters, whether of the whole or half blood;
- the widow or widower or surviving civil partner of a child of the donor;
- the donor's grandchildren;
- the children of the donor's brothers and sisters of the whole blood;
- the children of the donor's brothers and sisters of the half blood;

- the donor's uncles and aunts of the whole blood; and

- the children of the donor's uncles and aunts of the whole blood.

Where the attorney falls within a notifiable class, he counts as one of the relatives who has been notified, although he is not required formally to give notice to himself. For example, if the donor has a wife, one adult child who is the attorney, and one sister, the attorney must notify the wife and sister and no further relatives need to be notified. If, however, the donor also has two sisters, both sisters must be notified even though four relatives will have been notified in total.

If there are two or more attorneys applying to register the EPA then they do not need to notify each other, even though they may fall within a class of notifiable relatives. Thus if a donor appoints her husband and two sons to be attorneys and all three attorneys apply to register the EPA, no one (apart from the donor) needs to be notified. The requirement to notify a prescribed group of persons should not prevent a donor informing (for example) an unmarried partner, other concerned family members or close friends of what is happening.

If there are fewer than three relatives who must be notified, such relatives should be notified and the fact that there are no other relatives who can be notified should be clearly stated in Form EP2PG (using the additional information box).

Where more than one attorney has been appointed jointly and severally and not all the attorneys are applying to register the EPA, the attorney who is applying to register the EPA must give notice in Form EP1PG to the other attorneys unless notice can be dispensed with (Sch 4 para 11(1) and see **14.23** below).

Dispensing with notices

14.23 An attorney is not obliged to notify a relative or co-attorney if his or her address is not known to the attorney and cannot be reasonably ascertained by him or if the attorney believes the relative or co-attorney is under the age of 18 or mentally incapable (Sch 4 paras 6(2) and 11(2)).

In respect of any person entitled to receive notice, as well as the donor, the Court may also dispense with the requirement to give notice under Sch 4 paras 7(2) and 8(2) if the Court is satisfied that:

(a) it would be undesirable or impracticable for the attorney to give him notice, or

(b) no useful purpose is likely to be served by giving him notice.

For obvious reasons, the Court is unwilling to allow the requirement to give notice to be dispensed with, as the notice procedure is an essential safeguard of the EPA legislation. The donor's own rights to be notified of such an important step should also not be compromised. Where the donor is concerned, the Court will only dispense with the requirement to give notice in exceptional circumstances, for instance if there is clear medical evidence that service of a notice might cause psychological harm or endanger a relationship between donor and attorney which is already operating in the best interests of the donor.

After an application has been made, where it appears to the Court (on an application by the attorney) that a person has not been properly notified, the Court is not obliged to reject the application if the Court is satisfied that it was undesirable or impracticable for the attorney to give notice, or that no useful purpose is likely to be served by giving notice (Sch 4 para 13(4)).

An application to dispense with notice is made to the Court of Protection using the general form of application (COP1) in accordance with Part 9 of the Court of Protection Rules (Rule 68(1)). An application fee of £400 is also payable.

Payment of fee

14.24   As mentioned above, the registration fee of £120 must accompany the application to register the EPA. The cheque must be made payable to the 'Public Guardian'. If the attorney makes the payment personally, he is entitled to reimbursement from the donor's estate.

The fees due are set out in the Public Guardian (Fees, etc) Regulations 2007 (SI 2007/2051) (see **12.9** above). This not only prescribes the fees payable for registration of an EPA and searching the registers, but also provides for remission of fees where the donor is in receipt of a qualifying benefit.

Original power missing

14.25   The original EPA must accompany the application for registration. If, however, it cannot be located, the Public Guardian will consider registering a certified copy. The applicant should submit a copy properly certified on each page together with an affidavit explaining the circumstances of the loss, his belief that it has been lost and has not been revoked and undertaking to forward the original document to the Public Guardian in the event that the original is discovered.

Regulation 24 of the Lasting Power of Attorney, Enduring Power of Attorney and Public Guardian Regulations 2007 refers to the attorney producing with his application the original enduring power of attorney or a certified copy. The regulation also deals with a situation where neither the original nor a certified copy is available. In such a case the Public Guardian cannot register the instrument unless directed to do so by the Court.

Time limits

14.26   Curiously the Lasting Power of Attorney, Enduring Power of Attorney and Public Guardian Regulations 2007 make no reference to any time limits. By contrast, the Enduring Power of Attorney Rules 2001 (SI 2001/825) required notices to be given within 14 days of each other and registration to be made within 10 days of the last notice being given. The only time limits now in force are:

- the Public Guardian must not register an instrument if he receives a valid notice of objection before the end of the period of five weeks beginning with the date (or the latest date) on which the attorney gave notice of his intention to register the EPA; and

- the practice of the Public Guardian to allow a five-week period in which to receive a notice of objection.

Subsequent procedure

14.27   Applications for registration are dealt with by the Office of the Public Guardian. On receipt of the application, the registration team will check that the papers are correct and, unless there are any procedural defects, will write to the applicant to acknowledge the application and confirm that the power may be used under Sch 4 para 1(2). If the attorney needs to use the EPA during this period, then a copy of that letter is useful as evidence of the attorney's authority to act under the EPA. The letter will also contain an official reference number for the EPA which must be referred to in any further correspondence or in any proceedings concerning the EPA.

Assuming the papers are in order, the Public Guardian must register the EPA under Sch 4 para 13(1) unless one of the prescribed grounds arises:

- a deputy has been appointed and the powers of the deputy are inconsistent with the powers of the attorney; or

- a valid notice of objection is received by the Public Guardian within five weeks of the date of the last notice being given by the attorney.

If no one has been notified or the Public Guardian 'has reason to believe that appropriate enquiries might bring to light 'evidence on which he could be satisfied that one of the grounds of objection' could be satisfied, then the Public Guardian must not register the instrument until he has undertaken such inquiries 'as he thinks appropriate in all the circumstances'.

If no valid notice of objection is received and the instrument and registration procedure are correct, the Public Guardian must register the instrument as an EPA. The original EPA will be sealed and stamped with the date of registration. A copy will be retained by the Public Guardian who must retain a register of EPAs (Sch 4 para 14). The original is then returned with a covering letter to the applicant or his solicitor.

Competing applications

14.28   If an order appointing a deputy is already in place, the Public Guardian will – unless the Court directs otherwise – refuse the application to register the EPA. The Court would not normally interfere with a deputyship which is already in operation and providing adequate safeguards for a person's property. However, the Court is entitled to transfer control of a person's property to an attorney provided it is satisfied that the EPA was validly created, provides adequate safeguards for the person and it is in the best interests of the person to discharge the deputy.

If only an application to appoint a deputy has been made , then the Public Guardian must still go ahead and register the EPA, notwithstanding the application to appoint the deputy, unless a valid objection to registration is received. It is therefore possible for an EPA to be registered if the person applying for the appointment of a deputy is not a notified relative who is aware of the application. If there is a conflict between the deputy and the attorney, the Court will generally prefer the attorney as reflecting the donor's preferred arrangement. However, the Court must be satisfied that the EPA is valid and the donor's affairs can be properly dealt with in this way. For instance, where the donor has received a personal injury award and also created an EPA, the attorney may be unsuitable for the purposes of administering a substantial sum of money which was not anticipated at the time the EPA was made (*Cretney & Lush*, 5th edition, at paragraphs 1.5 and 3.5.3).

No application made by attorney

14.29   A problem arises if an attorney refuses to apply to register an EPA and either that attorney might be unsuitable or the intervention of the Court is required. The interim measures available under Sch 4 para 4(5) (see **14.18** above) do not assist as they only apply in favour of an attorney. In such a situation, a concerned party should apply for the appointment of a deputy and request the Court to make an order revoking the EPA. The attorney must be notified (see Practice Direction 9B para 10(c)) and given an opportunity to apply to register the EPA, which will then provide the applicant with an opportunity to apply to object to registration.

Objections to registration

Grounds for objection

14.30   There are only five grounds on which a person may object to the registration of an EPA. These are set out in Sch 4 para 13(6):

That the power purported to have been created by the instrument was not valid as an enduring power of attorney

14.31   This ground is appropriate where it is alleged that the donor lacked capacity to create a valid EPA, that the instrument is a forgery or fails to comply with the formal requirements for the creation of an EPA, for instance if it was not properly executed or was not in the prescribed form.

Challenging an EPA on the grounds of lack of capacity has been made more difficult following the case of *Re W* [2001] 1 FLR 832, which placed the burden of proof on the objector to show why the Court should not direct the registration of the EPA. The objector must provide as much evidence as possible to support his objection. Medical evidence must also be supplied which should be as near as possible to the events in question. The Public Guardian and the Court may make their own enquiries and request evidence from a solicitor who prepared the EPA or direct that one of the Lord Chancellor's Medical Visitors attend on the patient.

That the power created by the instrument no longer subsists

14.32   This ground may be used where the objector believes that the EPA has been terminated by revocation or by the bankruptcy of the attorney. Disputes frequently arise where there is more than one EPA in existence appointing different attorneys. However, a later EPA does not automatically revoke an earlier EPA (see *Re E* [2000] 3 All ER 1004). There must be some evidence of the express revocation of the EPA by the donor and that this fact was communicated to the attorney. A statement in a later EPA that it revokes all previous EPAs is ineffective unless the attorney under the earlier EPA is duly notified.

If it is alleged that an EPA has been revoked, the objector must also demonstrate that at the time the revocation was made, the donor had sufficient capacity to revoke the EPA. The capacity to revoke an EPA is specific to the particular act, and the requirements in such a case may well be different from those relevant to capacity to create an EPA. The donor must at the very least be capable of understanding the instrument being revoked, the consequences of its revocation, the formalities required and the further action that would be required as a result.

That the application is premature because the donor is not yet becoming mentally incapable

14.33   An application to register only arises when the attorney has reason to believe that the donor 'is or is becoming mentally incapable' but clearly the registration cannot take place if the donor is still mentally capable. However, following the case of *Re W* [2001] 1 FLR 832, the burden is on the objector to demonstrate that the donor is still capable. An objection on these grounds will require clear medical evidence in support.

That fraud or undue pressure was used to induce the donor to create the power

14.34   If fraud is alleged, the objection will be considered very carefully with the Court expecting all available evidence to be placed before it. Although the Court of Protection has wide powers to summon witnesses and cross-examine them, it is not an appropriate venue for a detailed investigation into an alleged fraud. If the EPA has been used improperly to commit a fraud then the police should be notified and the Court may revoke the EPA. If fraud is merely alleged, then it is more likely to indicate a breakdown in relations between relatives or other persons concerned with the donor's welfare and the objection can be dealt with under the fifth ground, relating to the unsuitability of the attorney with regard to all the circumstances.

Similar considerations arise where 'undue pressure' is alleged. Pressure may be brought which is not 'undue pressure', for instance where an elderly client is regularly advised by his solicitor that he should make an EPA. 'Undue pressure' is a matter of degree and requires a subjective assessment of whether the pressure was extreme or disproportionate to the extent that the donor could not have made the EPA of his own free will.

That, having regard to all the circumstances and in particular the attorney's relationship to or connection with the donor, the attorney is unsuitable to be the donor's attorney

14.35 The fifth ground is the most commonly used 'catch all' ground and allows the Court a very wide discretion to make a subjective assessment of the suitability of the attorney in the light of all the circumstances. The EPA may have been properly created and the need for registration arisen, but problems arise subsequently which can be dealt with under this ground:

- the attorney is unable to carry out his duties correctly resulting in loss or potential loss to the patient's estate;

- there is a significant conflict of interest due to the attorney's self-dealing or other financial dealings as attorney which call for explanation and need to be investigated;

- the attorney has abused his powers as attorney or committed a fraud against the donor;

- there is a clear conflict of interest, for instance where the attorney is the owner of the nursing home where the donor lives;

- the EPA was granted in particular circumstances or for particular purposes which no longer exist and the donor's affairs can be dealt with more conveniently in some other way;

- relations between the donor and the attorney have broken down and this has adversely affected the ability of the attorney to co-operate with the donor, even though the attorney's conduct is beyond reproach;

- there is a conflict between two or more attorneys, making it difficult for the donor's affairs to be administered properly.

In determining whether an attorney is suitable or not, the Court may have regard to all the factors pertinent to the choice of a suitable deputy, considered in more detail at **4.11–4.17**. Although the Court has a wide discretion to consider these factors, greater regard must be given to the wishes of the donor, who chose the attorney to carry out the duties entrusted to him. In *Re W (Enduring Power of Attorney)* [2000] 3 WLR 45, Jules Sher QC considered the concept of unsuitability in the context of the hostility of two siblings to their sister acting as sole attorney. Although his decision was appealed against, the Court of Appeal upheld his decision and his comments are on this point are very helpful:

'The second ground of unsuitability is the hostility between the three children. The Master concluded that that fact alone rendered any one of them unsuitable to be Mrs. W's attorney. In my judgment such hostility may well have such consequences but it all depends upon the circumstances. For example, had the estate of Mrs. W been complex and had it required strategic decisions in relation to its administration, one would expect the attorney to have had to consult and work with her siblings in relation to the administration. In such circumstances the evident hostility between them would impact adversely on the stewardship of the attorney, no matter who was at fault in creating the hostility in the first place.

But in this case the estate is simple. I asked counsel what the position was and was told that there are the following assets: (1) a portfolio of investments of a value (as at 23 December 1998) of £211,189; (2) £20,000 in premium bonds; (3) a life policy (written in trust) of £30,000. As to the outgoings there is the cost of the nursing home at some £2,000 a month, and then, simply, the need for a modest amount to cover a regular hairdo, telephone bills and the like. And, of course, on the income side there is the old age pension.

In other words there is nothing of any significance left to be done. The assets are under proper control. The income simply needs to be fed through to the nursing home. The evidence is that this has been done by Mrs. X very efficiently. She has indicated more than once that she has never intended to charge for her services under the power of attorney and she does not intend to do so. Against this, if the Public Trustee were to come in, there would be an appointment fee and an annual fee of between £2,350 and £3,600 per annum. If a solicitor were appointed the total cost would be likely to be somewhat less than that.

It seems to me that it is not right to say that (irrespective of the background) hostility of the kind we have seen in this case between the children renders any one of them unsuitable to be Mrs. W's attorney. In this case the hostility will not impact adversely on the administration. It would, in my judgment, be quite wrong to frustrate Mrs. W's choice of attorney in this way. Whether it is or is not a good idea for a parent in Mrs. W's position, when such hostility exists, to appoint one child alone as attorney is another question. But Mrs. W did so and, on the evidence, did so knowing of the hostility. That is her prerogative and in my judgment, when the hostility does not interfere with the smooth running of the administration, the court should not interfere of the ground of unsuitability.'(pp 51 and 52)

The decision was subsequently upheld by the Court of Appeal, reported as *Re W (Enduring Power of Attorney)* [2001] 2 WLR 957, and was later applied in *Re E (Enduring Powers of Attorney)* [2000] 3 WLR 1974 and in *Re F* [2004] 3 All ER 277. In *Re F* (at page 284), Patten J commented as follows:

'It seems to me that to remove a chosen attorney because of hostility from a sibling or other relative, in the absence of any effective challenge to his competence or integrity, should require clear evidence either that the continuing hostility will impede the proper administration of the estate or will cause significant distress to the donor which would be avoided by the appointment of a receiver. Neither of these conditions is satisfied by the evidence in this case.'

Although these cases were decided before the MCA 2005 came into force, the grounds on which they were dealt with are contained in Sch 4 of the MCA 2005 and still apply to EPAs. However, the Court must also consider the 'best interests' of the donor and exercise a balancing act between the wishes of the donor in choosing the individual to act as attorney and the wider interests of the donor and his estate.

The ground of unsuitability is not used where lasting powers of attorney are concerned. Instead, s 22(3) only allows the Court to refuse to register or revoke an instrument if it is satisfied that the donee has behaved or proposes to behave in a way that contravenes his authority or is not in the donor's best interests.

Procedure on an objection

14.36   Although a valid notice of objection must be made to the Public Guardian to prevent registration, only the Court can determine that one or more of the grounds of objection has been satisfied and therefore direct the Public Guardian to register or not register the EPA. A formal objection is therefore made to the Court, with notice given to the Public Guardian. The guidance to the application form (COP8) advises the objector in forceful terms as follows:

> 'If you have not already done so, you should notify the Public Guardian of your objection within five weeks of receiving the EP1PG notice. Upon notification the Office of the Public Guardian will suspend the registration until the court provides further directions. If the Public Guardian is not notified there is a risk that the EPA will be registered.

> You should also notify the Public Guardian of your application to the court.'

A person wishing to object to registration of an EPA must anticipate a high procedural threshold. It is no longer possible, as it was prior to 1 October 2007, to make an objection by letter or statement of facts. An application must be made in form COP8, setting out the grounds for objection and providing a witness statement in support using form COP24. If the applicant (for the purposes of the objection) is not one of the notified persons, he must also pay an application fee of £400 (Court of Protection Fees Order 2007 (SI 2007/1745), r 4(3)(b)).

The applicant must also notify the Public Guardian. There is no prescribed form of notice or objection to give the Public Guardian but the applicant must comply with reg 25 of the Lasting Power of Attorney, Enduring Power of Attorney and Public Guardian Regulations 2007 and provide the Public Guardian with a notice in writing stating (a) the name and address of the objector, (b) if different, the name and address of the donor of the power, (c) if known, the name and address of the attorney (or attorneys), and (d) the ground for making the objection. The simplest way of notifying the Public Guardian is to serve a copy of form COP8 directly on the Public Guardian.

Once an application has been made, it proceeds under Part 9 of the Court of Protection Rules. Proceedings are dealt with in more detail in Chapter 3. At the end of those proceedings, unless the Court is satisfied that a valid objection to registration has been made, the Court must direct the Public Guardian to register the EPA under Sch 4 para 13(10).

Powers of the Court after registration

14.37   The Court has wide powers to intervene in the management of the donor's affairs, supervise the conduct of the attorney, assist the attorney by supplying further authority and may at any time cancel the registration of the EPA. All the available grounds for objection to registration are not voided simply because the EPA has been registered, but may be revisited at any time in response to an application to cancel the EPA or by the Court of its own motion. For instance, the Court may subsequently receive an application for the appointment of a deputy and on considering the evidence, direct that the EPA is revoked (Sch 4 para 2(9)(b)).

For as long at the EPA remains registered, Sch 4 para 16(2) also provides the Court with the following powers:

- *To determine any question as to the meaning or the effect of the instrument*

  The Court may clarify an issue of construction where an EPA has been restricted or altered in some way or the attorney is unsure of the scope of his authority. If the attorney is unsure of whether he can carry out a particular task, an application for determination should be accompanied by an application for the authority being sought in the event that the Court's consent is required.

- *To give directions with respect to (i) the management or disposal of property, (ii) the rendering and production of accounts, and (iii) the remuneration of the attorney*

  The Court has a general authority to authorise the sale or purchase of property due to a limitation in the power, a potential conflict of interest or if the proposed transaction might be open to challenge by other parties.

  Although an attorney has a duty to keep accounts, there is no statutory requirement for him to do so. However, the Court may impose such a requirement if it believes that such additional scrutiny or reassurance might be required. In the case of *Re C (Power of Attorney)* [2000] 2 FLR 1, the nominated judge directed that a report be prepared by a chartered accountant for the benefit of the Court and the attorneys (and at the expense of the donor's estate) which would investigate all transactions over a certain amount.

  Such orders are, however, extremely rare and it is one of the failings of the jurisdiction that the Public Guardian does not have adequate resources to monitor accounts in even a small proportion of cases. Where a report or account is required, the Court will usually direct that the report or account is prepared by an independent solicitor or forensic accountant and then delivered to the Court by the party seeking the order.

An attorney as a fiduciary cannot profit from acting as an attorney, although he may recover his out-of-pocket expenses for so acting. Remuneration of a professional attorney should therefore be agreed with the donor when the EPA is prepared and provided for in the EPA by way of a special condition. However, the Court can provide for remuneration where there is no provision in the instrument or the remuneration is far in excess of what might have been authorised, due perhaps to unforeseen complexities arising.

- *To require the attorney to furnish information or produce documents or things in his possession as attorney*

This power may be used if there are concerns about the attorney's conduct and these need to be investigated. It may also be necessary to require an attorney to deliver the donor's will. Whatever information is required, it should be established that the Public Guardian has insufficient powers to deliver this information or that the Public Guardian has received an insufficient response (see **14.43** below).

- *To give any consent or authorisation to act which the attorney would have to obtain from a mentally capable donor*

A capable donor would be able to authorise the attorney to perform an act which is otherwise excluded from the instrument appointing him or in potential conflict with his fiduciary duties. Where the donor is incapable, this authority can be supplied by the Court and would be appropriate where:

– there was a restriction in the EPA preventing the disposal of an asset without the donor's consent;

– the donor was entitled to consent to the disposal of another person's property; or

– a conflict of interest arose, for example where the attorney wished to buy a property belonging to the donor.

- *To authorise the attorney to act so as to benefit himself or other persons than the donor otherwise than in accordance with s 3(4) and (5) (but subject to any conditions or restrictions contained in the instrument)*

The Court's powers to direct the making of gifts and settlements to provide for 'other persons than the donor' are considered in more detail in Chapter 13. While this part of Sch 4 allows gifts beyond the scope of paras 3(2) and (3), it does not permit the attorney to make gifts beyond the scope of the EPA itself. Thus if the EPA contains a restriction preventing or limiting gifts, the Court cannot exercise its powers under this section (see *Re R (Enduring Power of Attorney)* [1990] 2 All ER 893; [1991] 1 FLR 128). The Court must in such cases use its powers under MCA 2005, s 18 to give authority to make gifts. The Court's powers under s 18 may also be used where the proposed decision is beyond the scope of the attorney's authority, such as the making of a statutory will.

- *To relieve the attorney wholly or partly from any liability which he has or may have incurred on account of a breach of his duties as an attorney*

  This power may be used to validate an action carried out by an attorney in good faith, but which may have been beyond the scope of his authority as an attorney.

Procedure

14.38 An application for the exercise of the Court's powers under Sch 4 para 16 may be made by the attorney or any other person. Permission is not required where the application concerns the EPA (Rule 51(2)(c)). Any application for the exercise of the Court's jurisdiction under Sch 4 must, however, be made in form COP1 setting out clearly the order or relief required and supplying such evidence as may be necessary to inform the Court. A fee of £400 is payable and the applicant must follow the Part 9 procedure (see Chapter 3). If the case is complex, it is more appropriate for the applicant to apply under MCA 2005, s 18; the provisions specific to EPAs are more appropriate in straightforward cases which would fall within the scope of Practice Direction 9D (see **3.43**).

Protection of attorney acting under enduring power of attorney

14.39 Unless and until the registration of the EPA is cancelled, the attorney can continue to act with all the powers of an attorney acting under an EPA subject to any restrictions and conditions contained in the power. No attempted revocation by the donor is valid unless confirmed by the Court. Where a party to a transaction does not know that the EPA is invalid or has been revoked, or that an event has occurred which would have the effect of revoking the EPA, the attorney and any person dealing with him in good faith enjoy the protection afforded by Sch 4 para 18.

Cancellation of registration by Court

14.40 Once the power has been registered, only the Court can authorise the cancellation of the power on the following grounds set out in Sch 4 para 16(4):

'(a) on confirming the revocation of the power under sub-paragraph (3) [where the Court has confirmed the revocation of the power by the donor];

(b) on directing under paragraph 2(9)(b) that the power is to be revoked [where the Court exercises any of its powers under sections 16 to 20 of the Act];

(c) on being satisfied that the donor is and is likely to remain mentally capable;

(d) on being satisfied that the power has expired or has been revoked by the mental incapacity of the attorney;

(e) on being satisfied that the power was not a valid and subsisting enduring power when registration was effected,

(f) on being satisfied that fraud or undue pressure was used to induce the donor to create the power,

(g) on being satisfied that, having regard to all the circumstances and in particular the attorney's relationship to or connection with the donor, the attorney is unsuitable to be the donor's attorney.'

The procedural or technical grounds on which the Public Guardian can cancel registration are dealt with at **14.42** below.

Role of Public Guardian after registration

14.41 Once the EPA has been registered, the Public Guardian is responsible for the supervision of the attorney. His powers are, however, limited to keeping a register of EPAs, dealing with technical cancellations and providing a limited degree of supervision.

Cancellation of powers

14.42 Once the EPA has been registered, the Public Guardian must cancel the registration if directed to do so by the Court. However, the Public Guardian has the power (as well as the obligation) to cancel registration on the technical grounds provided by Sch 4 para 17:

(a) on receipt of a disclaimer signed by the attorney;

(b) if satisfied that the power has been revoked by the death or bankruptcy of the donor or attorney or, if the attorney is a body corporate, by its winding up or dissolution;

(c) on receipt of notification from the Court that the Court has revoked the power;

(d) on confirmation from the Court that the donor has revoked the power.

Supervision of attorneys

14.43 The role of the Public Guardian and his statutory powers generally are considered at **2.40** above. However, in respect of attorneys acting an EPA, the Public Guardian has the following powers under the Lasting Power of Attorney, Enduring Power of Attorney and Public Guardian Regulations 2007. Regulation 47 provides as follows:

'(1) This regulation applies where it appears to the Public Guardian that there are circumstances suggesting that, having regard to all the circumstances (and in particular the attorney's relationship to or connection with the donor) the attorney under a registered enduring power of attorney may be unsuitable to be the donor's attorney.

(2)   The Public Guardian may require the attorney—

(a)   to provide specified information or information of a specified description; or

(b)   to produce specified documents or documents of a specified description.

(3)   The information or documents must be provided or produced—

(a)   before the end of such reasonable period as may be specified; and

(b)   at such place as may be specified.

(4)   The Public Guardian may require—

(a)   any information provided to be verified in such manner, or

(b)   any document produced to be authenticated in such manner, as he may reasonably require.

(5)   "Specified" means specified in a notice in writing given to the attorney by the Public Guardian.'

Under reg 48 the Public Guardian also has the following functions:

'(a)   directing a Court of Protection Visitor

(i)   to visit an attorney under a registered enduring power of attorney, or

(ii)   to visit the donor of a registered enduring power of attorney,

and to make a report to the Public Guardian on such matters as he may direct; and

(b)   dealing with representations (including complaints) about the way in which an attorney under a registered enduring power of attorney is exercising his powers.'

The problem in practice is that the Public Guardian has limited resources to investigate complaints or concerns about the conduct of attorneys. His powers are limited and any substantive action, especially where the EPA needs to be cancelled, requires the involvement of the Court. The Public Guardian must then either go to the effort and expense of making an application and becoming a party to the application or assuming that a concerned individual, firm or public body will take the risk of making a substantive application to the Court.

Problems with enduring powers of attorney

Extent of the problem

14.44   According to Cretney & Lush's *Enduring Powers of Attorney* (5th edition at para 12.1):

'. . . financial abuse probably occurs in about 10–15% of cases. Expressed as a percentage this may seem to be a relatively minor problem, and maybe even an acceptable price to pay for the 85–90% of cases where attorneys act lawfully.'

The problem with this analysis is that the majority may benefit from the convenience and low cost of the EPA jurisdiction, but at the expense of the minority who are vulnerable and deserving of greater protection. Most laws which are made for public safety benefit only a tiny minority of people yet the majority are prepared to pay this price for the benefit of those less able to look after themselves.

Nature of the problem

14.45   The main problem with the EPA jurisdiction is that it was designed for a perfect world in which donors and attorneys work together in permanent harmony. However, the one system must cover the whole range of human characteristics and situations, from happy families with children who get on with each other to families who argue and people who have no families, and from people with vast estates to people with modest savings who are in receipt of benefits. The principal problems with EPAs are, however, the lack of protection and supervision and the improper use of the power, by attorneys who either act beyond the scope of their authority or without authority where they fail to register the power after the donor has become incapable. The MCA 2005 introduces LPAs to address some of these concerns, but as shall be seen in Chapter 15, LPAs address only some of these concerns and create their own difficulties in practice.

Chapter 15

Lasting powers of attorney

Introduction

15.1   A lasting power of attorney (LPA) is in essence, like the enduring power of attorney (EPA) which it replaces, a mechanism contrived by statute to enable a person to delegate decision-making powers that remain effective despite the onset of incapacity. Any competent adult ('the donor') may grant a power of attorney to another person (the attorney or 'donee') to carry out one or more functions on behalf of the donor. As with the EPA, the donor is allowed to select the person who will make decisions on his behalf in the event that he lacks capacity. Without an EPA or LPA, decisions in such circumstances could only be taken by the Court of Protection or by a deputy appointed by the Court. Because the donor has selected his own attorney, the degree of supervision and accountability required of an attorney is significantly less than that which is required from a deputy. And as with EPAs, the Court of Protection retains overall responsibility for the LPA jurisdiction and the Public Guardian is responsible for a registration process.

Enduring powers of attorney compared

15.2   Although LPAs have a similar function to EPAs, and fall within the same statutory framework, there are some considerable differences. These can be summarised as follows:

- a separate LPA can be made to make welfare decisions;

- LPAs are an integral part of the Mental Capacity Act 2005 (MCA 2005) framework, providing for decisions to be made at different levels on behalf of persons without capacity and in their best interests;

- an LPA is not effective or valid as a power of attorney until it is registered, so that registration can be effected at an early stage regardless of the donor's capacity;

- the donor selects the persons he wishes to be notified on registration;

- the instrument that creates an LPA contains a certificate of capacity to provide a contemporary record of the donor's capacity at the time the instrument is made;

- a welfare power can only be used to make decisions the donor lacks capacity to make; and

- any decision made on behalf of a donor who lacks capacity must be made in his best interests.

Lasting powers of attorney and the Mental Capacity Act 2005

15.3   The LPA jurisdiction is an integral element of the MCA 2005 and cannot be dealt with in isolation. The principle influences of the Act can be summarised as follows:

- the Court of Protection retains jurisdiction to make decisions for persons who lack capacity and to supervise and interpret LPAs and the conduct of donees;

- the Public Guardian is responsible for administering the registration of LPAs;

- the prescribed forms of LPA, the registration forms and the powers of the Public Guardian in respect of LPAs are set out in the Lasting Powers of Attorney, Enduring Powers of Attorney and Public Guardian Regulations 2007;

- the Court of Protection Rules 2007 apply to applications made by attorneys to the Court of Protection;

- another person with standing in a matter may wish to apply to the Court to use its powers, because the donee cannot or will not exercise his powers under the LPA or the scope of the power is not sufficient to make the particular decision;

- there is a presumption that the Public Guardian will not register a LPA if a deputy has been appointed (Sch 1 para 12);

- the Court of Protection may revoke an LPA and exercise any of its other powers under the MCA 2005, for instance to replace an attorney with a deputy.

Nature of the lasting power of attorney

15.4   Section 9 of the MCA 2005 sets out the core characteristics of an LPA, which is a power of attorney that has no validity or effect until it has been registered:

'(1)   A lasting power of attorney is a power of attorney under which the donor ("P") confers on the donee (or donees) authority to make decisions about all or any of the following—

(a)   P's personal welfare or specified matters concerning P's personal welfare, and

(b)   P's property and affairs or specified matters concerning P's property and affairs,

and which includes authority to make such decisions in circumstances where P no longer has capacity.

(2)   A lasting power of attorney is not created unless—

(a)   section 10 is complied with,

(b)   an instrument conferring authority of the kind mentioned in subsection (1) is made and registered in accordance with Schedule 1, and

(c)   at the time when P [the donor] executes the instrument, P has reached 18 and has capacity to execute it.

(3)   An instrument which—

(a)   purports to create a lasting power of attorney, but

(b)   does not comply with this section, section 10 or Schedule 1,

confers no authority.'

An LPA is therefore a statutory power, which is made in a prescribed form and is registered. It is not therefore 'created' until these two stages – the 'making' and the 'registration' have been complied with. This marks an important departure from the EPA framework. The 'trigger' for registration is no longer the incapacity of the donor, but the fact of use by the attorney. Therefore if the attorney wishes to use the power, he must register it first. This respects the presumption contained in s 1 of the MCA 2005, that a person must be assumed to have capacity unless it can be established that he or she lacks capacity and that capacity is only relative to the matter and at the time that capacity needs to be determined. The LPA itself is silent as to the capacity of the donor.

Advantages of registration prior to use

15.5   The registration of an instrument as a LPA, before it can be used, offers a number of advantages:

*   The protection of the registration process is available to the donor before the power can be used. This should minimise the risk of LPAs being used prematurely without proper authority.

*   No assessment of the donor's capacity is required. Not only does this make life easier for the attorney, but it prevents the donor from being labelled and therefore stigmatised by a lack of capacity or presumed lack of capacity. Thus a donor and attorney can work together with each doing what he is able to do.

Disadvantages of registration prior to use

15.6   Unfortunately, the benefits introduced by the Act give rise to corresponding disadvantages:

*   It is harder for banks and other third parties to rely on the registered power to inform them how to act. As there is no presumption from the record for or against capacity, each transaction needs to be considered carefully on its own terms. While a third party should be able to rely on the authority of the attorney, a person relying on a welfare attorney must be satisfied that the donor lacks capacity. Where financial powers are concerned, a third party can rely on the authority of the donee, but it will

not necessarily be clear whether there are conflicting or even fraudulent instructions.

- There may be some reluctance on the part of donors to see their powers registered. Not only do they experience the delay and expense of registration, they may also feel stigmatised by the mere fact of an official process being used. They may also be concerned that once registered, they will need to provide the Public Guardian with evidence if they wish to revoke the power (see **15.27** below). This has not as yet proved to be the case, in that the Public Guardian has received more applications to register LPAs than had been predicted. However, this may be partly due to the novelty of the new forms and donors (and their solicitors) seeking the reassurance of registration to confirm that the LPAs are correct.

- If donors generally felt constrained by the complexity and cost of the forms and the registration process, they may avoid LPAs altogether and leave financial decisions to ordinary powers of attorney and welfare decisions to advance decisions made in accordance with s 24 of the Act.

- As the power is not created until it is registered, the attorney cannot act under the power in an emergency, during the registration process, as there is with EPAs (see **14.19**).

- There will doubtless be some confusion in terminology. An LPA is not an LPA until it is registered, even though the forms marked 'Lasting Power of Attorney' have been fully completed. Section 9 for instance refers to 'an instrument conferring authority of the kind mentioned in subsection (1)' and s 13 refers to 'an instrument with a view to creating a Lasting Power of Attorney'. There will therefore be many donors who believe they have granted LPAs without actually having done so!

Scope of lasting power of attorney

Personal welfare matters

15.7   Section 9(1) introduces a new provision, whereby a donee can be authorised to make decisions about 'personal welfare' or specified matters concerning 'personal welfare'. The term itself is not defined in detail, although s 11(7)(c) makes it clear that the authority to make decisions about the donor's personal welfare 'extends to giving or refusing consent to the carrying out or continuation of a treatment by a person providing health care'. The Act therefore allows the donee – where the donor lacks capacity – to give consent to how the donor is cared for or treated. In most cases this should be a fairly passive or reactive role. A doctor or healthcare professional responsible for treating the donor will recommend a particular treatment and it is for the donee to give consent on behalf of the donor. However, the donee can, if the LPA so allows, also refuse consent and that refusal may well lead to the death of the donor.

It is less clear from the Act whether a donee can take a assertive role in requiring a particular treatment or determining where the donor should live.

By comparison, the authority to decide where a person lives is referred to in the Act, but only in favour of the Court of Protection or a deputy appointed by the Court (s 17).

Limits on donee's powers

15.8   The Act does set out a number of important limits on what a donee of a welfare LPA can do. The authority of the donee does not:

- extend to circumstances in which the donee does not reasonably believe that the donor lacks capacity (s 11(7)(a));

- operate where there is a valid and applicable advance decision (s 11(7)(b));

- extend to life-sustaining treatment unless the instrument contains express provision to that effect (s 11(8));

- allow the donor to be restrained unless (s 11(1) to 11(5));

  (a)   the attorney reasonably believes that the donor lacks the capacity to do the act in question;

  (b)   the attorney reasonably believes that the act is necessary to prevent harm to the donor;

  (c)   the act is proportionate to the likelihood of the donor's suffering harm and the seriousness of that harm; and

  (d)   any restraint MUST NOT amount to a deprivation of liberty under Article 5;

- extend to acts outside the scope of the MCA 2005, principally:

  (a)   mental health: giving consent to medical treatment for mental disorder (s 28);

  (b)   family matters: giving consent to sexual relations, to marriage, civil partnership or divorce or dissolution based on two years' separation, to adoption and under the Human Fertilisation and Embryology Act 1990, and discharging parental responsibilities (except in relation to a child's property) (s 27); and

  (c)   voting: voting in an election for any public office or in a referendum (s 29).

Principles governing donee's actions

15.9   Any donee, whether acting under a financial or welfare power, must act in accordance with the Act's core principles, and in particular, in the best interests of the donor. A donee must for instance:

- consider whether the donor is likely to re-gain capacity;

- allow and encourage the donor to participate, so far as practicable;

- consider the donor's past and present wishes and feelings (particularly a written statement made when capable), the donor's beliefs and values, and other factors the donor would be likely to consider;

- when considering life-sustaining treatment, not be motivated by a desire for the donor's death; and

- take account of the views of anyone named by the donor to be consulted and anyone caring for the donor or interested in his welfare – so far as practicable and appropriate.

The difficulty facing a financial donee is that the principles that are not specific to welfare matters apply to a financial power as well. A financial donee may therefore need to act in accordance with two sets of principles. Firstly, the donee is bound by the common law relationship between a principal and his agent. This is based on a relationship of trust and confidence or a fiduciary relationship, which requires the agent to act for the benefit of the donor or his estate. This is an objective responsibility and applies equally to an attorney acting under an EPA (see **14.13**) and a deputy dealing with property and affairs (see **7.1**). However, where the donee is making a decision on behalf of a donor who lacks capacity, he must also act in his 'best interests' which at first sight appears to require a subjective analysis. In the majority of cases it is hoped that there is no conflict between the two approaches. But donors of LPAs come in all varieties and the awkward, capricious and eccentric may provide an interesting conflict for a donee between what is for the donor's material or physical benefit and what is in the donor's best interests. Where there is a conflict between the two, then this should be resolved in favour of an objective view of the donor's best interests (see the principles applied in *Re P* [2009] EWHC 163 (Ch) and described in more detail at **1.23**.

The Lasting Power of Attorney forms

15.10   Schedule 1 to the MCA 2005 requires an LPA to be in a prescribed form and to include a statement by the donor that he has read or had read to him certain prescribed information. Prescribed forms of LPA were set out in the Lasting Powers of Attorney, Enduring Powers of Attorney and Public Guardian Regulations 2007. Revised draft forms were put forward for consultation by the Ministry of Justice on 23 October 2008 (Consultation Paper CP26/08) with a view to new forms being available by 1 October 2009 (Response to Consultation CP(R)26/08 published on 11 March 2009).

Unlike EPAs which are restricted to property and affairs, an LPA enables welfare decisions and property and affairs decisions to be delegated to an attorney. The Regulations therefore provide for two separate forms: one for welfare matters and one for property and affairs. This is sensible in practice, for separate instruments may be made appointing different persons to act in relation to different decisions that need to be made at different times. Many donors will already have EPAs dealing with their property and affairs and wish to complete LPAs dealing with their personal welfare.

Although the prescribed forms are designed to be 'user friendly' for people to fill in for themselves, they are complex forms in their own right, before even considering:

- the scope of the LPA and the principles governing the donee's actions;

- the choices available to the donee;

- whether restrictions or conditions need to be included;

- the suitability of the persons named as donees or notifiable persons;

- issues of advice, pressure or undue influence;

- whether independent legal advice is needed;

- the capacity of the donor;

- completion of the certificate of capacity; and

- the likely costs of the exercise.

The forms are set out in four parts:

1.   The prescribed information which must be read by or to the donor.

2.   Part A – the information relevant to the donor and which must be signed by the Donor.

3.   Part B – the certificate of capacity.

4.   Part C – the attorney's statement.

Some of the issues that need to be addressed by the donor and donee and any professional advisers when completing the forms need to be considered in more detail.

Specific issues with the prescribed forms

Complying with section 10 of the Mental Capacity Act

15.11   The forms are designed to be filled in, using the guidance and choices clearly set out in the forms and explanatory notes. However, several factors and options must be considered, including the provisions of s 10. The conditions specified must be fulfilled or the options addressed must be answered clearly:

- A donee must be an individual who has reached 18, or if the power relates only to a donor's property and affairs, either an individual or a trust corporation.

- An individual who is bankrupt may not be appointed as donee in relation to a donor's property and affairs. However, an individual who is a bankrupt may be appointed in relation to a person's welfare.

- Where two or more persons are to act as donees of a lasting power of attorney, the instrument appointing them may appoint them to act:

(a) jointly,

(b) jointly and severally, or

(c) jointly in respect of some matters and jointly and severally in respect of others.

- To the extent to which the LPA does not specify whether two or more attorneys are to act jointly or jointly and severally, the instrument is to be assumed to appoint them to act jointly. The problems caused by joint appointments is considered at **15.12** below.

- If donees are to act jointly, a failure, as respects one of them, to comply with the requirements of s 10(1) or 10(2) or Part 1 or 2 of Sch 1 prevents an LPA from being created.

- If donees are to act jointly and severally, a failure, as respects one of them, to comply with the requirements of subsection (1) or (2) or Part 1 or 2 of Sch 1 prevents the appointment taking effect in his case, but does not prevent an LPA from being created in the case of the other or others.

- An instrument used to create an LPA cannot give the donee (or, if more than one, any of them) power to appoint a substitute or successor.

- An instrument used to create an LPA may itself appoint a person to replace the donee (or, if more than one, any of them) on the occurrence of an event mentioned in s 13(6)(a) to (d) which has the effect of terminating the donee's appointment. The difficulties that replacement attorneys may give rise to are considered at **15.13** below.

More than one attorney

15.12 Section 10(4) of the MCA 2005 allows a donor to appoint more than one donee provided that the donees are appointed to act 'jointly' or 'jointly and severally' or 'jointly in respect of some matters and jointly and severally in respect of others.' This may appear to be an unnecessary complication. In practice, a donor may for instance wish to appoint donees to act jointly and severally in respect of his investments but require them to act jointly where a major decision was required, for instance to sell his home or in a welfare power, to withhold consent to life-sustaining treatment. However, if the appointment of one of the joint donees were to fail due for instance to the death or (in the case of a financial power) bankruptcy of the donee, the appointment of the joint donees would fail. The LPA may therefore end up being effective in respect of some decisions but ineffective in respect of other decisions.

Where a donor wishes to protect his interests through the appointment of joint donees, he should consider carefully whether:

- he has appointed the right persons if potentially they cannot be relied upon to act individually;

- it is safer to appoint donees jointly and severally with a restriction or condition in the instrument requiring certain decisions to be taken by more than one person, subject to there being more than one person so capable; or

- replacement attorneys should also be appointed.

Replacement attorneys

15.13 The appointment of a replacement donee is often desirable. For instance an elderly donor may wish to appoint his spouse to act if willing and able and only appoint his two children if the spouse is unable or unwilling to act. Section 10(8)(b) therefore allows a donor to appoint a person to replace the donee (or one of the donees) on the occurrence of an event mentioned in s 13(6)(a) to (d) which has the effect of terminating the donee's appointment. The replacement attorney can, however, only operate the power if the first appointment fails on one of the statutory grounds: disclaimer, death, bankruptcy, divorce or lack of capacity of the donee. The replacement donee cannot be appointed to act if the appointment of the first donee were to fail on a different ground such as the revocation of the power in favour of one of the attorneys by the Court.

The situation becomes more complicated where multiple donees are appointed. The donor may for instance appoint his wife and elder son as donees jointly and his daughter as a replacement. His wife dies, with the result that the appointment of both wife and son is terminated, leaving the daughter as sole donee.

The appointment of a substitute donee therefore needs to be considered carefully, especially as the level of protection afforded to the donor may also be affected. . On the application for registration by the first donees, the replacement donee remains firmly in the background. He is not deemed to be a donee (even though he has completed a certificate for Part C). In the above example, the wife and son apply to register the LPA: at that point the daughter is not a donee and does not need to join in the registration process. The named persons have no indication that if the appointment of the wife and son were to fail, the donee with sole responsibility for looking after the donor's affairs will in fact be the daughter. This may cause some concern if the daughter is in fact unsuitable; it may also cause some concern if the wife and son are unsuitable. In that scenario, the daughter cannot be a named person who receives notice of registration (Sch 1 para 2(3)). The daughter may be unaware of, or denied a right to object to, the registration of the LPA.

Restrictions and conditions

15.14 The prescribed forms provide a great deal of space for the inclusion of restrictions and/or conditions, which are encouraged. The following restrictions and conditions might be considered:

- Restricting the operation of the LPA to being used in specified circumstances. If unrestricted, the LPA can be used – subject to registration – at any time by the donee. Many donors will be unhappy with going through the formalities and expense of registration when the

339

power only needs to be used for a limited time or function. They may also be unhappy with the prospect of the LPA being used while they are still capable. A donor might restrict the creation of the LPA to (for example) such time as he becomes mentally incapable of managing his property and affairs. This does, however, contradict the spirit of a property and affairs LPA which is that the LPA itself is neutral as to the donor's capacity. Questions might also be asked about the suitability of a donee who cannot be relied on to act sensitively in such a situation. There may also be less restrictive ways of dealing with a donor's concerns, such as having a solicitor to hold the LPA to the order of the donor so that while he is capable it is not released without his consent.

- Requiring medical evidence to be supplied on an application to register the LPA. Some donors will be uncomfortable with the idea of the donee registering and using the power without any formal medical evidence being supplied. There is, however, a danger of making the condition overly prescriptive, with the result that the condition does not meet a situation in which the LPA actually needs to be used.

- Authority for the delegation of investment powers to a professional fund manager. A donee cannot generally delegate his functions except where he cannot be expected to attend to them personally. A discretionary power of investment is probably beyond the scope of this implied power and should be provided for expressly.

- Professional fees. A donee acts in a fiduciary role in relation to the donor's estate and should not benefit from his so acting without the consent of the donor. It is therefore important for this to be expressly provided for in the instrument. The prescribed forms provide for this to be addressed.

- Authorising disclosure or safe custody of the donor's will. A solicitor holding a will owes a duty of confidentiality to the donor and would not normally release documents without the consent of the donor (if capable) or the Court (if incapable). A donee may, however, need to know the contents of the will especially if a property is to be sold or gifts made.

- Requiring the donee to keep accounts or to render an account to a second donee or to a third party such as another member of the family, a solicitor or accountant. Although a donee has a common law duty to keep accounts, this is not always followed in practice. The Court of Protection has authority to require a donee to deliver an account (s 23(3)(a)). However, this authority is rarely exercised. Many of the disputes that involve EPAs (and by implication, LPAs) have been caused by a lack of awareness of what an attorney is doing: a duty to disclose information and/or account to another party or to an independent professional often provides an adequate degree of reassurance in such cases.

- The donee's authority to make gifts under s 12 is considered at **13.6** above. The donor may wish to restrict the power to make gifts by setting a maximum amount for gifts or prohibiting the making of gifts without the consent of the Court or a third party. A donor can, however, only restrict the power to make gifts; he cannot expand it. It is therefore unlikely that the donee's power to make gifts could be extended to include a power of maintenance (see **13.8**). A donee requiring to pay maintenance may therefore need to consider an application to the Court under s 18(1)(b) or 23(4).

• Restricting the amount of capital which can be applied or limiting the value of transactions that may be entered into by the attorney.

• Confirming the revocation of an earlier LPA or EPA. One power of attorney does not automatically revoke an earlier power. There must be a clear act of revocation and the attorney under the earlier power must be notified. However, as an LPA is not created until it is registered, this formality would be required where the instrument has not yet been registered. Where the LPA has been registered, then the donor must notify the Public Guardian as well as the donee of the revocation (see reg 21(1) of the Lasting Powers of Attorney, Enduring Powers of Attorney and Public Guardian Regulations 2007). However, it may be good practice to ensure that there is a clear record of revocation of an earlier instrument.

• Requiring the consent of a third party to the disposal of a particular asset, such as the family home, heirlooms or shares in a family company.

• Restricting the scope of the LPA so that it does not apply to a particular asset, for instance that it should not apply to the sale of the family home.

• Where welfare decisions need to be made, certain important decisions – especially in relation to life-sustaining treatment – should require consultation with or concurrence with certain individuals.

Although the prescribed forms encourage the insertion of restrictions and conditions, great care needs to be taken with their drafting. In principle, they should be kept to a minimum. Restrictions and conditions sit uneasily with the principles behind the Act – of trusting and empowering donees to exercise their judgment. The clauses can be awkward to draft and can cause their own problems for the attorneys. Several cases have been referred to the Court by the Public Guardian to sever the provisions under Sch 1 para 11(4). A detailed account of some of the first decisions referred to the Court and the problems caused by home-made restrictions and conditions is contained in an informative and detailed article by Senior Judge Lush in the October 2008 Newsletter of the Association of Contentious Trust and Probate Specialists and the Trusts and Estates Law and Tax Journal (December 2008). Some of the cases referred to in these articles have since been summarised and published on the Public Guardian website at: http://www.publicguardian.gov.uk/forms/cop-lpa-orders.htm. They are reproduced below for ease of reference:

'Re Begum (an order of the Senior Judge made on 24 April 2008)

On the application of the Public Guardian, the court directed the severance from a Property and Affairs LPA instrument of the following clauses, on the ground that they were ineffective as part of an LPA:

All decisions about the use or disposal of my property and financial resources must be driven by what my Personal Welfare Lasting Power of Attorney(s) believe will support my long term interests.

Any decisions affecting assets (individually or together) worth more than £5,000 at any one time must be discussed and agreed with Dr X.

In the event of there being any disagreement between my Personal Welfare Lasting Power of Attorney(s) and/or Dr X this should be resolved by these parties appointing an independent advocate to adjudicate.

Re Jenkins (an order of the Senior Judge made on 2 September 2008)

The donor had appointed the attorneys of a property and affairs LPA to act "together and independently". She then directed that they must act together in relation to any bills, payments or costs exceeding £2,000 in any one calendar month and in relation to any single payment greater than £1,000 in any calendar month. The donor had also appointed a replacement attorney, and directed that she should act if the original attorneys were "not available through travel or living abroad or any other circumstances that may prevent or restrict their capacity to act on my behalf as attorneys".

The court ordered the severance of both clauses, on the application of the Public Guardian. The directions in the first clause were incompatible with an appointment to act "together and independently". The directions in the second clause were invalid because a replacement attorney may only act on the occurrence of an event mentioned in section 13(6)(a) to (d) of the MCA, for example where an original attorney disclaims, dies or loses mental capacity.

Re Patel (an order of the Senior Judge made on 1 December 2008)

The donor appointed a replacement attorney to act if the original attorney should be "mentally or physically incapable" or if the original attorney "is not in England at any time that my personal or financial affairs require attention". The words in bold were severed on the application of the Public Guardian on the ground that a replacement attorney may only act on the occurrence of an event mentioned in section 13(6)(a) to (d) of the MCA, for example where an original attorney disclaims, dies or loses mental capacity.

Re Bates (an order of the Senior Judge made on 3 December 2008)

The donor appointed two original attorneys and a replacement attorney, who would assume office in the following circumstances: "She may act at any time at the election of either attorney". These words were severed on the application of the Public Guardian on the ground that a replacement attorney may only act on the occurrence of an event mentioned in section 13(6)(a) to (d) of the MCA, for example where an original attorney disclaims, dies or loses mental capacity.'

If a donor is in any doubt as to whether a restriction or condition should be included, then it may be appropriate to include this as guidance. Restrictions and conditions may however be very relevant – and certainly need to be considered carefully – in welfare powers, especially where life and death decisions might need to be taken.

Guidance

15.15   The prescribed forms also contain space for the donor to provide guidance for the donees. A LPA should if possible provide a donee with discretion and autonomy, and it goes against the nature of the relationship between donor and donee to be overly prescriptive. However, a donee may well benefit from a record of the donor's wishes. While these may not be binding as such, the donee will be obliged by virtue of s 4(6) of the MCA 2005 to take them into account in determining the donor's best interests.

Life-sustaining treatment (welfare power)

15.16   The authority of a donee under a welfare LPA does not extend to 'giving or refusing of consent to the carrying out or continuation of life-sustaining treatment' unless the instrument so permits. Conversely, the power can extend to the giving or refusing of consent in such circumstances. Although the Act appears to set out a presumption in favour of one option – which can be replaced – the prescribed form simply sets out two choices (at paragraph 6 of Part A) and requires the donor to specify one of them. Thus in addition to executing the instrument at the end of Part A, he must also sign the box beside Option A or Option B specifying which option is to be chosen. As a further safeguard and to prevent the donor signing the wrong box in error, the signature beside the chosen box must be signed in the presence of a witness who must sign and complete the boxes at the foot of the same page.

Curiously the form treats the 'giving or refusing of consent' to life-sustaining treatment as part of the same option. There is no ready provision for a donor who wants his donee to be able to refuse consent to life-sustaining treatment but not to give such consent. Conversely, a donor may want the donee to be able to give consent to treatment but not to refuse it. The donor will have to choose this option and then qualify it with a restriction at paragraph 7.

Persons named in the power

15.17   A principal safeguard in the statutory power of attorney that survives the incapacity of the donor is the inclusion of a registration process, whereby certain people are given notice. They replace the need to involve doctors and judges and act as the guardians of the donor or the whistle-blowers of the Court, who will raise the alarm if there is any danger to the donor. As has been seen, EPAs require a prescribed class of relatives to be notified (see **14.22** above). Where LPAs are concerned, the donor must specify the names of persons to be notified on registration (Sch 1 para 2(1)(c)). Up to five persons can be named for this purpose. There is no restriction as to the relationship, age or even capacity of the named person: the only restriction is that the named person cannot be a donee (Sch 1 para 2(3)). A donee for these purposes includes a replacement donee (see the case of *Re Howarth* summarised on the OPG website at http://www.publicguardian.gov.uk/forms/cop-lpa-orders.htm).

The choice of persons to be notified on registration may appear to be a departure from an established practice and even more open to abuse. For those involved in drafting LPAs it may also make the forms more time consuming to prepare as donors consider who is to be notified. The prescribed forms also provide space for the names, addresses, telephone numbers and emails of the notified persons. The forms also make no allowance for the fact that they are made years in advance of being used, by which time the persons named in the power may well have married, moved home, died, disappeared or become incapable. The reason for this change of policy was set out by the Law Commission (Law Com 231 at 7.37), which was critical of the statutory list of notifiable relatives which:

> '… makes no acknowledgement that close and important relationships may exist outside of legal marriage and blood ties. It conflicts with the autonomy principle to require, regardless of the donor's wishes, that certain relatives must be notified of a private arrangement to govern future decision making.'

This approach was followed closely when the Mental Capacity Bill made its way through Parliament. For instance, speaking in the House of Lords at its third reading (*Hansard*, 15 March 2005, Col 1316), Baroness Ashton stated:

> 'I am also very clear that this provision is about the donor making a choice. Ultimately, the donor should say who they would like to have notified. It could be a relative, but there may not be any relatives around or the donor may be estranged from his or her family – so there would be little point in notifying a relative. Just because someone is related does not necessarily mean that he will care anything for the donor. He may even have his own selfish motives for showing an interest in trying to object to the donor's chosen attorney.'

What this fails to take into account is that not every donor will make an objective and fully informed choice that will last the passage of time. There has already been one case referred to the Court where an elderly gentleman appointed his nephew to be his attorney and named another nephew and a niece of the intention to register the instrument. The wife and four children of the donor had no knowledge of the power and no knowledge of its registration and only heard about it through a friend. They had no standing to object to the Public Guardian.

The Act also fails to address the possibility that the donor may lose touch with a named person or a named person may himself become incapable. There is no provision, as there is on registering an EPA, to avoid notifying a family member who is incapable or cannot be traced (see **14.23** above). The Act assumes that an LPA will be registered soon after the instrument is prepared in which case the notified persons will be fresh in the donor's memory. However, as time goes on, it is likely that more and more LPAs will be completed in instalments, with registration left to a later date. If on later registration, the notified person cannot be located, it seems the only remedies available to a donee are:

- to send the notice to the notified person at the address shown in the instrument; or

- apply to the Court of Protection (by way of a formal application) to dispense with the requirement to notify (Sch 1 para 10).

No persons named in the power

15.18 The donor may not want anyone to be named for the purposes of registration, in which case there must be two certificates of capacity in Part B (Sch 1 para 2(2)(b)). This does not seem unreasonable and it may be quite common for instance for someone with two children to appoint them as attorneys and not want to involve anyone else. However, this safeguard can be avoided very simply by including any named person who is alive at the time the instrument is executed. The donor who recently named Gordon Brown of 10 Downing Street, London SW1 as the person to be notified has not been able to benefit from this additional statutory safeguard.

Execution by donor

15.19 As well as completing the relevant parts of the instrument that apply to him, the donor must also read (or have had read to him) all the prescribed information contained in the form. As soon as reasonably practical, he must sign Part A as a deed in the presence of a witness (Lasting Powers of Attorney, Enduring Powers of Attorney and Public Guardian Regulations 2007, reg 9(3)).

Certificate of capacity (Part B)

15.20 Before the instrument is completed, there is a further safeguard to protect the interests of the donor. One of the principal concerns over the EPA jurisdiction was that EPAs were completed too readily, without sufficient attention being given to the capacity of the donor or the powers and duties of the attorneys. A presumption would then arise that the EPA had been validly made and as it might be several years before problems came to light, there was no contemporaneous evidence of the donor's understanding at the time the EPA was made.

To address this particular problem and to add a further safeguard, an instrument that is made in accordance with Sch 1 of the Act must include a certificate by a person of a prescribed description that, in his opinion:

'at the time when the donor executes the instrument:

(a) the donor understands the purpose of the instrument and the scope of the authority given under it;

(b) no fraud or undue pressure is being used to induce the donor to create a Lasting Power of Attorney; and

(c)   there is nothing else which would prevent a lasting power of attorney from being created.'

Sch 1 para 2(e) refers to the certificate being given in respect of the time 'when the donor executes the instrument'. There is, however, no time limit in which the certificate must be given, so long as it is given before the instrument is registered and becomes effective as a LPA. Regulation 9(4) of the Lasting Powers of Attorney, Enduring Powers of Attorney and Public Guardian Regulations 2007 refers to this being done 'as soon as reasonably practicable' after the instrument has been executed. Clearly, the longer the gap between execution and the completion of the certificate, the harder it is for the certificate provider to be able to certify the facts required by the Act. Ideally, the certificate of capacity should be completed at the same time as the donor executes Part A of the instrument, and there is nothing to prevent the certificate provider also witnessing the donor's signature when completing Part A. For instance, a solicitor who prepares a form for a client can oversee execution of Part A and completion of the certificate of capacity in Part B. However, this will not always be possible, for instance where a solicitor who prepares the instrument is a donee or the donor's capacity is in doubt and a doctor needs to complete the certificate.

Whether the certificate of capacity is completed contemporaneously or subsequently, the certificate provider has a responsibility to ensure that the statutory requirements have, to the best of his knowledge and belief, been complied with. It should not be necessary for the certificate provider to ensure that the donor understands every detail of the instrument; it is sufficient that he understands its purpose and the scope of the donee's authority. However, the certificate provider also has the responsibility, in effect providing a seal of authenticity. Once the certificate of capacity has been completed and the LPA has been created, it would be extremely difficult for any other person to overturn the presumption that the donor had capacity and that the instrument had been validly made.

Who can give a certificate of capacity

15.21   To anticipate donors making or executing LPAs and then being put off completing the power because of the difficulty of locating a certificate provider, the draft forms provide for as wide a class as possible of certificate provider. Regulation 8 of the Lasting Power of Attorney, Enduring Power of Attorney and Public Guardian Regulations 2007 determines who can or cannot be a certificate provider:

'(1)   Subject to paragraph (3), the following persons may give an LPA certificate—

(a)   a person chosen by the donor as being someone who has known him personally for the period of at least two years which ends immediately before the date on which that person signs the LPA certificate;

(b)   a person chosen by the donor who, on account of his professional skills and expertise, reasonably considers that he is competent to make the judgments necessary to certify the matters set out in paragraph (2)(1)(e) of Schedule 1 to the Act.

(2) The following are examples of persons within paragraph (1)(b)—

(a) a registered health care professional;

(b) a barrister, solicitor or advocate called or admitted in any part of the United Kingdom;

(c) a registered social worker; or

(d) an independent mental capacity advocate.

(3) A person is disqualified from giving an LPA certificate in respect of any instrument intended to create a lasting power of attorney if that person is—

(a) a family member of the donor;

(b) a donee of that power;

(c) a donee of—

(i) any other lasting power of attorney, or

(ii) an enduring power of attorney,

which has been executed by the donor (whether or not it has been revoked);

(d) a family member of a donee within sub-paragraph (b);

(e) a director or employee of a trust corporation acting as a donee within sub-paragraph (b);

(f) a business partner or employee of—

(i) the donor, or

(ii) a donee within sub-paragraph (b);

(g) an owner, director, manager or employee of any care home in which the donor is living when the instrument is executed; or

(h) a family member of a person within sub-paragraph (g).'

There is often some confusion over who can or cannot be a certificate provider and the prescribed forms are not as clear as they should be. It is important to note the following.

• A person 'chosen by the donor as being someone who has known him personally for the period of at least two years' is not required to show any particular skill or expertise. This places a burden on the donor to ensure that the certificate is credible if called into question and on the certificate provider to ensure that he has carried out his obligations in giving the certificate.

• The professional categories listed in the Regulations are examples of skills-based certificate providers. The certificate provider must first of all be someone who 'on account of his professional skills and expertise reasonably considers that he is competent to make the judgments necessary'. The onus is on the certificate provider to show why he considers himself to have the relevant skills. The fact that someone is a solicitor or barrister – or even a doctor – does not by itself qualify that person to assess the donor's capacity and understanding.

- A certificate provider cannot be 'a business partner or employee' of the donee. Thus where the donee (who includes a replacement donee) is a partner in a firm of solicitors, another partner or member of staff cannot act as a certificate provider. However, if the donee is a member of staff, then a partner in the donee's firm who is his employer, can be a certificate provider, however inadvisable it might be.

- A person acting as certificate provider in a professional capacity will need to consider carefully the extent of his obligations. Will he for instance be acting for the donee as a client? If a solicitor, will he need to obtain identification, prepare an attendance note and charge a fee? Is he under any obligation to offer advice, if the donor asks any questions or if there is a patent defect in the instrument? And where he is seeing a couple, should a husband and wife or civil partners be seen independently?

- The Regulations make no reference to the donee being interviewed by the certificate provider in private, although the LPA forms (annexed to the Lasting Powers of Attorney, Enduring Powers of Attorney and Public Guardian Regulations 2007) imply that this is necessary. It is, however, sensible for the certificate provider to spend some time alone with the donee.

The donee's certificate (Part C)

15.22   As with an EPA, there is a Part C for completion by the donee. This must be dealt with carefully and should not be signed as a formality. The donee's certificate provides the donee with a useful reminder of his obligations under the power and the MCA 2005 and Code of Practice as well as a point of reference if the donee fails to meet those obligations. The forms prescribed by the Lasting Powers of Attorney, Enduring Powers of Attorney and Public Guardian Regulations 2007 require the donee to certify to the following factors:

'1.   I have read the prescribed information on pages 2, 3 and 4 or have had the prescribed information read to me.

2.   I understand the duties imposed on me under this lasting power of attorney including the obligation to act in accordance with the Mental Capacity Act 2005 and the duty to have regard to the Code of Practice.

3.   I am not an undischarged bankrupt or an interim bankrupt.

4.   I understand that I cannot act under this lasting power of attorney until this form has been registered by the Public Guardian.'

Once component parts of the instrument have been completed, the LPA can be created on its registration by the Public Guardian.

The registration process

15.23   The registration process is a straightforward one and designed to give formal recognition to the power as well as provide a measure of protection to the donor. An application to register is made to the Public Guardian, in form LPA002, accompanied by a fee and the original instrument. The fee prescribed by the Public Guardian (Fees, etc) Regulations 2007 (SI 2007/2051) is currently £120 (reduced from £150 as at 1 April 2009) and the same fee is payable in respect of each LPA if two applications for registration are made at the same time.

Unlike the EPA registration process, an application to register an LPA can be made by the donor as well as by the donee.

The person making the application must give notice in form LPA001 to any persons named by the donor in the LPA for that purpose (see **15.17** above). However, it is the Public Guardian who must give notice in form LPA003 to the donor if, as will usually be the case, the application is made by the donee. The Public Guardian is also responsible for giving notice to the donees where the application is made by the donor or to a donee where the application is made by another donee.

Time for the notice period of six weeks begins on the date the Public Guardian gives the last notice which he is required to give (Lasting Powers of Attorney, Enduring Powers of Attorney and Public Guardian Regulations 2007, reg 12). Unless the Public Guardian receives a valid notice of objection (see **15.25** below) or there is a defect in the instrument preventing registration (see **15.26** below), the Public Guardian must register the instrument as a LPA (Sch 1 para 5). Once the LPA has been registered, the original instrument is stamped and returned to the applicant. The Public Guardian also gives notice in form LPA004 to the donor and donee that the LPA has been registered.

Objections to registration and cancellation by Public Guardian

15.24   Although the Public Guardian is the registration authority, he has a limited right or ability to determinate the validity of the power. His power is only to refuse registration on certain technical or factual grounds unless directed otherwise by the Court. He can also cancel the registration directly if satisfied that one of the specified grounds exists, whether due to a defect in the power or on receipt of a valid notice of objection. Where there is an objection on a substantive ground that might involve a determination of fact, then this must be dealt with by the Court.

Refusal of Public Guardian to register

15.25   The Public Guardian is obliged to refuse registration if:

- It appears to the Public Guardian that the instrument is not made in accordance with Sch 1 (Sch 1 para 11(1)). For example where the incorrect form was used or there was a technical defect in the form which prevented it from operating as a valid LPA. This provision has been relied on by the Public Guardian to refuse registration where boxes or fields in the prescribed form are omitted.

- The Court has already appointed a deputy and it appears to the Public Guardian that the powers conferred on the deputy would conflict with the powers conferred on the attorney in which case the power cannot be registered unless directed by the Court (Sch 1 para 12).

- It appears to the Public Guardian that there is a provision in the instrument which would be ineffective as part of a LPA or which would prevent the power from operating as a LPA, in which case the power must be referred to the Court for determination (Sch 1 paras 11 (2) and 11(3)). If the instrument contains a restriction or condition or other provision which would prevent the power from operating, then the Court has power to sever the offending provision under s 23(1).

- The Public Guardian receives a notice of objection from the donee or named person on one of the specified grounds (see **15. 27** below) and it appears to the Public Guardian that the ground for making the objection is satisfied, in which case the Public Guardian must not register the power unless directed by the Court (Sch 1 para 13).

- The Court receives a notice of objection from the donee or named person on one of the prescribed grounds, the Public Guardian must not register the power unless directed by the Court (Sch 1 paras 13(3) and 13(4)).

Objections to Public Guardian on factual grounds

15.26   An objection to registration on one of the factual grounds can only be made to the Public Guardian by a donor, donee or named person using form LPA007 (which complies with the requirements of the Lasting Powers of Attorney, Enduring Powers of Attorney and Public Guardian Regulations 2007, reg 14). A person making an objection must file his notice before the end of the period of five weeks beginning with the date on which the notice is given.

The 'factual' grounds on which a person entitled to notice can 'object' in this way are limited to the following cases (Sch 1 para 13(1)):

- insofar as the LPA relates to the property and affairs of the donor, the bankruptcy of the donor or the donee or where the donee is a trust corporation, its winding up or dissolution;

- the LPA has been disclaimed by the donee;

- the death of the donee;

- the dissolution or annulment of the donor's marriage or civil partnership between the donor and the donee (unless the power excludes revocation in these circumstances);

- the donee lacks capacity.

On receipt of an objection on the factual grounds, the Public Guardian will simply stop the registration process. It is then for the applicant to accept the situation or apply to the Court to consider the matter and to require the Public Guardian to register the power (Sch 1 para 13(2)).

Cancellation of registration by Public Guardian

15.27   The Public Guardian must cancel the registration of the power if:

- he is satisfied that the (financial) LPA has been revoked by the bankruptcy of the donor (Sch 1 para 17(1)(a));

- he is satisfied that the LPA has been revoked on one of the grounds mentioned in s 13(6)(a) to (d), namely: the LPA has been disclaimed by the donee, the donee has died, the marriage or civil partnership of the donor to the donee has been dissolved (unless provided otherwise by the instrument) or the donee lacks capacity (Sch 1 para 17(1)(b));

- the Court directs the Public Guardian to cancel the registration if it revokes the power, determines the power has been revoked by the donor or otherwise come to an end or it determines that a requirement for creating the power was not met (Sch 1 para 18);

- he is satisfied that the power has been revoked by the death of the donor (Lasting Powers of Attorney, Enduring Powers of Attorney and Public Guardian Regulations 2007, reg 22); or

- if he receives a notice that the donor has revoked the LPA and is satisfied that the donor has taken such steps as are necessary in law to revoke the power (Lasting Powers of Attorney, Enduring Powers of Attorney and Public Guardian Regulations 2007, reg 21).

Where a matter must be established to the satisfaction of the Public Guardian, it is for the Public Guardian to determine whether there is sufficient evidence. In most cases the evidence will speak for itself. For instance, if the donee has died, it will be clear from the death certificate that this is the case. If a donee disclaims the power, he must also give notice to the Public Guardian in form LPA005 (Lasting Powers of Attorney, Enduring Powers of Attorney and Public Guardian Regulations 2007, reg 20). If however, the donee has lost capacity or disclaimed the power, there may be an issue over whether the evidence is sufficient to determine whether or not this is the case, in which case the Public Guardian may unintentionally be expected to exercise a judicial function. In particular, where the donor has revoked the power, there may be an issue over whether the donor has sufficient capacity, in which case there may also be a conflict between the Public Guardian's powers under reg 21 and the Court's powers under s 22(2)(b) (see **15.28** below).

Revocation by Court of Protection

15.28   Where a donee or a named person receives a notice of registration and objects on one of the 'prescribed grounds' the Public Guardian cannot register the LPA until directed to do so by the Court of Protection. An objection on one of these grounds must be made by way of application to the Court in Form

COP7 and notice must also be given to the Public Guardian in form LPA008. The person making the objection must make an application to the Court before the end of the period of five weeks beginning with the date on which the notice is given (Lasting Powers of Attorney, Enduring Powers of Attorney and Public Guardian Regulations 2007, reg 15).

If an objection to registration on these grounds is made by any other person or any person (including a donor, donee or named person) wishes to apply for revocation of the LPA after it has been registered, then a formal application needs to be made to the Court under Part 9 of the Court of Protection Rules.

The procedure for objections to registration and applications to the Court where LPAs are concerned is dealt with in more detail at **3.65–3.67** above.

The Court may direct that a power is not to be registered or if the donor lacks capacity, revoke the power (s 22(4)) on the following grounds:

- if the Court determines that the power has been revoked (by the donor) or otherwise come to an end;

- if the Court determines that one of the requirements for the creation of a LPA have not been met; or

- if the Court is satisfied that:

    (a)   fraud or undue pressure was used to induce or create the LPA (s 22(3)(a)); or

    (b)   the donee has behaved, is behaving, or proposes to behave in a way that contravenes his authority or is not in P's best interests (s 22(3)(b)).

At the time of writing, the Court has yet to receive an application to revoke a LPA on the grounds that the donor is or might behave in a way that contravenes his authority or is not in the donor's best interests. In part this is due to the LPA jurisdiction being new, but it is also due to this ground being a difficult one to establish, compared to the unsuitability ground used to justify the revocation of an EPA in favour of an attorney (see **14.37** above). The Court must be satisfied (and if it is not satisfied, it cannot act) that there is a breach or potential breach of the donee's duties or a failure or potential failure to act in the donor's best interests. It has been assumed that this would be straightforward where the donee makes gifts that are beyond the scope of his authority, but that it would be harder to prove a failure to act in a donor's best interests where the donee reasonably believes that he is acting in good faith in the best interests of the donor. However, the decision in *Re P* (see **1.23** above) permits the Court to take a more robust or objective view of a person's best interests and it is expected that decisions or proposed decisions by attorneys will where necessary be subject to these standards.

Powers of the Court after registration

15.29   The Court has wide powers to intervene in the operation of the LPA, similar to those available in respect of an EPA (and which are dealt with in more detail at **14.37** above). Section 23 of the Act provides the Court with the following powers:

(1)   The court may determine any question as to the meaning or effect of a lasting power of attorney or an instrument purporting to create one.

(2)   The court may—

    (a)   give directions with respect to decisions—

        (i)   which the donee of a lasting power of attorney has authority to make, and

        (ii)   which P lacks capacity to make;

    (b)   give any consent or authorisation to act which the donee would have to obtain from P if P had capacity to give it.

(3)   The court may, if P lacks capacity to do so—

    (a)   give directions to the donee with respect to the rendering by him of reports or accounts and the production of records kept by him for that purpose;

    (b)   require the donee to supply information or produce documents or things in his possession as donee;

    (c)   give directions with respect to the remuneration or expenses of the donee;

    (d)   relieve the donee wholly or partly from any liability which he has or may have incurred on account of a breach of his duties as donee.

(4)   The court may authorise the making of gifts which are not within section 12(2) (permitted gifts).'

Powers of Public Guardian after registration

15.30   The role of the Public Guardian and his statutory powers generally are considered at **2.4** above. The Public Guardian has no standing role in connection with donees of LPAs in the same way as deputies. His only statutory duty is to maintain a register of LPAs (s 58(1)(a)). However, the Public Guardian is also obliged, by s 58(1)(h), to deal with representations (including complaints) about the way in which a donee is exercising his powers. The Public Guardian therefore has limited investigatory powers under the Lasting Powers of Attorney, Enduring Powers of Attorney and Public Guardian Regulations 2007. Regulation 46 provides as follows:

'(1)   This regulation applies where it appears to the Public Guardian that there are circumstances suggesting that the donee of a lasting power of attorney may—

    (a)   have behaved, or may be behaving, in a way that contravenes his authority or is not in the best interests of the donor of the power

    (b)   be proposing to behave in a way that would contravene that authority or would not be in the donor's best interests, or

    (c)   have failed to comply with the requirements of an order made, or directions given, by the court.

(2)   The Public Guardian may require the donee—

    (a)   to provide specified information or information of a specified description; or

    (b)   to produce specified documents or documents of a specified description.

(3)   The information or documents must be provided or produced—

    (a)   before the end of such reasonable period as may be specified; and

    (b)   at such place as may be specified.

(4)   The Public Guardian may require—

    (a)   any information provided to be verified in such manner, or

    (b)   any document produced to be authenticated in such manner, as he may reasonably require.

(5)   "Specified" means specified in a notice in writing given to the attorney by the Public Guardian.'

Under regulation 48 the Public Guardian also has the following functions:

    (a)   directing a Court of Protection Visitor—

        (i)   to visit an attorney under a registered enduring power of attorney, or

        (ii)   to visit the donor of a registered enduring power of attorney,

    and to make a report to the Public Guardian on such matters as he may direct; and

    (b)   dealing with representations (including complaints) about the way in which an attorney under a registered enduring power of attorney is exercising his powers.'

Conclusion: lasting powers of attorney – better or worse?

15.31   The main practical consequence of the legislation and in particular new forms, incorporating so many alternatives and details to complete is that the forms are very time consuming to complete. Many potential donors are put off making LPAs by the length and complexity of the forms and the resultant costs. If they are not prepared professionally, they may either not be done at all or will be done badly. For all the reassurances from ministers and the former Public Guardian that the forms were extensively tested and suitable for their purpose, they have taken a great deal of getting used to. After 18 months of use, new revised forms are being prepared with a view to being available by October 2009. The official view remains that the forms can be obtained for free and completed easily without legal assistance. This may well work for those who are capable, educated or supported by honest relatives or friends. But the people who need to make LPAs are often those who need help: the elderly, the vulnerable, those without close family. It is possible that many will act alone or with the help of someone who may well be less than impartial. Unlike EPAs, it is not just a person's property that may be at stake. With a welfare LPA, it may be their life that is also at stake.

The MCA 2005 and the LPA regime set out to address many of the commonly perceived problems with EPAs (addressed at **14.44** above); while some of these have been addressed – for instance by the certificate of capacity – the LPA regime does create its own problems in turn. These have been dealt with above when looking at LPAs in detail, but in looking at these problems and comparing the results, it cannot yet be said that there is an overall net benefit.

There is perhaps a danger of a two-tier society for LPAs: between those who have professional expert and independent advice and those who make their own (or simply create ordinary powers of attorney which will turn out to be invalid when they come to be used). Many of those who could benefit from making LPAs will simply not bother and trust to luck (and their own efforts) to retain control over their affairs or to s 5 of the MCA 2005 to ensure that welfare matters are dealt with correctly. As the majority of LPAs made deal solely with property and affairs, the inference is that most donors will entrust their welfare to their carers acting in their best interests. But if their plans – or lack of plans – are inadequate, their affairs will need to be dealt with by the Court of Protection. Thus an attempt to create new safeguards for the vulnerable, could end up providing less protection and more work for the Court of Protection.

Time will tell whether LPAs will need a further legislative overhaul in the near future. It is certainly the experience of many practitioners that far fewer people create LPAs than was the case with their predecessors. They are no longer made as simple insurance policies as a 'bolt on' to another service such as the making of a will. While this is good for practitioners who should treat LPAs with the care and attention they require and the cost of the work needs to reflect this, quantity is sacrificed at the expense of quality. But is the LPA so much safer than its predecessor that it justifies the extra effort involved in 'making' the power? Is the potential donor better off without a power of attorney, leaving his affairs to be dealt with by the Court of Protection in the future? Time will tell.

Chapter 16

Foreign matters

Importance

16.1 Given the ease with which people move from one country to another and live and work without reference to national boundaries, it is surprising how little is understood about the interaction of different laws that relate to the property and affairs of persons who lack capacity. Each country has evolved its own customs and practices and while no one country claims that its domestic law is superior to another's, laws that relate to where people live and where they own property must be dealt with at a local level. The land needs to be dealt with according to the law of the territory in which it is situated, while the law of the territory in which a person is living will be needed to make decisions about how and where he is cared for and therefore how his assets should be used for his maintenance. A difficulty arises where the person is in one country and the property is in another. As it becomes more and more common for people to own property in other countries and in particular to retire to other countries, so the interdependence of different legal systems will become more important in this area of practice.

Assets in England and Wales where P was resident abroad

16.2 Where a person who lacked capacity was resident outside England and Wales and held assets within England and Wales, the authority of the Court of Protection may still have been required to deal with those assets. Traditionally, the jurisdiction to deal with a person's assets depended on the *lex situs* of the property. Therefore the Court of Protection retained jurisdiction over those assets. If a curator or guardian had been appointed by a foreign court, the Court of Protection was only obliged to recognise the authority of that person in England and Wales if there were no proceedings or proposed proceedings in the Court of Protection and the property in question was movable. The aim of the Court of Protection was not to interfere with a foreign court's jurisdiction but to ensure that the interests of the person concerned were adequately protected. There may be many reasons for a person to retain assets in England & Wales, for example if property is required for his own benefit or for the use of a relative or other dependant. The Court might also wish to consider where the person lived and was likely to continue to live, and whether there were any interests under a will that might be prejudiced by a disposal of the property.

The jurisdiction of the Court of Protection in such cases was considered by Hale J in the case of *Re S* [1995] 4 All ER 30 where a dispute arose over the residence of a Norwegian citizen who, at the age of 70, had set up home with his companion who was English. After the elderly man suffered a stroke, his son applied to the High Court for a declaration that his father had Norwegian domicile and that it was in his best interests to be returned to and cared for in Norway. The Court of Protection also had to consider an application by a guardian, appointed by the Norwegian court, to take control of the assets in England and Wales. The Court of Protection rejected that application, and its discretion in the matter was upheld by the judge who stated:

'... the Court of Protection has jurisdiction if the person or any of his property is here. If there are proceedings in that court, it is not automatically bound to recognise the appointment of a foreign guardian or curator. There are currently proceedings relating to S in the Court of Protection and an order was made ... appointing the Official Solicitor receiver ad interim with a view to the hospital bills being paid ... The master did not consider it appropriate to make no order on the basis that [Mrs Bjorn, the Norwegian guardian] had all the authority she needed. She considered either appointing Mrs Bjorn as interim receiver or giving Mrs Bjorn appropriate directions or appointing the Official Solicitor but with a duty to render accounts to Mrs Bjorn as well as to the court. She chose the latter'.

In most cases there was no need to appoint a deputy to deal with movable assets in England and Wales. The assets needed to be realised and transferred to the foreign curator, guardian or court to administer in accordance with the laws of the country of residence of the person concerned. Therefore the Court of Protection would issue a direction in favour of the foreign guardian or his agent if it was satisfied as to the ownership of the property, that the person lacked capacity to make decisions in respect of the property and affairs that needed to be dealt with and that a valid appointment had been made authorising that person to collect and give a receipt for such assets in England and Wales. However, a deputy would need to be appointed in relation to immovable assets in England and Wales.

Movable property

16.3   The case of *Re S* concerned a person's movable property. The foreign curator had no power to execute a transfer of stock or shares, although the Court of Protection could specifically authorise this (and this power is still provided by MCA 2005 Sch 2 para 7) However, the Court's jurisdiction in such cases presupposes that there are already proceedings or possible proceedings in the Court of Protection. Where a single or straightforward act needs to be performed by a foreign guardian or curator then his authority is still valid (*Didisheim v London and Westminster Bank* [1900] 2 Ch 15). Thus where the foreign guardian or curator wishes to close a bank account then his authority should be recognised, subject to the bank's terms and conditions.

Immovable property

16.4   Where immovable property is concerned then the Court did expect a deputy to be appointed to deal with the sale of the property and his authority would, if appropriate, provide for the proceeds of sale to be transferred to the foreign jurisdiction. The deputy may be the foreign guardian or curator, or may be a local relative or professional person. The overriding consideration will be the best interests of the person who lacks capacity, and in that context, the administration of the estate. For instance the Court has appointed a deputy in England and Wales where:

- the estate consisted of a number of farms, many of which were let. The person concerned was resident in California where he had lived his entire life and was being cared for. It was more appropriate to manage the property locally and to transfer the rents and profits from time to time to the conservator in the United States;

- a property had to be sold, while the person concerned went to live with her husband in the Middle East. Given her age and limited life expectancy, the proceeds of sale were held in the special account and the deputy arranged to transfer funds to the husband from time to time to pay for her care. On the lady's death, her remaining property passed under her will made in England and Wales.

The Hague Convention

16.5   The international protection of adults without capacity is also addressed by s 63 of the MCA 2005 which incorporates Sch 3 to give effect to the Hague Convention on the International Protection of Adults (the 'Convention'). The Convention has only recently been formally ratified on 1 January 2009 by France, Germany and Scotland. However, the Netherlands, Switzerland, Finland, Greece, Ireland, Luxembourg and Poland have all signed and there are proposals that the whole of the European Union might ratify the Convention. Switzerland may also ratify soon. However, where a country is not a party to the Convention the principles outlined above will still apply to the property of a person habitually resident in such a country.

The provisions of the Convention have statutory force within the MCA 2005. The aims of the Convention and Sch 3 to the MCA 2005 are to provide for the mutual recognition of protective measures made in other countries. Schedule 3 to the MCA 2005 extends the Convention in two ways. Firstly, the Convention applies to adults over the age of 18 whereas the MCA 2005 applies to persons over the age of 16. Secondly, the Convention only applies to adults who, by reason of an impairment or insufficiency of their personal faculties, are not in a position to protect their interests, whilst the MCA 2005 also applies to the donors of powers of attorney even if there is no impairment or insufficiency of their personal faculties.

The Court will have regard to the principles set out in Sch 2 para 7 to the MCA 2005 (which repeals the provisions of s 100 of the Mental Health Act 1983). Paragraph 7 provides statutory authority for 'the vesting of stock in a foreign curator'. The Court of Protection must be satisfied that under the laws of the foreign jurisdiction a person has been appointed to exercise powers over the property and affairs of a person (P) on the ground '(however formulated) P lacks capacity to make decisions with respect to the management of his property and affairs'. The Court must also 'have regard to the nature of the appointment and to the circumstances of the case' and be satisfied that it is 'expedient that the Court should exercise his powers under this paragraph'. Although Sch 2 para 7 refers only to the vesting of stock, its principles are reflected in Sch 3 which deals specifically with the international protection of adults and can therefore be applied to other assets (see **16.2** above).

It should be remembered that the Sch 3 para 33 specifically disapplies the Convention in relation to the matters set out in Article 4 of the Convention including trusts and succession. The jurisdiction of the Court of Protection in relation to these matters may therefore be limited.

Domicile and residence

Habitual residence

16.6   Traditionally, under English law the applicable law in a case where a person lacked capacity would be the law of the person's domicile.

However, the Convention now uses 'habitual residence' as the relevant connecting factor. Thus Sch 3 paras 7 and 8 of MCA 2005 allow the Court to exercise its powers in respect of:

- an adult habitually resident in England and Wales;

- an adult's property in England and Wales;

- an adult present in England and Wales or who has property there, if the matter is urgent;

- an adult present in England and Wales, if a protective measure which is temporary and limited in its effect to England and Wales is proposed in relation to him;

- an adult present in England and Wales whose habitual residence cannot be ascertained, is a refugee, or has been displaced as a result of disturbance in the country of his habitual residence;

- he is a British citizen, who has a closer connection with England and Wales than with Scotland or Northern Ireland, and Article 7 of the Convention has, in relation to the matter concerned, been complied with.

This flexible approach is required by the European Convention on Human Rights. Article 5 sets out the principle:

'The judicial or administrative authorities of the Contracting State of the habitual residence of the adult have jurisdiction to take measures directed to the protection of the adult's person or property.'

The Convention does not define the term 'resident' as each case will be determined on its own terms. Lord Scarman in *R v Barnet London Borough Council ex parte Shah* provided the following helpful comments:

'I unhesitatingly subscribe to the view that "ordinarily resident" refers to a man's abode in a particular place or country which he has adopted voluntarily and for settled purposes as part of the regular order of his life for the time being, whether of short or long duration' ([1983] 1 All ER 226 at 235)

The recent case of *Marinos v Marinos* [2007] EWHC 2047 (Fam) is a helpful summary as to the definition of habitual residence for the purposes of European legislation. It is not clear as to whether the definition for Hague Convention purposes might in some circumstances be different.

Conflicts between jurisdictions

16.7   In the event of a conflict between jurisdictions, the Convention allows each territory to apply its own law in relation to the protection of the person or the property. There may then be a potential for each territory to claim precedence. In the case where the person concerned is resident abroad and an order or protective measure has been made in that territory, it will be recognised by the Court of Protection by virtue of Sch 3 para 19 of the MCA 2005. However, para 19 goes on to allow the Court of Protection to disapply that order or protective measure, if it thinks that:

●   the case in which the measure was taken was not urgent;

●   the adult was not given an opportunity to be heard, and that omission amounted to a breach of natural justice;

●   recognition of the measure would be manifestly contrary to public policy;

●   the measure would be inconsistent with a mandatory provision of the law of England and Wales; or

●   the measure is inconsistent with one subsequently taken, or recognised, in England and Wales in relation to the adult.

Foreign assets of a person resident in England and Wales

16.8   Although the Court of Protection may have technical jurisdiction under Sch 3 to the MCA 2005, traditionally it would not make an order directly affecting property in another jurisdiction if such order would not be recognised in that other jurisdiction or if it would infringe another court's jurisdiction. The Court of Protection must also have regard to the convenience of the case. Where different languages and legal systems are concerned it is often simpler for each territory to deal with its own property according to its own laws.

Except where the Convention applies, there are no universal rules which apply where a person who lacks capacity has assets which are situated in a foreign jurisdiction. Most jurisdictions, however, contain similar or equivalent authorities for the management of the property and affairs of persons without mental capacity. Just as the Court of Protection will consider the rights of the foreign person with assets in England and Wales, foreign courts may recognise the authority of their counterparts. This is consistent with the principles of private international law which provide that the capacity of a person is determined by the person's domicile or nationality. Many jurisdictions may therefore apply similar principles to those contained in the Convention.

Where a person who lacks capacity who is habitually resident in England and Wales has assets in another jurisdiction, the requirements of that jurisdiction will be different in each case and an agent in that jurisdiction should be instructed. Other jurisdictions will generally recognise the jurisdiction of the Court of Protection and will authorise the transfer of assets to a deputy appointed by the Court of Protection. However, this is not an automatic process and many jurisdictions will require a formal application to the territorial court of equivalent jurisdiction. This will need to include, inter alia:

- formal evidence of the proposed deputy's authority to act and to recover or receive the assets in question. Where a deputy has been appointed, a sealed and certified copy of the order needs to be supplied. The application should also provide an explanation of the deputy's authority to act and the arrangements made for the custody of the property and affairs in England and Wales;

- confirmation of the person's domicile and residence;

- details of the assets for which authority is required and whether they are movable or immovable;

- confirmation that the assets are not required in the territory for the maintenance or benefit of the person or any creditors or dependants of the person (including under any testamentary disposition); and

- confirmation that no person has been appointed to administer those assets in the jurisdiction where they are situated.

The foreign court will then either confirm the deputy's authority, provide the deputy with authority to act or appoint a local guardian with authority to administer and then remit assets back to the deputy or the Court of Protection.

Similar principles apply to a registered enduring power of attorney, as was illustrated by the Guernsey case of *Greenwood v NatWest Offshore Limited* (2000) 25 February. The donor, who was domiciled in England and Wales had appointed a solicitor to act as his attorney under an enduring power of attorney. The donor also had investments with a trust company in Guernsey. After the donor's enduring power of attorney was registered by the Court of Protection, the attorney applied to the Royal Court of Guernsey for a declaration confirming his authority to act in respect of the Guernsey investments. The Bailiff agreed to the declaration but affirmed a common principle in such cases, that the territorial court retained its jurisdiction and was exercising its discretion:

'... I am in principle happy that this Court should recognise [the attorney] in the same way as if this money had been deposited in the City of London. From what Dicey says it does appear that the courts have a discretion in these matters and clearly had the extent of [the donor's] estate in Guernsey extended to realty or other items of personalty which required a local guardian to be appointed to administer them, then the rights of the guardian to call in all the estate, including the bank accounts with NatWest Offshore would override the rights of [the attorney . . .'

Reciprocal arrangements

16.9   Section 110 of the Mental Health Act 1983 (which provided for reciprocal arrangements in relation to Scotland and Northern Ireland) has not been carried into the MCA 2005. Instead, Sch 3 applies principles of international law to Scotland and Northern Ireland. An order of the Court of Protection will therefore be recognised in those territories unless in Scotland a guardian has been appointed for or in Northern Ireland powers have been exercised under Part VIII of the Mental Health (Northern Ireland Consequential Amendments) Order 1986 (SI 1986/596).

Northern Ireland

16.10   The law relating to adults without capacity is governed by the Mental Health (Northern Ireland Consequential Amendments) Order 1986 (SI 1986/596). Part VIII deals with the property and affairs of a person who is 'incapable, by reason of mental disorder, of managing and administering his property and affairs' (who is defined as a 'patient'). The provisions of the Order are similar to Part VII of the Mental Health Act 1983, save that the powers that would be exercised by a judge (of the Court of Protection) are exercisable by the Office of Care and Protection (which is part of the Family Division of the High Court). A person appointed to make decisions in respect of a patient's property and affairs is a Controller.

The Office of Care and Protection is situated at:

Room 2.2A, Second Floor
Royal Courts of Justice
Chichester Street
Belfast
BT1 3JF
Telephone (028) 9072 4733
Fax (028) 9032 2782
http://www.courtsni.gov.uk

The legislation pertaining to Northern Ireland has not been updated as it has in Scotland and England and Wales. The Bamford Review, published in November 2007, put forward a new comprehensive legislative model on the lines of the MCA 2005. This will be dealt with by the devolved Assembly and is expected to be enacted by April 2011.

Scotland

16.11   The Adults with Incapacity (Scotland) Act 2000 came into effect on 2 April 2001. This was the result of extensive consultation and aimed to create a modern and comprehensive legal framework for persons without capacity.

The Act allows a person to create a continuing power of attorney as well as a welfare power of attorney, which extends to welfare decisions being made on behalf of the incapable person. The courts also have power to appoint a guardian to make welfare decisions or to make welfare decisions in its own right. The legislation was for many years ahead of that available in England and Wales, although it is questionable whether it had been in force for long enough for lessons to be learned before other jurisdictions borrowed heavily from it. It has incorporated some of the ideas set out by the Law Commission in 1995 in *Making Decisions* (Law Com 231) but with a number of safeguards which make it a more considered and protective piece of legislation than the MCA 2005. However, those safeguards are more in the legislation than in the supervisory framework. Court appointed guardians have a great deal of autonomy, without being restricted and supervised in the same way as deputies appointed by the MCA 2005. Various shortcomings in the legislation have been acknowledged and the Act has been heavily amended by the Adult Support & Protection (Scotland) Act 2007.

The Act is of interest in its own right but also as a legislative and practical framework to be compared with that for England and Wales. The main features of the Act provide for:

- *Clear statements of policy*

  Section 1 of the Act lays down simply and clearly that no intervention is to be carried out unless it is for the benefit of the incapable adult and that the benefit cannot be achieved without intervention. There is therefore less scope for argument over 'benefit' as this is an objective term. However, the person carrying out the intervention shall at least take account of the incapable adult's past wishes and feelings, the views of relatives and carers, the views of attorneys or guardians and the views of any other person appearing to 'have an interest' in the person's welfare.

- *A functional definition of capacity*

  A person shall be deemed incapable in respect of a particular act or function if he is incapable by reason of mental disorder or of inability to communicate a decision, of:

  (a)   acting; or

  (b)   making decisions; or

  (c)   communicating decisions; or

  (d)   understanding decisions; or

  (e)   retaining the memory of decisions

  The approach of the Act is to define capacity in terms of function rather than the mental state of the person. Thus a person who cannot communicate as a result of a stroke who otherwise retains capacity can still be the subject of an intervention.

- *Intervention should be as limited as possible*

As is clear from the very first section of the Act, intervention should be as limited as possible. Where the court appoints a guardian, the guardian shall only have power to deal 'with such particular matters' as may be specified in the order (s 66). Any matters not within the order will therefore be capable of being dealt with by the person concerned. A guardian also has the very useful facility of being able to authorise the incapable person to carry out particular transactions or types of transactions.

● *A continuing power of attorney has various safeguards*

The continuing power of attorney must be made in a prescribed form, and contain a statement that the power is a continuing power as well as a certificate from a solicitor or other person (being a member of a prescribed class and who is not the attorney) stating that:

(a) he has interviewed the granter immediately before the granter subscribed the document;

(b) he is satisfied that at the time the continuing power of attorney is granted the granter understands its nature and extent; and

(c) he has no reason to believe that the granter is acting under undue influence or that any other factor prevents the granting of the power.

Once the power is made it must be registered with the Public Guardian immediately its use is required by the attorney, or if the power contains a condition that it should not be registered except on the happening of an event, then it may only be registered on the happening of such an event. However, no more than two persons (whose details are set out in the power) shall be given notice of the registration.

● *The creation of an office of Public Guardian*

Scotland has a Public Guardian who has certain statutory functions (ss 6 and 7). These include the registration of powers of attorney and the maintenance of a register. The Public Guardian has more extensive powers than his English counterpart. Not only is he responsible for the supervision of guardians appointed by the courts, he must approve management plans prepared by guardians (Sch 2). The Public Guardian must also approve any gifts, the sale or purchase of property and the guardian's accounts.

● *Guardian is appointed by the court*

The appointment of a guardian for a person who lacks capacity is made by the sheriff. The aim of the Act is to enable decisions to be made locally through the courts, with the follow up administration and supervision dealt with by the central registry provided by the Public Guardian. When appointing a guardian, the sheriff may appoint 'any individual whom he considers to be suitable for appointment and who has consented to be appointed' (s 59) but the sheriff must have regard to various factors laid down by the Act, including the adult's wishes and feelings.

● *Other safeguards*

As the Scottish legislation is more comprehensive and touches on more personal and potentially controversial welfare interests, the Act contains numerous safeguards. Thus:

● the Public Guardian has a statutory duty to investigate complaints regarding the conduct of attorneys and guardians (s 6);

● a Mental Welfare Commission may exercise protective functions where a personal welfare order or power is in place (s 9);

● local authorities have a statutory responsibility to investigate complaints relating to the conduct of welfare attorneys or guardians and to investigate any circumstances where a person is alleged to be at risk (s 10);

● the Act provides for detailed codes of practice to be published (s 13);

● any person 'claiming an interest in the property, financial affairs or personal welfare' of the granter of a continuing power of attorney may apply to the sheriff who has wide powers to investigate the case and make orders for supervision by the Public Guardian, the rendering of accounts or the revocation of the power. The sheriff is not required to find fault, but may take such action as is necessary to 'safeguard or promote' the interests of the incapable person (s 20);

● the Act does not contain any provision for the making or recognition of advance directives;

● the Act encourages doctors to take responsibility for medical decisions and to encourage consultation and consensus with the welfare attorney or guardian. If there is no disagreement, any other person having an interest in the personal welfare may appeal to the Court of Session. If there is a disagreement, the doctor may refer the decision to another doctor nominated for the purpose by the Mental Welfare Commission. The nominated medical practitioner must consult with the other parties and may authorise the treatment to be given or withheld. There is a right of appeal to the Court of Session (s 50);

● the jurisdiction of the sheriff must be based on his being satisfied that the person is incapable of taking the action for which authority is required. Where an application is made for the appointment of a guardian, the Act provides for detailed medical evidence to be submitted from two doctors. Where the application relates to personal welfare, a personal welfare report must be obtained and if the application relates to property or financial affairs a report from an independent third party who has interviewed and assessed the incapable person and dealing with the appropriateness of the order sought and the suitability of the prospective guardian (s 57).

For further information, the Office of the Public Guardian can be contacted at:

Hadrian House
Callendar Business Park
Callendar Road
Falkirk
FK1 1XR
Tel: 01324 678300
http://www.publicguardian-scotland.gov.uk

Index

[All references are to paragraph number]